# Eating Disorders in Public Discourse

## LANGUAGE, DISCOURSE AND MENTAL HEALTH

*Series Editors*:



*Mental Health Ontologies*
*How We Talk About Mental Health, and Why it Matters in the Digital Age*
Janna Hastings, 2020

*Madness and Literature*
*What Fiction Can Do for the Understanding of Mental Illness*
ed. Lasse R. Gammelgaard, 2022

*Eating Disorders in Public Discourse*
*Exploring Media Representations and Lived Experiences*
ed. Laura A. Cariola, 2023

# EATING DISORDERS IN PUBLIC DISCOURSE

## Exploring Media Representations and Lived Experiences

**Edited by**
**Laura A. Cariola**

UNIVERSITY
*of*
EXETER
PRESS

First published in 2023 by
**University of Exeter Press**
Reed Hall, Streatham Drive
Exeter EX4 4QR, UK

www.exeterpress.co.uk



*Language, Discourse and Mental Health*

**British Library Cataloguing in Publication Data**
A catalogue record for this book is available from the British Library.

https://doi.org/10.47788/QSAU5913

ISBN 978-1-80413-009-4 Hardback
ISBN 978-1-80413-010-0 ePub
ISBN 978-1-80413-011-7 PDF

Cover image: https://www.istockphoto.com

Typeset in Caslon and Myriad by Deanta Global Publishing Services, Chennai, India

# Contents

# Contributors

**Prof. Kimberly Bissell** is the Associate Dean for research in the College of Communication and Information Sciences at the University of Alabama. She also directs its Institute for Communication and Information Research. Bissell studies health communication.

**Dr Matt Bowen** is a Senior Lecturer in the Mental Health and Learning Disabilities Department at the University of Chester. He was previously the Clinical Nurse Specialist at a National Centre for Excellence that provided treatment to people with personality disorder. As a clinician and researcher, he has conducted research into staff competencies when working with people with personality disorder, and the functioning of specialist treatment services. Matt's PhD examined the representation of people with personality disorder in the red-top tabloid press. Since then, he has gone on to examine how the UK press discuss and represent people with a diagnosis of schizophrenia and how mental health is represented in newspaper Twitter feeds. His media analysis research is characterized by drawing on a range of qualitative and quantitative approaches.

**Dr Dawn Branley-Bell** is a Chartered Psychologist, Medical Research Foundation Fellow and Chair of the British Psychological Society (BPS) Cyberpsychology Section. She is based within the Psychology and Communication Technology Lab (PaCT Lab) and Centre for Digital Citizens at Northumbria University. Dr Branley-Bell specializes in health- and cyber- psychology, with a keen interest in remote healthcare, online social and peer support, cybersecurity, and the use of technology to promote positive behaviours.

**Dr Laura A. Cariola** is Lecturer in Applied Psychology at the School of Health in Social Science at the University of Edinburgh. She studied Applied Linguistics and Psychology. She is a chartered member of the British Psychological Society, Division of Academics, Researchers and Teachers in Psychology, and a member of the Division of Counselling Psychology. Her research focuses on the intersection of language, discourse and mental health using both linguistic and psychological approaches to explore the language of individuals affected by mental health problems and the presentation of mental health in the media.

**Dr Pamara F. Chang** is an Assistant Professor of Communication at the University of Cincinnati. Her research programme is at the intersection of health communication and computer-mediated communication. Her research focuses on how people manage stigmatized identities using various information communication technologies in the context of invisible disabilities.

**Dr Kate Davenport** works as a clinical psychologist within a physical health setting at Broomfield Hospital in Essex. Her clinical and research interests are around 'visible differences', including burns, limb loss, cancer, cleft lip and palette, and weight management.

**Nicholas Eckhart** is a doctoral student in the College of Communication and Information Sciences at the University of Alabama.

**Dr Elizabeth V. Eikey** is an Assistant Professor in the Department of Family Medicine and Public Health as well as the Design Lab at the University of California, San Diego. Her research is at the intersection of mental health, technology and equity. Dr Eikey is also the Assistant Director of the iSchool Inclusion Institute (i3).

**Dr Carolina Figueras Bates** is Associate Professor of Spanish Philology at the University of Barcelona. She is author of the book *Pragmática de la puntuación* (2001), and the editor, with Adrián Cabedo, of *Perspectives on Evidentiality in Spanish: Explorations across Genres* (2018). Her research interests are focused on the discursive construction of eating disorders and the pro-anorexia movement. Specifically, her publications have addressed the construction of identity through metaphors and evidential markers in mental illness narratives, and the mitigating operations used to cope with an eating disorder in online support groups.

**Oliver Golden** is an undergraduate student in the Department of Psychological Science at the University of California, Irvine and a researcher in the Mental Health in Design (MiD) Lab.

**Dr Hayriye Gulec** received her PhD in clinical psychology from Ruprecht Karls University in Heidelberg, Germany. She is an Assistant Professor in the Department of Psychology at Bursa Uludag University, Turkey. Her areas of research include e-mental health applications, eating disorders and psychotherapy research.

**Prof. Stephen M. Haas** is a Full Professor of Communication at the University of Cincinnati. His research explores uncertainty, stigma, self-advocacy and social support in health communication. His work has been funded by the US National Institutes of Health agencies and has received several National Communication Association awards.

**Prof. Nancy A. Jennings** is a Professor in the Department of Communication at the University of Cincinnati. She studies the impact of media on the lives of youth and their families, applying both qualitative and quantitative methods. She also addresses public policies and media practices involved with youth media.

**Dr Billy Lee** is a Lecturer in Psychology at the University of Edinburgh. His research enquires into the phenomenology of marginal and special life experiences, especially in relation to the talking therapies. He uses experience-near interviewing methods to facilitate people to communicate their lived experience and personal meanings. His current research explores issues around culture and ethnocentricity in theory and practice of the talking cure. He is interested in supervising research using a phenomenological approach to explore any aspect of marginal or different experience including race, ethnicity, gender and sexuality.

**Dr Irene López-Rodríguez** holds a BA and MA in English Language and Literature and an MEd from the University of Extremadura, Spain. Currently, she holds the Joseph-Armand Bombardier doctoral fellowship (Canadian Research Agency) at the University of Ottawa, where she works as a part-time Professor for the Department of Modern Languages and concluded her PhD dissertation on the representation of gender through animal metaphors in Francoist Spain (2020). Her current research explores the connection between the animalization of female victims in (non-)fictional accounts of gender violence in contemporary Spain.

**Dr Allyn Lueders** is an Associate Professor in the Communication Studies Department at Wayne State College, Nebraska. She teaches courses in Public Relations, Leadership, and Interpersonal Communication, and is the faculty adviser of the school's chapter of PRSSA. Her research interests include health and interpersonal communication, especially in online contexts.

**Dr Gareth Lyons** is a man who has experienced purging anorexia; he undertook a PhD study to find out about the illness and to try to answer questions about his own illness. He is a former teacher and currently works in a brand marketing role in the outdoor industry.

**Prof. Sue McAndrew** is Professor of Mental Health and Young People at the University of Salford. Sue's research interests include young carers and service users, childhood sexual abuse and its impact on mental health, self-harm and suicide, and therapeutic engagement. Sue has published extensively and presented papers at local, national and international conferences.

**Dr Joanne McDowell** is a Principal Lecturer in English Language and Linguistics at the University of Hertfordshire. She specializes in workplace discourse, gender studies, identity construction, classroom discourse and interactional sociolinguistics. She has published in numerous edited collections and journals including *Gender, Work and Organisation*, *Gender and Language* and *Gender and Education*, and is the editor of *De-Gendering Gendered Occupations: Analysing Professional Discourse* (2021).

**Emma O'Rourke** obtained an MSc in Children and Young People's Mental Health and Psychological Practice at the University of Edinburgh. Currently she is a mental health nurse at the Child and Adolescent Mental Health Services (CAMHS) inpatient unit of NHS Lothian, Scotland.

**Bumsoo Park** is a doctoral student in the College of Communication and Information Sciences at the University of Alabama.

**Dr Scott Parrott** is an Associate Professor and Reese Phifer Fellow at the University of Alabama in the College of Communication and Information Sciences. Parrott studies media representations of mental illness and how exposure to media content nurtures or mitigates stigmatization.

**Dr Wendy Solomons** is a Clinical Psychologist and the Academic Lead on the Doctoral Programme in Clinical Psychology at the University of Hertfordshire. Her research focuses on critical and constructionist approaches to health, social and clinical psychology, with a particular interest in contested positions and the social construction of identities.

**Dr Rhian Waller** has a background in journalism and post-compulsory education. She re-entered academia after working in regional print journalism for five years, where she wrote about everything from politics to police operations to deadly parasites. She was shortlisted for a Mind Media Award in 2013 for her features on mental health issues. Her research interests include media depictions of mental health, female figures in pop culture and literary approaches to journalism.

**Prof. Tony Warne** is Professor Emeritus in Mental Health at the University of Salford, and former Pro-Vice Chancellor and Dean of the School of Health and Society. His research focused on inter-personal, intra-personal and extra-personal relationships, using psychodynamic and managerialist analytical discourses. He has published extensively in these areas.

# Abbreviations

| | |
|---|---|
| **APA** | American Psychiatric Association |
| **AN** | Anorexia nervosa |
| **BED** | Binge eating disorder |
| **BN** | Bulimia nervosa |
| **CDP** | critical discursive psychology |
| **ED** | Eating disorder |
| **EDNOS** | Eating disorders not otherwise specified |
| **FA** | Fat acceptance |
| **IPA** | Interpretative Phenomenological Analysis |
| **UFED** | Unspecified Feeding or Eating Disorder |
| **OSFED** | Other Specified Feeding and Eating Disorder |

# Introduction

*Laura A. Cariola*

Eating disorders (EDs) are serious and multifaceted mental health conditions associated with changes in eating behaviour and potentially grave health consequences, including mortality. While statistics have observed a consistent rise of ED rates in the last twenty-year period (Galmiche et al., 2019), the coronavirus pandemic and its lockdown measures have resulted in a sharp and unprecedented surge in children and adolescents being referred for treatment to ED services (Solmi, Downs & Nicholls, 2021). Prevalence statistics on EDs vary widely, and it is estimated that approximately 1.25 million people in the UK and 28.8 million people in the USA, of whom approximately 25% are male, are affected by an ED (ANAD 2021; Beat, 2021). Despite these statistics, it is somewhat unclear how common EDs are in the general population, as 'true' EDs that meet all clinical criteria of an ED are relatively rare, whereas subthreshold EDs that meet many but not all criteria are relatively common (Field et al., 2012; Machado, Gonçales & Hoek, 2012).

Although Western contemporary psychiatry, positioned within a twentieth-century positivist discourse of scientific knowledge, relies predominantly on numerical data and quantitative techniques, it is evident that language and qualitative approaches are central features in clinical practice (Galasiński, 2018, 2021). For example, language is used to group together a set of common symptoms and describe psychological states in relation to classification systems, such as the Diagnostic and Statistical Manual of Mental Disorders (DSM-5)

Laura A. Cariola, 'Introduction' in: *Eating Disorders in Public Discourse: Exploring Media Representations and Lived Experiences*. University of Exeter Press (2023). © Laura A. Cariola. DOI: 10.47788/BASF7279

(APA, 2013). Similarly, clinicians use language in developing formulations and treatment plans, assessing patients, implementing triage, applying diagnostic tools, conducting therapeutic sessions, writing patient notes and so forth. The way clinicians speak with patients and interpret their unique experiences is fundamental to the therapeutic process, and the forming of a strong therapeutic alliance is the most important component linked to successful therapeutic outcomes (Ardito & Rabellino, 2011).

Language is central, not only to how mental health and social problems are communicated in the consultation room, but also to public discourse, including newspapers and online communications, which have a strong influence in shaping what the general public knows and thinks about mental health (Anderson, 2003; Ohlsson, 2017). The media tend to discuss mental health problems via sensationalist stories that convey negative and stereotypical messages. It comes as no surprise that EDs are not widely understood by the public, who often hold simplistic and reductionist views about them. A common myth, for instance, is that people with EDs are responsible for their illness and that their difficulties are self-inflicted; this view is often perpetuated in place of recognizing EDs as biologically influenced illnesses (Schaumberg et al., 2017).

Language-based analysis has long been recognized as a powerful method for obtaining a better understanding of healthcare settings (e.g., doctor–patient interactions, therapeutic processes), cognition in mental health problems (e.g., thought disorder in schizophrenia) and lived experiences of mental health problems (e.g., depression). Although the role of language has also been recognized as a key component in the complex relationship between the media and EDs, there is a dearth of research exploring the representation of EDs in the media and how this relates to the subjective experiences of EDs. With the aim of addressing this gap in empirical literature, this edited volume provides insights into the ways in which individuals with EDs are affected by media texts and their representations of the topic.

The various chapters in this book put forward a range of arguments, conclusions and contextualizing information, showcasing how language is used as the privileged mode to analyse public discourses about EDs. This volume makes a collective and interdisciplinary effort to provide empirical, theoretical and critical insights, and presents explorations of the ways EDs are discussed and represented in public discourse. Attention is given to stigmatizing stereotypes, discourse frames and metaphors, identity construction in online spaces, the ways individuals affected by EDs make sense of media representations, including on social media, and how parents write about their experiences of caring for children with EDs. These topics are explored through the lens of qualitative, quantitative and mixed-methods language-based approaches, which differ in their theoretical orientations and philosophical assumptions. The majority of chapters in this volume are empirical studies using language-based approaches, including thematic analysis, critical discursive psychology, content analysis, interpretative phenomenological analysis, metaphor analysis, fantasy theme analysis and Natural Language Processing. To obtain a multifaceted understanding of ED discourses, this volume synthesizes evidence obtained from a range of data types, including the UK and international newspapers, social media, online communities, blogs and forums, apps and in-depth interviews. The studies in this volume also reflect different cultural perspectives, including those held in the USA, the UK, Spain and Turkey. The book brings together a group of researchers from a variety of disciplinary backgrounds, including communication and information studies, journalism, linguistics, medicine, mental health, nursing, psychology and public health, to engage in a conversation on how language-based approaches can be used to showcase and explore the relationship between EDs and the media. This provides a fisheye view of ED media discourses from different disciplinary perspectives.

While there is a growing body of language-based studies on mental health discourses in the media, there has been much less investment in research on the use of language in media discourses, and the ensuing stigmatization of those affected by EDs. This is unusual considering that EDs are a prevalent mental health problem, and their aetiology has been linked with social factors, including depictions of the 'thin body ideal' in print and social media. It is also difficult to establish why this aspect of ED research has not received more attention from an interdisciplinary perspective.

Traditionally, research on EDs has offered powerful evidence of the effectiveness of treatment intervention, using controlled trials. The last decade, however, has seen an expanding interest in widening our understanding of EDs by exploring language-based data through the lens of various disciplines, using language-based approaches. Such research draws on a variety of concepts, theories, paradigms and methodologies from psychiatry, psychology, critical theory, sociology and communication studies. As such, language-based perspectives on ED research traverse narrow disciplinary boundaries to provide a more comprehensive understanding of EDs. Any interdisciplinary endeavour requires researchers to position themselves as the learners of theories and approaches belonging to another discipline, and by doing so, to move beyond the confines of their own discipline (Smith & Carey, 2007). Interdisciplinary research prevents disciplinary blindness, whereby linguists only discuss with other linguists, psychologists only discuss with other psychologists, and so on, with some disciplines perceiving themselves as more expert and competent than others. Such an inclusive framework also acknowledges the pluralistic identity of modern linguistics that concerns itself with those parts of other academic domains that focus on language, which nowadays form part of 'linguistics' but historically belonged to other fields. For instance, traditionally linguistics formed part of philology (e.g., English, Classics, Oriental studies); Chomsky's early work on grammar originated from the field of mathematical logic; authors of major theories that influenced pragmatics (e.g., John L. Austin, Paul Grice, John R. Searle) were philosophers, not linguists; and psycholinguistics was developed in psychology, not linguistics departments (Wilson, 2021).

The aim of an inclusive framework in this edited volume is to break down communication barriers and power structures between disciplines. All disciplines are positioned as equal and transcend hierarchical perceptions of evidence that often regard disciplines using quantitative methodologies as producing knowledge of higher importance than that generated from qualitative-orientated disciplines. Interdisciplinary perspectives may address research questions and lead to a more comprehensive understanding of 'real-world problems', such as EDs, that are not confined to a single discipline and cannot be wholly explained using the existing traditional disciplinary approaches within psychiatry and clinical psychology. For example, randomized controlled trials are often perceived as the gold standard in the hierarchy of evidence because of their ability to limit bias. Within ED research, these traditional controlled approaches also tend to conceptualize EDs as 'objects' or medical artefacts, without acknowledging the value of naturally occurring data, including the subjective experience of those affected (O'Connor et al., 2019). Exploring ED discourses from a broad and interdisciplinary perspective offers the space to identify novel insights that can inform the development of effective evidence-based interventions and policy-making to meet the needs and expectations of a diverse population, including those affected by inequality (Kivits, Ricci & Minary, 2019).

In the light of the above view, this volume assumes an inclusive and pluralistic stance that adopts a broad perspective on what constitutes 'evidence' and embraces a diverse range of research approaches to advance knowledge relevant to EDs, including qualitative and quantitative approaches. Ideologically it also opposes 'methodolatry' and the blind reification of certain qualitative or quantitative methods, or conventions associated with any one academic discipline alone (Chamberlain, 2000). This inclusive approach to 'evidence' will offer a basis for a reflective inquiry that encompasses a wide range of theoretical and philosophical assumptions and provides a framework to develop innovative approaches to ED treatment and policy development. It is hoped that this volume will offer an interdisciplinary insight that contributes to a better understanding of the relationship between the media and EDs. Before introducing the individual chapters of this volume, the following section will offer a brief overview of the literature on ED diagnosis, ED stigma, EDs in newspapers and on pro-ED websites, and language-based approaches to the understanding of EDs in the media.

## Overview of Eating Disorders

EDs are the central theme of this book. EDs are serious mental health problems of great public health concern, characterized by disturbances in eating behaviours, including dieting, restrictive food intake, self-induced vomiting and binge eating, to mention but a few. EDs relate to a range of negative physical outcomes, and are associated with a heightened risk of mortality (Fichter & Quadflieg, 2016) due to medical complications, suicidality (Mandelli et al., 2019), health problems (e.g., osteoporosis and cardiovascular disease) (Mehler & Krantz, 2003), psychiatric comorbidities (e.g., obsessive compulsive disorder; APA, 2013) (Ulfvebrand et al., 2015), psychosocial impairments (Stice, Marti & Rohde, 2013), and reduced quality of life (Jenkins et al., 2011).

The Diagnostic and Statistical Manual of Mental Disorders, 5th Edition (DSM-5) (APA, 2013) and the International Classification of Diseases, 11th Revision (ICD-11) (WHO, 2018) describe a range of EDs that are characterized by abnormal eating habits and behaviours. The DSM is the official classification in the USA for clinical diagnosis, which nowadays is used worldwide, and the ICD is the official world classification tool published by the World Health Organization (WHO) (Tyrer, 2014). As outlined by Galmiche and colleagues (2019), EDs were first included in the DSM-III in 1980, with revisions of the diagnostic criteria occurring in 1982 and again in the DSM-IV in 1994, until its latest classification in the DSM-5 in 2013. Similarly, EDs were first included in the ICD-9 (1977), with revised criteria in the ICD-10 (1990), and the current revised classification was included in the ICD-11. These classification systems use a categorical rather than a dimensional model to describe and label problematic eating behaviours (Grilo, 2006). The DSM-5 and ICD-11 both include three diagnostic categories of ED—Anorexia Nervosa, Bulimia Nervosa and Binge Eating Disorder. The DSM-5 also refers to Other Specified Feeding and Eating Disorder (OSFED) and Unspecified Feeding or Eating Disorder (UFED); the former includes a mixture of different ED symptoms, and the latter refers to eating problems that are not included as formal disorders in the classification system (APA, 2013).

According to the medical framework, anorexia nervosa is characterized by three criteria: (1) a restriction of energy intake that leads to significantly low body weight, (2) an intense fear of weight gain or becoming fat even if the individual is substantially underweight, and (3) disturbance in the ways in which the body weight or shape are experienced or the inability to recognize the seriousness of the low body weight (APA, 2013). There are also two subtypes of anorexia nervosa: the majority of cases are classified as the restricting subtype, characterized by individuals achieving weight loss through dieting and fasting and/or excessive exercise, whereas the binge eating/purging subtype of anorexia nervosa is characterized by recurrent episodes of binge eating or purging behaviour (e.g., self-induced vomiting; the misuse of laxatives, enemas or diuretics) (APA, 2013).

Bulimia nervosa is characterized within the medical framework by five criteria: (1) recurrent episodes of binge eating (i.e., large amounts of food in a discrete period of time), (2) a sense of lack of control over eating, (3) recurrent inappropriate compensatory behaviours to prevent weight gain, (4) self-evaluation influenced by body shape and weight, which must occur at least once a week for three months to be diagnosed as bulimia nervosa, and (5) that the disturbance does not occur during episodes of anorexia nervosa (APA, 2013). Although DSM-5 criteria are mutually exclusive as only one diagnosis can be assigned, in clinical practice, individuals with anorexia tend to develop bulimia over time (Carr & McNulty, 2016).

Binge eating was officially recognized and included as an independent ED diagnosis in the DSM-5 to describe recurrent bingeing episodes that are not associated with compensatory behaviours, as is the case with bulimia nervosa.

Five criteria characterize binge eating disorder (APA, 2013): (1) recurrent episodes of consumption of a large amount of food in a discrete period of time, (2) the presence of three or more of the following behaviours: eating much more rapidly than normal, eating until uncomfortably full, eating large amounts of food when not feeling hungry, eating alone out of embarrassment of how much food is consumed, and negative mood state after food intake, (3) marked distress, (4) binge eating occurring on average at least once a week for three months, and (5) binge eating which is not associated with the recurrent use of inappropriate compensatory behaviour, and does not occur during the course of bulimia nervosa or anorexia nervosa (APA, 2013).

OSFED refers to the presence of symptoms associated with feeding and EDs that cause clinically significant distress or impairment in social, occupational and other important areas of functioning, but do not meet the full criteria of the feeding and ED diagnostic rubrics. These include atypical anorexia nervosa, bulimia nervosa of low frequency and/or duration, binge eating disorder of low frequency and/or duration, purging disorder and night eating syndrome. UFED, in contrast, relates to various non-clinical eating behaviours, such as orthorexia (an unhealthy obsession with eating 'pure' food) and diabulimia (an ED that affects individuals with Type-1 diabetes). Other eating and feeding disorders that are mentioned in the DSM-5 are Pica, Rumination Disorder, and Avoidant/Restrictive Food Intake Disorder (APA, 2013), which do not require further evaluation in this edited volume.

The estimated prevalence of EDs varies across studies. A comprehensive review by Galmiche and colleagues (2019) based on ninety-four studies identified that EDs as a broad category have an averaged point prevalence of 5.7% (0.9–13.5%) in women and 2.2% (0.2–7.3%) in men, and a lifetime prevalence of 8.4% (3.3–18.6%) in women and 2.2% (0.8–6.5%) in men.

For anorexia nervosa, the averaged point prevalence is greater in women, with 2.8% (0–4.8%) compared to 0.3% (0–0.4%) in men, and a lifetime prevalence of 1.4% (0.1–3.6%) in women and 0.2% (0–0.3%) in men. Similarly, for bulimia nervosa, the averaged point prevalence is 1.5% (0–8.4%) in women, which is higher than the 0.1% (0–1.3%) in men, with a lifetime prevalence of 1.9% (0.3–4.6%) in women and 0.6% (0.1–1.3%) in men. For binge eating disorder, the averaged point prevalence is 2.3% (0–9.8%) in women and 0.3% (0–0.5%) in men, with a lifetime prevalence of 2.8% (0.6–5.8%) in women and 1.0% (0.3–2.0%) in men (Galmiche et al., 2019). The onset for binge eating disorder is in late adolescence, between 16 and 20 years (Stice, Marti & Rohde, 2013). The prevalence of EDs also showed an increase from 3.5% in 2000–2006 to 7.8% for the period of 2013–2018, indicating the rising challenge of EDs as a public health concern (Galmiche et al., 2019).

Based on a study by Volpe and colleagues (2016), anorexia nervosa has a mean age onset at 18 years, and bulimia nervosa has a mean age onset at 18.2 years; however, 75.3% of the anorexia group had an early onset, with an average age of 16.2 years, and 83.3% of the binge eating group had an early peak at 16.7 years. Peak onset statistics vary, with other findings proposing a lower peak age for anorexia (10–14 years) and bulimia nervosa (15–19 years) (Micali et al., 2013). The statistics also clearly indicate that EDs are less common among males and are typically regarded as a feminine mental health problem (Nagl et al., 2016). Because of this, men have been underrepresented in ED research (Limbers, Cohen & Gray, 2018). However, there is a growing recognition that men are also at risk of developing of EDs (Lipson & Sonneville, 2017) and that a substantial minority of men report ED symptoms, yet the diagnostic criteria may not meet men's presentations with a focus on muscularity (Allen et al., 2013; Flament et al., 2015).

Although the exact causes of EDs are not entirely understood (NIMH, 2021), clinicians agree that EDs and body dissatisfaction are multifaceted constructs that develop through a complex dynamic of multiple influences, including biological factors (e.g., age, gender, puberty; Jacobi et al., 2004; Jacobi & Fittig, 2010), personality factors such as perfectionism, negative self-critical evaluation, rejection and interpersonal sensitivity, and harm avoidance (Hilbert et al., 2014; Jacobi & Fittig, 2010). Environmental risk factors, such as abuse, trauma and dysfunctional family dynamics, may also predispose the development of EDs (Backholm, Isomaa & Birgegård, 2013; Hilbert et al., 2014). Parental criticism about weight and appearance is also an important risk factor (Dodge & Simic, 2014). There is growing awareness of the role of familial genetic transmission, which has been identified as a predisposing risk factor through interaction with life stressors in the environment (Mayhew et al., 2018). Twin studies demonstrated that heritability explains up to 83% of the development of EDs, with anorexia in particular having a high genetic loading (Thornton, Mazzeo & Bulik, 2011). Epigenetic studies have also shown that genetic and environmental influences on EDs are related to sex and developmental stage, with an increase of EDs during puberty (APA, 2013).

The influence of the mass media and the exposure to images of idealized bodies as part of the developmental trajectory of EDs have been heavily associated with the sociocultural model. Conversely, only a small proportion of individuals exposed to the media develop an ED or body dissatisfaction, indicating the complex interplay between a combination of risk factors.

One of the key assumptions of the sociocultural model is that exposure to the media's idealized body types predisposes one to the development of EDs through various factors, including internalization of the thin body ideal, pressure for thinness and self-deprecating appearance comparison. These factors have been associated with the experience of body dissatisfaction that would precede weight concerns and the development of unhealthy eating behaviour in those at risk (Tiggemann & Miller, 2010). Prolonged exposure to the media's unrealistic and narrowly defined beauty standard of a 'perfect thin body' results in the perception of these 'perfect thin body' depictions as valid representations of reality, which drives the need to conform to this idealized yet unrealistic societal standard, which is often unattainable (Grabe, Ward & Hyde, 2008). The ensuing perceived discrepancy between the internalized unrealistic thin body ideal and one's own real yet not 'perfect' body has been associated with body dissatisfaction, low self-esteem, appearance comparison and unhealthy weight loss behaviour, constituting risk factors for the development of EDs (Fardouly & Vartanina, 2015; Sidani et al., 2016).

Early studies that focused on the emergence of the media's idealization of the thin body identified that women depicted on *Playboy*, beauty pageant contestants, fashion models and actresses between the 1930s and the 1990s became thinner and less curvaceous over time (Garner et al., 1980; Kaufman, 1980; Silverstein et al., 1986; Wiseman et al., 1992). This preference for a thinner body shape in the media, however, coincided with an increasing average body weight in the North American female population in the late 1980s and early 1990s, thus reflecting an increased discrepancy between the body ideal and women's actual body sizes (Garner et al., 1980; Wiseman et al., 1992). This coincided with an increase in magazine and television advertisements for diet foods, reflecting how the diet industry perpetuated this thin ideal for marketing purposes, which impacted on high levels of dieting in women (Wiseman et al., 1992). Paradoxically, this contrasted with an increase of media content that focused on food, such as food preparations and advertisements for snacks (Ogletree et al., 1990; Silverstein et al., 1986). The consumption of beauty fashion magazines rose in the 1990s, meaning that women were positioned between contrasting discourses of food consumption and dieting, actual and idealized bodies, thinness and fatness, which over time defined the social expectations of what women's bodies 'should look like'. This coincided with the development of young women's sense of self, and an increased preoccupation with physical appearance, attainment of the thin body ideal, and weight loss (Kilbourne, 1994). While body image and appearance concerns predominantly affect young women, there is an increasing proportion of men with muscularity-orientated body image concerns that reflect a stereotypical masculine-associated body ideal (Griffiths et al., 2016; Kinnaird et al., 2019). Thus, body dissatisfaction tends to be qualitatively different between genders, where women are predominantly concerned with the desire to attain a thin body through dieting, but men exhibit a stronger desire to attain a muscular ideal through weight training (Kinnaird et al., 2019; Limbers, Cohen & Gray, 2018).

Drawing on Bandura's (2009) social cognitive theory of mass communication, it seems that recurrent exposure to images of unrealistically thin bodies leads to attitude, behaviour and cognitive changes in the way individuals think and feel about their eating habits and bodily self-perceptions. Proponents of cultivation theory (Gerbner, Gross & Morgan, 2002) and the illusory truth effect (Hasher, Goldstein & Toppio, 1977) also propose that repeated exposure to media information leads viewers to perceive the messages conveyed as being accurate and truthful presentations of reality. After viewers have accepted media portrayals of thin bodies as normative, based on the mere exposure effect (Zajonc, 1968), they tend to develop a preference for slender body shapes.

As achieving an 'ideal' body shape is often unattainable for many people, this may lead some individuals to develop skewed self-perceptions and body dissatisfaction, and to adopt unhealthy eating behaviours (Grabe, Ward & Hyde, 2008). As early as 1992, Myers and Biocca recognized that exposure to the media's unrealistic body representations provided individuals with distorted perceptions of their own bodies. Their experimental study demonstrated a causal relationship between exposure to television portrayals of the ideal thin body and an unstable self-perceived body image in young women. A study by Stice and Shaw (1994) also showed that exposure to pictures of ultra-thin models had a negative impact on young women's mood states and caused dissatisfaction with their own body shapes, compared to those who were shown pictures of average-sized or normal models. The results mirror the relationship between body dissatisfaction as an underlying risk factor for eating pathology, and its links to self-esteem and mood disorders (Brechan & Kvalem, 2015).

With the increasing pervasiveness of the World Wide Web beginning in the 1990s and the subsequent facilitation of communication without geographical constraints, there has been a growing interest in interrogating the relationship between people's access to social networking sites, body image concerns and EDs (Tiggemann & Slater, 2013). As young people connect to social media, they are exposed to celebrities and influencers who promote the thin body ideal and dieting culture. Young people also actively engage in the following: the creation and sharing of selfies that are perfected with photoshopping and filters (Tiggemann & Zinoviev, 2019), the monitoring of negative and positive feedback on uploaded selfies (Chua & Chang, 2016), the consumption of content promoting diet culture and cosmetic interventions (Sorice et al., 2017), the use of food intake, weight loss and fitness-tracking technology (Lupton, 2018), attempting to conform to stereotypical ideals of beauty (Slater & Tiggemann, 2012), and involvement with social media 'trends' (e.g., thinspiration, pro-anorexia) that promote and glamourize unhealthy eating behaviours and the thin body ideal (Cavazos-Rehg et al., 2020).

Evidently, social media engagement is not solely responsible for the onset and maintenance of body dissatisfaction and eating behaviour, as it 'merely' reflects the internalization of body attitudes and stereotypes that exist within society (Derenne & Beresin, 2018). These stereotypes are continuously recreated, reproduced and reinforced by social media users who share selfies and other images that conform to and reinforce societal norms of bodily appearance. This at least partly explains why young people engage in unhealthy weight loss practices to gain social approval and avoid rejection from peers (Lewallen & Behm-Morawitz, 2016; Tiggemann & Slater, 2013). As such, the drive for thinness and having a desirable body may be also conceptualized as a reflection of Western culture's competitiveness, and its illusion that it is possible to control one's social standing through dieting and achieving a body ideal (Ferreira, Pinto-Gouveia & Duarte, 2013).

ED pathology is sometimes assumed to affect predominantly white populations living in Western, post-industrialized, high-income countries that emphasize the thin body ideal. In these countries, thinness is synonymous with attractiveness and its links to perceptions of success, health and happiness (Ferreira, Pinto-Gouveia & Duarte, 2013). Empirical studies have revealed that white adults are at an increased risk of internalizing a thin ideal, experience greater body dissatisfaction, and have a higher lifelong tendency to develop EDs compared to many other ethnic groups globally (Pike et al., 2001; Striegel-Moore et al., 2003; Udo & Grilo, 2018; Wildes, Emery & Simons, 2001). Such ethnic differences might be related to different cultural influences and perceptions regarding a desirable body ideal (Kolar et al., 2016; Perez, Ohrt & Hoek, 2016). Conversely, some studies have identified inconsistent findings regarding ethnic differences in the prevalence and risk factors of EDs, which challenge the sociocultural model of ED and body dissatisfaction. For example, Cheng and colleagues' (2019) longitudinal study of women with body image concerns did not find any reliable ethnic differences in relation to prevalence, onset or risk factors of EDs, indicating more similarities than differences across ethnic groups.

Due to the process of Westernization and globalization, non-Western cultures are increasingly exposed to Western media that promote the thin ideal, and there is increased sociocultural pressure to effect body dissatisfaction and internalization of the thin ideal among non-Western cultural communities. The impact of Western media on non-Western communities has been demonstrated in a study by Becker (2004), who identified that ethnic Fijian adolescent girls had significantly more indicators of bulimic-based behaviours following exposure to Western television, and their weight loss was motivated by the desire to model themselves after the television characters. Although research found little evidence of thinness being desirable in Arab countries (Khaled, Kimmel & Le Trung, 2018), some studies do indicate an increase of EDs in Arab and Asian countries among young females, which might be associated with increasing globalization and industrialization (Pike, Hoek & Dunne, 2014; Tong et al., 2013). Epidemiological studies in Africa identified low incidence rates of anorexia nervosa, but the prevalence rate of bulimia nervosa in African women was within the range reported for Western populations, including African Americans and Latin Americans (van Hoeken, Burns & Hoek, 2016); and a small proportion of a subpopulation with increased exposure to Western culture reported ED pathology (Eddy, Hennessey & Thompson-Brenner, 2007; Njenga & Kang'ethe, 2004).

One of the challenges in protecting people from the negative influence of the media relates to the difficulty in regulating its content. Several policy recommendations have been proposed to regulate media content with the aim of protecting those at risk of poor body image. In the UK, for instance, a key recommendation of the All Party Parliamentary Group on Body Image (APPG) (2012) was for advertisers and the fashion industry to reflect greater diversity in appearance, such as including models with body sizes consistent with the general population. Despite these recommendations, in 2020, shortly after the first national Covid-19 lockdown, the UK Government launched a new review to better understand the rise of body image problems and EDs (GOV, 2021). The ensuing APPG report, 'Changing the Perfect Picture: An Inquiry into Body Image', recommended greater representation of diverse people and body shapes in the fashion and beauty industry; continued restriction of online content and activity that harms body image; clearer information for users from the Advertising Standards Authority on how to report posts that breach regulations; restrictions on harmful media content through advertising rules and community guidelines for social media companies with Ofcom as a regulator; restrictions on algorithm-informed advertising to users under the age of 18, and restricted use of altered images in advertising. In response to media and legislative pressure, some social media companies have introduced safeguarding and advertising policies to protect users from being exposed to harmful content that may promote body dissatisfaction. For example, in 2012, Instagram banned hashtags such as 'anorexia', 'proana', 'thinspiration', 'thigh gap' and 'imugly', whereby anyone searching these terms will be met with a blank screen and information about supportive resources. Since 2019, Instagram has also restricted users under the age of 18 from accessing posts that promote weight loss or cosmetic surgery. Some progress has also been made in the advertisement and fashion industry, with a more diverse representation of body shapes, but there is a need to further diversify body representations.

EDs are one of the most misunderstood and stigmatized mental health problems, and the way they are thought and talked about has profound consequences on attitudes, leading to the marginalization of individuals who have disordered eating behaviours. In this volume, stigma is defined as an 'attribute that is deeply discrediting', which reduces the stigmatized individual 'from a whole and usual person to a tainted, discounted one' (Goffman, 1963, p. 3). Public stigma can be perceived as a process that involves labelling, stereotyping and social distancing, leading to discrimination and status loss (Link & Phelan, 2006). As such, stigma is a social and attributional process (Jones et al., 1984) in which the person is perceived as socially invalid and thereby subtly or overtly excluded from participation (Elliott et al., 1982). Stigma may occur through knowledge acquisition or its failure (e.g., ignorance and misinformation), attitude formation (e.g., prejudice) and verbal and nonverbal behaviours (e.g., discrimination and hostility) (Thornicroft et al., 2007).

Stigmatization may be further understood as a phenomenon of public stigma versus self-stigma, both having far-reaching implications, particularly for individuals affected by a mental health condition (Corrigan et al., 2000). The experience of self-stigma involves the internalization of societal prejudices, leading to negative experiences (e.g., shame, low self-esteem, negative emotions) and self-devaluation (Corrigan, 2007; Corrigan & Watson, 2002; Whitley & Campbell, 2014). Similarly, family members and friends may experience prejudices and discrimination merely by association with individuals with a mental health problem (Ostman & Kjellin, 2002), so-called courtesy stigma (Goffman, 1963). Public stigma and self-stigma are reflections of a broader structural stigma—discriminatory attitudes towards mental health problems ingrained at cultural, political and institutional levels (Corrigan et al., 2005; Knifton, 2012).

As such, not only do individuals with EDs experience debilitating symptoms, but they also endure the stigma of having a mental health problem (O'Connor et al., 2019). Although in the early days EDs may feel like a helpful coping strategy to those affected, stigma and the experience of shame have long been recognized as some of the barriers to treatment-seeking in individuals with an ED, and they inhibit the disclosure of symptoms to family, friends and healthcare professionals (Ali et al., 2017). Telling others of an ED might also coincide with a fear of others wanting to take away the ED, indicating the important function of the ED to the individual. Fear of negative judgement, disapproval and others' control over their ED may lead those affected to distance and conceal their ED from others, causing them to seek out alternative support, including from online pro-ED communities (Mulveen & Hepworth, 2006). In these online communities, they are able to explore their experiences and receive support anonymously, while also being encouraged to engage in disordered eating, which might prolong the duration of EDs (Griffiths et al., 2015; Yeshua-Katz & Martins, 2013). Research has also revealed that healthcare professionals hold stigmatizing perceptions towards individuals with EDs, which has been associated with reduced quality of psychiatric service delivery and patients' lack of improvement (Thompson-Brenner et al., 2012).

Stigma towards individuals with EDs is more prevalent compared to those with other common mental health problems, and may be based on the beliefs that they are responsible for their disorder, are attention-seeking, have a weak character or are difficult to communicate and empathize with (Crisp et al., 2000; Crisp, 2005; Griffiths et al., 2015; Roehrig & Mclean, 2010). Rather than perceiving EDs as severe conditions that require psychological treatment, the public also tends to perceive them as trivial and a lifestyle choice, motivated by vanity and the desire to emulate celebrities (Dimitropoulos et al., 2016). As pointed out by Foran and colleagues (2020), stigmatization of those with anorexia nervosa is like a pendulum that swings between attaining a socially perceived 'high-status' thin body ideal that is admired, and a 'low-status' body that is pathologized and stigmatized. However, those who experience the greatest stigma and associated psychological distress are individuals with EDs who are at a higher weight, and who also experience weight-based discrimination (Ashmore et al., 2008).

The way language is used in representations of EDs is a central theme of this volume. Language use has been identified as an important factor in the reduction of public stigma (Corrigan et al., 2005). The way language is used in print and social media has been recognized as a powerful vehicle in shaping our attitudes and beliefs about mental health problems, and through it, keeping stereotypes, prejudices and stigma alive (McGinty et al., 2016).

Newspaper coverage of serious mental health problems, in particular psychotic disorders, tends to portray those affected as perpetrators of violence and crimes (Corrigan et al., 2005; Whitley & Berry, 2013), or to position them as hopeless victims (Coverdale, Nairn & Claasen, 2002). In contrast to these portrayals, individuals with EDs are rarely linked with aggressive behaviour, and are portrayed more sympathetically (Bowen, Lovell & Waller, 2019; O'Hara & Smith, 2007; Shepard & Seale, 2010). Evidence from longitudinal studies exploring chronological changes in newspaper reporting indicates that anti-stigma campaigns and newspaper reporting guidelines, such as Time to Change, can result in an overall reduction in stigmatizing newspaper content (Anderson et al., 2018; Rhydderch et al., 2016; Thornicroft et al., 2013).[1] Representations of EDs as a broad category are significantly less stigmatizing compared to other diagnoses (e.g., schizophrenia and depression), but overall, the newspaper coverage has not changed significantly over time (Hildersley et al., 2020).

Although the news media are a central influence in propagating the thin body ideal and stigmatizing attitudes about EDs, only a few empirical studies have explored how EDs are presented in newspapers. Of these studies, the majority focused predominantly on anorexia and bulimia nervosa, prior to the inclusion of binge eating disorder as a clinical disorder with diagnostic criteria. As such, there is only limited information on the more nuanced understanding of EDs, and binge eating disorder still remains a highly neglected, marginalized and stigmatized mental health problem. To some extent, the focus on newspaper representations of anorexia and bulimia nervosa—to the exclusion of other ED types such as binge eating disorder—may unintentionally reinforce stereotypical views of ED in the public domain, and it is evident that further investigation is required within this field of ED research.

An early study by Mondini and colleagues (1996) included 347 articles on EDs and topics associated with ideal feminine beauty (e.g., nutrition, fitness, beauty, fashion models) published in Italian newspapers and magazines between 1985 and 1995. The results showed that the media provided information about clinical symptoms that were consistent with scientific reports; however, EDs were not presented as genuine mental health problems, and reports emphasized positive personality traits of those affected by EDs (e.g., intelligence, perfectionism, ambition). In relation to ED aetiology, there was an emphasis on sociocultural factors (e.g., the fashion industry) and family factors (e.g., disordered family dynamics). Despite these reports, seemingly contradictory articles about fashion models also detailed their 'ideal characteristics and physical characteristics' and thus highlighted the perceived discrepancy between real and ideal images of beauty.

Further newspaper studies that focused on ED representation in the USA (O'Hara & Smith, 2007), the UK (Shepard & Seale, 2010) and Chinese newspapers (Sun et al., 2019) identified that EDs were primarily depicted as a female and young person's problem. In all three countries, ED stories were portrayed as trivial and associated with the entertainment and gossip sections, indicating that newspaper reporting was predominantly driven by a populist agenda (Shepard & Seale, 2010). EDs were also frequently associated with troubled childhoods (e.g., verbal and sexual abuse) and psychological causes (e.g., stress, low self-esteem), with under-reporting of genetic and biological causes. Information about the seriousness of the conditions and subsequent medical complications was superficial or under-reported, and the ED treatment and recovery were depicted as over-optimistically simple compared to the medical literature. As discussed by O'Hara and Smith (2007), newspapers are contributing to the perception gap between the medical conceptualization of ED aetiology, which focuses on biomedical and multifactorial models, and the lay public view, which assumes environmental causes. This creates and reinforces public stigma about EDs and therefore may negatively impact prevention as well as patients' treatment and recovery processes.

Very few studies have specifically explored the stigmatization of EDs in newspapers, and those that have have produced mixed findings. One study, for instance, showed that EDs were mainly presented in a stigmatizing context, with an emphasis on the hopelessness of those affected (Rhydderch et al., 2016). Conversely, other studies have found no evidence of stigmatization, with one study demonstrating that the newspaper coverage of EDs has become less stigmatizing (Goulden et al., 2011). More recently, a study by Bowen and colleagues (2020) with a focus on anorexia nervosa showed that the UK newspapers and Twitter feeds were typically not stigmatizing, but that the use of sensationalistic images may contribute to the stigmatization and marginalization of those individuals affected.

To counteract existing public stigma towards mental health problems, mental health charities have issued guidelines on balanced and responsible reporting on the topic in newspapers. Notably, in 2017, Beat (a large UK ED charity) published media guidelines for journalists and broadcasters who provide information about EDs, covering areas such as terminology, common myths and reporting tips, to inform truthful and compassionate coverage. The guidelines discourage the use of sensationalist or shocking images, information about body weight and details about disordered eating behaviour, without considering the harmful effect this information may have on those affected by EDs. Rather than creating misinformation about EDs, journalists are also encouraged to use the media as a platform to promote and communicate information to the public—for example, dispelling myths about EDs by raising awareness of their complexity, causes and risks, disseminating information to support early help-seeking, and offering advice to those directly affected and their families and friends.

Consistent with the global expansion of the internet in the late 1990s to early 2000s, a Web of Science bibliometric search on literature that utilized language-based approaches to ED media discourse identified a steep increase in peer-reviewed empirical studies. Of these, the greatest proportion of articles was published in journals with a predominant focus on EDs, body image and health, such as *International Journal of Eating Disorders*, *Health Communication*, *Qualitative Health Research* and *Body Image*. This itself may reflect the marginalized and stigmatized status of ED research within the mental health domain, where it is positioned as niche and limited to ED journals rather than being considered for generic higher-impact mental health publications (Solmi et al., 2020).

Other relevant articles appear in a range of journal outlets, representing a wide spread of academic disciplines, including communication studies, computer science, healthcare science, information science, linguistics, medicine, psychology, psychiatry, sociology and women's studies, to mention but a few. Of the published literature, qualitative and quantitative language-based approaches have contributed to the existing clinical literature by providing an in-depth understanding of the content of ED online communities, including the identity construction of the community and its users, experiences of recovery, linguistic characteristics and conversational interactions. It is possible to differentiate between various types of ED websites, including pro-ana, pro-mia and thinspiration. For the purpose of this introduction, I will be using the term 'pro-ED' to refer to all pro-ED content and sites, including those specific to anorexia, bulimia or other disordered eating behaviours.

Although a minority of pro-ED online groups promote extreme and unhealthy encouragement of ED behaviours, the majority of pro-ED sites offer individuals affected by EDs a space to validate and speak about their ED experiences with like-minded people in a safe, supportive and anonymous space (Borzekowski et al., 2010; Mulveen & Hepworth, 2006). Individuals with EDs often experience loneliness and social isolation (Dias, 2003), and the pro-ED sites offer an opportunity to bring together those with shared experiences to form a community of peer support (Yeshua-Katz & Martins, 2013). Although pro-ED sites are virtual, they share characteristics with non-virtual communities (Boero & Pascoe, 2012), such as group values, pro-ED language and rituals to sustain their community and reinforce the group identity of their users (Fox, Ward & O'Rourke, 2005). Pro-ED sites also empower users by offering an alternative model that resists and counterbalances conventional medical and sociocultural perspectives, that positions EDs as a lifestyle, and provides users with a sense of identity, safety, stability and control (Day &

Keys, 2008). Despite these benefits, the exposure on pro-ED sites to sensational thinspiration imagery that glorifies the thin body ideal and anorexia, and active encouragement among pro-ED members to engage in ED behaviour, have been recognized as serious risk factors in the maintenance of body dissatisfaction and EDs (Mento et al., 2021).

In relation to the content of pro-ED sites, systematic content analysis studies demonstrate that rather than pathologizing problematic eating behaviour, there is a tendency to present EDs to users as a lifestyle choice (Borzekowski et al., 2010; Norris et al., 2006). In relation to anorexia nervosa, this is underpinned by the sharing of graphic images that encourage their users to engage in problematic eating behaviours, offering accessories to control food intake and physical activity (e.g., calorie calculators), sharing of suggestions on how to lose weight (e.g., diet, safe foods, exercise, purging) and tips on how to conceal the condition from others (Borzekowski et al., 2010; Harshbarger et al., 2009; Norris et al., 2006). Pro-ED site communities also tend to reframe disordered eating behaviour in terms of success, control, perfection, solidarity, self-hate and starvation, elevating it to something akin to a pseudo-religious belief through the use of religious metaphors such as the 'Ana Psalm and Creed' (Borzekowski et al., 2010; Norris et al., 2006).

The identity of the individual user and group member appears to be central in pro-ED sites. An early discursive study of an online anorexia message board by Hardin (2003) identified that some young women positioned themselves as 'wanting to be anorexic and desiring to become emaciated', which was perceived as 'fake' by 'authentic and legitimate' members who simply 'have anorexia'. Giles's (2006) discourse analysis of pro-ED sites posits that users perceive themselves as being part of an online community of like-minded individuals. These communities are not homogenous but there is a distinctive hierarchy of pro-ED identities (e.g., anorexia 'anas', bulimia 'mias', EDNOS), all of which associate themselves with specific values that are used to police their distinct identity boundaries, to determine in- or out-group community membership, and to defend themselves from 'fakers' and 'wannabes' (those who claim to have an ED but do not) and 'haters' (those who perceive the community as dangerous). Day and Keys' (2008) discourse analysis of pro-ED sites demonstrated how users would use two discursive subject positions—'the feminine saint' who conforms to the thin body ideal and the pursuit of perfection and virtue, and 'the feminine rebel' who resists medical authorities and control over the body. Gavin, Rodham and Poyer's (2008) interpretative phenomenological analysis of postings on pro-ana support forums indicated that pro-anorexic identities were normalized both through the normalization of participants' thoughts and behaviour, and the creation of a group bond by sharing their secret ED identity. A grounded theory study by Haas and colleagues (2010) identified that the co-construction of a pro-ED identity involves two strategies—'staying true to ana' through disclosure of eating habits and activities, and 'creating an audience for ana' through disclosing personal daily activities and intimate feelings. Other aspects associated with the communication strategies relate to self-loathing, communication of advice and group-orientated encouraging engagement.

A few studies have also focused on the identity of the pro-ED newbie, who may be considered a form of a 'wannarexic'. Notably, Stommel and Koole's (2010) conversation analysis of a German ED site provides a closer insight into group membership legitimacy by demonstrating that although ED groups are welcoming, they demand that novices align with their group norms and 'ED ideology', and refusal means they risk rejection and falling back into social isolation. Stommel and Meijman's (2011) follow-up conversation analysis described how the discursive process of entering a pro-ED group begins with a hesitant expression of wanting to join, followed by a self-presentation in terms of a diagnosis to legitimize joining the group, whereas the absence of a diagnosis may lead to being rejected from joining. An ethnographic study of pro-ED sites by Boero and Pascoe (2012) investigated how new members negotiate the seemingly precarious terrain of pro-ED sites by having to prove their authentic participation. For this they need to engage in group rituals to verify their 'authentic and legitimate anorexic identity' that sets them apart from the unwanted 'wannarexics'. Rituals include demonstrating their familiarity with weight loss strategies, posting pictures of themselves, engaging in 'check-in' rituals to report their food intake and activities, offline group activities (e.g., fasts) and aggression in reinforcing community boundaries (e.g., self-aggression, motivational aggression and other-aggression). Through these rituals, participants create a sense of embodied identity, and actively participate in community building.

Maloney (2013) further expands on the above studies, suggesting that pro-ED site users engage in an interactive ritual chain (e.g., ability to assemble, common linguistic norms and behaviours, shared focus of attention) to manage their pro-ED identity and to create an in-group that acts as a boundary to outsiders. As pointed out by Crowe and Watts (2016), this sense of a group boundary reinforces a positive sense of self where 'everyone strives to become more like an ideal self, the closer one is to an ideal self, the happier one will be' (p. 387). The notion of a group boundary and the striving towards an ideal self are also evident in Figueras Bates' (2015) metaphor analysis, which identifies four embodied identity schemas in pro-ED site users, of which the schemas 'self as space' and 'self and weight' align with the collective pro-ED identity, and the schemas 'improving/perfecting the self' and 'social self' align with the users' individual identities, as part of the pro-ED community.

Pro-ED sites are often ambivalent about recovery. Riley, Rodham and Gavin's (2009) discourse analysis of 'body talk', produced in a pro-ED forum and a recovery forum, identified that pro-ED participants described their body in terms of their weight, whereas users of the recovery forum made use of medical and psychological discourses reflecting the overt aims and ideology aligned with recovery. Both forums used descriptions around food preparation and weight as part of their identity, and described bodily experiences associated with their ED or recovery.

Branley and Covey (2017) conducted a thematic analysis to characterize differences between pro-ED, anti-ED and pro-recovery posts on two social media platforms (Twitter and Tumblr). Pro-ED posts related to users' desires to engage in disordered eating behaviour, offering or requesting support to encourage ED behaviour, and positioning EDs as a lifestyle choice. Anti-ana posts showed explicit disapproval of the pro-ED mentality as a lifestyle and challenged pro-ED material. Pro-recovery posts encouraged recovery in other users by sharing their own recovery progress and struggle, involving mixed emotions about wanting to engage in ED behaviour and wanting to recover (Branley & Covey, 2017). This resistance or ambivalence to change reflects the ego-syntonic stance of EDs compared to an ego-dystonic stance associated with most other mental health problems, and the wish for recovery and alleviation of the experience of negative symptoms (Williams & Reid, 2010).

The difficulty and ambivalence of those engaging in recovery was also evident in a computerized content analysis that compared the homepages of pro-ED and recovering individuals with anorexia (Lyons, Mehl & Pennebaker, 2006). The findings showed that pro-anorexics represented themselves in a distinctively different way from those in recovery; they had more positive emotions, less anxiety, a lower degree of cognitive reflection and lower levels of self-directed attention than recovering individuals with anorexia. Conversely, one quantitative text analysis study explored the psychological condition of pro-ED bloggers, identifying that their writing featured lower cognitive processing, a more close-minded writing style, and fewer terms associated with emotional expression and social references, but more ED references than those found in recovery blogs (Wolf, Theis & Kordy, 2013).

A more holistic picture of recovery is provided in the thematic analysis of lived experience narratives in ED recovery blogs by Kenny and colleagues (2019). They describe how bloggers do not necessarily perceive recovery as being confined to the management of symptoms, but as a conscious decision, a uniquely subjective experience and a complex process. For example, bloggers felt that they had lost their identity to the EDs, and that their recovery allowed them to find themselves again by relinquishing a false sense of control and connecting with others, as a means to finding new meaning in life beyond their appearance. There was also the perception that a lack of diversity in the blogs and the diet culture would be barriers to recovery, and hinder help-seeking. It is also evident that easy access to pro-ED sites presents a challenge to recovery and treatment. For instance, Hilton's (2018) thematic analysis of pro-ED messages showed that users believed that ED sites do not cause mental health problems or EDs but may be a trigger, and that pro-ED sites provide support, and the community cannot be reduced to the desire of wanting to be thin. Firkins and colleagues' (2019) narrative inquiry explored users' disengagement from pro-ED sites, and identified two overarching storylines that reflected 'disengagement by choice as a necessary step to recovery' and 'disengagement due to doubt about the legitimacy of their ED'. It is evident that disengagement is a complex process and clinicians need to be mindful of what disengagement means to the individual before making assumptions.

A central focus of this volume is the application of language-based approaches to ED representations in public discourse, including traditional media and online communities. The above brief outline of the studies that have analysed newspaper representations of EDs, and the content of pro-ED sites and experiences of their users, showcases the broad application of methodological approaches that use language as their unit of analysis.

Unlike any other entity that is amenable to scientific interrogation, language is unique to the extent that it does not prescribe a particular theory or research methodology. Language is a flexible variable that can be analysed using approaches following different orientations across the ontological and epistemological spectrum. Any language-based approach to data analysis reflects a philosophical assumption that aligns with an ontological and epistemological position, the former referring to the nature of being and reality ('What is there?'), and the latter to the nature of knowledge ('What do you know?' and 'How do you know it?'). Both ontology and epistemology interrogate the position of the researcher and their understanding of reality, to frame the research questions and to identify an appropriate research approach that answers the research questions.

Ontological assumptions can be perceived as being on a continuum, with realism—assuming that reality is independent from human practice—at one end, and relativism—assuming that reality is dependent on human practice—on the other. Whereas realism is associated with the natural sciences and their understanding of truth as rational, predictable and based on universal laws, relativism is associated with the social sciences, which reject the notion of an 'objective truth'. As such, relativism assumes that reality is subjective, and that there are multiple coexisting realities based on interpretations, rather than one single objective reality (Slevitch, 2011).

Language-based approaches also move along an epistemological continuum, between a constructivist and interpretative stance in qualitative research, which stems from a relativistic outlook, and the positivist stance associated with quantitative research (de Gialdino, 2009). Whereas positivism assumes that concepts in the world can be assessed and measured using scientific instruments, with the researcher being positioned as unbiased and objective, the constructivist stance perceives truth and knowledge to be socially constructed through discourse and language, and contextually situated.

Computer-assisted word frequency measures, for example, reflect a realist and positivist position, based on the perception that language is a behaviour that can be isolated and objectively studied as a psychological construct. The use of language dictionaries focuses on counting semantic content, or the manifest surface meaning of language, to describe psychological processes that can be broken down and isolated into constituent parts within a realist framework, using reliable measures to gather quantitative evidence (Smith & Ceusters,

2010). This approach to data analysis assumes the existence of an objective and value-free truth within a rational world, where objects that we can perceive with our senses may be measured and reduced to a set of codes to predict future behaviour. Such a realist approach to language analysis is deductive and theory driven, or 'top down', perceiving the data through the lens of the researcher's theoretical interest.

Similarly to computer-assisted content analysis, qualitative content analysis utilizes a coding scheme to systematically analyse language, with a focus on quantifying the presence of content that requires the researcher's subjective interpretation of the meaning of phrases and words in texts. Qualitative content analysis often involves both manifest and latent coding, which indicate a dynamic interplay between the positivist and interpretivist epistemological positions associated with content analytic approaches. Due to its use of a coding scheme, qualitative content analysis has often been associated with a positivist stance (Baxter, 2009). Arguably, qualitative content analysis appears to be situated between positivism and constructivism (Krippendorff, 2004; Neuendorf, 2002), reflecting a 'critical realist' or 'subtle realist' stance that assumes the existence of objects in an external, independent reality, but posits that this reality can only be partially understood through the individual's sense-making and interpretation of it (Dieronitou, 2014).

Qualitative approaches, including discourse analysis and interpretative phenomenological analysis, are situated at the constructivist/interpretivist end of the epistemological continuum, which perceives language as an intersubjective and social construct that is contextually situated. This contextualist stance is consistent with Smith's (2015) view that the reflective analysis of language provides a tool for the researcher, allowing them to describe, interpret and make meaning from the symbolic system of the verbalized experiences. The ontological and epistemological stance of qualitative research positions the researcher as an intrinsic part of the research process. For instance, approaches that involve interviews between the researcher and participant, such as interpretative phenomenological analysis or thematic analysis, obtain an in-depth understanding of participants' experiences, and how these are embedded and situated within their social, cultural and historical context. Although interviews are powerful ways of capturing information and understanding participants' lived experiences, the research interview is a process in which the researcher maintains an idealist stance, while recognizing that any interpretations are subjective and influenced by personal attitudes, ideologies and experiences (Braun & Clarke, 2016; Brinkman & Kvale, 2018). Such qualitative approaches to language analysis reflect an inductive approach that is data-driven or 'bottom-up', by focusing on exploring the meaning of the observed patterns in the data. Compared to descriptive approaches to language analysis that use data detailing linguistic frequencies, qualitative approaches focus on the deeper meaning conveyed in the data.

This volume aims to apply language-based approaches along the ontological and epistemological spectrum to discourses about EDs in the media, with the aim of better understanding how media portrayals and stigmatization of ED influence experiences of body dissatisfaction and disordered eating behaviour. The aims of this multi-methodological and interdisciplinary endeavour are twofold: first, to critically evaluate key insights, such as meanings and interpretations, obtained from the different data and methodological angles used; and second, to propose recommendations for accurate and non-sensationalist media reporting that would meet the wellbeing needs of the public.

## Contributions to this Volume

Each chapter in this volume uses a language-based approach to explore how EDs are represented in the media or spoken about by individuals with lived experiences. Two chapters also provide a theoretical and self-reflective framework on ED media discourses. The chapters have been organized into two parts according to the source of textual data investigated.

Part I focuses on traditional media representations of EDs including in the Canadian, UK, USA, Spanish and Turkish press, and the perception of newspapers by individuals with lived experiences of EDs. Part II concerns itself with discourses about EDs in online communities, participatory media and user-generated discourses.

The first part, Traditional Media and Public Discourse, covering newspaper and magazine representations of EDs, comprises seven chapters, of which the first is 'Eating Disorder Metaphors in the American and Spanish Press' by Carolina Figueras Bates. This chapter uses a cross-cultural metaphorical analysis to assess how EDs and individuals with EDs are depicted in the Spanish and American news medias, and what metaphors are shared or relate to their specific cultural landscapes. By exploring two subcorpora of two newspapers, *El País* in Spain and the *New York Times* in the USA, the results identify a core set of metaphorical constructions for each culture and an overarching metaphorical frame of 'AN EATING DISORDER IS A PROBLEM' in both cultures.

The second chapter in this section, 'Animal Metaphors in Women's Magazines: Their Potential Link with Eating Disorders' by Irene López-Rodríguez, studies the use of figurative fauna expressions in 8,976 articles from women's magazines. The results demonstrate that women's magazines utilize zoomorphic tropes to frame and communicate ideas pertaining to women's eating behaviours and physical appearances. Figurative expressions such as 'the beast inside', or 'whale', disparage women who cannot control their appetites and/or do not conform to the ultra-thin beauty standard, reinforcing stigmatizing and unhealthy body image attitudes, and potentially establishing a link to the development of disordered eating.

In 'Challenging the Stigma of a "Woman's Illness" and "Feminine Problem": A Cross-Cultural Analysis of News Stories about Eating Disorders and Men' by Scott Parrott, Kimberly Bissell, Nicholas Eckhart and Bumsoo Park, the authors acknowledge that although EDs present serious health consequences for men, they may not seek treatment because EDs are stigmatized by the lay population as being feminine. By examining how news organizations in Canada, the UK and the USA covered EDs between 2010 and 2019, their content analysis study of 279 articles found that, in fact, journalists often provide men with a platform through which to communicate their experiences with EDs, challenging assumptions concerning these so-called feminine problems.

The fourth chapter is Matt Bowen and Rhian Waller's study, 'Representations of Anorexia Nervosa in National Media: A Frame Analysis of the UK Press'. This explores the representation of anorexia in the UK national press and the degree to which underlying ideological positions may influence readers. In composing this chapter, the authors adapted an existing coding frame for Twitter data to print press data, which was then applied to 482 articles that included the words 'anorexic' or 'anorexia' in any the UK national broadsheet or tabloid newspaper. The results showed four news frames: illness, social, stress-recovery, and trivialization. Compared to social media, there was a near absence of clickbait frames, thus reflecting the traditional print media format.

In 'Representations of Eating Disorders in Turkish News Media', Hayriye Gulec analyses media representations of EDs in Turkish newspapers, to address a broader gap in existing literature on the portrayal of mental health problems in the Turkish media. A qualitative content analysis of over 199 articles published between 2000 and 2016 from two broadsheet Turkish newspapers (*Milliyet* and *Cumhuriyet*) showed that representations of EDs related predominantly to sensationalist coverage of the fashion industry and celebrities. There was also a greater focus on women and Western celebrities than on men and individuals from diverse backgrounds, contributing to the misconception that EDs only affect certain populations and cultures.

The sixth chapter, 'Experiencing Newspaper Representations of Eating Disorders: An Interpretative Phenomenological Study' by Laura A. Cariola and Billy Lee, explores how individuals with an ED make sense of newspaper discourses in relation to their lived experience. The results show that participants experienced newspaper reporting as sensationalizing and drawing on shock value. There was a sense of extreme loneliness, and of feeling muted by other people's assumptions and beliefs. The results demonstrate a fracture between newspaper discourses and first-hand experiences, which has been a major source of trouble for the participants. The authors also present recommendations for ethical reporting on EDs in the newspapers.

The seventh and last chapter in this section, Gareth Lyons, Sue McAndrew and Tony Warne's contribution, 'Narrative Experiences of Social Media and the Internet from Men with Eating Disorders', examines the lived experiences of men with EDs who had directly engaged with media outlets to share their stories. Applying interpretivist principles to thematic analysis, seven in-depth interviews with men diagnosed with anorexia nervosa about their experiences of living with the illness revealed several themes, including the lack of media representation of male EDs, working with the media, male anorexia on the internet, social media, internet forums/blogging and pro-anorexia and thinspiration sites/forums. The men's stories also indicated a lack of insight into ED symptoms, thus clearly demonstrating the need for greater public awareness of male EDs.

Part II of this book, Participatory Media and User-Generated Discourse, includes six chapters. The first is theoretical, 'Online Negative Enabling Support Group (ONESG) Theory: Understanding Online Extreme Community Communication Promoting Negative Health Behaviours' by Stephen M. Haas, Nancy A. Jennings and Pamara F. Chang. This chapter seeks to further explicate the theoretical propositions underpinning Online Negative Enabling

Support Group (ONESG) theory (Haas et al., 2010), which was developed using grounded theory to examine messages exchanged in the online pro-anorexia movement. In this chapter, the authors propose that ONESG theory has heuristic potential to increase understanding of the communication observed in groups that use the internet to promote negative health behaviours, for example self-injury, cutting and suicide, in the growing global information-based society.

In Chapter 9, 'Eating Disorder Discourse in a Diet and Fitness App Community: Understanding User Needs Through Exploratory Mixed Methods', Elizabeth V. Eikey, Oliver Golden, Zhuoxi Chen and Qiuer Chen conduct a computational and thematic analysis of ED-related posts from diet and fitness app users to better understand how to support users. Based on a dataset of over 27,900 posts, the results demonstrate that ED-related posts tend to solicit social support, and regardless of the type of health goal, users express concern around changing their weight in a healthy way, and not resorting to extreme measures or slipping back into ED behaviours or unhealthy approaches.

Dawn Branley-Bell's contribution, 'Using Qualitative and Mixed-Methods Approaches to Investigate Online Communication about Eating Disorders: A Reflective Account', draws upon her experience and lessons learned from using mixed-methods research to investigate social media communication around EDs. The author describes some of the techniques she applied in these studies, and throughout the chapter she critically reflects upon the design and ethical challenges she encountered as part of her research.

In her chapter, '"I'll Never Be Skinny Enough": A Fantasy Theme Analysis of Pro-Anorexia Discourse', Allyn Lueders investigates the social reality of fantasy themes on the pro-ED forum site Myproana.com. The data, which includes 1,652 posts by pro-ED site members published in the two-month period between February and April 2020, provides evidence of three fantasy themes in this community—'Us versus them', 'I'll never be skinny enough' and 'Openness to recovery'—indicating the coexistence of both pro-recovery or healthy eating choices and pro-ED sentiments on the same forum.

In 'Lived Experiences of Parents Raising Children with Eating Disorders: A Thematic Analysis', Emma O'Rourke and Laura A. Cariola use a thematic analysis of Mumsnet posts to obtain a better understanding of the everyday lived experiences of parents whose children have EDs. Based on sixty-seven discussion threads, published between January 2010 and November 2020, the authors' findings identified four themes—'Understanding, helplessness and self-blame', 'Control of the eating disordered behaviour', 'Abusive behaviour, self-harm and communication' and 'Mental health needs and lack of support'—highlighting how parents' experiences are challenged as they raise their child with a complex mental health condition, with minimal support and resources.

The last chapter in this section, by Wendy Solomons, Kate Davenport and Joanne McDowell, is titled '"Anorexia is Seen as a GOOD Thing When You're Fat!": Constructing "Eating Disorders" in Fat Acceptance Blogs'. It uses a critical discursive psychology approach within a social constructionist framework to explore how EDs, and those who live with them, are constructed within the 'fatosphere'. Drawing on a corpus of three fat acceptance blogs representing the voices of those with lived experiences of EDs, this study provides an insightful understanding of how 'fat acceptance' discourses represent a powerful and marginalized voice that challenges the homogenous societal 'thinness' conversation.

## Note

1 https://www.time-to-change.org.uk/media-centre/responsible-reporting

## References


Ali, K., Farrer, L., Fassnacht, D.B., Gulliver, A., Bauer, S., & Griffiths, K.M. (2017). Perceived barriers and facilitators towards help-seeking for eating disorders: a systematic review. *International Journal of Eating Disorders* 50: 9–21. https://doi.org/10.1002/eat.22598

All Party Parliamentary Group on Body Image (APPG) (2012). *Reflections on Body Image*. YMCA.

Allen, K.L., Byrne, S.M., Oddy, W.H., & Crosby, R.D. (2013). DSM-IV-TR and DSM-5 eating disorders in adolescents: prevalence, stability, and psychosocial correlates in a population-based sample of male and female adolescents. *Journal of Abnormal Psychology* 122(3): 720–32. https://doi.org/10.1037/a0034004

American Psychiatric Association (2013). *Diagnostic and Statistical Manual of Mental Disorders* (DSM-5®). Arlington, VA: APA. https://doi.org/10.1176/appi.books.9780890425596

ANAD (2021). *Eating Disorder Statistics*. https://anad.org/get-informed/about-eating-disorders/eating-disorders-statistics

Anderson, C., Robinson, E.J., Krooupa, A.M., & Henderson, C. (2018). Changes in newspaper coverage of mental illness from 2008 to 2016 in England. *Epidemiology and Psychiatric Science* 4(29): e9. https://doi.org/10.1017/S2045796018000720

Anderson, M. (2003). 'One flew over the psychiatric unit': mental illness and the media. *Journal of Psychiatric and Mental Health Nursing* 10: 297–306. https://doi.org/10.1046/j.1365-2850.2003.00592.x

Ardito, R.B., & Rabellino, D. (2011). Therapeutic alliance and outcome of psychotherapy: historical excursus, measurements, and prospects for research. *Frontiers in Psychology* 2: 270. https://doi.org/10.3389/fpsyg.2011.00270

Ashmore, J.A., Friedman, K.E., Reichmann, S.K., & Musante, G.J. (2008). Weight-based stigmatization, psychological distress, & binge eating behaviour among obese treatment-seeking adults. *Eating Behaviours* 9(2): 203–209. https://doi.org/10.1016/j.eatbeh.2007.09.006

Backholm, K., Isomaa, R., & Birgegård, A. (2013). The prevalence and impact of trauma history in eating disorder patients. *European Journal of Psychotraumatology* 4. https://doi.org/10.3402/ejpt.v4i0.22482

Bandura, A. (2009). Social cognitive theory of mass communication. In J. Bryant & M.B. Oliver (eds), *Media Effects: Advances in Theory and Research* (pp. 94–124). Mahwah, NJ: Lawrence Erlbaum.

Baxter, J. (2009). Content analysis. In R. Kitchin & N. Thrift (eds), *International Encyclopedia of Human Geography* (Vol. 1, pp. 275–80). Oxford: Elsevier.

Beat (2017). *Media Guidelines for Reporting Eating Disorders.* https://www.beateatingdisorders.org.uk/uploads/documents/2017/9/beat-media-guidelines.pdf

Beat (2021). *Statistics for Journalists.* https://www.beateatingdisorders.org.uk/media-centre/eating-disorder-statistics

Becker, A.E. (2004). Television, disordered eating, and young women in Fiji: negotiating body image and identity during rapid social change. *Culture, Medicine and Psychiatry* 28(4): 533–59. https://doi.org/10.1007/s11013-004-1067-5

Boero, N., & Pascoe, C.J. (2012). Pro-anorexia communities and online interaction: bringing the pro-ana body online. *Body and Society* 18(2): 27–57. https://doi.org/10.1177/1357034x12440827

Borzekowski, D.L.G., Schenk, S., Wilson, J.L., & Peebles, R. (2010). E-Ana and e-Mia: a content analysis of pro-eating disorder websites. *American Journal of Public Health* 100(8): 1526–34. https://doi.org/10.2105/ajph.2009.172700

Bowen, M.L., & Lovell, A. (2013). Representations of mental health disorders in print media. *Journal of Mental Health Nursing* 2: 198–202. https://doi.org/10.12968/bjmh.2013.2.4.198

Bowen, M., Lovell, A., & Waller, R. (2020). Stigma: the representation of anorexia nervosa in UK newspaper Twitter feeds. *Journal of Mental Health* 15: 1–8. https://doi.org/10.1080/09638237.2020.1793128

Branley, D.B., & Covey, J. (2017). Pro-ana versus pro-recovery: a content analytic comparison of social media users' communication about eating disorders on Twitter and Tumblr. *Frontiers in Psychology* 8: 1356. https://doi.org/10.3389/fpsyg.2017.01356

Braun, V., & Clarke, V. (2016). Thematic analysis. *The Journal of Positive Psychology* 12: 297–98. https://doi.org/10.1080/17439760.2016.1262613

Brechan, I., & Kvalem, I.L. (2015). Relationship between body dissatisfaction and disordered eating: mediating role of self-esteem and depression. *Eating Behaviours* 17: 49–58. https://doi.org/10.1016/j.eatbeh.2014.12.008

Brinkman, S., & Kvale, S. (2018). *Doing Interviews*. London: Sage.

Carr, A., & McNulty, M. (2016). *The Handbook of Adult Clinical Psychology: An Evidence-Based Practice Approach*. London: Routledge.

Cavazos-Rehg, P.A., Fitzsimmons-Craft, E.E., Krauss, M.J., Anako, N., Xu, C., Kasson, E., Costello, S.J., & Wilfley, D.E. (2020). Examining the self-reported advantages and disadvantages of socially networking about body image and eating disorders. *International Journal of Eating Disorders* 53(6): 852–63. https://doi.org/10.1002/eat.23282

Chamberlain, K. (2000). Methodolatry and qualitative health research. *Journal of Health Psychology* 5(3): 285–96. https://doi.org/10.1177/135910530000500306

Cheng, Z.H., Perko, V.L., Fuller-Marashi, L., Gau, J.M., & Stice, E. (2019). Ethnic differences in eating disorder prevalence, risk factors, and predictive effects of risk factors among young women. *Eating Behaviours* 32: 23–30. https://doi.org/10.1016/j.eatbeh.2018.11.004

Chua, T.H.H., & Chang, L. (2016). Follow me and like my beautiful selfies: Singapore teenage girls' engagement in self-presentation and peer comparison on social media. *Computers in Human Behaviour* 55: 190–97. https://doi.org/10.1016/j.chb.2015.09.011

Corrigan, P.W. (2007). How clinical diagnosis might exacerbate the stigma of mental illness. *Social Work* 52: 31–39. https://doi.org/10.1093/sw/52.1.31

Corrigan, P.W., & Watson, A.C. (2002). Understanding the impact of stigma on people with mental illness. *World Psychiatry: Official Journal of the World Psychiatric Association (WPA)* 1(1): 16–20.

Corrigan, P.W., Watson, A.C., Gracia, G., Slopen, N., Rasinski, K., & Hall, L.L. (2005). Newspaper stories as a measure of structural stigma. *Psychiatric Services* 56: 551–56. https://doi.org/10.1176/appi.ps.56.5.551

Coverdale, J., Nairn, R., & Claasen, D. (2002). Depictions of mental illness in print media: a prospective national sample. *Australian and New Zealand Journal of Psychiatry* 36(5): 697–700. https://doi.org/10.1046/j.1440-1614.2002.00998.x

Crisp, A. (2005). Stigmatization of and discrimination against people with eating disorders including a report of two nationwide surveys. *European Eating Disorder Review* 139(3): 147–52. https://doi.org/10.1002/erv.648

Crisp, A.H., Gelder, M.G., Rix, S., Meltzer, H.I., & Rowlands, O.J. (2000). Stigmatisation of people with mental illnesses. *British Journal of Psychiatry* 77: 4–7. https://doi.org/10.1192/bjp.177.1.4

Crowe, N., & Watts, M. (2016). 'We're just like Gok, but in reverse': Ana Girls—empowerment and resistance in digital communities. *International Journal of Adolescence and Youth* 21: 379–90. https://doi.org/10.1080/02673843.2013.856802

Day, K., & Keys, T. (2008). Starving in cyberspace: a discourse analysis of pro-eating-disorder websites. *Journal of Gender Studies* 17(1): 1–15. https://doi.org/10.1080/09589230701838321

de Gialdino, I.V. (2009). Ontological and epistemological foundations of qualitative research. *Forum: Qualitative Social Research* 10(2). https://www.qualitative-research.net/index.php/fqs/article/view/1299

Derenne, J., & Beresin, E. (2018). Body image, media, and eating disorders: a 10-year update. *Academic Psychiatry* 42(1): 129–34. https://doi.org/10.1007/s40596-017-0832-z

Dias, K. (2003). The ana sanctuary: women's pro-anorexia narratives in Cyberspace. *Journal of International Women's Studies* 4: 31–45.

Dieronitou, I. (2014). The ontological and epistemological foundations of qualitative and quantitative approaches to research. *International Journal of Economics, Commerce, and Management* 2(10). http://ijecm.co.uk/volume-ii-issue-10

Dimitropoulos, G., Freeman, V.E., Muskat, S., Domingo, A., & McCallum, L. (2016). 'You don't have anorexia, you just want to look like a celebrity': perceived stigma in individuals with anorexia nervosa. *Journal of Mental Health* 25(1): 47–54. https://doi.org/10.3109/09638237.2015.1101422

Dodge, E., & Simic, M. (2014). Anorexia runs in families: does this make the families responsible? A commentary on 'Anorexia runs in families: is this due to genes or the family environment?' *Journal of Family Therapy* 37(1): 93–102. https://doi.org/10.1111/1467-6427.12065

Eddy, K.T., Hennessey, M., & Thompson-Brenner, H. (2007). Eating pathology in East African women: the role of media exposure and globalization. *Journal of Nervous and Mental Disease* 195(3): 196–202. https://doi.org/10.1097/01.nmd.0000243922.49394.7d

Elliott, G., Ziegler, H.L., Altman, B.M, & Scott, D.R. (1982). Understanding stigma: dimensions of deviance and coping. *Deviant Behavior* 3: 275–300. https://doi.org/10.1080/01639625.1982.9967590

Fardouly, J., & Vartanina, L.R. (2015). Negative comparisons about one's appearance mediate the relationship between Facebook usage and body image concerns. *Body Image* 12: 82–88. https://doi.org/10.1016/j.bodyim.2014.10.004

Ferreira, C., Pinto-Gouveia, J., & Duarte, C. (2013). Self-compassion in the face of shame and body image dissatisfaction: implications for eating disorders. *Eating Behaviours* 14(2): 207–10. https://doi.org/10.1016/j.eatbeh.2013.01.005

Fichter, M.M., & Quadflieg, N. (2016). Mortality in eating disorders: results of a large prospective clinical longitudinal study. *International Journal of Eating Disorders* 49(4): 391–401. https://doi.org/10.1002/eat.22501

Field, A.E., Sonneville, K.R., Micali, N., Crosby, R.D., Swanson, S.A., Laird, N.M., Treasure, J., Solmi, F., & Horton, N.J. (2012). Prospective association of common eating disorders and adverse outcomes. *Pediatrics* 130(2): e289–e295. https://doi.org/10.1542/peds.2011-3663

Figueras Bates, C. (2015). 'I am a waste of breath, of space, of time': metaphors of self in a pro-anorexia group. *Qualitative Health Research* 25: 189–204. https://doi.org/10.1177/1049732314550004

Firkins, A., Twist, J., Solomons, W., & Keville, S. (2019). Cutting ties with pro-ana: a narrative inquiry concerning the experiences of pro-ana disengagement from six former site users. *Qualitative Health Research* 29(10): 1461–73. https://doi.org/10.1177/1049732319830425

Flament, M.F., Henderson, K., Buchholz, A., Obeid, N., Nguyen, H.N., Birmingham, M., & Goldfield, G. (2015). Weight status and DSM-5 diagnoses of eating disorders in adolescents from the community. *Journal of American Academy of Child and Adolescent Psychiatry* 54(5): 403–411.e2. https://doi.org/10.1016/j.jaac.2015.01.020

Foran, A.-M., O'Donnell, A.T., & Muldoon, O.T. (2020). Stigma of eating disorders and recovery-related outcomes: a systematic review. *European Eating Disorders Review* 28(4): 385–97. https://doi.org/10.1002/erv.2735

Fox, N.J., Ward, K., & O'Rourke, A. (2005). Pro-anorexia, weight-loss drugs and the internet: an 'anti-recovery' explanatory model of anorexia. *Sociology of Health & Illness* 27(7): 944–71. https://doi.org/10.1111/j.1467-9566.2005.00465.x

Galasiński, D. (2018). Language and psychiatry. *The Lancet* 5(3): 200–201. https://doi.org/10.1016/s2215-0366(18)30040-3

Galasiński, D. (2021). No mental health research without qualitative research. *The Lancet* 8(4): 266–67. https://doi.org/10.1016/s2215-0366(20)30399-0

Galmiche, M., Déchelotte, P., Lambert, G., & Tavolacci, M.-P. (2019). Prevalence of eating disorders over the 2000–2018 period: a systematic literature review. *The American Journal of Clinical Nutrition* 109(5): 1402–13. https://doi.org/10.1093/ajcn/nqy342

Garner, D.M., Garfinkel, P.E., Schwartz, D., & Thompson, M. (1980). Cultural expectations of thinness in women. *Psychological Reports* 47: 483–91. https://doi.org/10.1080/106402601753454903

Gavin, J., Rodham, K., & Poyer, H. (2008). The presentation of 'pro-anorexia' in online group interactions. *Qualitative Health Research* 18(3): 325–33. https://doi.org/10.1177/1049732307311640

Gerbner, G., Gross, L., Morgan, M., Signorielli, N., & Shanahan, J. (2002). Growing up with television: cultivation processes. In J. Bryant & D. Zillmann (eds), *Media Effects: Advances in Theory and Research* (pp. 43–67). Mahwah, NJ: Lawrence Erlbaum.

Giles, D. (2006). Constructing identities in cyberspace: the case of eating disorders. *British Journal of Social Psychology* 45: 463–77. https://doi.org/10.1348/014466605x53596

Goffman, E. (1963). *Stigma: Notes on the Management of Spoiled Identity*. Englewood Cliffs, NJ: Prentice Hall.

Goulden, R., Corker, E., Evans-Lacko, S., Rose, D., Thornicroft, G., & Henderson, C. (2011). Newspaper coverage of mental illness in the UK, 1992–2008. *BMC Public Health* 11: 796. https://doi.org/10.1186/1471-2458-11-796

GOV (2021). Changing the perfect picture: an inquiry into body image. *Sixth Report of Session 2019–21*. https://committees.parliament.uk/publications/5357/documents/53751/default

Grabe, S., Ward, L.M., & Hyde, J.S. (2008). The role of the media in body image concerns among women: a meta-analysis of experimental and correlational studies. *Psychological Bulletin* 134(3): 460–76. https://doi.org/10.1037/0033-2909.134.3.460

Griffiths, S., Mond, J.M., Murray, S.B., & Touyz, S. (2015). The prevalence and adverse associations of stigmatization in people with eating disorders. *International Journal of Eating Disorders* 48(6): 767–74. https://doi.org/10.1002/eat.22353

Griffiths, S., Hay, P., Mitchison, D., Mond, J.M., McLean, S.A., Rodgers, B., Massey, R., & Paxton, S.J. (2016). Sex differences in the relationships between body dissatisfaction, quality of life and psychological distress. *Australian and New Zealand Journal of Public Health* 40(6): 518–22. https://doi.org/10.1111/1753-6405.12538

Grilo, C.M. (2006). *Eating and Weight Disorders (Clinical Psychology: A Modular Course)*. London: Psychology Press.

Haas, S., Irr, M.E., Jennings, N.A., & Wagner, L.M. (2011). Communicating thin: a grounded model on online negative enabling support groups in the pro-anorexia movement. *New Media and Society* 13(1): 40–57. https://doi.org/10.1177/1461444810363910

Hardin, A. (2003). Constructing experience in individual interviews, autobiographies and on-line accounts: a poststructuralist approach. *Journal of Advanced Nursing* 41(6): 536–44. https://doi.org/10.1046/j.1365-2648.2003.02565.x

Harshbarger, J.L., Ahlers-Schmidt, C.R., Mayans, L., Mayans, D., & Hawkins, J.H. (2009). Pro-anorexia websites: what a clinician should know. *International Journal of Eating Disorders* 42(4): 367–70. https://doi.org/10.1002/eat.20608

Hasher, L., Goldstein, D., & Toppio, T. (1977). Frequency and the conference of referential validity. *Journal of Verbal Learning and Verbal Behavior* 16: 107–12. https://doi.org/10.1016/s0022-5371(77)80012-1

Hilbert, A., Pike, K.M., Goldschmidt, A.B., Wilfley, D.E., Fairburn, C.G., Dohm, F.A., Walsh, B.T., & Striegel Weissman, R. (2014). Risk factors across the eating disorders. *Psychiatry Research* 220(1–2): 500–506.

Hildersley, R., Potts, L., Anderson, C., & Henderson, C. (2020). Improvement for most, but not all: changes in newspaper coverage of mental illness from 2008 to 2019 in England. *Epidemiology and Psychiatric Sciences* 29: e177. https://doi.org/10.1017/s204579602000089x

Hilton, C.E. (2018). 'It's the symptom of the problem, not the problem itself': a qualitative exploration of the role of pro-anorexia websites in users' disordered eating. *Issues in Mental Health Nursing* 39(10): 865–75. https://doi.org/10.1080/01612840.2018.1493625

Jacobi, C., & Fittig, E. (2010). Psychosocial risk factors for eating disorders. In W.S. Agras (ed.), *The Oxford Handbook of Eating Disorders* (pp. 106–25). Oxford: Oxford University Press.

Jacobi, C., Hayward, C., de Zwaan, M., Kraemer, H.C., Agras, W.S. (2004). Coming to terms with risk factors for eating disorders: application of risk terminology and suggestions for a general taxonomy. *Psychological Bulletin* 130(1): 19–65. https://doi.org/10.1037/0033-2909.130.1.19

Jenkins, P.E., Hoste, R.R., Meyer, C., & Blissett, J.M. (2011). Eating disorders and quality of life: a review of the literature. *Clinical Psychology Review* 31: 113–21. https://doi.org/10.1080/10640266.2013.779176

Jones, E.E., Farina, A., Hastorf, A.H., Markus, H., Miller, D.T., & Scott, R.A. (1984). *Social Stigma: The Psychology of Marked Relationships*. London: Freeman.

Kaufman, L. (1980). Prime-time nutrition. *Journal of Communication* 30: 37–46. https://doi.org/10.1111/j.1460-2466.1980.tb01989.x

Kenny, T.E., Boyle, S.L., & Lewis, S.P. (2019). #recovery: understanding recovery from the lens of recovery-focused blogs posted by individuals with lived experience. *International Journal of Eating Disorders* 53(8): 1234–43. https://doi.org/10.1002/eat.23221

Khaled, S.M., Kimmel, L., & Le Trung, K. (2018). Assessing the factor structure and measurement invariance of the eating attitude test (EAT-26) across language and BMI in young Arab women. *Journal of Eating Disorders* 6: 14. https://doi.org/10.1186/s40337-018-0199-x

Kilbourne, J. (1994). Still killing us softly: advertising and the obsession with thinness. In P. Fallon, M. Katzman, & S. Wooley (eds), *Feminist Perspectives on Eating Disorders* (pp. 395–419). New York: Guilford Press.

Kinnaird, E., Norton, C., Pimblett, C., Stewart, C., & Tchanturia, K. (2019). 'There's nothing there for guys': do men with eating disorders want treatment adaptations? A qualitative study. *Eating and Weight Disorders—Studies on Anorexia, Bulimia and Obesity* 24: 845–85. https://doi.org/10.1007/s40519-019-00770-0

Kivits, J., Ricci, L., & Minary, L. (2019). Interdisciplinary research in public health: the 'why' and the 'how'. *Journal of Epidemiology and Community Health* 73(12): 1061–62. https://doi.org/10.1136/jech-2019-212511

Knifton, L. (2012). Understanding and addressing the stigma of mental illness with ethnic minority communities. *Health Sociology Review* 21(3): 287–98. https://doi.org/10.5172/hesr.2012.21.3.287

Kolar, D.R., Rodriguez, D.L.M., Chams, M.M., & Hoek, H.W. (2016). Epidemiology of eating disorders in Latin America: a systematic review and meta-analysis. *Current Opinion in Psychiatry* 29(6): 363–71. https://doi.org/10.1097/yco.0000000000000279

Krippendorff, K. (2004). *Content Analysis: An Introduction to Its Methodology* (2nd edn). Thousand Oaks, CA: Sage.

Lewallen, J., & Behm-Morawitz, E. (2016). Pinterest or thinterest? Social comparison and body image on social media. *Social Media and Society* 2(1). https://doi.org/10.1177%2F2056305116640559

Limbers, C.A., Cohen, L.A., & Gray, B.A. (2018). Eating disorders in adolescent and young adult males: prevalence, diagnosis, and treatment strategies. *Adolescent Health, Medicine and Therapeutics* 10(9): 111–16. https://doi.org/10.2147/ahmt.s147480

Link, B.G., & Phelan, J.C. (2006). Stigma and its public health implications. *The Lancet* 367(9509): 528–29. https://doi.org/10.1016/s0140-6736(06)68184-1

Lipson, S.K., & Sonneville, K.R. (2017). Eating disorder symptoms among undergraduate and graduate students at 12 U.S. colleges and universities. *Eating Behaviours* 24: 81–88. https://doi.org/10.1016/j.eatbeh.2016.12.003

Lupton, D. (2018). 'I just want it to be done, done, done!' Food tracking apps, affects, and agential capacities. *Multimodal Technologies and Interaction* 2: 29. https://www.mdpi.com/2414-4088/2/2/29

Lyons, E.J., Mehl, M.R., & Pennebaker, J.W. (2006). Pro-anorexics and recovering anorexics differ in their linguistic internet self-presentation. *Journal of Psychosomatic Research* 60(3): 253–56. https://doi.org/10.1016/j.jpsychores.2005.07.017

Machado, P.P.P., Gonçales, S., & Hoek, H.W. (2012). DSM-5 reduces the proportion of EDNOS cases: evidence from community samples. *International Journal of Eating Disorders* 46(1): 60–65. https://doi.org/10.1002/eat.22040

Maloney, P. (2013). Online networks and emotional energy: how pro-anorexic websites use interaction rituals to (re)form identity. *Information, Communication and Society* 16(1): 105–24. https://doi.org/10.1080/1369118x.2012.659197

Mandelli, L., Arminio, A., Atti, A.R., & De Ronchi, D. (2019). Suicide attempts in eating disorder subtypes: a meta-analysis of the literature employing DSM-IV, DSM-5, or ICD-10 diagnostic criteria. *Psychological Medicine* 49(8): 1237–49. https://doi.org/10.1017/s0033291718003549

Mayhew, A.J., Pgueyre, M., Couturier, J., & Meyre, D. (2018). An evolutionary genetic perspective of eating disorders. *Neuroendocrinology* 106(3): 292–306. https://doi.org/10.1159/000484525

McGinty, E.E., Kennedy-Hendricks, A., Choksy, S., & Barry, C.L. (2016). Trends in news media coverage of mental illness in the United States: 1995–2014. *Health Affairs* 35: 1121–29. https://doi.org/10.1377/hlthaff.2016.0011

Mehler, P.S., & Krantz, M. (2003). Anorexia nervosa medical issues. *Journal of Women's Health* 12: 331–40. https://doi.org/10.1089/154099903765448844

Mento, C., Silvestri, M.C., Muscatello, M.R., Rizzo, A., Celebre, L., Pratico, M., Zoccali, R. A., & Bruono, A. (2021). Psychological impact of pro-anorexia and pro-eating disorder websites on adolescent females: a systematic review. *International Journal of Environmental Research and Public Health* 18(4): 2186. https://doi.org/10.3390/ijerph18042186

Micali, N., Hagberg, K.W., Petersen, I., & Treasure, J.L. (2013). The incidence of eating disorders in the UK in 2000–2009: findings from the General Practice Research Database. *BMJ Open* 3(5). https://doi.org/10.1136/bmjopen-2013-002646

Mondini, S., Favaro, A., Santonastaso, P. (1996). Eating disorders and the ideal of feminine beauty in Italian newspapers and magazines. *European Eating Disorders Review* 4(2): 112–20. https://doi.org/10.1002/(SICI)1099-0968(199606)4:2<112::AID-ERV152>3.0.CO;2-6

Mulveen, R., & Hepworth, J. (2006). An interpretative phenomenological analysis of participation in a pro-anorexia internet site and its relationship with disordered eating. *Journal of Health Psychology* 11(2): 283–96. https://doi.org/10.1177/1359105306061187

Myers, P.N., & Biocca, F.A. (1992). The elastic body image: the effect of television advertising and programming on body image distortions in young women. *Journal of Communication* 42(3): 108–33. https://doi.org/10.1111/j.1460-2466.1992.tb00802.x

Nagl, M., Jacobi, C., Paul, M., et al. (2016). Prevalence, incidence, and natural course of anorexia and bulimia nervosa among adolescents and young adults. *European Child and Adolescent Psychiatry* 25: 903–18. https://doi.org/10.1007/s00787-015-0808-z

Neuendorf, K.A. (2002). *The Content Analysis Guidebook*. Thousand Oaks, CA: Sage.

Nevin, S.M., & Vartanian, L.R. (2017). The stigma of clean dieting and orthorexia nervosa. *Journal of Eating Disorders* 5: Article 37. https://doi.org/10.1186/s40337-017-0168-9

Njenga, F., & Kang'ethe, R. (2004). Anorexia nervosa in Kenya. *East African Medical Journal* 81(4): 188–93. https://doi.org/10.4314/eamj.v81i4.9153

NIMH (2021). Eating disorders: about more than food. https://www.nimh.nih.gov/health/publications/eating-disorders

Norris, M.L., Boydell, K.M., Pinhas, L., & Katzman, D.K. (2006). Ana and the Internet: a review of pro-anorexia websites. *International Journal of Eating Disorders* 39(6): 443–47. https://doi.org/10.1002/eat.20305

O'Connor, C., McNamara, N., O'Hara, L., McNicholas, M., & McNicholas, F. (2019). How do people with eating disorders experience the stigma associated with their condition? A mixed-methods systematic review. *Journal of Mental Health* 11: 1–16. https://doi.org/10.1080/09638237.2019.1685081

O'Hara, S.K., & Clegg Smith, K. (2007). Presentation of eating disorders in the news media: what are the implications for patient diagnosis and treatment? *Patient Education and Counselling* 68: 43–51. https://doi.org/10.1016/j.pec.2007.04.006

Ogletree, S.M., Williams, S.W., Raffeld, P., Mason, B., & Fricke, K. (1990). Female attractiveness and eating disorders: do children's television commercials play a role? *Sex Roles* 22: 791–97. https://doi.org/10.1007/bf00292061

Ohlsson, R. (2017). Public discourse on mental health and psychiatry: representations in Swedish newspapers. *Health* 22(3): 298–314. https://doi.org/10.1177/1363459317693405

Ostman, M., & Kjellin, L. (2002). Stigma by association: psychological factors in relatives of people with mental illness. *British Journal of Psychiatry* 181(6). https://doi.org/10.1192/bjp.181.6.494

Perez, M., Ohrt, T.K., & Hoek, H.W. (2016). Prevalence and treatment of eating disorders among Hispanics/Latino Americans in the United States. *Current Opinion in Psychiatry* 29(6): 378–82. https://doi.org/10.1097/yco.0000000000000277

Pike, K.M., Dohm, F.A., Striegel-Moore, R.H., Wilfley, D.E., & Fairburn, C.G. (2001). A comparison of black and white women with binge eating disorder. *American Journal of Psychiatry* 158: 1455–60. https://doi.org/10.1176/appi.ajp.158.9.1455

Pike, K.M, Hoek, H.W., & Dunne, P.E. (2014). Cultural trends and eating disorders. *Current Opinion in Psychiatry* 27(6): 436–42. https://doi.org/10.1097/yco.0000000000000100

Rhydderch, D., Krooupa, A.-M., Shefer, G., Goulden, R., Williams, P., Thornicroft, A., Rose, D., Thornicroft, G., & Henderson, C. (2016). Changes in newspaper coverage of mental illness from 2008 to 2014 in England. *Acta Psychiatrica Scandinavica* 134: 45–52. https://doi.org/10.1111/acps.12606

Riley, S., Rodham, K., & Gavin, J. (2009). Doing weight: pro-ana and recovery identities in cyberspace. *Journal of Community & Applied Social Psychology* 19(5): 348–59. https://doi.org/10.1002/casp.1022

Roehrig, J.P., & McLean, C.P. (2010). A comparison of stigma toward eating disorders versus depression. *International Journal of Eating Disorders* 43(7): 671–74. https://doi.org/10.1002/eat.20760

Schaumberg, K., Welch, E., Breithaupt, L., Hübel, C., Baker, J.H., Munn-Chernoff, M.A., Yilmaz, Z., Ehrlich, S., Mustelin, L., Ghaderi, A., Hardaway, A.J., Bulik-Sullivan, E.C., Hedman, A.M., Jangmo, A., Nilsson, I.A.K., Wiklund, C., Yao, S., Seidel, M., & Bulik, C.M. (2017). The science behind the academy for eating disorders' nine truths about eating disorders. *European Eating Disorder Review* 25(6): 432–50. https://doi.org/10.1002/erv.2553

Shepard, E., & Seale, C. (2010). Eating disorders in the media: the changing nature of UK newspaper reports. *European Eating Disorders Review* 18(6): 486–95. https://doi.org/10.1002/erv.1006

Sidani, J.E., Shensa, A., Hoffman, B., Hanmer, J., & Primack, B.A. (2016). The association between social media use and eating concerns among U.S. young adults. *Journal of the Academy of Nutrition and Dietetics* 116(9): 1465–72. https://doi.org/10.1016/j.jand.2016.03.021

Silverstein, B., Perdue, L., Peterson, B., & Kelly, E. (1986). The role of the mass media in promoting a thin standard of bodily attractiveness for women. *Sex Roles* 14(9/10): 519–32. https://doi.org/10.1007/bf00287452

Slater, A., & Tiggemann, M. (2012). Just one click: a content analysis of advertisements on teen web sites. *Journal of Adolescent Health* 50(4): 339–45. https://doi.org/10.1016/j.jadohealth.2011.08.003

Slevitch, L. (2011). Qualitative and quantitative methodologies compared: ontological and epistemological perspectives. *Journal of Quality Assurance in Hospitality and Tourism* 12(1): 73–81. https://doi.org/10.1080/1528008x.2011.541810

Smith, B., & Ceusters, W. (2010). Ontological realism: a methodology for coordinated evolution of scientific ontologies. *Applied Ontologies* 5(3–4): 139–88. https://doi.org/10.3233/ao-2010-0079

Smith, J.A., & Carey, G. (2007). What is the role of an interdisciplinary researcher? *International Journal of Epidemiology* 36(3): 690. https://doi.org/10.1093/ije/dym106

Smith, J.A. (2015). *Qualitative Psychology: A Practical Guide to Research Methods.* London: Sage.

Solmi, F., Bould, H.E., Lloyd, E.C., & Lewis, G. (2020). On the limited visibility of eating disorder research. *Lancet Psychiatry* 8(2): 91–92. https://doi.org/10.1016/s2215-0366(20)30423-5

Solmi, F., Downs, J.L., & Nicholls, D.E. (2021). COVID-19 and eating disorders in young people. *Lancet Child and Adolescent Health* 5: 316–18. https://doi.org/10.1016/s2352-4642(21)00094-8

Sorice, S.C., Li, A.Y., Gilstrap, J., Canales, F.L., & Furnas, H.J. (2017). Social media and the plastic surgery patient. *Plastic and Reconstructive Surgery* 140(5): 1047–56.

Stice, E., & Shaw, H.E. (1994). Adverse effects of the media portrayed thin-ideal on women and linkages to bulimic symptomatology. *Journal of Social and Clinical Psychology* 13(3): 288–308. https://doi.org/10.1521/jscp.1994.13.3.288

Stice, E., Marti, C.N., & Rohde, P. (2013). Prevalence, incidence, impairment, and course of the proposed DSM-5 eating disorder diagnoses in an 8-year prospective community study of young women. *Journal of Abnormal Psychology* 122(2): 445–57. https://doi.org/10.1037/a0030679

Stommel, W., & Koole, T. (2010). The online support group as a community: a micro-analysis of the interaction with a new member. *Discourse Studies* 12(3): 357–78. https://doi.org/10.1177/1461445609358518

Stommel, W., & Meijman, F.J. (2011). The use of conversation analysis to study social accessibility of an online support group on eating disorders. *Global Health Promotion* 18(2): 18–26. https://doi.org/10.1177/1757975911404764

Striegel-Moore, R.H., Dohm, F.A., Kraemer, H.C., Taylor, C.B., Daniels, S., Crawford, P.B., & Schreiber, G.B. (2003). Eating disorders in white and black women. *American Journal of Psychiatry* 160(7): 1326–31. https://doi.org/10.1176/appi.ajp.160.7.1326

Sun, S., He, J., Fan, X., Chen, Y., & Lu, X. (2019). Chinese media coverage of eating disorders: disorder representations and patient profiles. *International Journal of Eating Disorders* 53(1): 113–22. https://doi.org/10.1002/eat.23154

Thompson-Brenner, H., Satir, D.A., Franko, D.L., & Herzog, D.B. (2012). Clinician reactions to patients with eating disorders: a review of the literature. *Psychiatric Services* 63: 73–78. https://doi.org/10.1176/appi.ps.201100050

Thornicroft, G., Rose, D., Kassam, A., & Sartorius, N. (2007). Stigma: ignorance, prejudice or discrimination? *British Journal of Psychiatry* 190: 192–93. https://doi.org/10.1192/bjp.bp.106.025791

Thornicroft, A., Goulden, R., Shefer, G., Rhydderch, D., Rose, D., Williams, P., Thornicroft, G., & Henderson, C. (2013). Newspaper coverage of mental illness in England 2008–2011. *British Journal of Psychiatry* 202: s64–s69. https://doi.org/10.1192/bjp.bp.112.112920

Thornton, L.M., Mazzeo, S.E., & Bulik, C.M. (2011). The heritability of eating disorders: methods and current findings. *Current Topics in Behavioural Neurosciences* 6: 141–56. https://doi.org/10.1007/7854_2010_91

Tiggemann, M., & Miller, J. (2010). The Internet and adolescent girls' weight satisfaction and drive for thinness. *Sex Roles: A Journal of Research* 63(1–2): 79–90. https://doi.org/10.1007/s11199-010-9789-z

Tiggemann, M., & Slater, A. (2013). NetGirls: the Internet, Facebook, and body image concern in adolescent girls. *International Journal of Eating Disorders* 46(6): 630–33.

Tiggemann, M., & Zinoviev, K. (2019). The effect of #enhancement-free Instagram images and hashtags on women's body image. *Body Image* 31: 131–38. https://doi.org/10.1002/eat.22141

Tong, S.T., Heinemann-Lafave, D., Jeon, J., Kolodziej-Smith, R., & Warshay, N. (2013). The use of pro-ana blogs for online social support. *Eating Disorders* 21: 408–22. https://doi.org/10.1080/10640266.2013.827538

Tyrer, P. (2014). A comparison of DSM and ICD classifications of mental disorder. *Advances in Psychiatric Treatment* 20(4): 280–85. https://doi.org/10.1192/apt.bp.113.011296

Udo, T., & Grilo, C.M. (2018). Prevalence and correlates of DSM-5-defined eating disorders in a nationally representative sample of U.S. adults. *Biological Psychiatry* 84(5): 345–54. https://doi.org/10.1016/j.biopsych.2018.03.014

Ulfvebrand, S., Birgegård, A., Norring, C., Högdahl, L., & von Hausswolff-Juhlin, Y. (2015). Psychiatric comorbidity in women and men with eating disorders results from a large clinical database. *Journal of Psychiatric Research* 230(2): 294–99. https://doi.org/10.1016/j.psychres.2015.09.008

van Hoeken, D., Burns, J.K., & Hoek, H.W. (2016). Epidemiology of eating disorders in Africa. *Current Opinion of Psychiatry* 29(6): 372–77. https://doi.org/10.1097/yco.0000000000000274

Volpe, U., Tortorella, A., Manchia, M., Monteleone, A.M., Albert, U., & Monteleone, P. (2016). Eating disorders: what age at onset? *Journal of Psychiatric Research* 238: 225–27. https://doi.org/10.1016/j.psychres.2016.02.048

Whitley, R., & Berry, S. (2013). Trends in newspaper coverage of mental illness in Canada: 2005–2010. *Canadian Journal of Psychiatry* 58: 107–12. https://doi.org/10.1177/070674371305800208

Whitley, R., & Campbell, R.D. (2014). Stigma, agency and recovery amongst people with severe mental illness. *Social Science and Medicine* 107: 1–8. https://doi.org/10.1016/j.socscimed.2014.02.010

WHO (World Health Organization) (2018). International Classification of Diseases for Mortality and Morbidity Statistics (11th Revision). Geneva: WHO.

Wildes, J.E., Emery, R.E., & Simons, A.D. (2001) The roles of ethnicity and culture in the development of eating disturbance and body dissatisfaction: a meta-analytic review. *Clinical Psychology Review* 21: 521–51. https://doi.org/10.1016/s0272-7358(99)00071-9

Williams, S., & Reid, M. (2010). Understanding the experience of ambivalence in anorexia nervosa: the maintainer's perspective. *Psychology and Health* 25(5): 551–67. https://doi.org/10.1080/08870440802617629

Wilson, A. (2021). Personal communication, 25 October 2021.

Wiseman, C.V., Gray, J.J., Mosimann, J.E., & Ahrens, A.H. (1992). Cultural expectations of thinness in women: an update. *International Journal of Eating Disorders* 11(1): 85–89. https://doi.org/10.1002/1098-108x(199201)11:1<85::aid-eat2260110112>3.0.co;2-t

Wolf, M., Theis, F., & Kordy, H. (2013). Language use in eating disorder blogs: psychological implications of social online activity. *Journal of Language and Social Psychology* 32(2): 212–26. https://doi.org/10.1177/0261927x12474278

Yeshua-Katz, D., & Martins, N. (2013). Communicating stigma: the pro-ana paradox. *Health Communication* 28(5): 499–508. https://doi.org/10.1080/10410236.2012.699889

Zajonc, R.B. (1968). Attitudinal effects of mere exposure. *Journal of Personality and Social Psychology* 9: 1–27. https://doi.org/10.1037/h0025848

# Part I

## Traditional Media and Public Discourse

# 1 Eating Disorder Metaphors in the American and Spanish Press

*Carolina Figueras Bates*

## Introduction

The news media constitute the most common source of health information available to the public (Ma, 2017). News stories play a critical role in raising awareness of certain health issues and framing them in ways that shape people's attitudes, knowledge and opinion (Ray & Hinnant, 2009; Slopen et al., 2007). At the same time, the media inform about the views, opinions and positions taken by policy-makers, advocacy groups, researchers, patients and their families (McGinty et al., 2016). By foregrounding some aspects and backgrounding others, the coverage of particular illnesses impacts how these conditions are socially understood and treated.

In the realm of mental health, much of the research has focused on three main areas: media constructions of mental disorders, media effects of those constructions, and recommendations to reduce and to prevent stigmatization of afflicted individuals (Ma, 2017). The result is a large body of literature exploring how mental health conditions are reported in the news (e.g., Oostdyk, 2008; Stout, Villegas & Jennings, 2004; Wahl, 1992, 2003). Conversely, intercultural analysis of media representations and their influence on the public's perception of mental health problems are still scarce. Most of the research has been generally limited to a particular country, although in recent years there has been an increasing interest in carrying out contrastive analysis across mass media of different countries (cf. Nawková et al., 2012; Vengut, 2018).

Carolina Figueras Bates, 'Chapter 1: Eating Disorder Metaphors in the American and Spanish Press' in: *Eating Disorders in Public Discourse: Exploring Media Representations and Lived Experiences*. University of Exeter Press (2023). © Carolina Figueras Bates. DOI: 10.47788/QWOM4518

For the USA, descriptive studies on media content from the 1980s and 1990s revealed that the news tended to emphasize interpersonal violence and criminal acts performed by people with psychiatric disorders (Wahl, Wood & Richards, 2002). Looking at the period from 1995 to 2014, McGinty et al. (2016) found that in the USA there had been an increase in the mention of mass shootings committed by individuals experiencing severe mental disorders, whereas fewer news stories were dedicated to successful treatments for these conditions. These findings are consistent with other media reporting in countries such as Canada, New Zealand, the UK and Spain (Vengut, 2018).

In the specific case of Spain, Lima, Sáez and Lima (2011) examined the digital version of the popular newspaper *El País* between 1998 and 2009 and concluded that no improvement was made in the representation of persons with mental conditions, particularly about schizophrenia. Relatedly, the more detailed study by Aragonès et al. (2014) confirmed that a significant part of the news insisted on the relationship between mental health issues and danger and crime, and that much less attention was dedicated to the aetiology of these disorders from a biological standpoint.

These results support the need to perform more qualitative studies on the news coverage of specific disorders. One set of conditions that deserves further attention is eating disorders (EDs). The limited investigation conducted so far has revealed that the media construction of EDs is based on a deficient reporting of the severity, complex aetiology and difficulties in treating them (Mondini, Favaro & Santonastaso, 1996; O'Hara & Smith, 2007; Shepherd & Seale, 2010; Sun et al., 2019). Contrary to the dangerousness and violence commonly associated with psychosis, schizophrenia or bipolar disorders (Ross et al., 2021), EDs have often been part of the media content of entertainment and fashion (O'Hara & Smith, 2007).

More recent studies, however, have widened the scope of the scholarly work on media representations of EDs to include other groups of experiencers and conditions. For instance, MacLean et al. (2015) and Parrott et al. (this volume) investigated how men with EDs were described in the news, while Saguy and Gruys (2010) explored the characterization of obesity and EDs in the US press, stressing the contrasting social and moral meanings attributed to binge eating and anorexia. Little is still known, however, about the ordinary ways people talk about EDs in different cultural environments. This chapter aims to contribute to this area of research by examining the recurrent metaphors projected in the American and Spanish press. The rationale for such a comparison came from the realization that there were some differences in how EDs were reported; namely, the depiction of ED experiencers, the kind of social factors involved in the aetiology and prevalence of EDs and the nature of the interventions devised to deal with them.

I assumed that those variations emanated from differing cultural values. The USA is usually characterized as an individualistic society (Hofstede, 1980). American social life is more person-centred, that is, more orientated towards the individual, their personal achievements and their unique attributes and independence. Spain, instead, is generally associated with more collectivist cultures, such as other Southern European and Latin American countries (Benet & Waller, 1995). In collectivist societies, social existence is more communal or public-orientated, and affiliation is a value (Markus & Kitayama, 1991). Because of this dissimilarity in cultural values, a systematic comparison between the metaphorical constructions of EDs in the US and Spanish press seemed beneficial to shed light onto the mainstream understandings of these conditions in each country.

### *Metaphors in discourse*

Metaphors play an essential role both in cognition and in communication, since they convey particular meanings on how we make sense of the social world. Metaphors are linguistic devices that are rooted in language, thought and action (Lakoff & Johnson, 1980). They pervade our everyday life. From a cognitive standpoint, they operate as mechanisms of thought that are organized in conceptual structures and processes. At the same time, they can be used as persuasive tools to define reality, because they bring out a network of entailments that highlight some aspects of reality, while leaving others in the background. In a sense, metaphors are always ideologically charged. This is why metaphors are not only an essential component of human cognition but also a critical factor in political behaviour and social interaction.

Metaphors facilitate conversations about abstract, subjective, sensitive and sometimes taboo subjects (Semino, 2008), such as mental health issues (Tay, 2017). As powerful communicative devices, they influence the public's attitude to support or oppose governmental policies on a wide range of matters (Barry et al., 2009). This key function is often described as 'framing' (Demjén

& Semino, 2016; Semino, 2008; Semino, Demjén & Demmen, 2018a).[1] For instance, living with cancer is often described either as a 'fight' or as a 'journey', which has consequences for how the person and others around her/him experience and understand the illness (Demjén & Semino, 2016). The framing power of metaphors thus has a significant impact on healthcare (Semino, Demjén & Demmen, 2018a). Metaphorical references to an illness that trigger negative associations in the public might stigmatize the person with the condition and contribute to social rejection (López-Rodríguez, this volume). On the contrary, there is evidence confirming the benefits of metaphors in the personal narratives of afflicted individuals to comprehend the illness experience, as is the case with EDs (Burton, Hands & Bulsara, 2015; Garret, 1996; Mathieson & Hoskins, 2005; Skårderud, 2007).

Frames constructed and propagated in the media determine what social topics are relevant and why some factors are more important than others. As a result, the more coverage a public issue is given in the news, the higher the perceived salience of that particular problem (Carter, 2013). Different metaphorical framings are conducive to different ways of thinking and reasoning about the subjects presented to the audience, as well as to a different emotional appraisal of the illness experience (Hendricks et al., 2018; Bowen & Waller, this volume). In the present study, the issue at hand is the media representation of EDs by means of metaphors in different cultures (American and Spanish), a topic that has not been addressed in the literature. My main research questions are the following:

*RQ1:* What are the core metaphors employed in US and Spanish news media to represent EDs and people with EDs?

*RQ2:* What are the common metaphors, and which of those are specific for each cultural landscape?

*RQ3:* What are the frames to report on EDs that emerge from the key metaphors in both countries (the USA and Spain)?

## Methods

### *Corpus*

Two sample news items from two of the most widely circulated general newspapers in the USA and Spain—the *New York Times* (NYT) and *El País* (EP)—were selected. Both publications share similar political ideology (more left-leaning), and both are considered authoritative and professional references for English and Spanish-speaking countries. The bilingual corpus comprised 50 written pieces from the NYT (53,798 words) and 61 written pieces from EP (53,380 words). The time period of these two samples ranged from 2000 to 2020. The texts were drawn from the electronic database of each publication, using a search string of keywords (anorexia, eating disorders, trastornos de la conducta alimentaria, bulimia). Ethical approval was not required for this study because it involved information freely available in the public domain (newspaper accounts).

### *Procedure*

The corpus was manually coded for metaphorical expressions applying the three-step procedure devised by the Pragglejaz Group (2007, p. 3). The 'metaphor identification procedure' (MIP) calls for:

1. Reading of the text-discourse to achieve a general understanding of the meaning.
2. Detailed contextual analysis to determine if each lexical unit of interest has a more concrete, more precise, or historically older meaning in other contexts different than the one in the given context.
3. If so, the lexical item is marked as metaphorical.

With the Pragglejaz method (MIP), I highlighted all the metaphorical linguistic expressions used in each sample to talk about EDs. The corpus-based *Merriam-Webster Dictionary* (www.merriam-webster.com) was taken as a point of reference for the establishment of basic meanings in English. For Spanish, I resorted to the online version of *Diccionario de la lengua española* (dle.rae.es). Once the metaphorical expressions were identified, the next step was to organize them into meaningful clusters. I proceeded to carefully determine the main thematic areas of meaning upon which each newspaper drew to explain the notion of EDs. I classified and coded the linguistic metaphorical expressions underlined in each sample according to these main areas of meaning.

### *Analysis*

I conducted a qualitative analysis of the main metaphors in both publications (the NYT and EP) in the framework of conceptual metaphor theory (CMT;

Lakoff & Johnson, 1980), together with the metaphor framing approach developed by Semino and colleagues (Semino, Demjén & Demmen, 2018a; Semino et al., 2018b; Demjén & Semino, 2016; Demjén, Semino & Koller, 2016; Demjén et al., 2019). Within CMT, metaphors are conceived as mappings (sets of correspondences) between different domains in conceptual structure.[2] Thus, an expression such as 'She destroyed my argument' is analysed as the linguistic projection of the conceptual metaphor ARGUMENT IS WAR. This conceptual metaphor emerges from the mapping of certain elements of the 'source' (WAR) onto particular elements of the 'target' domain of ARGUMENT. In a conceptual metaphor, some elements of the source domain are in the spotlight, while others remain hidden (Lakoff & Johnson, 1980), resulting in a biased process of conceptualization. This bias is, in fact, what becomes the 'framing' power of metaphor (Semino, Demjén & Demmen, 2018a). So, the conceptual metaphor ARGUMENT IS WAR highlights the confrontational and competitive character of arguments, while it suppresses the potential cooperative side of the activity. This conceptual organization shapes the way we think of arguments and it potentially impacts the way we act in the world regarding arguments as well.

Illnesses are generally target domains, because they represent complex, subjective and sensitive experiences. Source domains are usually simpler, more concrete or less subjective. To be able to make legitimate claims about what functions metaphors play in cognition and discourse, however, conceptual metaphors have to be systematically evaluated in corpora that contain authentic linguistic data, as is the case in the present study (cf. Semino et al., 2018b).

## Results and Discussion

### *EDs as problems*

The analysis of the corpus revealed that EDs were generally defined with the overarching and highly conventional metaphor, AN ED IS A PROBLEM. This conceptual metaphor was identified in both samples (65 occurrences of the metaphor in the NYT; 83 occurrences in EP). To understand its framing implications, we should take into consideration the original meaning of 'problem'. According to the *Merriam-Webster Dictionary*, a problem is 'a question raised for inquiry, consideration, or solution' (www.merriamwebster.com/dictionary/

problem). It follows then that EDs are framed in both newspapers as questions to be solved. This is the view conveyed in examples (1) and (2):

(1) one reason the panel wants to change the guidelines is to help patients with eating **problems** recognize them even if they do not exhibit any of the traditional symptoms (NYT, 18 January 2010)

(2) Muchas veces las personas que lo sufren no pueden salir del pozo por sí mismas. La comunicación para afrontar este terrible **problema** es vital [*Often people who suffer from it cannot get out of the hole by themselves. Communication to overcome this terrible problem is vital*] (EP, 3 April 2019)

In (1), people with EDs are generically described as patients in need of assistance. A relevant aspect of the ED, understood as a problem, is abnormal eating behaviour, which is always alluded to as a characteristic symptom that must be 'treated' to recover. The excerpt in (2) offers a similar faceless portrait of (all) individuals living with an ED. They are collectively labelled as sufferers and the condition is metaphorically referred to as the 'well' (that is, a container) in which those sufferers are trapped and from which they are unable to escape. This media representation construes ED experiencers as helpless subjects lacking the ability to solve 'the problem of the ED' on their own. The delivery of a solution to this question is the prerogative of those who are vested with the authority to make decisions. Clinical experts belong, according to the NYT and EP, to the category of legitimized problem-solvers. Government and policy-makers are also attributed the role of problem-solvers (e.g., approving regulations to prevent EDs), but only in the Spanish subcorpus.

Focusing on the NYT, EDs are often labelled as 'psychological problems', a characterization that limits the area of intervention against the illness to the personal sphere of the individual. This positioning is made clear in statements such as 'people tend to underreport their **problems** with eating disorders' (NYT, 6 February 2007), which construct EDs in terms of difficulties and troubles experienced by those with the condition. In contrast, in the EP sample, the conceptual metaphor EDs ARE PROBLEMS is raised to the level of social concern, which explains the calls for joint action to deal with the ED problem made in (3) and (4):[3]

(3) Montse Graell, psiquiatra responsable del servicio de psiquiatría del Niño Jesús de Madrid, afirma que 'los TCA son un **problema** de todos, a los que deben aportarse **soluciones** drásticas por parte de todos' [*Montse Graell, psychiatrist at the psychiatry service of Niño Jesús in Madrid, claims that 'EDs are everybody's problem, and everybody should provide drastic solutions to them'*] (EP, 10 January 2019)

(4) 'La anorexia sigue siendo un problema de salud pública que arruina la vida de las pacientes y sus familiares', ha reiterado la experta en un comunicado [*'Anorexia is still a public health problem that ruins the lives of patients and their families', the expert has reiterated in a statement*] (EP, 4 April 2017)

In (3), the claim 'los TCA son un **problema** de todos' (*EDs are everybody's problem*) construes EDs as social issues that must be resolved collectively. This generalization has the effect of overshadowing the agentivity of those living with the condition, to the point that the ED experiencer is not even mentioned or acknowledged. In the scenario created in (3), the only agents with the capacity to tackle the problem (the ED) are external to the person and seemingly operating without their participation or collaboration. Relatedly, in (4), anorexia is framed by the clinical expert being quoted as a public health concern, as a force that destroys patients' lives and their families. Once again, the person with an ED is assigned the passive role of standing as a suffering patient.

The conceptual construction of EDs as problems is so recurrent in both publications (the NYT and EP) that it can be considered a systematic metaphor to frame the ideas, attitudes and values of discourse participants (Semino, Demjén & Demmen, 2018a). This systematic metaphor comes to represent the dominant way of conceiving EDs, which makes this evaluative stance the common sense or natural view of these disorders. This metaphor is so conventional that it has become part of the set of common beliefs (ideology) that society holds about EDs, in particular, and about mental health, in general. Thus, in parallel with physical ailments, mental health conditions tend to be perceived in black and white fashion as systems to be fixed, like any other mechanical object that must be repaired. Framing EDs as problems in need of adjustment represents, as a matter of fact, the adaptation of the metaphor THE BODY IS A MACHINE (Johnson, 1987), which is a central tenet of the acute biomedical model prevalent in Western healthcare (Loftus, 2011). In the same vein, the machine metaphor is used in the medical arena to account for the workings of the mind. The implication is that the person with an ED should surrender to a health professional who is able to treat the condition and fix the problem.

This mechanistic gaze makes the individual with an ED invisible and suppresses their lived experience. It places them in the backstage and focuses on the health professionals who, playing the role of engineers or technicians, operate on the ED (Coulehan, 2003). In this framework, the way to solve the ED problem is to 'treat the illness' (rather than the person as a whole), a business conducted only by socially legitimized health experts, as claimed in (5) and (6):

(5) Cuanto más afectado estaba el cerebro, más difícil era **tratar** la enfermedad [anorexia] [*The more the brain was affected, the more difficult it was to treat the illness*] (EP, 4 April 2017)

(6) Dr S. Bryn Austin, a professor at Boston Children's Hospital and Harvard T.H. Chan School of Public Health, said [:] 'Eating disorders can be successfully **treated**, they just need to take the first step in reaching out for care' (NYT, 14 July 2017)

Expressions such as 'tratar'/ 'treated' can be interpreted as discursive realizations of conceptual metaphors involving ENGINEERING as the main domain. Within the engineering frame, another pervasive metaphor in the Western medical culture emerges in excerpts (5) and (6), and that is DISEASES ARE OBJECTS (Hodgkin, 1985). This conceptual metaphor features illnesses as objects that have an independent existence apart from the individuals experiencing them. This highly conventional metaphor is present in both the NYT and EP samples (16 and 17 occurrences, respectively).

### *Specific metaphors for defining EDs in the US and Spanish press*

Beyond the systematic metaphor AN ED IS A PROBLEM, a more fine-grained analysis of the metaphorical constructions in the two newspapers revealed fundamental similarities, as well as significant differences, in the semantic domains applied to represent EDs in each country. The main meaning groupings of the metaphors identified in both publications are the following:

- Organism metaphors
- Change metaphors

- Vision metaphors
- Order metaphors
- Control metaphors
- Hiding/Invisibility metaphors
- Behaviour metaphors
- Violence metaphors

One of the most recurrent discursive constructions of EDs in the NYT as well as in EP is the Organism metaphor, according to which EDs are living organisms that evolve and develop over time. Twenty-five occurrences of this conventional metaphor were identified in the EP sample, as opposed to 34 occurrences in the NYT. The Organism metaphor is recognizable in statements such as 'the more infections or hospitalizations a girl had, the more likely she was to **develop** an eating disorder' (NYT, 2 May 2019). The anthropomorphic conceptual metaphor in this case is EDs ARE LIVING ORGANISMS, a conceptualization consistent with the mechanistic view of body and mind. The usefulness of this metaphor lies in the functionality of personification, which allows us to 'comprehend a wide variety of experiences with nonhuman entities in terms of human motivations, characteristics, and activities' (Lakoff & Johnson, 1980, p. 33).[4]

The notion of LIVING ORGANISM to make sense of the onset and progression of the illness is closely related in the Spanish corpus to Change metaphors that discursively produce EDs as modifications of eating behaviours that deviate from what is deemed as 'normal', as is claimed in (7):

(7) La anorexia y la bulimia son enfermedades que se caracterizan por **alteraciones** en la conducta alimentaria, la regulación del peso corporal y la percepción de la imagen [*Anorexia and bulimia are illnesses characterized by alterations in eating behaviour, body weight regulation and body perception*] (EP, 16 June 2004)

The Change metaphor was unique to the EP sample (8 occurrences). No cases were found in the NYT sample. The basis for this metaphor is the more basic meaning of 'alterar' in Spanish. According to *Diccionario de la lengua española*, 'alterar' signifies changing the essence or the shape of something (dle.rae.es/alterar). Understood as radical transformations, EDs then become abnormalities or aberrations actualized in certain behaviours (such as body weight regulation or eating anomalies). From this stance, 'solving the ED problem' naturally amounts to the normalization of food intake and weight, as is explicitly stated in (8) and (9):

(8) 'Si el paciente está desnutrido, el primer paso es conseguir una motivación y **normalizar** su peso', apunta el médico [*'If the patient is malnourished, the first step is to motivate her/him and normalize her/his weight', notes the doctor*] (EP, 16 July 2019)

(9) [Entre los objetivos terapéuticos está] la **normalización** de los hábitos alimentarios [*Normalization of eating habits is among the therapeutic goals*] (EP, 27 December 2015)

These media constructions are fundamentally rooted in the clinical definitions that connect EDs to disorder and aberration, and that problematize this association (Feuston & Piper, 2019). This deviation from normalcy is also conveyed, both in Spanish and English, by metaphorical expressions such as 'distorsión'/'distortion'. The Spanish lexical item 'distorsión', as well as the English equivalent 'distortion', come from the late Latin expression *distorsio, -ōnis*, with the original meaning of 'twist'. This more basic content is shared in these two languages, albeit the metaphorical use of each term differs slightly in the English and Spanish samples.

For the EP subcorpus, the concept denoted by 'distorsión' and 'distorsionado/a' (7 occurrences) points to visual perception, whereas, in the NYT, the expressions 'distorted' (9 occurrences) and 'distortions' (1 occurrence) are more bounded to the set of practices featured in EDs (in particular, deviant eating habits). Thus, in the USA sample, 'distorted' and 'distortion' are terms generally applied to behaviours ('distorted eating behaviours', for instance), whereas, in the Spanish body of news, 'distorsión' and 'distorsionado/a' always imply the visual domain, as illustrated in statements such as: 'la **distorsión de ver** una imagen que no es real' [*the distortion of seeing an image that is not real*] (EP, 4 April 2017).[5]

The difference between the US and Spanish versions of the Visual metaphor arises from nuanced distinctions between the basic definitions of these two words in each language. For the lexical item 'to distort', the oldest meaning in English is 'to twist out of the true meaning or proportion: to alter to give a false or unnatural picture or account' (www.merriam-webster.com/dictionary/distort). Instead, the basic meaning of 'distorsión' in Spanish is 'deformación de imágenes, sonidos, señales, etc., producida en su transmisión o reproducción' [*alteration of images, sounds, signals, etc., produced in their transmission or reproduction*] (dle.rae.es/distorsión). The comparison between those two definitions brings to the fore a component of deception or falsehood in the English expression 'distortion' that is absent in its Spanish counterpart 'distorsión'. This singular property activates another metaphor, the Hiding/Invisibility metaphor, unique to the USA sample.

Admittedly, in the NYT, EDs are occasionally portrayed as conditions that afflicted individuals hide or conceal on purpose, a characterization that incorporates the trait of deception to the behavioural definition of the illness. Some examples of this depiction of ED patients as misleaders are provided in (10) and (11):

(10) One concern, she and other experts say, is that as women get older they are more adept at **concealing** the problem, and symptoms may be attributed to aging rather than to an eating disorder (NYT, 28 March 2011)

(11) Even the best-trained psychologist can have a difficult time filtering through the **deceptive** acts and statements that can accompany an eating disorder (NYT, 14 September 2006)

News reports in which the Hiding/Invisibility metaphor becomes prominent, like in (10) and (11), validate, support and perpetuate mainstream views of individuals with an ED as lacking transparency and integrity. Even the person who has lived with an ED is likely to resort to the Hiding/Invisibility metaphor by consistently referring to the condition as a secret that had to be withheld from others. The metaphorical construction of EDs as covert acts was only found in the NYT (10 occurrences).[6] As one ED experiencer acknowledged, 'People around me started discovering my **secret** years before I got better, but there was no socially acceptable way to get me professional help, so they didn't try' (NYT, 14 July 2017). The implication of framing EDs as 'secrets' is that family members, sports coaches, counsellors, teachers or friends are in charge of the daunting task of 'discovering' or 'unveiling' the truth of the illness that the person is so eagerly concealing.

This understanding of EDs as private, undisclosed activities, both in the mainstream media and in the personal accounts by those experiencing them, is also part of the clinical literature on those conditions. In fact, clinicians often accuse sufferers of 'tactical denial' or 'deliberate concealment' of their struggles with EDs. These patients are even labelled as 'manipulative' by their physicians because they tend to camouflage certain behaviours and practices to lose weight, trying actively to avoid detection (Hambrook & Tchanturia, 2008).

The deviant nature of EDs is captured in the Order metaphor with which these illnesses are featured in the USA sample (32 occurrences in the NYT). Since EDs are routinely pictured as a set of aberrant behaviours (eating, in particular), the Order metaphor pervades the clinical descriptions of EDs in the press, as the following statement provided by a well-known expert proves: '"The eating has to be **disordered** in some way, as does the behaviour relating to eating," said Ruth H. Striegel-Moore, a professor of psychology at Montana State University' (NYT, 18 January 2010).[7] As this assertion makes clear, behaviours are central to the current definitions of EDs, as well as core features for their clinical assessment, which means that Order and Behaviour metaphors are intertwined. In the Behaviour metaphor, exemplified in excerpts (12) and (13), the condition is equated with the behaviour:

(12) But a new study suggests that the extreme dieting characteristic of anorexia may instead be a well-entrenched habit—**behavior** governed by brain processes that, once set in motion, are inflexible and slow to change (NYT, 12 October 2015)

(13) La anorexia y la bulimia son enfermedades que se caracterizan por alteraciones de la **conducta** alimentaria [*Anorexia and bulimia are illnesses characterized by alterations of eating behaviour*] (EP, 16 June 2004)

The conceptual metaphor projected in the excerpts in (12) and (13) takes the form THE ILLNESS (THE ED) IS THE BEHAVIOUR. Sixty-eight occurrences of this metaphor were found in the NYT sample, as opposed to 85 occurrences in EP. Within this metaphorical construction, EDs are reduced to a set of disordered behaviours, a representation that expands on the construction of EDs as irregular, undesirable or even destructive actions, habits and practices rather than holistic experiences. This conception is consistent with the behaviouristic approach typical of the biopsychological model of mental illnesses.[8]

The Behaviour metaphor, in turn, is linked to the Control metaphor, deployed in both samples either to explain some of the ways people with EDs conduct themselves, or to refer to some external action (by the government, for instance) aimed at limiting the spread of EDs. As a matter of fact, each publication resorts to the Control metaphor, stressing one meaning or the other. Thus, all cases of 'control' in the NYT (55 occurrences) point to the symptomatology of the ED. The person living with an ED may feel in control (meaning that diet and exercise become tools to discipline their bodies) or out of control (when the person is unable to govern their food intake). Each scenario is respectively typified in (14) and (15):

(14) 'It's so easy to get that adrenaline rush off your perfectionism, of **controlling** what you can control, which is your food intake' (NYT, 3 May 2020)

(15) **Out of Control**: A True Story of Binge Eating (NYT, 20 February 2007)

In the Spanish subcorpus, contrastingly, the Control metaphor is projected not only to make sense of the symptoms of the ED, as in the USA sample, but also to promote the external disciplinary actions of medical and government authorities to eliminate the condition, either from individuals or from the society at large (e.g., ordering the shut-down of pro-anorexia sites on the internet). Twenty-one occurrences of 'control' with the latter sense (out of 63 occurrences of the lexical item) were identified in EP. The fragment in (16) exemplifies this specific use of the Control metaphor:

(16) Las subvenciones [del gobierno] van dirigidas al desarrollo de actividades para la promoción de hábitos de vida saludables, con especial atención [...] al estudio y **control** de los trastornos del comportamiento alimentario [*The government aids are aimed at the development of activities for the promotion of healthy lifestyles, with a special focus on the study and control of eating disorders*] (EP, 27 August 2004)

In essence, the discrepancy between the contents of the Control metaphor in both samples is based on two factors: the site and the direction of the control that is being exercised. If the site of control is the experiencer, and the direction is inwards, the Control metaphor is applied to refer to the symptoms of the ED. If, instead, the site of control is the condition itself, the action comes from outside the person, and the direction of the control is top down, then the metaphorical construction 'control de los TCA' ('control of EDs') is combined in the EP subcorpus with the Violence metaphor. There are, hence, specific applications of the Control metaphor that lead to different approaches on how to deal with EDs.

In the Violence metaphor (Demjén & Semino, 2016; Semino, Demjén & Demmen, 2018a), the fight ('lucha') is against EDs. The warriors are the Spanish (or some other European) government, representatives of the fashion industry or public associations. Twenty-nine occurrences of this metaphor were retrieved from the EP sample, such as the ones in (17) and (18):

(17) El Congreso reaviva la **lucha contra** la anorexia [*Congress brings back the fight against anorexia*] (EP, 25 May 2011)

(18) la Asociación contra la Anorexia y la Bulimia firmó ayer un acuerdo con el Consorcio de Comercio y Moda de Cataluña para unir esfuerzos en la **lucha contra** los trastornos alimentarios en el marco de la pasarela 080 Barcelona Fashion [*The Association against Anorexia and Bulimia signed an agreement yesterday with the Catalan Consortium of Commerce and Fashion to join efforts in the fight against eating disorders in the context of the Barcelona Fashion runway 080*] (EP, 17 January 2017)

The broad source domain that is being captured in the headline in (17) and the fragment in (18) is VIOLENT CONFRONTATION. Within the framework of EDs as problems to be solved, the controversial solution offered in Spain has been to regulate the standards of beauty in the fashion industry and to prosecute and close down those online sites that promote EDs.[9] As a result, the battlefields of this violent confrontation with EDs are both the runway and the internet. Two are the locus of the Spanish authorities' actions: models' weight and clothes sizing (example in 19); and/or the pro-anorexia content on the web (excerpt in 20).[10]

(19) Sanidad pacta con el mundo de la moda una regulación de las tallas de la ropa para **combatir** la anorexia [*The Department of Health makes a deal with the fashion industry to regulate clothing sizing to fight against anorexia*] (EP, 23 January 2007)

(20) Para **combatir** la proliferación de páginas web y contenidos que promueven los trastornos alimentarios, Salud y el CAC han elaborado una guía de recomendaciones para que los medios de comunicación no perpetúen estigmas ni favorezcan el desarrollo de trastornos alimentarios [*In order to fight the spread of websites and contents that promote EDs, the Department of Health and CAC published a list of recommendations preventing the media from perpetuating stigmas or from promoting the development of EDs*] (EP, 13 July 2015)

The events described in (19) and (20) instantiate two different frames for the Violent metaphor: the beauty frame and the crime frame. In the beauty frame, the goal of authorities is to erode the metaphor BEAUTY IS THINNESS, publicized by the fashion industry. As contended in one of the articles, what Spanish health authorities seek is 'cambiar la imagen del cuerpo en la sociedad para evitar la promoción de ideales de belleza inaccesibles, y evitar la anorexia en los jóvenes' [*to change the body image in society to prevent the promotion of unattainable ideals of beauty and to prevent anorexia in young people*] (EP, 6 May 2017). In the crime frame, in contrast, the government targets the anonymous promoters of harmful pro-anorexia content on the web. Within this frame, some correspondence is established between EDs and the notional domain of PRO-ANOREXIA/PRO-BULIMIA PRACTICES, by which anorexia and bulimia nervosas are viewed as a collection of hazardous activities talked about and propagated through the internet. The concerns of the government are voiced in the following statement: 'Tal y como informa el Govern, [la] apología [de los TCA] se ha convertido en uno de los factores de riesgo más [...] peligroso' [*As the Government informs, inciting EDs has become one of the most dangerous risk factors*] (EP, 23 January 2019).

Both in the world of fashion and on the internet, authorities are endowed in Spain with agentic power to protect 'the most vulnerable'. This characterization is divulged in statements such the one in (21):

(21) [El contenido pro-anorexia] puede afectar a la salud de mucha gente, sobre todo aquellos que son vulnerables a padecer algún trastorno alimentario [*Pro-anorexia content might affect the health of many people, in particular those who are vulnerable to suffer from an eating disorder*] (EP, 26 November 2011)

The person experiencing an ED (or susceptible to developing one) is regularly portrayed in the EP sample as a submissive, unresisting subject who is entirely dominated by the thin media ideals of beauty or who is a credulous victim of the pro-anorexia discourse disseminated on the web. In either case, EDs are construed simultaneously as a reading and as a mental illness (Bray, 2005). These reading practices are then predicated on girls and young women,[11] featuring them as infantilized, irrational and dangerously influenceable versions of ED subjects (Bray, 2005). Making ED sufferers the inevitable outcome of media or internet consumption yields, in Holmes's (2018, p. 150) words, 'the most hyperbolic image of this devalued, feminine subjectivity'. In this media representation, ED experiencers are silent sufferers, and not real actors of change. This depiction is repeatedly put forward in the EP sample, with 78 occurrences of 'sufrir' and 'sufrimiento' and 46 occurrences of 'padecer' when introducing individuals with EDs (as opposed to only 26 cases of 'suffer' and 'suffering' in the NYT). The image of the person living with an ED that is rendered in the EP corpus is mostly generic and lacking any individualizing traits, as exemplified in (22):

(22) A los pacientes que sufren anorexia o bulimia [...] les resulta decisivo su lugar de residencia [*For patients who suffer anorexia or bulimia it is very critical where they live*] (EP, 16 April 2019)

Counter to these results, the US press elicits a different frame for the Violence metaphor. In the NYT sample, only four cases of metaphorical expressions invoke the conceptual domain VIOLENT CONFRONTATION WITH THE ED. In none of these occurrences is the action of fighting or combating performed by the ED experiencer, but rather by the families. Parents then become the 'warriors' to 'combat their daughter's anorexia' (NYT, 18 October 2010).

Compared to the Spanish sample, however, the American body of news brings out a more self-reliant, self-determined and agentive representation of the person with the condition. She/he is no longer a passive case or a vulnerable target, but a manager of her/his own symptoms. This discursive construction emerges in reports such as in (23):

(23) Roughly one in 10 Americans **struggle** with disordered eating, and the pandemic has created new hurdles for those **managing** difficult **relationships** with food (NYT, 5 May 2020)

The metaphorical expression 'struggle' here indicates a 'strenuous or violent' effort to overcome 'difficulties or opposition', according to the first definition of this lexical item offered by the *Merriam-Webster Dictionary* (www.merriam-webster.com/dictionary/struggle). In (23), those who experience an ED are represented more as handlers of the troubling manifestations of the illness than as fighters. The implication is that the concept of 'struggle' in the context of EDs includes those taxing efforts to 'manage' the set of typical behaviours indicative of the disorder, such as decisions about food intake. Forty-one occurrences of 'struggle' in the NYT carry this interpretation.[12] In addition, there are other aspects of the ED that the afflicted person should deal with, such as body image issues (as in 24), or thoughts caused by the illness (excerpt in 25):

(24) So how can you **manage** your own body-image **struggles**—and protect your kids from inheriting them? (NYT, 15 April 2020)

(25) I'm in my mid-40s and **I've struggled** with eating disorders since adolescence. Early on in the pandemic, my **'E.D. thoughts,'** as they are called, were trained on contamination (NYT, 12 May 2020)

The Struggle metaphor projected in (24) and (25) can be regarded as a variation of the Violence metaphor. In contrast to the cancer metaphors that conceptualize BEING ILL as a violent confrontation with the disease (Semino, Demjén & Demmen, 2018a), the notional domain of Struggle applied to EDs brings out the conceptual metaphor BEING ILL WITH AN ED IS SORTING OUT DIFFICULTIES. When these impediments or difficulties are expressed in discourse, they are always referred to as problematized mental issues. This is the case with 'difficult relationships with food' (in 23), 'body-image' (in 24) or 'ED thoughts' (in 25). Relatedly, this comprehensive metaphor is connected to a more basic metaphor that takes the form DIFFICULTIES ARE SYMPTOMS OF THE ED.

With EDs, the 'struggle' is not so much about destroying the condition (as it is in cancer), but to overcome it. Living with an ED is thus constructed as a long, solitary endeavour to regulate the symptoms. In this representation, the use of 'manage' and 'struggle' constitute the linguistic instantiations of a general conceptual metaphor that has a basis in a mental experience. The framing implication of the metaphor BEING ILL WITH AN ED IS SORTING OUT DIFFICULTIES is that the US representation of ED experiencers casts them as agents wrestling with a difficult matter (the ED problem) and looking for ways to resolve it. The ED is an undesirable condition that demands manipulation or substantial modification of some kind. This view consistently fits into the overarching conventional metaphor EDs ARE PROBLEMS (TO BE SOLVED), which is shared by the Spanish and US cultures. However, whereas in the latter, ED experiencers are endowed with the agency and willpower to deal with the problem, in the former, the government and other social institutions become the true agents in charge of 'fighting' EDs by regulating the conditions that 'create' them.

## Conclusion

In this chapter, we identified and discussed the metaphors deployed in two mainstream newspapers in Spain and the USA: *El País* and the *New York Times*. The focus of the investigation was the metaphorical construction of EDs in these two publications. The analysis yielded a core set of conventional metaphors for each culture, which, in turn, elicited specific frames in which they were organized. An overarching systematic metaphor—AN ED IS A PROBLEM—was used in both countries to structure other more concrete metaphors aimed at making sense of EDs. Specifically, we found that this conceptual framework encompassed the Organism, Change, Vision, Order, Control, Hiding/Invisibility, Behaviour, and Violence metaphors.

Framing EDs as problems implies that a solution must be devised, either to assist the person with the condition or to prevent the spread of EDs in the community. For each endeavour, two types of socially legitimate agents, clinical experts and health authorities, were recognized in the media. Each one delivers solutions of a different kind. At the individual level of the ED experiencer, medical solutions (that is, treatments) seek to help the patient overcome their psychological 'problem'. At the societal level, European governments censor certain 'harmful' content on the internet (the circulation of pro-anorexia/pro-bulimia materials) and/or regulate certain cultural standards about beauty (such as the prevailing assumption THINNESS IS BEAUTY) that endanger vulnerable, susceptible individuals. In either case, the person with an ED is represented as an anonymous subject, both powerless and highly influenceable by external pressures. The inevitable solution to this situation is to 'treat the disorder' within the traditional social control structures of power.

The examination of the specific notional domains to which each newspaper resorted to inform their readers about EDs revealed some commonalities between the two countries, but also some important differences related to their cultural values. The conceptualization of EDs as living organisms, as well as the assimilation of EDs to certain deviated behaviours, was present in both the NYT and EP. This association between abnormality and mental health is certainly not exclusive to EDs (it is common for mental health in general; cf. Feuston & Piper, 2019), albeit it becomes a prominent feature of the notion of EDs in the media. This pervasive characterization sensationalizes some ED symptoms while decontextualizing the individual's whole living experience. By doing so, it perpetuates stereotypes of ED experiencers as frivolous subjects and contributes to further public stigma with these conditions. In addition, linking the causes of EDs to the pressures to comply with cultural standards of beauty and/or associating EDs with celebrities, as the Spanish press recurrently did, trivializes the severity and significance of the illness for the person.

Beyond the shared component of deviance, the patterns to represent the relationship between the subject and their ED differed in each culture. Whereas in the Spanish sample, the individual with an ED was discursively construed as a patient lacking individualizing features and agency, in the USA sample, they were often represented as maintaining a contentious relationship ('struggle') with the mental condition. A component of agency was, therefore, predicated on the subject. What is more, the NYT gathered several personal testimonies of the ED experience, resulting in a kaleidoscope of voices to chronicle the transition to recovery. In comparison with the Spanish portrait of EDs, the picture in the USA seemed to provide a more nuanced understanding of the subjective and singular ways of living with and without these conditions.

These differences might stem from value orientations idiosyncratic of each culture. Individualistic or autonomous values are more prevalent in the American culture, which explains the emphasis on giving voice to an array of ED experiencers with different ethnic, social and professional backgrounds. A more collectivist orientation, with hierarchical and embeddedness values, could explain why in the Spanish press ED experiencers were rarely singularized, and why government interventions to curb the 'epidemics' of EDs were widely reported.

Due to limitations of space, the present research restricted its scope to the most recurrent metaphors in newspapers in the USA and Spain. More intercultural and contrastive studies, however, should be conducted both on the media portrayals of EDs in different countries and on the original and subjective metaphorical meanings reported by ED experiencers to the media.

## Notes

1 According to Entman (1993, p. 52), framing 'involves selection and salience. To frame is to select some aspects of a perceived reality and make them more salient in a communicating text, in such a way as to promote a particular problem definition, causal interpretation, moral evaluation, and/or treatment recommendation for the item described.' In essence, frames are organizing structures to make sense of facts.

2 As Semino (2008, p. 30) contends, the most common function of metaphors (both in language and thought) is 'talking and thinking about something in terms of something else'.

3 The reference to EDs as social problems only appears in the NYT when reporting on the regulations approved in Europe (mainly France and Italy) to ban underweight models in the fashion industry, as in the following example: 'In Paris, no one at the French Federation of Couture was available for comment today. In an earlier statement made after Ms. Reston's death, the group said that anorexia was a **social problem** requiring public health information rather than regulation' (NYT, 22 December 2006).

4 The LIVING ORGANISM metaphor is very common in many disciplines, such as science, economics, architecture, politics, sociology and so on.

5 The visual metaphor is construed in the NYT sample by referring to the 'mirror' as the object that reflects the image of anorexia (14 occurrences vs. 2 occurrences of 'espejo' in the EP subcorpus). This more concrete construction of the illness is transmitted by statements such as 'you look in the mirror to see if you've mastered it' or 'The mirror became a cruel optical illusion: I kept crunching, tucking, sweating and squatting, but my reflection just got uglier.' Both the NYT and EP position the notion of 'image' as central to the definition of EDs (40 occurrences of 'imagen' in EP; 38 occurrences of 'image' in the NYT).

6 Only the NYT (as opposed to EP) published articles with personal stories of ED (6 articles).

7 Influenced by English, examples of 'desorden alimentario' (*disordered eating*) were found in the EP subcorpus (8 occurrences). 'Desorden' is an Anglicism not yet admitted in Spanish (cf. *Diccionario de la lengua española*).

8 In fact, cognitive behavioural psychology has become a widespread intervention for EDs (see Linardon et al., 2017 for a review of the literature).

9 For the same period of time, in the EP subcorpus up to 11 news articles were dedicated to the pro-anorexia movement and the actions taken by the Spanish government to ban these contents, as opposed to the NYT subcorpus, in which only 7 news articles reported on this topic.

10 Such government regulations about a minimum size for fashion models and the prohibition of pro-anorexia material on social media are not, however, part of the actions pursued in the American culture to curb the 'problem of EDs'.

11 Actually, in the Spanish sample, a higher number of references to children and adolescents was found than in the USA sample: 123 occurrences of 'niños' vs. 79 occurrences of 'children', and 73 occurrences of 'adolescente(s)' vs. only 4 occurrences of 'teenager(s)'. In addition, EP contains more references to 'chica(s)' (51 occurrences) and 'niña(s)' (31 occurrences) than the NYT (only 22 occurrences of 'girl'). These contrasts reveal a strong tendency to identify potential ED sufferers as very young females in the Spanish press.

12 There are also two occurrences of 'wrestle', a synonym of 'struggle', in the NYT sample.

## References

Aragonès. E., López-Muntaner, J., Ceruelo, S., & Basora, J. (2014). Reinforcing stigmatization: coverage of mental illness in Spanish newspapers. *Journal of Health Community* 19(11): 1248–58. https://doi.org/10.1080/10810730.2013.872726

Barry, C., Brescoll, V.L., Brownell, K.D., & Schlesinger, M. (2009). Obesity metaphors: how beliefs about the causes of obesity affect support for public policy. *The Milbank Quarterly* 87(1): 7–47. https://doi.org/10.1111/j.1468-0009.2009.00546.x

Benet, V., & Waller, N.G. (1995). The big seven factor model for personality description: evidence for its cross-cultural generality in a Spanish sample. *Journal of Personality and Social Psychology* 60(4): 701–18. https://doi.org/10.1037/0022-3514.69.4.701

Bray, A. (2005). The anorexic body: reading disorders. In T. Atkinson (ed.), *The Body: Readers in Cultural Criticism* (pp. 115–28). Basingstoke: Palgrave.

Burton, T., Hands, B.P., & Bulsara, C. (2015). Metaphors used by eating disordered women to describe their experience of being pregnant. *Evidence Based Midwifery* 13(4): 126–32.

Carter, M.J. (2013). The hermeneutics of frames and framing: an examination of the media's construction of reality. *SAGE Open* 1–12.

Coulehan, J.L. (2003). Metaphor and medicine: narrative in clinical practice. *The Yale Journal of Biology and Medicine* 76(2): 87–95. https://doi.org/10.1353/pbm.1988.0064

Demjén, Z., Marszalek, A., Semino, E., & Varese, F. (2019). Metaphor framing and distress in lived-experience accounts of voice-hearing. *Open Access*. Retrieved from: https://doi.org/10.1080/17522439.2018.1563626

Demjén, D., & Semino, E. (2016). Using metaphor in healthcare. In Z. Demjén and E. Semino (eds), *The Routledge Handbook of Metaphor and Language* (pp. 385–99). New York: Taylor and Francis.

Demjén, Z., Semino, E., & Koller, V. (2016). Metaphors for 'good' and 'bad' deaths: a health professional view. *Metaphor and the Social World* 6(1): 1–19. https://doi.org/10.1075/msw.6.1.01dem

Entman, R. (1993). Framing: toward clarification of a fractured paradigm. *Journal of Communication* 43(4): 51–8. https://doi.org/10.1111/j.1460-2466.1993.tb01304.x

Feuston, J.L., & Piper, A.M. (2019). Everyday experiences: small stories and mental illness on Instagram. *CHI Paper*, 4–9 May, Glasgow, Scotland, UK.

Garrett, C.J. (1996). Transformations in time and space: social theory and recovery from eating disorders. *Eating Disorders* 4: 245–55. https://doi.org/10.1080/10640269608251179

Hambrook, D., & Tchanturia, K. (2008). A pilot study exploring Machiavellianism in anorexia nervosa: eating and weight disorders. *Studies on Anorexia, Bulimia and Obesity* 13: 137–41. https://doi.org/10.1007/bf03327614

Hendricks, R.K., Demjén, Z., Semino, E., & Boroditsky, L. (2018). Emotional implications of metaphor: consequences of metaphor framing for mindset about cancer. *Metaphor & Symbol* 33(4): 267–79. https://doi.org/10.1080/10926488.2018.1549835

Hodgkin, P. (1985). Medicine is war and other medical metaphors. *British Medical Journal* 291: 1820–21. https://doi.org/10.1136/bmj.291.6511.1820

Hofstede, G. (1980). *Culture's Consequences: International Differences in Work-Related Values*. Beverly Hills, CA: Sage.

Holmes, S. (2018). (Un)twisted: talking back to media representations of eating disorders. *Journal of Gender Studies* 27(2): 149–64. https://doi.org/10.1080/09589236.2016.1181539

Johnson, M. (1987). *The Body in the Mind: The Bodily Basis of Meaning, Imagination, and Reason*. Chicago: University of Chicago Press.

Lakoff, G., & Johnson, M. (1980). *Metaphors We Live By*. Chicago: University of Chicago Press.

Lima, M., Sáez, A., & Lima, J. (2011). ¿Contribuye la prensa al estigma de personas con trastorno mental? Análisis de contenidos de *ElPais.com*. *Revista Presencia* 7(14).

Linardon, J., Wade, T.D., de la Piedad, X., & Brennan, L. (2017). The efficacy of cognitive-behavioural therapy for eating disorders: a systematic review and meta-analysis. *Journal of Consulting and Clinical Psychology* 85(11): 1080–94. https://doi.org/10.1037/ccp0000245

Loftus, S. (2011). Pain and its metaphors: a dialogical approach. *Journal of Medical Humanities* 32: 213–30. https://doi.org/10.1007/s10912-011-9139-3

Ma, X. (2017). How the media cover mental illnesses: a review. *Health Education* 117(1): 90–109. https://doi.org/10.1108/he-01-2016-0004

MacLean, A., Sweeting, H., Walker, L., Patterson, C., Räisänen, U., & Hunt, K. (2015). 'It is not healthy and it's decidedly not masculine': a media analysis of UK newspaper representations of eating disorders in males. *BMJ Open* 5: e007468. https://doi.org/10.1136/bmjopen-2014-007468

Markus, H.R., & Kitayama, S. (1991). Culture and the self: implications for cognition, emotion, and motivation. *Psychological Review* 98(2): 224–53. https://doi.org/10.1037/0033-295x.98.2.224

Mathieson, L.C., & Hoskins, M.L. (2005). Metaphors of change in the context of eating disorders: bridging understandings with girls' perceptions. *Canadian Journal of Counselling/Revue canadienne de counseling* 39: 260–74.

McGinty, E.E., Kennedy-Hendricks, A., Choksy, S., & Barry, C.L. (2016). Trends in news media coverage of mental illness in the United States: 1995–2014. *Health Affairs* 35(6): 1121–29. https://doi.org/10.1377/hlthaff.2016.0011

Mondini, S., Favaro, A., & Santonastaso, P. (1996). Eating disorders and the ideal of feminine beauty in Italian newspapers and magazines. *European Eating Disorders Review* 4: 112–20. https://doi.org/10.1002/(sici)1099-0968(199606)4:2<112::aid-erv152>3.0.co;2-6

Nawková, L., Nawka, A., Adamkova, T., Rukavina, T.V., et al. (2012). The picture of mental health/illness in the printed media in three Central European countries. *Journal of Health Communication* 17(1): 22–40. https://doi.org/10.1080/10810730.2011.571341

O'Hara, S.K., & Smith, K.C. (2007). Presentation of eating disorders in the news media: what are the implications for patient diagnosis and treatment? *Patient Education and Counseling* 68: 43–51. https://doi.org/10.1016/j.pec.2007.04.006

Oostdyk, A.M. (2008). Portrayal of mental illness on television: a review of the literature. Master's thesis, University of Pittsburgh, Pittsburgh, available at: http://dscholarship.pitt.edu/7009

Pragglejaz Group (2007). MIP: a method for identifying metaphorically used words in discourse. *Metaphor and Symbol* 22(1): 1–39. https://doi.org/10.1207/s15327868ms2201_1

Ray, L., & Hinnant, A. (2009). Media representation of mental disorders: a study of ADD and ADHD coverage in magazines from 1985 to 2008. *Journal of Magazine & New Media Research* 11(1): 1–21. https://doi.org/10.1353/jmm.2009.0004

Ross, A.M., Morgan, A.J., Wake, A., Jorm, A.F., & Reavley, N.J. (2021). Key stakeholders' recommendations for improving Australian news media reporting of people with severe mental illness, violence and crime. *Advances in Mental Health*, doi:10.1080/18387357.2021.1942101

Saguy, A.C., & Gruys, K. (2010). Morality and health: new media constructions of overweight and eating disorders. *Social Problems* 57(2): 231–50. https://doi.org/10.1525/sp.2010.57.2.231

Semino, E. (2008). *Metaphor in Discourse.* Cambridge: Cambridge University Press.

Semino, E., Demjén, Z., & Demmen, J. (2018a). An integrated approach to metaphor and framing in cognition, discourse, and practice, with an application to metaphors of cancer. *Applied Linguistics* 39(5): 625–45. https://doi.org/10.1093/applin/amw028

Semino, E., Demjén, Z., Hardie, A., Payne, S., & Rayson, P. (2018b). *Metaphor, Cancer and the End of Life: A Corpus-Based Study.* New York: Routledge.

Shepherd, E., & Seale, C. (2010). Eating disorders in the media: the changing nature of UK newspaper reports. *European Eating Disorders Review* 18: 486–95. https://doi.org/10.1002/erv.1006

Skårderud, F. (2007). Eating one's words, part I: 'concretised metaphors' and reflective function in anorexia nervosa—an interview study. *European Eating Disorders Review* 15: 163–74. https://doi.org/10.1002/erv.777

Slopen, N.B., Watson, A.C., Gracia, G., & Corrigan, P.W. (2007). Age analysis of newspaper coverage of mental illness. *Journal of Health Communication* 12: 3–15. https://doi.org/10.1080/10810730601091292

Stout, P.A., Villegas, J., & Jennings, N.A. (2004). Images of mental illness in the media: identifying gaps in the research. *Schizophrenia Bulletin* 30(3): 543–61. https://doi.org/10.1093/oxfordjournals.schbul.a007099

Sun, S., He, J., Fan, X., Chen, Y., & Lu, X. (2019). Chinese media coverage of eating disorders: disorder representations and patient profiles. *International Journal of Eating Disorders* 53: 113–22. https://doi.org/10.1002/eat.23154

Tay, D. (2017). Using metaphor in healthcare: mental health interventions. In E. Semino and Z. Demjén (eds), *Routledge Handbook of Metaphor and Language* (pp. 371–84). New York: Routledge.

Vengut, E. (2018). Newspaper portrayal of mental illness in England, Canada, Portugal. *Revista Española de Comunicación en Salud* 9(2): 176–87. https://doi.org/10.20318/recs.2018.4495

Wahl, O.F. (1992). Mass media images of mental illness: a review of the literature. *Journal of Community Psychology* 20(4): 343–52. https://doi.org/10.1002/1520-6629(199210)20:4<343::aid-jcop2290200408>3.0.co;2-2

Wahl, O.F. (2003). Depictions of mental illnesses in children's media. *Journal of Mental Health* 12(3): 249–58. https://doi.org/10.1080/0963823031000118230

Wahl, O.F., Wood, A., & Richards, R. (2002). Newspaper coverage of mental illness: is it changing? *Psychiatric Rehabilitation Skills* 6(1): 9–31. https://doi.org/10.1080/10973430208408417

# 2 Animal Metaphors in Women's Magazines: Their Potential Link with Eating Disorders

*Irene López-Rodríguez*

## Introduction

Animal metaphors have been explored in discourses of eating disorders (EDs) (Burns, 2004; Fathallah, 2006; Treasure et al., 2010). The etymology of 'bulimia', from Greek 'ox' and 'hunger' (OED), serves to exemplify the close relationship between these mental ailments and fauna. Zoomorphic symbols, indeed, appear to inform people's experiences with anorexia, bulimia and binge eating, both in medicine (Johnston, 2000; Metcalfe, 2006; Tiell, 2018) and in the media (Stommel, 2007; McCurley, 2014; Figueras Bates, 2018).

In the medical field, physicians and patients alike tend to describe an individual's struggle with food in terms of 'defeating a beast'. The former can use this analogy to transmit a message of hope to overcome the disease, as reported in the works *The Eating Disorder Beast Can be Beaten* (Tiell, 2018) and *Dying to Be Thin: Tools for Battling the Bulimia Beast* (Gilbert, 2020). Patients, on the other hand, frequently recur to this simile to express the destructive effects of such ailments, as seen in excerpts from the journals of individuals with anorexia and bulimia: 'It [anorexia] has fallen over me like a beast and I am helpless against it' (as cited in Hawton & van Heeringen, 2000, p. 269) or 'An eating disorder is a beast that resides deep within, destroying a person slowly from the inside out' (Richards, 2016, p. 39).

Irene López-Rodríguez, 'Chapter 2: Animal Metaphors in Women's Magazines: Their Potential Link with Eating Disorders' in: *Eating Disorders in Public Discourse: Exploring Media Representations and Lived Experiences*. University of Exeter Press (2023). © Irene López-Rodríguez. DOI: 10.47788/HKAQ8861

Healthcare professionals can also resort to animal metaphors as pedagogical tools to introduce concepts of EDs and to coach family members of ill individuals. The labels 'kangaroo' (overprotective), 'rhinoceros' (critical), 'jellyfish' (anxious), 'ostrich' (disengaged), 'dolphin' (gentle) and 'St Bernard' (warm), for instance, have been devised to explain the various interactive styles of carers so that guardians can understand their pivotal role in facilitating the patient's recovery through their guidance and support (Treasure et al., 2010). Similarly, therapists may use the allegory of the hungry wolf to address and solve complex issues related to bulimia and binge eating (McCubbrey, 2003). The website of the Eating Disorder Institute (2012), which defines bulimia as 'the big, bad wolf', recommends using the iconic canid to account for a person's compulsive eating, and so does the Institute for the Psychology of Eating (2014) when appealing to control those hunger urges through the archetype of the wolf: 'the key to taming that hungry wolf within is to listen to it deeply'.

People with disordered eating also recur to the bestial iconography to come to terms with their maladies. Their narratives related to food frequently incorporate their views of hunger as 'an uncontrollable beast going berserk inside their bodies' (Twohig & Kalitzkus, 2008), as attested in *Soothing the Beast Within: A Loving Path to End Food Addiction* (Routley, 2012) and *Taming the Feast Beast* (Trimpey & Trimpey, 1995). Their corporeal depictions are likewise rife with images of gross and large creatures that somehow reflect their experience of body dysmorphia (Metcalfe, 2006). Even their memoirs are given significant titles, with animal names that epitomize disgust towards their bodies and yearning for change—such as *Chrysalis: A Dark and Delicious Diary of Emergence* (Chartrand, 2014), *Monkey Taming: You've Eaten Too Much, You Fat Pig* (Fathallah, 2006), *Butterflies are Free... What About Me: One Woman's Battle with Anorexia Nervosa* (Levine, 2018) and *Beauty Comes With a Beast: Overcoming an Eating Disorder* (Vance, 2019).

At some points, individuals with anorexia and bulimia may personify their sickness via animalization. 'Ana, the bitch', 'Ana, the parasite', 'the bulimic bulldog' and 'a bulimic boa constrictor' serve to project their feelings and thoughts regarding their complex ailment onto unpleasant and dangerous animals (Bernhardsson, 2010). In artistic therapies, patients frequently speak of their relationship with their physique and food through similar metaphors. Drawings of devouring creatures and circular worms feeding themselves (Levens, 1995) along with theatrical performances displaying animals' movements (Wood, 2016) attest to the prevalence and significance of the bestial iconography in the medical jargon of EDs.

In like manner, the media can provide a good insight into the binomial animal metaphors-eating disorders (Stommel, 2007; McCurley, 2014). Magazines and newspapers often approach these pathologies from a zoomorphic perspective. The *Los Angeles Times*, for example, represents anorexia and bulimia as ravaging beasts when reporting on a young gymnast's death from EDs: 'Beasts of anorexia nervosa, bulimia ravaged gymnast's body: Christy Henrich was 22 and weighed less than 60 pounds when she died' (21 August 1994). *The Huffington Post* employs the same beastly symbol when interviewing a person who formerly had bulimia: 'Part of healing is understanding the beast that takes over lives' (26 February 2016). Even the medicine-orientated magazine *Psychology Today* defines orthorexia as 'a new beast in the eating disorder world' (10 March 2019).

On other occasions, the print news media include autobiographical extracts of individuals with disordered eating that similarly display animal metaphors to refer to their body image and food intake. In the *Chicago Tribune*, a woman with binge eating disorder speaks of her nightly binge as 'pig out': 'At night when I'm alone I pig out like you wouldn't believe. Then I force myself to throw up' (23 December 1987). In the fitness magazine *Shape*, another woman with bulimia refers to her compulsive eating as 'wolfing down': 'If you look at me, you wouldn't guess I was a binge eater. But four times a month, I find myself wolfing down more food than I can handle' (17 November 2019).

As far as the internet is concerned, research in German forums for people with anorexia has shown that some of the most common nicknames of their users pertain to fauna. Terms such as 'small snap dragon', 'small lion's mouth' and 'small bear' seem to reflect the participants' desire to connect with their natural essence and their thrive for thinness (Stommel, 2007, p. 150). Other studies on pro-anorexia and pro-bulimia websites have equally revealed the currency of zoomorphic images in the formation of the participants' identities (McCurley, 2014, p. 25). For instance, the metaphoric pig exhibited in their profile descriptions appears to corroborate their disgust towards their bodies and eating practices: 'I'M A FAT PIG' (qtd. in Figueras Bates, 2018, p. 175) or 'I AM A FAT PIGGY' (qtd. in Brown, 2017, p. 45). Analogously, the understanding of their bodies as obstacles preventing individuals with anorexia from finding their true inner self is translated into depictions of their anatomical frames as 'a cage' or 'a shell' in which they feel 'trapped' (Figueras Bates, 2014, p. 7).

In addition, the animal world seems to enable pro-ana users to detach themselves from the physical realm of all living entities that depend on foodstuffs. Their longing for spiritual perfection through food deprivation, which nicely corresponds with Knapton's (2013) metaphorical construction of anorexia as a religion, is visible in their comments: 'Do not reward yourself with food, you are not a dog' (cited in Arseniev-Koehler et al., 2016, p. 9) or 'Ana sets us distinctly—and irrevocably—apart from, and above, the herd' (cited in Knapton, 2013, p. 18). Finally, on their personal blogs and sites, people who have recovered from EDs may recall their previous pathologies and give advice to (re-)establish a healthy lifestyle through figurative fauna, as shown in 'Dog toys and other eating disorder metaphors' (Rzemieniak, 2018).[1]

Animal symbols, it appears, have become instrumental in the discursive construction of disordered eating. As carriers of conceptual meanings, cultural values and ideologies (Goatly, 2006), zoomorphic metaphors not only provide mental frameworks to apprehend these mental ailments, but as noted, they can also offer a window onto the construction of the identities of individuals with these maladies.

According to research in human cognition, culture and communication, people constantly draw from the colourful animal world as a way of explaining human behaviour, human feelings and human relations. Figurative fauna can certainly shed some light onto people's construction of the self and the Other (López-Rodríguez, 2009, pp. 78–79). In fact, animal metaphors help individuals address the duality of being part of nature yet, at the same time, somehow removed from and above it (Lévi-Strauss, 1968, p. 26). The conceptualization of PEOPLE AS BEASTS (Kövecses, 2006) is generally embedded in the context of humans as evolved animals able to refrain from their innate impulses thanks to their superior rational capacity.[2] Underpinning most faunistic metaphors is the notion of (lack of) control that presupposes that the animal side of a person must be hidden or kept at bay as part of civilized behaviour.[3] There is a wide repertoire of figurative expressions drawing from the domain of animals that highlight the inability to restrain emotions and drives, such as bodily functions (e.g., *pig*), sexual desire (e.g., *cougar*), anger (e.g., *unbridled* rage) and hunger (e.g., *wolf down*). Falling within the scope of the so-called control metaphors (Pérez, 2001, p. 180; MacArthur, 2005), faunistic icons have thus become powerful mechanisms that help in the (self-) regulation of people's conduct in accordance with societal norms (López-Rodríguez, 2016, p. 81).

Notwithstanding that animal metaphors have been documented in the (hate) speech of individuals with anorexia, bulimia and binge eating (Hanne, 2015; Tiell, 2018), little attention has been paid to the deployment of bestial iconography in women's magazines. Perhaps except for Tartakovsky (2009), and López-Rodríguez (2016), who have underscored the negative messages conveyed through such images, there is a lack of critical studies examining the functions of zoomorphic tropes in publications that have been explicitly linked to body dysmorphia and disordered eating (Swiatkowski, 2016). Building upon these works, this chapter aims to explore figurative fauna in women's magazines published in the UK, the USA, Canada and Australia. The goals of the study are to understand the use(s) and function(s) of animal metaphors in this sort of media frequently credited with the promotion of disordered eating. This is particularly relevant considering Figueras Bates's study in this book, underscoring how the media's use of specific metaphorical framings to refer to EDs may trigger negative general associations in the public, which, in turn, may contribute to social rejection.

## Method: Procedure and Analysis

Data for this study were collected from twenty-four magazines, namely: *Best Health Magazine*, *Cosmopolitan*, *Ebony*, *Fitness*, *Fitness First*, *Glamour*, *Marie Claire*, *Martha Stewart Living*, *Now*, *O* (*The Oprah Magazine*), *Oxygen*, *People*, *Real Simple*, *Romper*, *Runners*, *Self*, *Shape*, *Star*, *Top Fitness*, *US*, *Vogue*, *Woman's Day*, *Women's Health* and *Women's Lifestyle*. These publications were intentionally chosen because they are mainly aimed at a female audience, tend to cover topics related to physical appearance, beauty, fitness and diets, and have often been credited with fostering thin ideal internalization, body dissatisfaction, unhealthy dieting and even disordered eating (Conradie, 2011; Swiatkowski, 2016). Thus, they lend themselves nicely to an analysis of the uses and functions of animal metaphors.[4] Furthermore, published in English, these print news media have international coverage and distribution. Their apparently wide readership also justifies their use as valuable sources of information, given that they provide influential contexts for socialization and identity formation among the female population (López-Rodríguez, 2008).

This study did not require ethical approval by the University of Ottawa given that all the data analysed is published in magazines and, therefore, available to the public. Besides not receiving any type of funding for undertaking this project, the author has no conflict of interest. The results of this study will, hopefully, pave the way for future empirical research concerning the detrimental impact that animal metaphors in women's magazines may have on the physical and mental wellbeing of their intended female audience.

Data collection and sampling were purposive, guided by the objectives to explore the research questions. The study conducted a qualitative analysis of the animal metaphors used in women's magazines to talk about diets, health, fitness and beauty. All the articles dealing with one of the abovementioned topics were registered and considered for future metaphoric coding. Note that not all the monthly issues of each magazine were consulted due to time and financial constraints to access them. A total of four magazines (whether in print or online) were consulted each month over the course of seventeen years (2003–2020). This selection was made randomly, depending on the availability of each publication, but always with the desire to encompass a wider variety of journals to enrich data. A total of 816 magazines were consulted (48 magazines annually) with an average of 11 articles per issue covering the key topics of diets, health, fitness and beauty. This yielded a final corpus of 8,976 articles. The animal-based metaphors were manually coded using the metaphor identification procedure (MIP) (Pragglejaz Group 2007). The description of this method—the only one, so far, formally tested and found reliable and valid in the discipline of metaphor studies (Steen et al., 2010)—is as follows:

1. Read the entire text-discourse to establish a general understanding of the meaning.
2. Determine the lexical units in the text-discourse.
3. (a) For each lexical unit in the text, establish its meaning in context, that is, how it applies to an entity, relation, or attribute in the situation evoked by the text (contextual meaning). Take into account what comes before and after the lexical unit.
   (b) For each lexical unit, determine if it has a more basic contemporary meaning in other contexts than the one in the given context. For our purposes, basic meanings tend to be

- More concrete; what they evoke is easier to imagine, see, hear, feel, smell, and taste.
- Related to bodily action.
- More precise (as opposed to vague).
- Historically older.

Basic meanings are not necessarily the most frequent meanings of the lexical unit.

(c) If the lexical unit has a more basic current-contemporary meaning in other contexts than the given context, decide whether the contextual meaning contrasts with the basic meaning but can be understood in comparison with it.

4. If yes, mark the lexical unit as metaphorical. (Pragglejaz Group, 2007, p. 3)

Having identified and marked all the animal metaphors used in the representation of women's physiques and eating behaviours in the above corpus according to MIP, the next step required their organization into meaningful clusters. The identification and formulation of the conceptual structures underlying the tokens labelled as metaphorical were carried out considering that the primary function of metaphor is the understanding of abstract ideas in terms of more concrete, bodily or familiar ones (Lakoff & Johnson, 1980; Semino, 2008). With this premise of conceptual metaphor theory (CMT) in mind, the project thoroughly examined the main zoomorphic scenarios to which these magazines recurred when illustrating complex ideas related to women's body image and dietary practices.

The resulting corpus was comprised of 584 metaphorical items. Note that all these linguistic metaphors were regarded as the surface manifestation in language of conceptual metaphors. Hence, once retrieved and noted, the former were grouped thematically, so that conceptual metaphors could be put forward to explain them.

In addition, the qualitative analysis of the main animal metaphors that women's magazines deployed was framed within a discourse analytic approach orientated to news media, as described by Fairclough (2003), Charteris-Black (2004), Chilton (2005) and Mussolf (2012). Implementing cognitive semantics, this view considers the social influence of ideology, culture and history to provide a more convincing account of why particular metaphors are chosen in specific discourse contexts (Charteris-Black, 2004, p. 6). The selection of a specific metaphor, then, functions as a 'representational strategy' (Fairclough, 2003, p. 145), fulfilling what Halliday (2013) terms 'ideational function' of language. In fact, the preference of a metaphor over others not only reflects different ways of representing reality, but it can also create (social) realities that may influence thoughts and actions. To put it in Fairclough's words:

> [w]hen we see the world with a particular metaphor, it then forms basis of our action [...] our perception of the world and behaviour will change according to the use of a particular metaphor. (2003, p. 39)

Consistent with this approach, then, the focus of the study was placed on how animal metaphors in women's magazines can shape readers' perceptions of themselves and motivate changes in their eating behaviours and actions.

The present chapter discusses the use(s) and function(s) of this metaphorical animalesque talk in the construction of female physiques and dietary practices in women's magazines. Special attention will be paid to the wider psychological, cultural and social discourses from which these metaphors are drawn.

## Findings and Discussion

This section combines the report of the research findings and the discussion of their significance in order to explore the implications of the animal metaphors employed in women's magazines to describe female physical appearance and eating behaviours. The table below reflects the main conceptual animal metaphors identified in this research, along with their frequency. Following typographical conventions, the conceptual metaphors outlined in this study are written in small caps. Besides, to enhance the input visually, the linguistic metaphors are highlighted in bold and presented in context (i.e., with the relevant co-text). Additionally, this research employs 'metaphor' as an umbrella term that also encompasses metonymies, synecdoches and idioms, since they tend to contain metaphorical expressions as well.

### *HUNGER IS A BEAST INSIDE A WOMAN*

The experience of hunger in relation to an uncontrollable beast inside a female body is one of the most frequent metaphorical themes to which women's

**Table 2.1** Metaphoric conceptualizations of women's physiques and their eating behaviours in the corpus

| *No.* | *Conceptual Metaphors* | *Frequency* | *Percentage* |
|---|---|---|---|
| 1. | HUNGRY WOMEN ARE PIGS | 225 | 38.52% |
| 2. | HUNGER IS A BEAST INSIDE A WOMAN | 193 | 33.04% |
| 3. | HUNGRY WOMEN ARE WOLVES | 107 | 18.32% |
| 4. | OVERWEIGHT/PREGNANT WOMEN ARE COWS | 32 | 5.47% |
| 5. | OVERWEIGHT/PREGNANT WOMEN ARE WHALES | 27 | 4.62% |
| | | 584 | 100% |

magazines resorted to promote dieting. HUNGER IS A BEAST INSIDE A WOMAN accounts for 33.04% of all the animal-based metaphors of the corpus. This zoomorphic scenario, which corresponds with the more general conceptual metaphors THE BODY IS A CONTAINER FOR THE EMOTIONS and PASSIONS ARE BEASTS INSIDE US (for the container and passions metaphors, see Lakoff & Johnson, 1989), allowed these publications to personify hunger as a captive animal trying to break free from the control of women. Appealing to this beastly construction of emotions brought to the forefront the dichotomy of rational human/instinctual beast (Kövecses, 2006). As a matter of fact, in the corpus, the metaphoric 'beast' was generally embedded in passages tinged with sensorial verbs (e.g., see, sense, feel, hear) to encourage women to keep hunger at bay:

(1) Thanksgiving leftovers are too tempting [...] no wonder you can see the **beast** coming during the holiday season (*Self*, October 2011, p. 37)

(2) After your workout you can sense the **beast**. What to eat and not to eat to maximize your exercise routine (*Runners*, June 2013, p. 15)

The metamorphosis of hunger into a fierce beast also enabled women's magazines to recreate the painful effects of food deprivation on the female anatomy. The following extract details how different parts of an animal ('claws') can damage a woman's body ('tears your stomach'):

(3) When you are on a diet, you often have that **beast** inside you asking for ice-cream, cookies, and fast food. It **tears** your stomach with its **claws**, and it is painful, but you must resist the urge (*Cosmopolitan*, March 2014, p. 82)

This painful scene evoked through the personification of hunger is commonplace in the discourse of people with EDs. As already mentioned, research has shown how patients with anorexia, bulimia and binge eating tend to describe their state of being hungry as a menacing animal going berserk inside their bodies (Twohig & Kalitzkus, 2008).

The understanding of hunger as a captive animal in need of human subjugation, which falls within the scope of the so-called control metaphors (Pérez, 2001) aimed at the (self-) regulation of people's behaviours, translated into the symbolic 'taming' in these publications. This faunistic terminology was applied to women who use the different strategies publicized in the press to curb their cravings.

(4) TIPS TO **TAME** YOUR APPETITE. Plan ahead. Schedule your meals and snacks for times you're a little peckish, but not ravenous (*Fitness First*, 12 February 2020)

(5) The Cosmo Bikini Diet: Lose 15 Pounds & Get a Sexy Body. Sipping water is an **appetite-taming** move (*Cosmopolitan*, April 2015, p. 10)

Framing hunger as a ferocious uncontrollable beast often resulted in the representation of females as vulnerable prey succumbing to food:

(6) Don't **fall prey to a snack attack**! Healthy (and tasty) snack ideas (*Cosmopolitan*, May 2014, p. 35)

(7) Despite our best intentions, we all **fall prey to habits that are plumping us up**—even if we don't realize they are (*Woman's Day*, March 2015, p. 26)

This predator–prey relationship that allegorically represents social relations of domination and subjugation (Hart & Long, 2011) served women's magazines to explain female food weaknesses. In addition to conveying a threatening image of hunger, this hunting scenario transpired in the corpus through metaphorical usages of 'trap' to refer to the different nutritional habits (and often workout routines) that might lead to weight loss plateau or gain:

(8) Here, sneaky **traps** that can sabotage weight loss and what you can do about them (*Woman's Day*, March 2015, p. 26)

(9) Weight Loss **Traps** to Avoid at All Costs (*Women's Health*, 20 June 2016)

The representation of women as easy prey falling into the traps of foodstuffs to some degree resembles the hunting metaphors that individuals with disordered eating deploy to express their vulnerability to their disease, as registered in *The Eating Disorder Trap: A Guide for Clinicians and Loved Ones* (Goldberg, 2020). Furthermore, as already seen, images of cages also surfaced in the language of people with anorexia and bulimia to denote their bodies and their inner struggle with their EDs (Figueras, 2014). In this sense, it is worth mentioning the award-winning photography exhibition on anorexia, 'Cage', by David Arribas. The Spanish photographer declared that he had purposefully chosen this animal term to illustrate his project after interviewing numerous women with anorexia who continuously used it to refer to their pathological conditions.

## *HUNGRY WOMEN ARE PIGS*

The most recurrent metaphorical theme in the corpus was to account for women's eating behaviours in terms of pigs. Around 38% of the articles scrutinized contained some form of this metaphor. Therefore, with excerpts such as 'Don't **pig out** at weddings' (*Glamour*, 28 June 2010), 'We eat like **pigs** while on our periods' (*Self*, May 2014, p. 37), 'Some mothers-to-be use pregnancy as a license to **pig out**' (*Ebony*, August 1998, p. 136) or 'A Workout Doesn't Merit a Post-Gym **Pig-Out**' (*Real Simple*, 8 June 2018), women's magazines discursively constructed dietary practices through porcine imagery. The adoption of pig-based metaphors to transmit women's undesirable eating practices reflects the negative cultural load attached to this farmyard animal in Western cultures (Stibbe, 2003). Generally associated with greediness, dirtiness and fatness, the largely taboo pig (Leach, 1964, p. 51) recurred in articles devoted to food consumption during special celebrations, such as weddings, Thanksgiving or Christmas:

(10) How to **Pig Out** on Thanksgiving (But Without the Guilt) (*Cosmopolitan*, November 2009, p. 24)
(11) It's the holiday season, and many of us are tempted to **pig out** on turkey, dressing and cherry pie (*Ebony*, 16 December 2019)
(12) Do You **Pig Out** at Weddings? Here's the scene: You're all dressed up, you're inches away from equally put-together guests (whom you may not even know), and there's a plate with a heaping portion of the most

> yummy-looking (fill in the blank) right in front of you. Do you eat the whole thing? If you're me, you're damn right I do! I'm not a big drinker, so you won't see me up at the bar all night, but I love, love, love to eat and, if the food is good, don't be surprised if every full plate that's served to me winds up looking like it's been licked clean once I've had my way with it. (Just so we're clear, I don't *actually* lick plates clean!) Of course, if I'm full, I won't eat every last bite available to me. Usually, though, there's enough room in this body of mine for several hors d'oeuvres (and a whole roll of sushi at the cocktail hour), a salad, a pasta, most of the entree, some of the side veggies, and a thin(-ish) slice of cake or other desserts. (Wow, I really do sound like a **piggy**!) Maybe that's not very ladylike (*Glamour*, 28 June 2010)

Embedded in narratives that detail meals and their calories, the metaphoric *pig out* not only alerts women of potential weight gain, but also appears to connote dirtiness—notice the lack of manners of the woman who acknowledges her food excess in the last excerpt. In addition to casting aspersions on women's table manners, the porcine trope clearly belittles females by reducing them to the category of gluttonous beasts, as observed in the last comment: 'Maybe that's not very ladylike.'

Data analysis also revealed a tendency to categorize women's nutritional choices after exercising as pigs gobbling (19%). Although acoustic considerations might play a role in the encoding of the metaphoric 'pig out' in its collocation with 'work out', since, as Koller (2004, p. 2) has argued, metaphors are often used playfully to gain consumers' attention in the media, most fitness articles deploying this animal-derived verb appear to shame women who eat after exercising:

(13) Don't **pig out** after your work out (*Women's Health*, 30 March 2015)

(14) Why Do You **Pig Out** After Your Work Out? It's a vicious cycle: You sweat your butt off at the gym, then stuff your face when you get home. Follow our seven simple strategies to end the **oink-fests** (*Shape*, June 2015, p. 11)

The last writer exploits pig imagery in its acoustic dimension to sanction women's eating behaviours after doing sports. The coinage of the onomatopoeic compound 'oink-fests' to denote a massive consumption of food, far from being an isolated linguistic product (registered nine times in the corpus), seems to reflect the creation of a metaphorical network in accordance with the cognitive processes that inform our understanding of women's eating behaviours in the guise of pigs. Interestingly, the corpus showed another collocation of *pig out* with the animal verb 'graze' to judge eating behaviours among the female population:

(15) Don't **pig out** after your work out [...] To stave off **grazing** after exercising, have a healthy snack (*Real Simple*, 8 June 2018)

(16) Prevent love chub. So, while you want to feel comfortable in your relationship, you don't want to get so comfy that you **pig out** on ice-cream while wearing stretch pants every night [...] B moms tend to **graze** instead of sitting down for proper meals (*Fitness*, October 2014, pp. 107–108).

Considering the role of metaphors as 'attention-getters' in the print news media (Koller, 2004, pp. 2–6), it appears that women's magazines have generated a series of spin-offs from the archetypal pig to stigmatize women who do not adhere to strict diets. Hence, taking for granted that eating with debauchery is usually unavoidable, many articles speak of 'post pig-out plans' to compensate for the extra calories consumed with strict dieting, and of 'pig-out proof places' to keep food out of the reach of women:

(17) Party's over: Time for the **post-pig out plan**. A 3-day detox diet to purge holiday pounds even before the tree's down (*Women's Health*, September 2016)

(18) Your **Post-Pig-Out Plan**. Had two giant slices of cake and a couple glasses of wine at a friend's birthday party last night? Don't panic! Try this five-step fix (*Shape*, 6 November 2014)

(19) **Pig-Out Prevention Plan**: **PIG-OUT PROOF YOUR KITCHEN**. Sniff Essential Oils. New research shows that the smell of grapefruit can help curb hunger pangs, so keep a bottle of this essential oil in your bag and inhale whenever the urge to snack strikes. **PIG-OUT PROOF YOUR DESK** and **PIG-OUT PROOF YOUR HANDBAG**. Eat Dried Figs. Fiber fills you up and takes the edge of cravings, and a

dried fig contains nearly as much fibre as one square of Weetbix. Keep a couple of figs wrapped in cling film in a zipped-up pocket of your handbag for a perfect in-between snack (*Cosmopolitan*, 13 July 2020)

Ranked as one of the most offensive animal names applied to humans according to psychological studies (Haslam et al., 2011, p. 322), pig carries a strong sense of shame (Leach, 1964; Stibbe, 2003) that extends to feeding habits. To some degree, this disapproving metaphor forms part of the broader discourse of food shaming that negatively impacts people's health (Duarte et al., 2017). As a matter of fact, in 'Cos girls aren't supposed to eat like pigs, are they? Young women negotiating gendered discursive constructions of food and eating' (Woolhouse et al., 2011), researchers working in the realm of disordered eating have registered the high frequency of pig imagery in teenage girls' conversations about dieting, even establishing a link between this type of self-disparaging language with their development of a toxic relationship with food. Along the same lines, the USA's Child Mind Institute includes this deprecating metaphor as an alarm sign that might suggest an eating disorder in its section 'Signs a college student may have an eating disorder' (Jacobson, 2018).

### *HUNGRY WOMEN ARE WOLVES*

In discussing female dietary habits, women's magazines sometimes turned to wolf metaphors to transmit their (usually speedy and voracious) consumption of foods. Statements such as 'You **Wolf Down** Your Food to Get the Meal Over With' (*Women's Health*, May 2014, p. 48) or 'a power walk isn't an excuse to **wolf down** a bagel every day' (*Self*, 15 April 2016) are illustrative of 18% of the corpus.

In general terms, articles rendered women's uncontrollable appetite even to the point of sickness through the ravenous canid. The metaphoric *wolf down*, indeed, usually appeared with expressions of quantity (e.g., dozens of, large, a truckload of) to exaggerate food intake.

(20) You can **wolf down** large quantities of food when over-hungry and get way past the point of fullness (*Shape*, 7 March 2012)

(21) **wolf down** a truckload of **cupcakes** the day after you start your diet (*Oprah*, May 2010)

In addition to its occurrence with this hyperbolic language, the corpus revealed another set of collocations of *wolf down* with products laden with calories, such as fast food, pasta, sweets or chips (22) and (23). This interplay between a wild animal and edibles potentially hazardous for a woman's waistline might obey to the human tendency to categorize problems and threats as dangerous animals (Pérez, 2001). In fact, anthropological works (López, 1979) have highlighted the emotions of fear and loathing traditionally surrounding the predatory wolf, which might certainly explain its negative import.

(22) When your goal is to lean down, aim to make 20 to 25 percent of your calories come from fat. But don't use that as an excuse to **wolf down** a plate of fettuccine alfredo (*Oxygen*, 19 May 2017)

(23) How To Crank Up Your Metabolism. Don't settle for a sluggish system. Boost your calorie-burning superpowers with these expert tips to smoke fat 24/7. Have you ever watched a slim woman **wolf down** a giant bag of Kettle Chips and then wondered where she puts it all? (You may also have other thoughts about this **breed** of woman but let's skip over that) (*Women's Health*, June 2015, p. 90)

Data analysis also showed the development of wolf-related metaphors to instil fear of weight gain. Several articles turned hungry women into 'a pack of wolves' awaiting their food and even referred to their physical exercise to compensate for the extra calories with the metonymic 'hoof'.

(24) It's Friday night and like **a pack of hungry wolves** you and your friends eat pizza (*Cosmopolitan*, February 2015)

(25) How Your Metabolism Changes in Your 20s, 30s, and 40s [...] When you're a kid, you can **wolf down** candy bars, fast food and frozen pizza bagels without a second thought—you know it won't impact your weight... Most women enjoy their highest basal metabolic rate (the number of calories you burn by just being alive), in their late teens or early twenties [...] Some women will hit it a bit earlier, others later, which has a lot to do with genetics, but your activity level also plays a big role. After all, the more you **hoof** it around campus, play on intramural teams, and hit up the university weight room, the more calorie-torching muscle you'll build and the higher your metabolism will be (*Women's Health*, 29 October 2015)

Judging from the corpus analysed, the deployment of wolf imagery to stigmatize women's consumption of foods (whether large quantities or calorie-laden), to some extent, resembles the use of wolf metaphors in the discourse of people with EDs. As stated in the introduction, individuals with bulimia and binge eating constantly refer to their eating patterns through wolf symbolism. After all, statements such as 'It was like a wild hungry wolf took over my eating', compiled on the website of the Institute for the psychology of eating (2014), and excerpts like 'I turn into a wild hungry wolf at night' (*Shape*, 2017), taken from a women's health magazine, are virtually identical, despite their provenance, in their negative transmission of unhealthy eating patterns through wolf metaphors.

### *OVERWEIGHT/PREGNANT WOMEN ARE COWS/WHALES*

Along with descriptions of eating behaviours in terms of animals, the analysis also showed occasional figurative usages of 'cow' and 'whale' in the representation of overweight (6%) and pregnant women (3%). Thus, for instance, statements such as 'Apocalypse **cow**! Gym time' (*US*, June 2014, p. 34), 'feeling like a **cow** during pregnancy' (*Star*, October 2009), 'Kim Kardashian looks like a real **whale**' (*Now*, July 2014, p. 5) or 'Celebrities that look like beached **whales**' (*US*, August 2013, p. 4) explicitly targeted heavy females through these hefty and large mammals.

Terms of opprobrium, both zoomorphic metaphors carry the senses of unattractiveness and, above all, fatness (López-Rodríguez, 2009, p. 79). Classified as insults for fat people (Cameron & Russell, 2016), thus, these faunistic symbols resonate in the obesity discourse that stigmatizes females with weight issues, as shown in Hardy's (2014) work 'Cows, pigs, whales: nonhuman animals, antifat bias, and exceptionalist logics'. In the articles scrutinized, *cow* and *whale* appear to be derisive, fat shaming women who do not adhere to the ultra-thin beauty standard and even mothers-to-be. Indeed, although pregnancy irremediably results in weight gain, women's magazines render expectant mothers who put on too much weight as cows (34–35).

(34) Jessica Simpson has certainly gained some weight during her pregnancy and looks like a **cow** (*US*, June 2014, p. 34)

(35) Britney confesses to feeling like a **cow** with her second pregnancy (*Star*, October 2009, p. 15)

## Conclusion

The aim of this study on animal metaphors in women's magazines was to analyse the use(s) and function(s) of the bestial iconography in publications that have been linked to the promotion of body dysmorphia and disordered eating. An analysis of a corpus consisting of 584 faunistic tropes has shown how this sort of media resort to the zoomorphic scenario to frame and communicate ideas pertaining to women's eating behaviours and physical appearance.

According to data analysis, figurative expressions such as 'the beast inside', 'pig out', 'wolf down', 'cow' and 'whale' tend to disparage women who cannot control their appetite and/or who do not conform to the ultra-thin beauty standard. In addition to their widespread usage, the success of these images is well-attested in their generation of metaphorical networks: beast (breed, graze, tame, trap), pig (piggy, pig out, pig out proof, post-pig-out plan, oink-fests), wolf (wolf down, a pack, hoof) and whale (beach). Apart from providing connectivity textually and cognitively speaking (Koller, 2004, p. 2), these metaphorical chains ultimately seem to forge and reinforce the trinity fauna–female–food that appears to hunger- and fat- shame females. In fact, documented in obesity discourses, these bestial symbols might be part of the 'fat talk' (Martz, 2019) often identified in women's magazines as a contributing factor to body dissatisfaction (Arroyo, 2015).

In addition, given that animal metaphors have been documented in the (hate) speech of people with anorexia, bulimia and binge eating, both in medical and media discourses, the deployment of the bestial iconography in women's magazines inevitably leads to questioning the detrimental impact of such zoomorphic images on the physical and mental wellbeing of their intended audience. In other words, whether there exists a correlation between this type of faunistic language and women's development of a toxic relationship with food and their bodies falls outside the scope of this paper, but it would be a powerful area for future empirical research, especially in light of studies underscoring that individuals with disordered eating not only engage in heavy media use, but they even describe their consumption of women's magazines as 'an addiction' (Thomsen et al., 2001).

Furthermore, because animal metaphors serve to categorize otherness in reinforcing the dichotomy human/beast, the bestial iconography in women's magazines seemingly marginalizes those who do not comply with strict diets or a slender body type. Hence, their categorization as an 'undesirable' out-group within the female community may perpetuate stigma, which might result in women's development of low self-esteem, unhealthy weight management behaviours and maybe even prompting disordered eating.

Finally, given that, in the words of Lévi-Strauss (1968, p. 10), animals are essential in people's lives not only because they are good to eat but, more importantly, because they are good to think with, the analysis of zoomorphic tropes recurring in women's magazines deserves closer examination considering the striking similarities between the use of animal metaphors in the language of people with EDs and in the language of these publications. Hence, notwithstanding the numerous shortcomings of the present research (i.e., its theoretical nature, its use of magazines that may not be representative of women of different races, ages, educational backgrounds and social status), this study has attempted, on the one hand, to shed some light onto the negative messages conveyed through the iconography of the beast in women's magazines, and, on the other hand, to establish a potential link between this type of language and the development of disordered eating based on the pervasiveness of zoomorphic symbols in medical discourses of EDs.

## Acknowledgements

I would like to express my gratitude to Dr Rosalia Cornejo-Parriego, Dr Juana Liceras and Dr Luis Abanto from the University of Ottawa.

## Dedication

To my daughter, Helena. Thanks for being in my life.

## Notes

1 On the website Metamia: Science Communication Using Analogy, one of the most frequent metaphors used to explain anorexia pertains to the animal kingdom. For example, people frequently refer to this mental ailment as 'a serpent', 'a spider' and 'a crocodile' (http://www.metamia.com).

2 The iconography of the beast must be understood within THE GREAT CHAIN OF BEING metaphor (Lovejoy, 1936). This folk cognitive model basically

presupposes a hierarchical organization of the universe, pictured as a chain vertically extended, where complex, more powerful beings stand above and dominate lower forms of life. From top to bottom there are celestial creatures, human beings, animals, flora and inanimate objects. In general terms, a shift downward in the chain entails physical and figurative degradation. Hence, the identification of people with beasts usually conveys negative connotations.

3 The animal kingdom is a common source for the expression of extreme behaviour, as attested in the conceptual metaphors HUMAN BEHAVIOUR IS ANIMAL BEHAVIOUR, ANGER IS ANIMAL BEHAVIOUR, PASSIONS ARE BEASTS INSIDE US or A LUSTFUL PERSON IS AN ANIMAL (Lakoff, 1987; Kövecses, 2006).

4 Despite the value of the authentic data compiled in this research, it should be noted that most of the magazines consulted—perhaps with the exception of *Ebony* and *Oprah*, intended for the African American community—are targeted to Western white heterosexual women and, therefore, might not represent the metaphors used in other types of print media addressed to other race and gender identifications.

## References


Arroyo, A. (2015). Magazine exposure and body dissatisfaction: the mediating roles of thin ideal internalization and fat talk. *Communication Research Reports* 32(3): 246–52. https://doi.org/10.1080/08824096.2015.1052905

Arseniev-Koehler, A., Lee, H., McCormick, T., & Moreno, M. (2016). #Pro-ana: pro-eating disorder socialization on Twitter. *Journal of Adolescent Health* 58: 659–64. https://doi.org/10.1016/j.jadohealth.2016.02.012

Bernhardsson, K. (2010). Devils, serpents, and zebras: metaphors of illness in Swedish literature on eating disorders (1987–2005). In I. Lange & Z. Norridge (eds), *Illness, Bodies and Contexts: Interdisciplinary Perspectives* (pp. 135–43). Leiden: Brill.

Brown, T. (2017). Examining the influence of social media on body image: miss perception, a misperception [Unpublished MA Thesis]. Colorado State University.

Burns, M. (2004). Eating like an ox: femininity and dualistic constructions of bulimia and anorexia. *Feminism and Psychology* 14: 269–95. https://doi.org/10.1177/0959353504042182

Cameron, E., & Russell, C. (eds) (2016). *The Fat Pedagogy Reader: Challenging Weight-Based Oppression through Critical Education*. Bern: Peter Lang.

Charteris-Black, J. (2004). *Corpus Approaches to Critical Metaphor Analysis*. New York: Macmillan.

Chartrand, R. (2014). *Chrysalis: A Dark and Delicious Diary of Emergence*. London: Balboa Press.

Chilton, P. (2005). Missing links in mainstream CDA: modules, blends and the critical instinct. In R. Wodak & P. Chilton (eds), *A New Agenda in (Critical) Discourse Analysis* (pp. 68–99). Amsterdam: John Benjamins.

Conradie, M. (2011). Constructing femininity: a critical discourse analysis of Cosmo. *Southern African Linguistics and Applied Language Studies* 29: 401–17. https://doi.org/10.2989/16073614.2011.651940

Duarte, C., Matos, M., Stubbs, R.J., Gale, C., Morris, L., Pinto, J., & Gilbert, P. (2017). The impact of shame, self-criticism and social rank on eating behaviours in overweight and obese women participating in a weight management programme. *PLoS ONE* 12(1): 4–39. https://doi.org/10.1016/j.comppsych.2016.01.003

Fairclough, N. (2003). *Analysing Discourse: Textual Analysis for Social Research*. London: Routledge.

Fathallah, J. (2006). *Monkey Taming: You've Eaten Too Much, You Fat Pig*. London: Red Fox.

Figueras Bates, C. (2014). 'I am a waste of breath, of space, of time': metaphors of self in a pro-anorexia group. *Qualitative Health Research* 25(2): 1–16. https://doi.org/10.1177/1049732314550004

Figueras Bates, C. (2018). Self-presentation processes in personal profiles in a pro-anorexia group. *Normas: Revista de Estudios Lingüísticos Hispánicos* 8(1): 168–83. https://doi.org/10.7203/normas.v8i1.13432

Gibbs, R., & Steen, G. (eds) (1999). *Metaphor in Cognitive Linguistics*. Amsterdam: John Benjamins.

Gilbert, N. (2020). *Dying To Be Thin: Tools for Battling the Bulimia Beast*. New York: Morgan James Publishing.

Goatly, A. (2006). Humans, animals, and metaphors. *Society & Animals* 14: 15–37. https://doi.org/10.1163/156853006776137131

Goldberg, R. (2020). *The Eating Disorder Trap: A Guide for Clinicians and Loved Ones*. Alpharetta, GA: BookLogix.

Halliday, M. (2013). *Introduction to Functional Grammar*. London: Routledge.

Hanne, M. (2015). Diagnosis and metaphor. *Perspectives in Biology and Medicine* 58: 35–52. https://doi.org/10.1353/pbm.2015.0010

Hardy, K. (2014). Cows, pigs, whales: nonhuman animals, antifat bias, and exceptionalist logics. In R. Chastain (ed.), *The Politics of Size: Perspectives from the Fat Acceptance Movement* (pp. 4–39). Santa Barbara, CA: ABC-CLIO.

Hart, K., & R. Long, J.H. (2011). Animal metaphors and metaphorizing. *Evolution: Education and Outreach* 4: 52–63. https://doi.org/10.1007/s12052-010-0301-6

Haslam, N., Loughnan, S., & Sun, P. (2011). Beastly: what makes animal metaphors offensive? *Journal of Language and Social Psychology* 30(3): 311–25. https://doi.org/10.1177/0261927x11407168

Hawton, K., & van Heeringen, K. (eds) (2000). *The International Handbook of Suicide and Attempted Suicide*. Hoboken, NJ: John Wiley & Sons Ltd.

Jacobson, R. (2018). Signs a college student may have an eating disorder. *U.S. Child Mind Institute*. Retrieved November 11, 2020, from https://childmind.org/article/signs-a-college-student-may-have-an-eating-disorder

Johnston, A. (2000). *Eating in the Light of the Moon: How Women Can Transform Their Relationship with Food Through Myths, Metaphors, and Storytelling*. Carlsbad, CA: Gurze Books.

Knapton, O. (2013). Pro-anorexia: extensions of ingrained concepts. *Discourse and Society* 24(4): 461–77. https://doi.org/10.1177/0957926513482067

Koller, V. (2004). *Metaphor and Gender in Business Media Discourse: A Critical Cognitive Study*. London: Palgrave Macmillan.

Kövecses, Z. (2006). *Language, Mind, and Culture: A Practical Introduction*. Oxford: Oxford University Press.

Lakoff, G., & Johnson, M. (1980). *Metaphors We Live By*. Chicago: University of Chicago Press.

Lakoff, G. (1987). *Women, Fire, and Dangerous Things*. Chicago: University of Chicago Press.

Lakoff, G., & Johnson, M. (1989). *Philosophy in the Flesh: The Embodied Mind and Its Challenge to Western Thought*. New York: Basic Books.

Leach E. (1964). Anthropological aspects of language: animal categories and verbal abuse. In E.H. Lenneberg (ed.), *New Directions in the Study of Language* (pp. 23–63). Cambridge, MA: MIT Press.

Levens, M. (1995). *Eating Disorders and Magical Control of the Body: Treatment through Art Therapy*. London: Psychology Press.

Levine, W. (2018). *Butterflies Are Free… What About Me: One Woman's Battle With Anorexia Nervosa*. Scotts Valley, CA: CreateSpace.

Lévi-Strauss, C. (1968). *The Savage Mind*. Chicago: University of Chicago Press.

López-Rodríguez, I. (2016). Feeding women with animal metaphors that promote eating disorders in the written media. *Linguistik* 75: 1–35. https://doi.org/10.13092/lo.75.2517

López-Rodríguez, I. (2009). Of women, bitches, chickens and vixens: animal metaphors for women in English and Spanish. *Culture, Language and Representation* 7: 77–100.

López-Rodríguez, I. (2008). The representation of women in teenage and women's magazines: recurring metaphors in English. *Estudios Ingleses de la Universidad Complutense de Madrid* 15: 15–42.

López, B. (1979). *Of Wolves and Men*. New York: Scribner.

Lovejoy, A.O. (1936). *The Great Chain of Being: A Study of the History of an Idea*. Cambridge, MA: Harvard University Press.

Martz, D. (2019). *Fat Talk: A Feminist Perspective*. Jefferson, NC: MacFarland.

MacArthur, F. (2005). The competent horseman in a horseless world: observations on a conventional metaphor in Spanish and English. *Metaphor and Symbol* 20(1): 71–94. https://doi.org/10.1207/s15327868ms2001_3

McCubbrey, D. (2003). *How Much Does Your Soul Weigh?* New York: HarperCollins.

McCurley, K. (2014). *Beauty Through Control: Forming Pro-Anorexic Identities in Digital Spaces*. MA Thesis. University of Massachusetts.

*Metamia: Science communication using analogy* (2020, January 27). Retrieved 21 December 2020, from http://www.metamia.com.

Metcalfe, K. (2006). *Anorexia: A Stranger in the Family*. Cardiff: Accent Press.

Mussolf, A. (2012). The study of metaphor as part of critical discourse analysis. *Critical Discourse Studies* 9(3): 301–310. https://doi.org/10.1080/17405904.2012.688300

Pérez, C. (2001). The emotional control metaphors. *Journal of English Studies* 3(2): 179–92. https://doi.org/10.18172/jes.76

Pragglejaz Group (2007). MIP: a method for identifying metaphorically used words in discourse. *Metaphor and Symbol* 22(1): 1–39. https://doi.org/10.1207/s15327868ms2201_1

Richards, R. (2016). *Hungry for Life: A Memoir Unlocking the Truth Inside an Anorexic Mind*. Scotts Valley, CA: CreateSpace.

Routley, N. (2012). *Soothing the Beast Within: A Loving Path to End Food Addiction*. Bloomington, IN: Trafford.

Rzemieniak, S. (2018). Dog toys and other eating disorders metaphors. Eating Disorder Recovery Coach Site. Retrieved 12 October 2020, from https://sarahrzemieniak.com/eating-disorder-metaphors.

Semino, E. (2008). *Metaphor in Discourse*. Cambridge: Cambridge University Press.

Steen, G., Biernacka, E., Dorst, A., Kaal, A., López-Rodríguez, I., & Pasma, T. (2010). Pragglejaz in practice: finding metaphorically used words in natural discourse. In G. Low, Z. Todd, A. Deignan & L. Cameron (eds), *Researching and Applying Metaphor in the Real World* (165–84). Amsterdam: John Benjamins.

Stibbe, A. (2003). As charming as a pig: the discursive construction of the relationship between pigs and humans. *Society & Animals* 11(4): 375–92. https://doi.org/10.1163/156853003322796091

Stommel, W. (2007). *Mein Nick bin ich!* Nicknames in a German forum on eating disorders. *Journal of Computer-Mediated Communication* 13(1): 141–62. https://doi.org/10.1111/j.1083-6101.2007.00390.x

Swiatkowski, P. (2016). Magazine influence on body dissatisfaction: Fashion vs. health? *Cogent Social Sciences* 2: 21–40. https://doi.org/10.1080/23311886.2016.1250702

Tartakovsky, M. (2009). Minding women's magazines: asinine advice. *Psychology Central* 21: 1–11.

Thomsen, S.R., McCoy, J.K., & Williams, M. (2001). Internalizing the impossible: anorexic outpatients' experiences with women's beauty and fashion magazines. *Eating Disorders* 9(1): 49–64. https://doi.org/10.1080/106402601300187731

Tiell, L. (2018). The eating disorder beast can be beaten. *Psychology Central* 10, 1–9.

Treasure, J. et al. (eds) (2010). *The Clinician's Guide to Collaborative Caring in Eating Disorders*. London: Routledge. https://doi.org/10.4324/9780203864685

Trimpey, J., & Trimpey, L. (1995). *Taming the Feast Beast: How to Recognize the Voice of Fatness and End Your Struggle with Food Forever*. New York: Dell.

Twohig, P., & Kalitzkus, V. (eds) (2008). *Social Studies of Health, Illness and Disease: Perspectives from the Social Sciences and Humanities*. Amsterdam: Rodopi. https://doi.org/10.1163/9789401205917

Vance, K.J. (2019). *Beauty Comes With a Beast: Overcoming an Eating Disorder*. Pennsauken, NJ: BookBaby.

Wood, L. (2016). The use of therapeutic theater in supporting clients in eating disorders recovery after intensive treatment: a qualitative study (Dissertation). University of Missouri-Saint Louis.

Woolhouse, M. et al. (2011). Cos girls aren't supposed to eat like pigs, are they? Young women negotiating gendered discursive constructions of food and eating. *Journal of Health and Psychology* 17(1): 46–56. https://doi.org/10.1177/1359105311406151

# Challenging the Stigma of a 'Woman's Illness' and 'Feminine Problem': A Cross-Cultural Analysis of News Stories About Eating Disorders and Men

*Scott Parrott, Kimberly Bissell, Nicholas Eckhart and Bumsoo Park*

## Introduction

About 30 million people in the USA will experience an eating disorder (ED) at some point in their lifetime (NEDA, 2020). Despite the stereotype that EDs are a female problem, about one in three people with an ED is male (NEDA, 2020). EDs will affect about 10 million males in the USA at some point in their lives, and NEDA research also indicates that LGBTQ+ teens may be at an even higher rate of developing an ED than their heterosexual peers. The National Institute of Mental Health reports that the age of onset for the clinical diagnosis of EDs like bulimia or anorexia is 18; however, girls younger than 18 are symptomatic as young as 13 and 14 (NIMH, 2017), and the age of onset for boys is similar, with a peak at age 14 (Forman-Hoffman, Watson & Anderson, 2008).

Disordered eating and behaviours are perceived to be a common occurrence for women and girls (Mitchison et al., 2014). Stigma is associated with men and boys who experience similar issues (Gorrell & Murray, 2019). EDs are

Scott Parrott, Kimberly Bissell, Nicholas Eckhart and Bumsoo Park, 'Chapter 3: Challenging the Stigma of a 'Woman's Illness' and 'Feminine Problem': A Cross-Cultural Analysis of News Stories About Eating Disorders and Men' in: *Eating Disorders in Public Discourse: Exploring Media Representations and Lived Experiences*. University of Exeter Press (2023). © Scott Parrott et al. DOI: 10.47788/LXVK2554 considered to be the most gendered psychiatric disorder, and clinical studies of EDs rarely account for men (Murray, Griffiths & Mond, 2016). While numerous factors contribute to the gendered perception of EDs, commenters have suggested mass media contribute to the cultural construction of EDs as feminine (e.g., MacLean et al., 2015). When it comes to news, journalists can shape public attitudes toward EDs through the information they highlight (or ignore), providing audiences with information about causes, symptoms, treatment and the people affected by EDs. While researchers have well-documented stereotypes concerning mental illness in the media (see Parrott, 2020, for a review), less empirical attention has been devoted to the representation of EDs in the press. The limited literature suggests news stories about EDs in the UK and the USA (a) focus on young white women, (b) provide unclear information concerning the likelihood of men being affected by EDs and (c) offer simplistic explanations concerning causes and treatments (MacLean et al., 2015; Shepherd & Seale, 2010; Sweeting et al., 2015). Commenters suggest media representations can nurture stigma (Strother et al., 2012), because men who experience EDs are perceived as different or abnormal. Given the media's prominence as an information source for mental health, it also stands to reason that the messages communicated by journalists may challenge the stigmatization of EDs by educating audiences and permitting parasocial contact with men who are affected by anorexia nervosa, bulimia nervosa, binge eating disorder and other illnesses.

Thus, the purpose of the present chapter is to examine news media coverage of men and EDs to determine how much, if at all, news media outlets report the story in a way that potentially nurtures or mitigates the stigmatization of the issue for men by discussing the issue in relation to women and presenting readers with an opportunity to 'meet' a man affected by EDs. The study compares stories from three English-speaking countries that frequently covered the subject between 2010 and 2019—Canada, the UK and the USA.

## Literature Review

Several studies have examined the relationship between body image distortion (BID) and related outcomes looking at possible social, psychological and biological correlates to disordered eating in American women, girls and increasingly men and boys. More recent studies have also found BID and disordered eating to be problematic for women and girls in other countries such as Canada (Park & Beaudet, 2007; Gadalla & Piran, 2007; Piran & Gadalla, 2007), Brazil (Nunes et al., 2006), Sweden (Sundquist et al., 2004) and Qatar (Bener, 2006). However, limited literature exists documenting men and various ED outcomes on a more global level. Of the empirical work that has been done examining the social effects of media specific to body image and men, much of the research is fifteen to twenty years old, and subsequently may not be reflective or representative of the many changes witnessed in media content and media use across demographic groups. Similarly, studies examining news media coverage of men and EDs are equally lacking (Sweeting et al., 2015).

## Mass Media and Stigma

While numerous studies examine news coverage of weight (e.g., Heuer, McClure & Puhl, 2011), scholars have devoted less research attention to media representations of EDs, especially among males. The limited evidence suggests that news media often associate EDs with white young women through the people interviewed, the statistics reviewed and other information highlighted or ignored (e.g., O'Hara & Clegg Smith, 2007). As Bowen and Waller describe in Chapter 4, the frames conveyed by news media may shape audience understanding of the cause, consequences and treatment of issues including EDs.

To illustrate, MacLean and colleagues (2015) examined how journalists covered EDs in men between 2002 and 2012 for ten newspapers in the UK. While stories conveyed that men develop EDs, journalists used language associating EDs with women, including statements such as 'normally associated with girls' and 'seen as a young woman's illness' (MacLean et al., 2015, p. 4). In addition, stories conveyed that EDs are more prevalent among men who are less masculine—reinforcing stereotypes concerning masculinity. Finally, stories described men's shame at seeking treatment for EDs. Encountering stereotypes within the media can nurture isolation, misunderstanding and other negative consequences for people affected by EDs, as described by Cariola and Lee in Chapter 6.

Shepherd and Seale (2010) compared news coverage of EDs in the UK and the USA between 1992 and 2008, noting that stories in both countries associated EDs with young, white, female celebrities. Meanwhile, O'Hara and Clegg Smith (2007) examined news reports concerning EDs in seven US news publications between 2004 and 2005 and found that news stories overwhelmingly profiled women (95% of individuals profiled). Such representations may contribute to the cultural construction of EDs as female illnesses (e.g., MacLean et al., 2015). In addition to affecting people with EDs, O'Hara and Clegg Smith (2007, p. 44) note that news reports may influence whether family and friends notice symptoms: 'Families and friends who hold a particular demographic picture of EDs may fail to recognise disease among people who fall outside this stereotype, preventing early diagnosis.'

Given the problems stigma presents for individuals and society, researchers have worked to identify effective approaches for challenging it (Rüsch et al., 2005). These strategies for stigma-reduction often involve formal initiatives, such as a letter-writing campaign or public service announcements designed to educate the public about mental health (Rüsch et al., 2005). However, news reports may provide an alternative approach to challenging stigma through the sources journalists interview and the messages they convey concerning mental health. One effective approach is parasocial contact, which involves introducing an in-group member to an out-group member with the intention of challenging stereotypes and highlighting commonalities between groups. For instance, an individual who has never experienced mental illness might incorrectly assume people with EDs are women or feminine. The person's beliefs might be challenged—and changed—after meeting a man with an ED who challenges the stereotype. Successful contact nurtures increased empathy and reduced intergroup anxiety (Pettigrew & Tropp, 2008).

A growing line of research suggests contact may even be successful via mass media. Schiappa, Gregg and Hewes (2005) proposed the parasocial contact hypothesis, suggesting that television and other mass media can challenge prejudice by introducing audience members to people from other social groups. The hypothesis has enjoyed considerable empirical support, as media effects scholars have found that exposure to non-stereotypical media personae in both fiction and non-fiction reduces stereotypical thinking and prejudice. Despite the promise of contact, media critics have questioned whether newspapers and other media outlets present the general public enough opportunity to experience contact with people affected by mental illness. In one study of New Zealand news content, a mental health consumer told researchers that 'people never see us living well' in the news, a reference to news stories generally focusing on stereotypical representations of mental illness (Nairn & Coverdale, 2005). Less prevalent, critics contend, are human interest stories in which people with mental illness are permitted to speak for themselves. Such lack of voice is problematic in at least two ways. First, it deprives the audience of an opportunity to 'meet' someone who has mental illness. Second, it removes people who are actually affected by illness from the conversation. In doing so, it silences perhaps the most important voice in the conversation.

## Research Questions

Given the potential role of news coverage in nurturing/mitigating the stigmatization of EDs among men, the present study examines research questions related to characteristics of news stories that might function to stigmatize or challenge stigma related to EDs and men.

First, estimates concerning the prevalence of EDs among men certainly vary, especially when taking into account differences in culture in Canada, the UK and the USA. Nevertheless, one can say thousands of men across the three nations are affected by EDs, despite the fact that cases are more prevalent among women. For example, in the USA, the National Eating Disorders Association (2020) estimates that men represent nearly one in three people affected by binge eating disorder (36%), one in four people affected by anorexia nervosa (25%) and one in four people affected by bulimia nervosa (25%). In the UK, the National Centre for Eating Disorders notes (2020, para. 21) that while EDs are important health problems for men, there is 'a tendency for EDs in males to go unrecognized or undiagnosed, due to reluctance among males to seek treatment for these stereotypically female conditions. This may now be changing due to increased public information and awareness.' One route by which such awareness may be raised is through news coverage identifying anorexia and bulimia as illnesses affecting both males and females. Therefore, the study first examines news-based communication about EDs to examine the following:

**RQ1.** When journalists write about EDs and men, which disorders are referenced most often in Canada, the UK and the USA? How does the focus compare?

A 'complex interaction' of factors contributes to EDs (NIMH, 2020). Psychological factors may include genetics, social factors may include cultural norms such as mass media content that perpetuate thin ideals, and family factors may include pressure from parents (Shepherd &

Seale, 2010). News stories concerning EDs among men may inform the public of the aetiology of the illness, eliciting stigmatizing or counter-stigmatizing responses. Therefore, the present study next examines the following:

**RQ2.** Which contributing factors do journalists attribute to EDs among men in Canada, the UK and the USA?

The subject of EDs among men necessitates a conversation of its own; nevertheless, it is likely news stories that reference men and EDs place the subject within the context of femininity, rather than placing the focus squarely on men. Therefore, we ask:

**RQ3.** When journalists write about EDs and men, how often is the focus on men alone? How often do stories reference women and EDs?

Finally, news stories may act as a communicator of cultural norms, conveying to men with EDs the likelihood they would experience prejudice or discrimination should they disclose their illness to others. We ask the following:

**RQ4.** When stories discuss men and EDs, how often do they describe men experiencing prejudice and discrimination because of their disorder? Does this differ by country?

While stigma researchers have primarily focused on the negative consequences of media exposure, a budding line of research suggests the media may afford audiences the opportunity for parasocial contact. Therefore, we ask:

**RQ5.** Which sources are most often quoted in stories about EDs and men in Canada, the UK and the USA?

It is important to note that contact in itself does not necessarily translate into positive outcomes. Therefore, we also examine stories to see how they humanize men who have personally experienced EDs.

**RQ6.** How often do stories provide personal testimonies concerning EDs, and what information do they convey?

## Methods

To answer the research questions, the authors conducted a content analysis of news stories about EDs and men, focusing on Canada, the UK and the USA.

### *Sample*

The authors used the database NexisUni to search for stories published by English-language news organizations worldwide between 2010 and 2019 with the words 'eating disorder' and 'men' in the headline. The search initially returned 323 stories; duplicates were culled, producing a final sample of 279 articles. Publications included a mix of tabloid, broadsheet and local publications. Journalists in the UK afforded the subject the most coverage during this period, producing 124 stories, followed by news organizations in the United States (73 stories) and Canada (31 stories). Therefore, the analysis focused on these countries. The remaining 53 articles were published in thirteen countries, led by Ireland with 19 articles, Australia with 8, India with 4 and South Africa with 4. IRB approval was not required because the study examined publicly available newspaper texts.

### *Coding procedure*

Two lead authors developed the coding protocol, while graduate students in communication performed the coding. Coders conducted two practice runs on sample articles from outside the dataset. The protocol was refined. Coders then separately examined 10% of the 279 articles ($n=28$) to formally examine intercoder reliability using percent agreement and Cohen's kappa (listed below).

## Unit of Analysis

The text of individual news stories served as the unit of analysis.

## Variables

### *Disorders referenced*

Coders indicated (0=no, 1=yes) whether a story specifically referenced each of the following: anorexia nervosa ($\kappa=.1$; 100% agreement), bulimia nervosa ($\kappa=.78$, 96%), binge eating ($\kappa=.93$, 96%), purging ($\kappa=.91$, 96%), restrictive eating ($\kappa=1$, 100%), orthorexia (0, 96%) and body dysmorphia ($\kappa=.87$, 96%).

### *Contributing factors of EDs*

Coders noted (0=no, 1=yes) whether a news story referenced each of the following as contributing factors of EDs: genetics (κ=.67, 89%), mass media (κ=.78, 89%), pressure from friends (κ=0, 93%), pressure from family (κ=.46, 93%), pressure from romantic partners (no variation, 100%) and stress (κ=.91, 96%).

### *References to men and women*

Coders answered two questions related to gender in the stories. First, coders determined whether men represented the primary focus of the story (0=no, 1=yes), marking no if men were simply referenced in the story or if the article equally mentioned women and men (κ=1, 100%). Second, coders noted whether the story directly referenced women and EDs (0=no, 1=yes; κ=.64, 93%).

### *Prejudice and discrimination*

Coders indicated (0=no, 1=yes) whether the story referenced a person experiencing differential treatment (i.e., prejudice and discrimination) from others because of an ED (κ=.92, 96%).

### *Personal experience*

Coders noted (0=no, 1=yes) whether a story permitted a man with an ED to communicate information concerning his personal experiences with an ED (κ=.78, 89%). This variable documented whether the person communicated specific anecdotes concerning his experience with an illness, rather than a story simply quoting a man with an ED.

### *Sources quoted*

Coders documented (0=no, 1=yes) whether a story directly quoted—in other words, placed in quotation marks—statements from a man who experienced an ED (κ=.64, 82%); a woman who experienced an ED (κ=1, 100%); medical professionals (κ=.46, 79%); government officials (κ=1, 100%); advocates (κ=.63, 82%); a friend of someone with an ED (κ=1, 100%); or a family member of someone with an ED (κ=.52, 89%).

## Results

The first research question sought to identify the disorders most often referenced. Stories most often referenced anorexia (*n*=189, 67%), followed by bulimia (*n*=173, 61%), binge eating (*n*=79, 28%), purging (*n*=64, 23%), body dysmorphia (*n*=28, 10%), restrictive eating (*n*=22, 8%) and orthorexia (*n*=4, 1%).

Countries largely followed the same pattern. In Canada, coverage most often referenced bulimia (22 of 31 articles, 71% of Canadian coverage), followed by anorexia (*n*=21, 68%), binge eating (*n*=8, 26%), purging (*n*=8, 26%), restrictive eating (*n*=3, 10%), body dysmorphia (*n*=2, 6%) and orthorexia (*n*=0).

In the UK, coverage focused primarily on anorexia (89 of 123 articles, 72%), bulimia (*n*=86, 70%), binge eating (*n*=27, 22%), purging (*n*=22, 18%), body dysmorphia (*n*=14, 11%), restrictive eating (*n*=9, 7%) and orthorexia (*n*=3, 2%).

In the USA, coverage most often referenced anorexia (42 of 73 articles, 58%), followed by bulimia (*n*=32, 44%), binge eating (*n*=23, 32%), purging (*n*=19, 26%), restrictive eating (*n*=9, 12%), body dysmorphia (*n*=7, 10%) and orthorexia (*n*=0).

A chi square analysis suggested no statistically significant difference among the proportions, with one exception: Canadian news publications were more likely than US publications to reference bulimia in news stories about EDs and men, $x^2$ (1, *N*=104) = 7.42, $p<.01$. Similarly, the UK publications were more likely than US publications to reference bulimia, $x^2$ (1, *N*=196) = 13.00, $p<.001$.

Answering the second research question, stories most often blamed the mass media for causing EDs among men (69 of 283 stories, 24%), followed by stress (*n*=29, 10%), genetics (*n*=24, 9%), pressure from friends (*n*=17, 6%), pressure from family (*n*=12, 4%) and pressure from romantic partners (*n*=9, 3%).

In Canada, news stories most often blamed mass media (11 of 31 stories, 35%), genetics (*n*=6, 19%), stress (*n*=5, 16%), pressure from romantic partners (*n*=1, 3%), pressure from friends (*n*=0) and pressure from family (*n*=0). Similarly, in the UK, stories most often blamed mass media (*n*=31 of 124, 25%), stress (*n*=12, 10%), pressure from family (*n*=8, 6%), genetics (*n*=5, 4%), pressure from friends (*n*=4, 3%) and pressure from romantic partners (*n*=3, 2%). Finally, stories in the USA blamed mass media (12 of 73 stories, 16%), pressure from friends (*n*=8, 11%), genetics (*n*=7, 10%), stress (*n*=5, 7%), pressure from romantic partners (*n*=5, 7%) and pressure from family (*n*=2, 3%). Chi square analyses suggest differences in one category. Publications in Canada were more likely to blame genetics than publications in the UK, $x^2$ (1, *N*=155) = 8.83, $p<.01$.

Journalists rarely referenced only men when writing about EDs, addressing the third research question. Across countries, 183 of 283 news stories also referenced women's EDs (65%). Nonetheless, 220 stories focused primarily on men (78%). In the UK, 73 of 124 stories (59%) referenced women's EDs, while 48 of 73 stories (66%) in the USA and 25 of 31 stories in Canada (71%) did so. Meanwhile, 101 of 124 stories (81%) in the UK focused primarily on men, while 46 of 73 stories (63%) in the USA and 27 of 31 stories in Canada (87%) did so. Stories in the UK were more likely than stories in the USA to focus on men, $x^2$ (1, *N*=197) = 8.25, $p<.01$. Canadian stories were also more likely than stories in the USA to focus on men, $x^2$ (1, *N*=104) 6.03, $p<.05$.

The fourth research question sought to identify how often stories referenced prejudice when describing men's experiences. Overall, 50 of 283 stories (18%) referenced prejudice experienced by men who have EDs. In the UK, 21 stories (17%) referenced prejudice, while 10 stories in the USA (14%) and 10 stories in Canada (32%) referenced it.

When it came to sources, the fifth research question, journalists most often consulted men who experienced EDs (*n*=121, 43%), medical professionals (*n*=112, 40%), advocates (*n*=69, 24%), women who experienced EDs (*n*=32, 11%), family of someone who experienced an ED (*n*=20, 7%), friends of someone with an ED (*n*=7, 3%) and government officials (*n*=7, 3%).

Canadian news publications most often quoted medical professionals (21 of 31 stories, 68%), men who experienced an ED (*n*=15, 48%), advocates (*n*=9, 29%) and a family member of someone with an ED (*n*=1, 3%). Canadian stories never quoted women who experienced an ED (*n*=0), friends of someone with an ED (*n*=0) or government officials (*n*=0).

Publications in the UK most often quoted men who experienced an ED (65 of 124 stories, 52%), advocates (*n*=39, 31%), medical professionals (*n*=35, 28%), women who experienced an ED (*n*=19, 15%), a family member of someone with an ED (*n*=9, 7%), government officials (*n*=3, 2%) and friends of someone with an ED (*n*=3, 2%).

The US publications most often quoted medical professionals (28 of 73 stories, 38%), men who experienced an ED (*n*=24, 33%), advocates (*n*=10, 14%), women who experienced an ED (*n*=9, 12%), a family member of someone with an ED (*n*=6, 8%), government officials (*n*=4, 5%) and friends of someone with an ED (*n*=2, 3%). Overall, stories from the UK were more likely than the US stories to quote a man who experienced an ED, $x^2$ (1, *N*=197) 108,

$p$<.01. Meanwhile, stories from the UK were more likely to quote medical professionals than Canadian news stories, $x^2$ (1, $N$=155) 16.78, $p$<.001, while the US stories were also more likely than Canadian stories to quote medical professionals, $x^2$ (1, $N$=104) 7.54, $p$<.01. Finally, stories from the UK were more likely than the US stories to quote advocates, $x^2$ (1, $N$=197) 7.75, $p$<.01.

Answering the final research question, the analysis found that almost 1 in 3 stories (107 of 283, 37%) provided readers first-person, personal testimonies from men with EDs. This was the case for 11 of 31 stories in Canada (35%), 61 of 124 stories in the UK (49%) and 20 of 73 stories in the USA (27%). Stories from the UK were more likely than those in the USA to communicate men's personal stories about their experience with ED, $x^2$ (1, $N$=197) 9.01, $p$<.01.

The personal stories often communicated men's experiences with stereotypes, prejudice and discrimination related to EDs. Men described EDs as being perceived as a 'woman's illness' by everyone from family members to health professionals, including one man who told the *Manchester Evening News* in the UK that 'One of the first questions I was asked was: "Do you feel like you were meant to be born a girl?" They assumed I was confused about my gender. One nurse even made a joke about whether I had started my periods' (Dobson, 2014, para. 34). Another man told the *Bury Times* in the UK that 'When I see photos of myself, I am very obviously ill—but boys don't look at each other and talk about their bodies in that way' (Holbrook, 2019, para. 16). Men reported not seeking help because they feared humiliation. The shame men felt often had to do with EDs as being perceived as feminine. Shame often led men to either remain silent, not seek help, or actively deceive friends, family, teachers and others. 'A big part of anorexia is deception', one man told *The Times* in the UK (Rose, 2019, para. 23). 'I did everything to cover it up because it's such an inherently embarrassing illness, especially if you're a boy. The idea of tricking my family and friends into thinking I wasn't ill became so normal.'

## Discussion

While scholars in media studies, psychology and other fields have thoroughly documented stereotypes concerning mental illness in mass media worldwide, far less empirical attention has been devoted to understanding representations of EDs, particularly among men. Unlike other mental illnesses, which are associated with violence and erratic behaviour, EDs are perceived as 'feminine', still presenting the potential for serious downstream consequences for boys and men. It is paramount we understand whence these stereotypes emerge and how they might be challenged; the present study was designed with the aim of understanding one potential route—news coverage of men and EDs. Specifically, we examined two key characteristics of news content concerning EDs and men: whether stories primarily focused on men, or simply referenced men in a larger conversation about EDs, and whether journalists permitted men who experienced EDs to 'speak' to readers through first-person interviews.

The latter question is important because research suggests contact represents one of the most effective methods for challenging out-group stereotypes and prejudice. Further, research suggests contact may occur via mediated means, a phenomenon described as parasocial contact. Narratives may be effective for at least two primary reasons. First, personal narratives may generate empathy and understanding among audience members for men who experience EDs, especially when they lack real-world contact with such men. Second, by highlighting the stories of men who have experienced EDs, journalists are potentially showing male readers affected by EDs that they are not alone, challenging the sense of isolation that people affected by EDs have described to researchers, including Cariola and Lee in Chapter 6. Indeed, a common refrain among the men interviewed for these stories involved loneliness: they described feeling as though other men did not go through comparable experiences. As one man told the *Irish Times* (Kelleher, 2017, para. 4), 'I read a lot of books' about EDs, 'but they were all very gender specific. They were all about women. There was no mention of "he" in any of the books, it was all "she" and "her," and that was kind of soul destroying in a way. It's like you don't exist, there's nothing to describe you at all. You're off the radar.' By sharing their experiences, these men helped put the subject 'on the radar'.

While differences did emerge between countries, journalists often permitted men who experienced EDs an opportunity to describe for readers their personal experiences with symptoms, treatment and even prejudice and discrimination. Commonalities emerged in men's stories. Men often spoke about stigma and keeping secrets from family members and close friends—until their weight loss or other behaviours reached a crisis stage. In addition, most of the men appeared 'on the record', permitting journalists to use their real names in news articles because they felt that they could show other boys and men that there are others in the community who have been through comparable struggles. By shining light on EDs among men, they said they hoped others would reach out for help sooner. Finally, both the men and medical professionals often acknowledged treatment-related challenges for men who experience EDs: men recounted prejudice from medical providers, treatment groups in which they were surrounded by women, and being asked to complete questionnaires and read treatment literature clearly targeting women. 'If you go for treatment and you're in a group with 10 or 12 women and you're the only man, it's very difficult to feel like you're not different', a clinical director told the *Vancouver Province* in Canada (Kirkey, 2013, para. 4). The DSM specifically notes that the prevalence of anorexia nervosa and bulimia nervosa are less common in men compared to women, but also notes (APA, 2013, p. 24) that for bulimia, 'Males are especially underrepresented in treatment-seeking samples, for reasons that have not yet been systematically explained.' One explanation, based on the anecdotes shared in these news stories, might lie in stigma.

The news stories also served an educational role by sharing information about the factors that contribute to EDs among men, whether those stories appeared in Canada, the UK or the USA. Stories often acknowledged the diversity of factors that might contribute to anorexia, bulimia, binge eating and other EDs. Journalists—and the sources they interviewed—cited social norms, pressure from family and friends, and stress-related factors such as bullying, while also discounting stereotypes that the disorders are rooted in personal weakness. Nonetheless, one cause rose to the forefront of conversation: the mass media. One in three stories centred around the potential role of television, celebrities, magazines and social media in leading men to adopt negative views toward themselves and, in turn, seeking solace through behaviour such as excessive dieting and excessive exercise. In addition to skewing people's self-esteem, the mass media can nurture misperceptions over whether a boy or man's symptoms represent an ED. As one man told the *St. Petersburg Times* in the USA (Rodriguez, 2011, p. 1), 'I was aware of EDs due to media coverage, but they're usually presented as female problems so I never made the connection with myself.'

Regarding education, the news stories generally missed an opportunity to teach the public about the prevalence of specific disorders, which might be due in part to clinicians' own uncertainty concerning the frequency with which men experience the disorders. Nonetheless, we found that news stories most often referenced anorexia, followed by bulimia and binge eating. The result is interesting, in part, because of the actual prevalence of these illnesses among men: binge eating appears to be most prevalent among men, followed by bulimia and anorexia. This might very well be a remnant of the amount of public and clinical attention these disorders have received in the past. Binge eating, for instance, represents the 'newest' disorder in that it was the last one added (in 2013) to the DSM, an 'authoritative volume' of the American Psychiatric Association that 'defines and classifies mental disorders in order to improve diagnoses, treatment, and research' (APA, 2020). To compare, anorexia nervosa appeared in the first DSM in 1952 (National Eating Disorders Association, 2020). An alternative explanation involves gender: binge eating is described as 'eating your emotions', which might be considered more female than male, given stereotypical associations concerning men, women and emotionality (Fabes & Martin, 1991).

Among these three countries, the subject of EDs among men generated fairly consistent news coverage. There was not a noticeable increase in stories over time that might indicate greater public attention to the subject. We note this because the coverage generally adopted an educational, 'challenge readers' expectations' approach: stories often started with a journalist describing a man's experiences with an ED, employed a transition along the lines of 'he's not alone', featured a statement challenging the stereotype that EDs are a 'feminine illness' and transitioned to statistics concerning EDs among boys and men. Indeed, while the majority of the stories focused primarily on men, 65% also referenced women's experiences with EDs. The approach potentially carries positive and negative consequences. An important step in challenging stigma involves normalization. While the stories are educational, it would be helpful for journalists to reach the point where men and EDs may be discussed in their own right. Perhaps the issue is rooted in society: until social norms acknowledge the prevalence of EDs among men, journalists and mental health advocates will no longer feel the need to challenge the feminization of EDs.

## Limitations

As with any study, the present research had its limitations. In one limitation, the study did not examine the specific context of the parasocial contact. For example, research suggests news stories can be problematic when they provide readers with 'instructions' on how to achieve weight loss by sharing details of a man's experience with EDs; we sought to examine this variable but were unsuccessful after failing to achieve intercoder reliability. This area certainly warrants future investigation.

## Conclusion

The present study sought to understand how English-language print journalists covered EDs and men in Canada, the UK and the USA. Overall, journalists provided readers with a similar representation of anorexia, bulimia, binge eating and other EDs among men. Across countries, while differences emerged, journalists generally provided men affected by EDs with an opportunity to communicate their personal stories, which introduces the potential for prejudice-reducing contact. Further, stories across countries often adopted a 'challenge assumptions' approach to informing the public about EDs among men, providing anecdotes of men's experiences followed by statements along the lines of 'EDs affect both men and women', and statistics concerning the prevalence of EDs among men. The present study highlights ways in which journalists may challenge stigma through education and 'putting a human face' on disorders.

## References

American Psychiatric Association (2013). *Diagnostic and Statistical Manual of Mental Disorders* (DSM-5®). Arlington, VA: APA.

American Psychiatric Association (2020). https://www.psychiatry.org/psychiatrists/practice/dsm

Bener, A. (2006). Prevalence of obesity, overweight, and underweight in Qatari adolescents. *Food and Nutrition Bulletin* 27(1): 39–45. https://doi.org/10.1177/156482650602700106

Dobson, C. (2014, Nov. 20). 'Righteous eating' and the shocking rise in men with food disorders like anorexia and bulimia. *Manchester Evening News*. https://www.manchestereveningnews.co.uk/news/health/righteous-eating-shocking-rise-men-8135114

Fabes, R.A., & Martin, C.L. (1991). Gender and age stereotypes of emotionality. *Personality and Social Psychology Bulletin* 17(5): 632–540. https://doi.org/10.1177/0146167291175008

Forman-Hoffman, V.L., Watson, T.L., & Andersen, A.E. (2008). Eating disorder age of onset in males: distribution and associated characteristics. *Eating and Weight Disorders* 13: e28-e31.

Gadalla, T., & Piran, N. (2007). Co-occurrence of eating disorders and alcohol use disorders in women: a meta analysis. *Archives of Women's Mental Health* 10(4): 133–40. https://doi.org/10.1007/s00737-007-0184-x

Gorrell, S., & Murray, S.B. (2019). Eating disorders in males. *Child and Adolescent Psychiatric Clinics of North America* 28(4): 641–51. https://doi.org/10.1016/j.chc.2019.05.012

Heuer, C.A., McClure, K.J., & Puhl, R.M. (2011). Obesity stigma in online news: a visual content analysis. *Journal of Health Communication* 16(9): 976–87. https://doi.org/10.1080/10810730.2011.561915

Holbrook, K. (4 May 2019). What this male writer wants you to know about being a teenage boy with an eating disorder. *Bury Times.* https://www.burytimes.co.uk/news/17614104.male-writer-wants-know-teenage-boy-eating-disorder

Jones, W., & Morgan, J. (2012). Eating disorders in men: a review of the literature. *Journal of Public Mental Health* 9(2): 23–31. https://doi.org/10.5042/jpmh.2010.0326

Kelleher, P. (7 March 2017). Off the radar: the men who suffer from eating disorders—'Eating disorders in men have always been there, we just didn't see them.' *The Irish Times.*

Kirkey, S. (21 January 2013). Eating disorders aren't just a 'girl's problem': one case in three of anorexia nervosa is a man, study finds. *The Vancouver Province* (British Columbia). http://www.canada.com/health/men/face+eating+disorders+starving+themselves+look+like+pictures/7848692/story.html

Link, B.G., & Phelan, J.C. (2001). Conceptualizing stigma. *Annual Review of Sociology* 27(1): 363–85. https://doi.org/10.1146/annurev.soc.27.1.363

MacLean, A., Sweeting, H., Walker, L., Patterson, C., Räisänen, U., & Hunt, K. (2015). 'It's not healthy and it's decidedly not masculine': a media analysis of UK newspaper representations of eating disorders in males. *BMJ Open* 5(5): 1–8. https://doi.org/10.1136/bmjopen-2014-007468

Mitchison, D., Hay, P., Slewa-Younan, S. (2014). The changing demographic profile of eating disorder behaviours in the community. *BMC Public Health* 14(943): 1–9.

Murray, S., Griffiths, S., & Mond, J. (2016). Evolving eating disorder psychopathology: conceptualising muscularity-oriented disordered eating. *British Journal of Psychiatry* 208(5): 414–15. https://doi.org/10.1186/1471-2458-14-943

Nairn, R.G., & Coverdale, J.H. (2005). People never see living well: an appraisal of the personal stories about mental illness in a prospective print media sample. *Australian & New Zealand Journal of Psychiatry* 39(4): 281–87. https://doi.org/10.1080/j.1440-1614.2005.01566.x

National Eating Disorders Association (2020). https://www.nationaleatingdisorders.org/sites/default/files/ResourceHandouts/InfographicRGB.pdf

National Institute of Mental Health (2017). Eating disorders. https://www.nimh.nih.gov/health/statistics/eating-disorders.shtml

Nunes, M.A., Olinto, M.T.A., Camey, S., Morgan, C., & de Jesus Mari, J. (2006). Abnormal eating behaviours in adolescent and young adult women from southern Brazil: reassessment after four years. *Social Psychiatry and Psychiatric Epidemiology* 41(12): 951–56. https://doi.org/10.1007/s00127-006-0116-5

O'Hara, S.K., & Clegg Smith, K. (2007). Presentation of eating disorders in the news media: what are the implications for patient diagnosis and treatment? *Patient Education and Counseling* 68(1): 43–51. https://doi.org/10.1016/j.pec.2007.04.006

Park, J., & Beaudet, M.P. (2007). Eating attitudes and their correlates among Canadian women concerned about their weight. *European Eating Disorders Review: The Professional Journal of the Eating Disorders Association* 15(4): 311–20. https://doi.org/10.1002/erv.741

Parrott, S. (2020). Media stereotypes of mental illness: the role of the media in nurturing (and mitigating) stigma. In A.C. Billings & S. Parrott (eds), *Media Stereotypes: From Ageism to Xenophobia*. Bern: Peter Lang Publishing.

Pettigrew, T.F., & Tropp, L.R. (2008). How does intergroup contact reduce prejudice? Meta-analytic tests of three mediators. *European Journal of Social Psychology* 38(6): 922–34. https://doi.org/10.1002/ejsp.504

Piran, N., & Gadalla, T. (2007). Eating disorders and substance abuse in Canadian women: a national study. *Addiction* 102(1): 105–113. https://doi.org/10.1111/j.1360-0443.2006.01633.x

Rodriguez, L. (27 August 2011). Eating disorders affect men as well as women. *St. Petersburg Times* (Florida), p. 9.

Rose, H. (19 September 2019). Anorexia and the men who suffer in silence. *The Times*. https://www.thetimes.co.uk/article/anorexia-and-the-men-who-suffer-in-silence-k73jjlrbw

Rüsch, N., Angermeyer, M.C., & Corrigan, P.W. (2005). Mental illness stigma: concepts, consequences, and initiatives to reduce stigma. *European Psychiatry* 20(8): 529–39. https://doi.org/10.1016/j.eurpsy.2005.04.004

Schiappa, E., Gregg, P.B., & Hewes, D.E. (2005). The parasocial contact hypothesis. *Communication Monographs* 72(1): 92–115. https://doi.org/10.1080/0363775052000342544

Shepherd, E., & Seale, C. (2010). Eating disorders in the media: the changing nature of UK newspaper reports. *European Eating Disorders Review* 18(6): 486–95. https://doi.org/10.1002/erv.1006

Strother, E., Lemberg, R., Stanford, S.C., & Turberville, D. (2012). Eating disorders in men: underdiagnosed, undertreated, and misunderstood. *Eating Disorders* 20(5): 346–55. https://doi.org/10.1080/10640266.2012.715512

Sundquist, K., Qvist, J., Johansson, S.E., & Sundquist, J. (2004). Increasing trends of obesity in Sweden between 1996/97 and 2000/01. *International Journal of Obesity* 28(2): 254–61. https://doi.org/10.1038/sj.ijo.0802553

Sweeting, H., Walker, L., MacLean, A., Patterson, C., Räisänen, U., & Hunt, K. (2015). Prevalence of eating disorders in males: a review of rates reported in academic research and UK mass media. *International Journal of Men's Health* 14(2): 1–27. https://doi.org/10.1136/bmjopen-2014-007468

# 4 Representations of Anorexia Nervosa in National Media: A Frame Analysis of the UK Press

*Matt Bowen and Rhian Waller*

## Introduction

While printed press figures over the last decade have declined (Watson, 2021), combined print and online press readership in the UK has remained strong, with the most popular tabloid paper, *The Sun*, having a readership of over 38 million readers and the most popular broadsheet, the *Guardian*, a combined paper and online readership of over 24 million per month (Watson, 2021). Consequently, while the press is considered part of the legacy media (Perreault & Ferrucci, 2020), it is too soon to relegate their influence to historical value compared to social media. In this context, this study explores the representation of anorexia nervosa in the UK press, to consider its impact, the insights it may offer as a barometer of public opinion and opportunities to consider developments in clinical practice. The study is a development of a previous study by the researchers (Bowen, Lovell & Waller, 2020), which employed an inductive approach to analysis of anorexia nervosa in newspaper Twitter accounts, to test the viability of using those findings in a deductive study that would offer future opportunities for longitudinal analysis.

The researchers in this study come from different disciplinary backgrounds—one from mental health clinical practice and research, and the other from journalism practice and research. The shared interests and approaches between the researchers are the ones central to this book of exploring language, stigma and

Matt Bowen and Rhian Waller, 'Chapter 4: Representations of Anorexia Nervosa in National Media: A Frame Analysis of the UK Press' in: *Eating Disorders in Public Discourse: Exploring Media Representations and Lived Experiences*. University of Exeter Press (2023). © Matt Bowen and Rhian Waller. DOI: 10.47788/UBYL4471

EDs, specifically, how different news frames (Entman, 1993) have been used by the UK press and how these may impact people's lives. However, as noted in the introductory chapter, the interdisciplinary nature of the approaches has enabled a braiding of perspectives that we believe creates strengths. The differences have meant that the findings are understood in the context of both wider cultural influences and models of understanding used in clinical practice and research. Further consideration is given to how the insights from exploring media representations could be used both to consider impact on individuals' lives and possibly to enhance and develop clinical approaches. This has allowed an interplay between cultural and clinical perspectives.

This type of research is underpinned by an understanding of knowledge as social production, rather than an asocial discovery of truth. As Berger and Luckman carefully elaborated in 1966 (and revised in 1991), knowledge is socially constructed and needs to be continually refreshed and reproduced to continue to have social saliency. The distinctions then between domains such as clinical practice, academia and mass media start to blur in terms of authority and the impact on the lives of individuals with an ED. This is not to suggest a model of absolute relativism. However, it does emphasize that the production of knowledge is in a constant state of flux, critique and dispute, and further, that there are potential dangers involved in one model dominating over other perspectives and thereby stifling the development of new understandings and practices, including treatment practices. Within mental health, in Western European societies, there is concern that a 'reductive' focus on a neurobiological model has excessive power over the variety of perspectives that can form an understanding of mental distress (Munro, Randell & Lawrie, 2017). An analysis of the media therefore can contribute to an understanding of power and hegemony, including the impact of stigma (Link & Phelan, 2013).

The media, including the press, are understood to play an important role in the public's knowledge and awareness of mental health disorders (Bowen & Lovell, 2013), and what is known as psychiatric literacy (Bullivant et al., 2020). As such, they can be considered as having an important public health function within society. However, there is not a singular view among clinical experts in understanding mental disorders: these are often disputed territories. Anorexia nervosa (which will be abbreviated to anorexia throughout) is an example where there are several different commonly held models about the aetiology and appropriate treatments. Broadly speaking, there are three fields of knowledge: biological, psychological and sociocultural. Biological research has highlighted the links to genomes that predispose people to genetic vulnerability to developing anorexia (Saffrey, Novakovic & Wade, 2013). A psychological perspective has emphasized the understanding of personality traits and parenting (Martinez & Craighead, 2015), often with a particular focus on trauma. Finally, some research develops a sociocultural understanding that has highlighted the meaning of body shape and size in society and the structures within society that promote low weight and the impact that this has on individuals (Yom-Tov & Boyd, 2014), particularly on women but increasingly on men as well (see Parrott, Bissell, Eckhart & Park, this volume). Many clinicians and researchers in the field argue that aetiology is multifactorial and typically arises from combinations of biological, psychological and social factors (Munro, Randell & Lawrie, 2017).

## Approaches to Frame Analysis

To undertake this type of research, it is necessary to have an approach that can identify the use of different models of understanding. One such approach is frame analysis, which was originally developed from the sociological work of Goffman (1974) and sits with research into the framing of social objects in society (Boda, 2017) and research into the cognitive frames that individuals use to understand their world (Ocelík et al., 2017). Media frame analysis is concerned with identifying the dominant ways in which the media represent an issue, rather than highlighting all the nuances of diversity and heterogeneity. The rationale for this is put succinctly by Entman (1993): 'if the text frame emphasises in a variety of mutually reinforcing ways that the glass is half full, the evidence of social science suggests that relatively few in the audience will conclude it is half empty' (p. 56).

Frame analyses of newspaper articles that discuss issues about mental health have explored how articles are constructed and how they encourage readers to adopt a particular stance towards an issue (Sieff, 2003). Research into the representations of mental health in the media have provided some, at times contrasting, evidence about the degree to which the presentations are stigmatizing (Hildersley et al., 2019; Bowen & Lovell, 2019; Rhydderch et al., 2016). As noted in the introductory chapter, there is relatively little research that specifically examines how anorexia has been represented. Saukko (2008) has remarked on an 'infantilising' tendency in the 1980s and 1990s coverage of people with eating disorders, wherein women, in particular, are framed as 'simply sick or under false consciousness' (p. 60). In contrast, Ferris unpicks a narrative of anorexia heroism in her reading of case study media articles, wherein anorexia is depicted as an external threat, its effects, treatment and the anorexic person's recovery-seeking are framed as elements of a battle and anorexic bodies are read as existing 'outside the bounds of cultural intelligibility' (2003). While useful, these observations rest on isolated case studies and do not look at broader depictions of anorexia.

## Method

The research design for this project was strongly influenced by Van Gorp's use of a news frame matrix (Van Gorp, 2007; Vossen, Van Gorp & Schulpen, 2016) and Entman's (1993) work on reasoning devices within a news frame, which function to present an issue 'in such a way as to promote a particular problem definition, causal interpretation, moral evaluation, and/or treatment recommendation' (p. 52). Sieff (2003) advised that a common structure in newspaper representation is referred to as a syntactical structure in which the most important point(s) are highlighted in the headline. The opening line of a standard hard news article summarizes the remit and angle of the article and refers to the key entities within the story, establishing the who, what, when, where and why (Mast, Coesemans & Temmerman, 2019). The angle is typically devised as something that should be 'fresh and tied to something of interest to the audience' (Parcell, Lamme & Cooley, 2011) functioning both as an entry-point for the reader, who is introduced to a perspective on a subject, and as a thematic core around which the rest of the text is assembled. The article then follows an inverted pyramid structure, where the issues considered most important are introduced first and increasingly less significant points are added to the article as it progresses. Both the hierarchical ordering of information and the formulation of an angle which prioritizes or de-prioritizes elements of the article as points of central concern are understood to be relevant to the framing issue of saliency, so that even if two articles include very similar material, the position of the material contributes to the salience as readers attribute greater significance to material that appears earlier in the article (Sieff, 2003).

This study arose from two previous studies conducted by the researchers. The first of these was a study undertaken by one of the researchers who used content analysis as a method to examine the representation of mental health in the UK newspaper Twitter feeds (Bowen & Lovell, 2019). When conducting this research, it was observed that tweets about eating disorders were sometimes characterized by sensationalistic images. Informed by this observation, a second study was established that used frame analysis to examine the tweets from the UK national newspapers about anorexia (Bowen, Lovell & Waller, 2020). The findings from this study confirmed a pattern of use of sensationalistic images in some of the tweets, and also the use of three other news frames that were repeatedly utilized that we referred to as: society, stress-recovery and illness. The study identified that the textual messages in the tweets were not typically stigmatizing in their representation of anorexia; however, in some of the tweets, the textual message was undermined by sensationalistic visual images that were often sexualized. The latter was an inductive study that utilized thematic analysis to identify codes that developed into themes and ultimately a frame analysis matrix. This study builds on the preceding work and was established to test the usability of the developed matrix in the context of the UK national traditional press outputs. Accordingly, this is a deductive study that aimed to address the following research questions:

**RQ1.** Can the media frame matrix developed for Twitter outputs be adapted for print press outputs?

**RQ2.** To what extent is the UK national press's representation of anorexia nervosa dominated by one news frame?

**RQ3.** How may the blend of media frames used by the UK national press affect and influence readers' knowledge and attitude towards anorexia nervosa?

Question 2 was operationalized by identifying whether one news frame was used for 50% or more of all articles, as a marker that it dominated the discourse about anorexia.

To undertake the study, a dataset of articles was constructed using the LexisNexis database. All articles produced between 1 January 2019 and 31 December 2019 that included the words 'anorexic' or 'anorexia' in any the UK national broadsheet and tabloid newspapers were identified (i.e., *Daily/Sunday Telegraph*, *Daily/Sunday Times*, *Guardian*, *Independent*, *Daily /Sunday Mail*,

*Daily Express*, *The Sun*/*The Sun on Sunday*, *Daily Mirror*, *Daily Star*). All articles were downloaded and saved into Word documents, which produced a dataset of 522 articles. Articles that were not relevant were removed and this produced a final dataset of 482 articles. A sample of 35 articles from each of the newspapers was read through by both researchers to identify how the Twitter matrix needed to be adapted, which involved an iterative process. This sample was then coded by the two researchers to test the inter-rater reliability of the adapted coding framework. Each article was coded only in relation to its dominant news frame, though a proportion of articles were too brief to be aligned to an underlying perspective. Inter-rater reliability was calculated using Cohen's kappa test, which indicated very strong reliability, with all four of the identified new frames having a kappa value greater than 0.8. The whole dataset was coded by the two researchers, which led to the calculation of the portion of articles that used one of the four news frames (Landis & Koch, 1977). Full ethical approval for the study was not required from the University Research Ethics Board, as the study was based on publicly available data.

## Findings

The previous Twitter-based study identified four news frames: social model, illness model, stress-recovery model and clickbait model (Bowen, Lovell & Waller, 2020). As anticipated, the majority of these frames remained broadly applicable in a traditional press context, with several caveats. The most striking difference is the near absence of the clickbait framework, which was primarily a category of tweets where the images were sensationalistic or stigmatizing, irrespective of the content of the accompanying textual messages. This is largely because the research methodology of the current study relies on LexisNexis, an archive that does not store press images. Therefore, a fair and direct comparison with the early Twitter-based data set, which incorporated sometimes extreme images of people with anorexia, was not possible. Attention was directed, in this study, to the textual model of clickbait, that is, exaggerated, vague and potentially misleading 'news' prompts designed to encourage readers to access what lies beyond the bait (Andersen et al., 2019). Sensationalized headlines and lead lines may fulfil a similar role in traditional media. Indeed, Braun and Eklund (2019) note that alongside 'fake news' and hoax publishers, 'legitimate' publishers have turned to clickbait techniques to generate online audience interest. However, there was no substantial evidence of this format being used in the traditional press format. That said, a relatively small collection of articles were trivializing in their overall approach to anorexia. This included the use of the word anorexia as a metaphor, or its use to criticize celebrities. It was determined that there was a sufficient number of these articles to warrant a discrete news frame of trivialization.

A minor adaptation to the Twitter news frame matrix was to the stress-recovery news frame. This news frame was commonly used; however, a minority of the articles in this model were examples of individuals who experienced life stressors and did not recover and lost their lives. The underlying model was the same, with an emphasis on the impact of personal life stressors; however, adjusting the name of the news frame to 'personal stressors' was a more accurate reflection of the body of articles as a whole.

It had been anticipated that the transition from Twitter to traditional press outputs would involve a process of adaptation, and in response to Research Question 1, this study demonstrated that the Twitter anorexia news frame matrix could be adapted for printed press formats—see Table 4.1 for the UK press anorexia news frame matrix.

### *Illness model*

The most commonly used news frame was the illness model. From this perspective, an emphasis was placed on anorexia as a health disorder: 'I suffered with anorexia for 13 years. It wasn't a diet, it was a mental illness' (*Daily Express*, 5 January 2019); 'The illness is still there raging within me' (*Mail on Sunday*, Hastings, 2019). Typically, this emphasized research that supported a biological cause of anorexia, such as genetics: 'Anorexia down to genes' (*Daily Mail*, Allen, 2019); 'anorexia can be a genetic disorder' (*Daily Mirror*, Bagot, 2019) or hormones 'metabolic anorexia link' (*The Times*, 16 July 2019). While there is not a psychopharmacological treatment for anorexia, the emphasis within this model was seeking treatment from health providers, typically within a hospital, that at times the courts could impose, for example, 'Mr Justice Peter Kelly made orders yesterday for the 16-year-old's detention in hospital' (*Daily Mirror*, Faolain, 2019). However, there was hope that a biological treatment would be found, and this message was emphasized, alongside the need for further research in this area, for example, 'Anorexia gene find raises treatment

**Table 4.1** Matrix of anorexia nervosa news frames in the printed press

| *News frame* | *Definition* | *Causal reasoning* | *Consequences* | *Possible actions* | *Moral judgement* |
|---|---|---|---|---|---|
| Social model | The causes of anorexia lie in social factors | Social/cultural values and structures place undue pressures on individuals | People express the pressure of these structures through anorexia | Cultural shift in values and/or legislation to force change | Anger at social pressure |
| Illness model | Anorexia is a health condition | The causes of anorexia are a combination of biological and psychological | Biological and psychological treatment should be available | Further medical research into causes and investment in treatment | Frustration at inconsistent treatment and excitement at possible future |
| Personal stressors model | Anorexia arises from challengingpersonal life experiences | Experiences such as bullying, relationship breakdowns, social pressures | The distress caused is expressed through anorexia | Personal relationships and empowerment lead to recovery, or distress leads to fatality | Sympathy for the challenges and admiration at recovery, or sympathy for loss of life |
| Trivialization model | Anorexia used as a metaphor or in a flippant/ trivializing manner | Anorexia is both associated with oddness and has physical markers of its presence | Anorexia is something that can be used to add a quality of 'oddness' to something or someone | Anorexia is used either to add oddness to phenomena or to engage in trivializing celebrity speculation | Intention is to heighten reader engagement with the issues |

hopes' (*Daily Telegraph*, 16 July 2019); 'Brain hack: the quest for new treatments for eating disorders' (*Guardian*, Montague, 2019). In terms of a moral response to this message, the most common one was to highlight failings within the healthcare system. This was a repeated pattern, and the newspapers took a strong advocacy role in highlighting failings and the need for improved services, for example, 'Anorexia care crisis in NHS as coroner links 5 deaths' (*Sunday Telegraph*, Ward, 2019); 'NHS bed crisis sees anorexia patient living 400 miles from home' (*Independent*, Lintern, 2019).

### *Social model*

The social model was a commonly used news frame in the dataset. Within this perspective, social structures are heavily implicated in the causation of anorexia, for example, 'Amazon widely condemned for selling books that promote anorexia as a "healthy lifestyle"' (*Independent*, Young, 2019). There was a particular emphasis on the role of social media, for example, 'child anorexia rise blamed on social media' (*The Times*, Burgess, 2019) and particularly social media formats that are image-based, such as Instagram, for example, 'Instagram led Zoe to a dark place; we buried her in a beautiful spot' (*Sunday Times*, Griffiths, 2019); 'The number of Instagram posts that glamorise eating disorders is spiralling out of control, psychiatrists warn' (*The Sun*, 21 March 2019). However, it also included other institutions such as fashion, for example, 'I was working with a high fashion brand and they were measuring me and said, "If you were just a little bit smaller"' (*The Sun*, Bannon, 2019), and athletics, for example, 'Pressure on female distance runners to lose weight has left them vulnerable to eating disorders and brittle bones' (*Sunday Times*, Myers, 2019). Further, there was an example of a feminist perspective that the pervasive values of a patriarchal society have a causal responsibility in the aetiology of anorexia, for example, 'It didn't take me very long to learn part of being a girl is dieting, monitoring your appearance and being attractive' (*Daily Mirror*, Crabbe, 2019). Within this model, the social structures were seen as the causes of personal distress, and then a direction for individuals to express this stress through the preoccupation with weight and severe weight loss that characterizes anorexia. As these are structures rather than characteristics of individuals, the appropriate response proposed within the press was around legislation and control of the structures, for example, 'Facebook and Instagram will ban images of ribcages, concave stomachs and "thigh gaps" that glamorise eating disorders after pressure from charities and campaigners' (*Sunday Telegraph*, Dodds, 2019). The moral response to this was one of outrage and anger and by implication the need to protect, for example, 'Having survived anorexia in her teens, the actress Jameela Jamil is waging a war against the body-shaming of women' (*Sunday Times*, Hargrave, 2019).

### *Personal stressors*

Within the personal stressors model, articles emphasized how individual life experiences were implicated in the aetiology of anorexia. This often included experiences of bullying, for example, 'relentlessly bullied at school, Alisha, now 19, became anorexic and weighed just six stone at 13' (*Daily Mirror*, Small, 2019), and stressors at school, for example, 'she was stressed about her exams and felt isolated at school and home [...] it caused her to become obsessive about food and to stop eating' (*Daily Mail*, Hull, 2019). There was also a pattern of linking traumatic experiences such as sexual assault as a cause, for example, 'the alleged abuse resulted in long-term depression, anorexia' (*Independent*, Michallon, 2019); 'her life had been transformed for the worse after two sexual assaults at parties from the age of 11 and being raped by two men when she was 14' (*Sunday Times*, Conradi, 2019). Anorexia was seen as a response to and expression of the distress caused by these life stresses. Individuals' responses to their experiences of anorexia therefore often focused on a wider personal life journey rather than being limited to behaviours around eating and weight loss or gain, for example, '"Now I have this thing called life": How art, family and my dog helped me overcome anorexia' (*Independent*, Collins, 2019). This often included the importance of close and supportive relationships with friends and family, use of physical activity, and improving self-esteem, for example, 'I would say to anyone, if you don't feel OK in yourself the best medicine is fresh air and exercise. Go outside and do something physical. It is the best thing' (*The Sun*, O'Reilly, 2019). However, as noted earlier, there were also examples where the causation of an individual's anorexia was attributed to personal life stresses and these were then seen as the cause of their loss of life, for example, 'Successful student, 20, fell to death from department store as "life started to unravel"' (*Daily Star*, Blair, 2019). The moral response to this news frame was, therefore, divided between sadness at those who lost their lives and anger and at the causal stressors, and celebration and admiration for those who had recovered and established a different way of being-in-the-world.

### *Trivialization*

In the trivialization news frame, individuals with anorexia were not overtly stigmatized. However, there was a pattern of some trivialization of anorexia. This included examples of anorexia used as a metaphor, for example, 'The margins in the food industry are anorexically thin' (*Sunday Times*, Bowditch, 2019), or in a way that minimizes, for example, 'She added a couple of extracurricular eating disorders, too—anorexia from the age of 15' (*The Times*, Mulkerrins, 2019). It also included examples of excitable celebrity gossip when there was no formal diagnosis of anorexia, for example, 'she's not slavish about maintaining her slender frame. "I'm not anorexic—I'm eating French fries, everything"' (*The Telegraph*, Abraham, 2019) and as part of broader opinion pieces about body shape and size in society, for example, 'toxic obesity is akin to heroin chique [*sic*] anorexia' (*Daily Mirror*, O'Connor, 2019). As noted in the introductory chapter, these findings are consistent with previous studies that have highlighted the link with entertainment and gossip as part of process of trivialization (Shepard & Seale, 2010). It appeared that because anorexia includes physical and observable markers of the condition, this contributed to its employment in these more trivializing texts and at times added an oddness quality to the articles. The moral or attitudinal response that it attempted to evoke in readers was contextual to the overall message but typically it was used to heighten the emotional response, as a form of engagement.

### *The blend of news frames used*

The articles were all coded for their dominant news frame and when this process was completed, the number and proportion of articles that fell within each news frame was calculated. See Table 4.2 for results.

The results of coding the dataset indicated that the illness news frame was the most commonly used frame. However, in response to Research Question 2, the results did not indicate that the articles were dominated by the illness news frame and there was a reasonable balance between the three most commonly used news frames.

**Table 4.2** The number and proportion of articles that used each news frame

| *News frame* | *No. of articles* | *Proportion of dataset* |
|---|---|---|
| Illness model | 146 | 30% |
| Social model | 128 | 27% |
| Personal stressor model | 117 | 24% |
| Trivialization | 31 | 6% |
| Not enough information | 60 | 12% |
| Total | 482 | * |

* NB. Total of proportion does not add to 100% due to rounding up and down of each element.

## Discussion

The absence of textual clickbait content in the full articles surveyed here—many of which are simultaneously printed and circulated online—suggests traditional hard news, opinion and feature formats persist as the structures of choice in traditional media discussions of anorexia, both online and offline. It is worth noting this study also tracked the *Independent*, which is now an online-only entity. Here, too, clickbait was not in evidence. While there are sometimes stigmatizing, Othering, misleading and other problematic discourses evident in traditional media articles, there is little indication that these nationally syndicated newspapers have adopted the 'junk news' and 'low journalistic production standards' detected by Burger et al. on social media websites (2019) in relation to depictions of anorexia. An unanticipated outcome of this study, therefore, is that it has enabled some level of quality comparison between the overall Twitter outputs of the UK press and their traditional outputs. However, it should be noted that the results of the previous study identified that the clickbait tweets were limited to tabloid press Twitter outputs, rather than a reflection of the industry as a whole, and that they arose specifically through the use of sensationalistic images rather than stigmatizing language.

Overall, there was a relatively straightforward process of adapting the frame matrix from the earlier study to be used in this study and this offers an opportunity for future deductive research in both traditional and Twitter press representations of anorexia.

Perhaps the most striking feature of the findings of this study is that there was a fairly equitable mix of the three dominant news frames (illness, social, personal stressors) used to underpin the articles in the dataset. There has been concern expressed in some quarters about the medicalization of human distress and the pervasive—and at times hegemonic—power of a medical model (Mahaffey, 2019). For a model to truly exert a hegemonic influence, it would need to reproduce a particular vision in multiple domains, including academic, clinical, and cultural. It is this dominance of power that is of most concern. Natural sciences have produced great insights and knowledge into health conditions and with anorexia are striving to better understand the aetiology, with the reasonable hope that this will improve treatments for a clinical group that is characterized by high mortality (Moskowitz & Weiselberg, 2017). The illness model was certainly present, and indeed was the most commonly used frame, emphasizing the hope of improved treatment through a better understanding of genetics, for instance, 'Anorexia gene find raises treatment hopes' (*Daily Telegraph*, 16 July 2019) and 'brain hack: the quest for new treatments for eating disorders' (*Guardian*, Montague, 2019). As such, it was entirely appropriate that the press were emphasizing the importance of this perspective, but this was not the only perspective.

One of the interesting elements of the personal stressor model is that the emphasis on the impact of life experiences meant that articles were often centred around one or a small number of individuals, as part of a human interest genre of journalism. This meant that many of the articles included direct quotations from people with lived experience of anorexia, for example, 'Now I have this thing called life' (*Independent*, Collins, 2019). This is important because, as media guidelines have highlighted, it is an important mechanism for destigmatizing mental health by allowing readers to have direct access to individuals' thoughts and also presenting individuals as being inherently competent to contribute directly to the news (Time to Change, n.d.). This may well reflect another divergence between the representation of anorexia in the UK press and other mental health conditions. This study confirms that the representation of anorexia is not characterized by a theme of dangerousness that has been found in the representation of other disorders, particularly schizophrenia and personality disorder (Hildersley et al., 2020). The use of the journalistic technique of direct quotations can be viewed as a way of emphasizing a sympathetic stance from the readers towards people with anorexia.

An equally striking element of the personal stressor frame is that the reasoning devices employed within this model emphasize not only life events as having a causal factor, but also that a wider life journey plays a vital part in recovery. This message chimes strongly with a recovery model that has developed within clinical practice and research in the field of mental health broadly and has started to inform clinical practice with people with anorexia (Dawson, Rhodes & Touyz, 2014). What is interesting here is that a perspective that is still considered somewhat innovative in practice evidently is relatively easy for readers to understand, apparently without having to unpack the fact that it is innovative at all. It is unclear whether innovations in practice and research have filtered into the wider public or whether indeed such clinical innovations were catching up with more commonly held understandings in the public about the importance of life journey on the road to recovery. Further research may be able to explore this and the degree to which there is evidence of a recovery perspective in the cultural domain before its significant influence on research and practice.

Although within research there is a tradition of a sociocultural, and often feminist, perspective on understanding anorexia, researchers have often lamented that this has not readily translated into clinical practice (Holmes et al., 2017). The latter has been dominated by interventions that focus on individuals, or families, rather than interventions aimed at wider social structures or emphasizing the impact of these social structures on individuals within the treatment modality. It is interesting, therefore, to note that this somewhat marginalized perspective within practice appears to have a great deal of saliency for the public. There were repeated examples of concerns about different social structures such as athletics and the fashion industry, for instance, 'I was working with a high fashion brand and they were measuring me and said, "If you were just a little bit smaller"' (*The Sun*, Bannon, 2019). Whereas an overtly feminist perspective was barely present; the major focus of preoccupation was social media, and particularly image-based media, notably Instagram, for example, 'child anorexia rise blamed on social media' (*The Times*, Burgess, 2019). These findings have some resonance with Gulec's study (Chapter 5), which similarly found a pattern of frequent references to social factors as an explanatory model in the aetiology of EDs in Turkish newspapers. It could be argued that the general public take a more progressive view on anorexia than is commonly demonstrated in clinical practice, and indeed in research, in terms of identifying salient social structures and often supporting public health interventions around control of these structures as the appropriate way forward. This may well be true, and it may well be of use to be aware of this when developing clinical interventions. For example, if the public, including people with anorexia and their family and friends, see social structures as playing an important part in aetiology, then maybe treatment models should be addressing this. Ideally, this approach would operate both in terms of understanding and also in terms of developing resilience against social structures that pose a risk, and developing social skills to challenge the expression of the structures in individuals' interpersonal lives. These findings would suggest that such approaches would have resonance with individuals.

While the findings of this study highlight the use of a dominant news frame within each of the articles, it is important to note that many articles drew on more than one news frame within the article. As noted before, this is standard practice to present objectivity in journalism (Fahy, 2018). The overall impact of this mix of news frames appears to be positive. Several national and international advocacy groups for people with eating disorders argue that a more nuanced approach to depicting the causes of the disorder would be beneficial in terms of self-recognition of illness and encouraging help-seeking behaviours, as well as demythologizing anorexia and breaking down stereotypes (see beat .org, 2011; National Eating Disorders Collaboration, 2020). Framing anorexia as having a purely social, stress or biological-psychiatric cause may prevent self-recognition, as the lived experiences of individuals may not fall into the model depicted within singular news articles. However, individual publications display a blend of frames within their data sets, so regular readers are likely to encounter different models.

## Conclusion

The significance of the findings of this study is twofold. In the first instance, the findings from analysing the 2019 newspaper articles provide compelling evidence that the press draws on a range of underlying perspectives in their presentation of anorexia. This is both heartening in terms of the range of views presented to the public, and may provide some support for adaptations to practice in terms of the saliency of the social model. The second and equally significant outcome is that the study progressed a previously inductive study leading to an idiographic framing matrix to adapt and test its usability for future deductive studies of press representations of anorexia. This will enable future research to examine longitudinal changes concerning press representations of anorexia and establishes an approach that could be extended to other specific mental health disorders.

## References

Abrahams, T. (19 June 2019). 'If you are not doing something new, people get bored of you.' *The Telegraph*.

Andersen, E.M., Grønning, A., Hietaketo, M., & Johansson, M. (2019). Direct reader address in health-related online news articles: imposing problems and projecting desires for action and change onto readers. *Journalism Studies* 20(16): 2478–94. https://doi.org/10.1080/1461670x.2019.1603080

Allen, V. (16 July 2019). Anorexia down to genes. *Daily Mail*.

Anorexia gene find raises treatment hopes (16 July 2019). *Daily Telegraph*.

Bagot, M. (16 July 2019). Anorexia can be a genetic disorder. *Daily Mirror*.

Bannon, A. (2 October 2019). My general health was so bad. *The Sun*.

Beat.org (2011). Beat Media Guidelines. www.beateatingdisorders.org.uk. Retrieved from https://www.beateatingdisorders.org.uk/uploads/documents/2018/7/beat-media-guidelines.pdf

Berger, P.L., & Luckmann, T. (1991). *The Social Construction of Reality: A Treatise in the Sociology of Knowledge* (No. 10). London: Penguin.

Blair, A (3 July 2019). Successful student, 20, fell to death from department store. *Daily Star*.

Boda, C.S. (2017). Applying frame analysis and reframing for integrated conservation and development: example from Mumbai. *Development in Practice* 27(4): 528–43. https://doi.org/10.1080/09614524.2017.1308469

Bowditch, G. (25 August 2019). Restaurants must step up to plate on calories. *Sunday Times*.

Bowen, M., & Lovell, A. (2013). Representations of mental health disorders in print media. *British Journal of Mental Health Nursing* 2(4): 198–202. https://doi.org/10.12968/bjmh.2013.2.4.198

Bowen, M., & Lovell, A. (2019). Stigma: the representation of mental health in UK newspaper twitter feeds. *Journal of Mental Health* 30(4): 424–30. https://doi.org/10.1080/09638237.2019.1608937

Bowen, M., Lovell, A., & Waller, R. (2020). Stigma: the representation of anorexia nervosa in UK newspaper Twitter feeds. *Journal of Mental Health* 31(1): 131–38. https://doi.org/10.1080/09638237.2020.1793128

Braun, J.A., & Eklund, J.L. (2019). Fake news, real money: ad tech platforms, profit-driven hoaxes, and the business of journalism. *Digital Journalism* 7(1): 1–21. https://doi.org/10.1080/21670811.2018.1556314

Bullivant, B., Rhydderch, S., Griffiths, S., Mitchison, D., & Mond, J.M. (2020). Eating disorders 'mental health literacy': a scoping review. *Journal of Mental Health* 29(3): 336–49. https://doi.org/10.1080/09638237.2020.1713996

Burger, P., Kanhai, S., Pleijter, A., & Verberne, S. (2019). The reach of commercially motivated junk news on Facebook. *PloS One* 14(8). https://doi.org/10.1371/journal.pone.0220446

Burgess, K. (23 October 2019). Child anorexia rise blamed on social media. *The Times.*

Celebrity secrets (5 January 2019). *Daily Express.*

Collins, L. (27 February 2019). 'Now I have this thing called life.' *The Independent.*

Conradi, P. (19 June 2019). Not euthanasia—but a fatal run-in with red tape. *Sunday Times.*

Crabbe, M. (3 March 2019). 'I used to starve myself to be thin.' *Daily Mirror.*

Dawson, L., Rhodes, P., & Touyz, S. (2014). The recovery model and anorexia nervosa. *Australian & New Zealand Journal of Psychiatry* 48(11): 1009–16. https://doi.org/10.1177/0004867414539398

Dodds, L. (14 July 2019). Ribcages and 'thigh gaps' banned from Instagram. *Sunday Telegraph.*

Entman, R.M. (1993). Framing: toward clarification of a fractured paradigm. *Journal of Communication* 43(4): 51–58. https://doi.org/10.1111/j.1460-2466.1993.tb01304.x

Fahy, D. (2018). Objectivity as trained judgment: how environmental reporters pioneered journalism for a 'post-truth' era. *Environmental Communication* 12(7): 855–61. https://doi.org/10.1080/17524032.2018.1495093

Faolain, A.O. (10 October 2019). Anorexic teen critically ill, court is told. *Daily Mirror.*

Ferris, J. (2003). Parallel discourses and 'appropriate' bodies: media constructions of anorexia and obesity in the cases of Tracey Gold and Carnie Wilson. *Journal of Communication Theory* 27(3): 25. https://doi.org/10.1177/0196859903252848

Goffman, E. (1974). *Frame Analysis: An Essay on the Organization of Experience.* New York: Harper & Row.

Griffiths, S. (3 February 2019). 'Instagram led Zoe to a dark place; we buried her in a beautiful spot.' *Sunday Times.*

Hargrave, A. (11 August 2019). Having survived anorexia in her teens, the actress Jameela Jamil is waging a war against the body-shaming of women. *Sunday Times.*

Hasting, C. (16 September 2019). Eccleston: anorexia battle almost drove me to suicide. *The Mail on Sunday.*

Hildersley, R., Potts, L., Anderson, C., & Henderson, C. (2020). Improvement for most, but not all: changes in newspaper coverage of mental illness from 2008 to 2019 in England. *Epidemiology and Psychiatric Sciences* 29: e177. https://doi.org/10.1017/s204579602000089x

Holmes, S., Drake, S., Odgers, K., & Wilson, J. (2017). Feminist approaches to anorexia nervosa: a qualitative study of a treatment group. *Journal of Eating Disorders* 5(1): 36–15. https://doi.org/10.1186/s40337-017-0166-y

Hull, L. (16 August 2019). I was 4st at 16 until parents won right to force feed me. *Daily Mail.*

'I suffered with anorexia for 13 years. It wasn't a diet, it was a mental illness' (5 January 2019). *The Daily Express.*

Landis, J.R., & Koch, G.G. (1977). The measurement of observer agreement for categorical data. *Biometrics* 33(1): 159–74. https://doi.org/10.2307/2529310

Link, B.G., & Phelan, J.C. (2013). Labeling and stigma. In *Handbook of the Sociology of Mental Health* (pp. 525–41). Dordrecht: Springer.

Lintern, S. (28 November 2019). 'I cry every day': NHS bed crisis sees anorexia patient living 400 miles from home. *The Independent.*

Mahaffey, L. (2019). Why medicalizing madness has not worked: introducing a disability studies lens to mental-health service users and providers. *The American Journal of Occupational Therapy* 73(4_Supplement_1). 7311520432. https://doi.org/10.5014/ajot.2019.73s1-po6001

Martinez, M.A., & Craighead, L.W. (2015). Toward person(ality)-centered treatment: how consideration of personality and individual differences in anorexia nervosa may improve treatment outcome. *Clinical Psychology* 22(3): 296–314. https://doi.org/10.1111/cpsp.12111

Mast, J., Coesemans, R., & Temmerman, M. (2019). Constructive journalism: concepts, practices, and discourses. *Journalism* 20(4): 492–503. https://doi.org/10.1177/1464884918770885

'Metabolic anorexia link' (16 July 2019). *The Times.*

Michallon, C. (19 December 2019). Harvey Weinstein: former model accuses producer of sexually abusing her as a teenager. *The Independent.*

Montague, J. (19 October 2019). Brain hack: the quest for new treatments for eating disorders. *The Guardian.*

Moskowitz, L., & Weiselberg, E. (2017). Anorexia nervosa/atypical anorexia nervosa. *Current Problems in Pediatric and Adolescent Health Care* 47(4): 70–84. https://doi.org/10.1016/j.cppeds.2017.02.003

Mulerrins, J. (13 July 2019). Watch me crush a watermelon with my thighs. *The Times.*

Munro, C., Randell, L., & Lawrie, S.M. (2017). An integrative bio-psycho-social theory of anorexia nervosa. *Clinical Psychology & Psychotherapy* 24(1): 1–21. https://doi.org/10.1002/cpp.2047

Myers, R. (10 November 2019). 'You were told if you were thin or tired that was a good thing.' *Sunday Times.*

National Eating Disorders Collaboration (2020). Mindframe National Media Initiative: Reporting and Portrayal of Eating Disorders. Retrieved from: https://

www.nedc.com.au/assets/NEDC-Resources/Collaborative-Resources/NEDC-Mindframe-Reporting-Guidelines.pdf

O'Connor, S. (13 April 2019). Companies claim to be embracing all shapes and sizes. *Daily Mirror.*

O'Reilly, A. (16 August 2019). 'I was starving myself to death.' *The Sun.*

Ocelík, P., Osička, J., Zapletalová, V., Černoch, F., & Dančák, B. (2017). Local opposition and acceptance of a deep geological repository of radioactive waste in the Czech Republic: a frame analysis. *Energy Policy* 105: 458–66. https://doi.org/10.1016/j.enpol.2017.03.025

Parcell, L.M., Lamme, M.O., & Cooley, S.C. (2011). Learning from the trades: public relations, journalism, and news release writing, 1945–2000. *American Journalism* 28(2): 82–112. https://doi.org/10.1080/08821127.2011.10678196

Perreault, G.P., & Ferrucci, P. (2020). What is digital journalism? Defining the practice and role of the digital journalist. *Digital Journalism* 8(10): 1298–1316. https://doi.org/10.1080/21670811.2020.1848442

Rhydderch, D., Krooupa, A.M., Shefer, G., Goulden, R., Williams, P., Thornicroft, A. … & Henderson, C. (2016). Changes in newspaper coverage of mental illness from 2008 to 2014 in England. *Acta Psychiatrica Scandinavica* 134(S446): 45–52. https://doi.org/10.1111/acps.12606 doi:10.1111/acps.12606

Saffrey, R., Novakovic, B., & Wade, T. (2013). Assessing global and gene specific DNA methylation in anorexia nervosa: a pilot study. *International Journal of Eating Disorders* 47(2): 206–10. https://doi.org/10.1002/eat.22200

Saukko, P. (2008). *The Anorexic Self: A Personal, Political Analysis of a Diagnostic Discourse.* Albany, NY: University of New York Press.

Shepard, E., & Seale, C. (2010). Eating disorders in the media: the changing nature of UK newspaper reports. *European Eating Disorders Review* 18(6): 486–95. https://doi.org/10.1002/erv.1006

Sieff, E.M. (2003). Media frames of mental illnesses: the potential impact of negative frames. *Journal of Mental Health* 12(3): 259–69. https://doi.org/10.1080/0963823031000118249

Small, N. (3 February 2019). 'Instagram made me self-harm at age 13.' *Daily Mirror.*

The number of Instagram posts that glamorise eating disorders is spiralling out of control (21 March 2019). *The Sun.*

Time to Change (n.d.). Let's end mental health discrimination. Media guidelines.

Van Gorp, B. (2007). The constructionist approach to framing: bringing culture back in. *Journal of Communication* 57: 60–78. https://doi.org/10.1111/j.1460-2466.2006.00329_1.x

Vossen, M., Van Gorp, B., & Schulpen, L. (2016). In search of the pitiful victim: a frame analysis of Dutch, Flemish and British newspapers and NGO-advertisements. *Journal of International Development* [Online publication]. ttps://doi.org/10.1002/jid.3235

Ward, V. (22 September 2019). Anorexia care crisis in NHS as coroner links 5 deaths. *Sunday Telegraph.*

Watson, A. (2021). Monthly reach of leading newspapers in the UK from April 2019 to March 2020. https://www.statista.com/statistics/246077/reach-of-selected-national-newspapers-in-the-uk

Yom-Tov, E., & Boyd, D.M. (2014). On the link between media coverage of anorexia and pro-anorexic practices on the web. *The International Journal of Eating Disorders* 47(2): 196–202. https://doi.org/10.1002/eat.22195

Young, S. (1 May 2019). Amazon widely condemned for selling books that promote anorexia as a 'healthy lifestyle'. *The Independent.*

# 5 Representations of Eating Disorders in Turkish News Media

*Hayriye Gulec*

## Introduction

Eating disorders (EDs) are characterized by significant disturbances in eating behaviour accompanied by body image disturbance, which disrupt normal body functioning and daily activities. They are serious conditions with a high risk of morbidity, chronicity and mortality (Arcelus et al., 2011; Wonderlich et al., 2012). The adverse impact of EDs on health and psychosocial functioning, and their protracted course due to high rates of mortality, comorbidity and chronicity are associated with a substantial burden for the sufferers, carers and treatment providers (van Hoeken & Hoek, 2020). This chapter focuses on the representations of eating disorders in Turkish news media and provides an in-depth investigation into how these representations might shape public perceptions in a non-Western/in-between culture in the globalization of the media in today's world.

Mental illnesses are stigmatized conditions (Angermeyer & Dietrich, 2006; Crisp et al., 2000; Dey et al., 2020; Hinshaw & Stier, 2008; Parcesepe & Cabassa, 2013), and misconceptions related to their symptoms, epidemiology, causes, severity and treatment prevail in the general public (Angermeyer & Dietrich, 2006; Angermeyer et al., 2013; Jorm, 2000; Parcesepe & Cabassa, 2013; Speerforck et al., 2017). One of the common misconceptions about EDs includes the belief that EDs affect only young, white and upper-class women in Western countries. The accumulating evidence demonstrates, however, that eating disorders affect males (Hudson et al., 2007) (see Lyon et al., and Parrott

Hayriye Gulec, 'Chapter 5: Representations of Eating Disorders in Turkish News Media' in: *Eating Disorders in Public Discourse: Exploring Media Representations and Lived Experiences*. University of Exeter Press (2023). © Hayriye Gulec. DOI: 10.47788/UPWL9354 et al., this volume) and people from diverse ethnic backgrounds (Cheng et al., 2019). They occur in Western and non-Western countries (Makino et al., 2004), in women and men of all ages (Mangweth-Matzek & Hoek, 2017) and are equally distributed across socioeconomic status (Mulders-Jones et al., 2017). Another misconception is concerned with the higher endorsement of individual factors (e.g., personality characteristics and low self-esteem) and sociocultural factors (e.g., family and media influences) as the causes of EDs (Blodgett Salafia et al., 2015; Dryer et al., 2015; Mond & Hay, 2008; Mond et al., 2004; Stewart et al., 2006). Although individual and environmental factors are important in understanding EDs, the evidence confirms a complex aetiology in which a combination of biological, psychological and sociocultural factors interact in the development of EDs (Striegel-Moore & Bulik, 2007). The association between EDs and certain personality characteristics such as perfectionism and self-discipline is often misjudged in the general public, who sometimes believe that individuals with EDs have control over their disordered eating behaviours and that EDs are individual choices rather than serious mental illnesses (Anderson et al., 2016; Ebneter & Latner, 2013; Roehrig & McLean, 2010). Studies also indicate an association between stigmatization of EDs and the belief that they are caused by sociocultural factors such as parenting and lack of support (Crisafulli et al., 2008; Ebneter et al., 2011). The commonly observed stigmatizing attitudes include the beliefs that individuals with EDs could pull themselves together if they wanted to, and that they are to blame for their condition (Crisp et al., 2000; Griffiths et al., 2015; Reas, 2017).

Due to the negative impact of the frequent portrayal of thinness as the beauty ideal on body dissatisfaction, weight preoccupation and eating disturbances, the role of the media has been mostly discussed as a risk factor for the development and maintenance of eating disorders in women (Field et al., 1999). Yet, the media are among the primary sources of health-related information for the general public and contribute to shaping public perceptions of various health conditions (Young et al., 2008), including mental illnesses (Corrigan et al., 2013). As a significant source of public information, the mass media also have the power to shape lay knowledge, beliefs and attitudes about eating disorders (Levitt, 1997; Murray et al., 1990). Therefore, examining the media coverage related to eating disorders may provide data about the type of information provided about these conditions, their relevance to the current literature and the comparison of media content cross-culturally (see Figueras Bates, this volume).

Furthermore, the messages conveyed can be examined in terms of how they may shape public perceptions to improve media coverage of eating disorders.

The representations of eating disorders in the news media have been studied in only a few studies and mainly in Western countries (see Bowen & Waller, Figueras Bates, Cariola & Lee, López-Rodríguez, and Parrott et al., this volume). Mondini et al. (1996) examined 347 articles in Italian newspapers and magazines between 1985 and 1995. They found that sociocultural factors such as thin idealization and familial influences were reported frequently as the causes of EDs. In contrast, medical complications and medical treatments were rarely mentioned. O'Hara and Smith (2007) examined 252 articles from seven daily US newspapers between 2004 and 2005. They found that EDs were represented mainly as the problems of the young, female and white. The articles were mostly placed in the arts and entertainment sections of the newspapers. Sociocultural factors such as parental influence and individual factors such as low self-esteem and stress were frequently reported as the causes of EDs. However, the content lacked complexity by providing a single aetiological factor per article. The treatment and clinical severity of EDs were often neglected. Shepherd and Seale (2010) analysed 2,355 articles between 1992 and 2008 in the UK newspapers. They found an association between EDs and the representations of young, white, female celebrities in the UK newspapers over time. Similar to the US newspapers, the sociocultural and interpersonal factors were frequently mentioned as aetiological factors. The results indicated that the UK newspapers mentioned genetic and biological causes more frequently and portrayed recovery more pessimistically than the US newspapers. A recent study examined the news media coverage from 1998 to 2019 in more than 1,000 Chinese newspapers (Sun et al., 2020). The results indicated that EDs did not receive much attention in the news media in China compared to studies conducted in the UK and the USA. The coverage of binge eating disorder was limited. The information relating to the aetiology and treatment of EDs did not provide sufficient detail and comprehensiveness.

There is currently a lack of evidence on how EDs are represented in Turkish news media. Two previous studies investigated the media representations associated with mental illnesses in Turkish newspapers and concluded that the newspaper representations contributed to the negative public perception and stigmatizing attitudes towards mental illnesses (Aci et al., 2020; Boke et al., 2007). One of these studies examined the representations related to schizophrenia (Boke et al., 2007), and the other one was conducted on a general category of mental illnesses involving a range of mental disorders, but the representations related to EDs were not included (Aci et al., 2020). This study aimed to analyse articles about EDs in Turkish newspapers. In particular, media representations of EDs regarding their epidemiology, causes, symptoms, severity and treatment were examined in two Turkish broadsheet newspapers.

## Method

The content of the broadsheet Turkish newspapers is currently not available in the scholarly databases. Two broadsheet Turkish newspapers (*Milliyet* and *Cumhuriyet*) were selected for examination as they had archived their content in digital format and enabled keyword search. *Milliyet* is a mainstream centrist widely circulated newspaper, and *Cumhuriyet* is a leftist newspaper. The reported circulation rates between 16 November 2020 and 22 November 2020 were around 195,000 for *Milliyet* and 25,000 for *Cumhuriyet* (*Gazete tirajları*, n.d.). The online archiving period of *Milliyet* was between 1 January 1961 and 30 December 2007. The content of *Cumhuriyet* had been archived since 1 January 1930. For the purposes of the study, the articles were selected if they (1) included the equivalent Turkish terms for 'anorex' (anoreks), 'bulimi' (bulimi), 'binge eating disorder' (tıkınırcasına yeme bozukluğu) or 'eating disorder/s' (yeme bozukluğu/yeme bozuklukları) and (2) were published between 1 January 2000 and 30 December 2007 in *Milliyet*, or (3) were published between 1 January 2000 and 31 July 2016 in *Cumhuriyet*. This yielded a total of 250 articles where the respective keywords appeared.

The content was collected manually from the publicly available newspaper archive of Prof. Dr Fuat Sezgin Library at Bursa Uludag University. The study did not require ethical approval as it was conducted on publicly available data. Of 250 articles, 46 could not be accessed because (1) they were published in local supplements (17 articles), (2) the newspaper issues were not archived (7 articles) and (3) the content could not be found (19 articles). Thus, a total of 207 newspaper articles were available for coding. The articles were scanned, and then a program was used to convert the image format into an editable electronic format (ABBYY Production LLC, 2013). After the initial inspection, eight articles were deleted. Three of them were newspaper advertisements, and those remaining were not associated with EDs (e.g., part of multiple-choice questions or project titles). Deleting these documents yielded a total of 199 newspaper articles for coding.

Content analyses were conducted to analyse the print media representations of EDs. The coding scheme was based on previous research and included content associated with the epidemiology, causes, symptoms, severity and treatment of EDs. In the case of emerging themes not previously identified, new coding schemes were subsequently created. The newspaper sections and supplements and the source of evidence provided in each article were coded. The coding also included whether EDs appeared in passing or as the main theme in each article. The analyses were conducted using the QCAmap Qualitative Content Analysis Software (Mayring, 2014) and SPSS 23 (IBM Corp, 2015). The frequencies, percentages and 95% confidence intervals of the documents were reported. Chi square statistics or Fisher's exact test (when more than 20% of cells had expected frequencies $< 5$) were used to compare the percentages of media coverage in the newspapers between 2000 and 2007. The intra-coder agreement estimates were calculated for the main categories obtained from the initial content analyses.

## Results

Of 199 articles that mentioned EDs, there were 74 articles in *Milliyet* between 2000 and 2007, and 125 articles in *Cumhuriyet* between 2000 and 2016. Anorexia nervosa and bulimia nervosa appeared respectively in 64.8% and 33.7% of the documents assessed. Binge eating disorder was mentioned in five articles (2.5%). Fifty per cent of the documents (N=34) that involved 'eating disorder' or 'eating disorders' as keywords mentioned at least one specific type of ED. In addition, five articles mentioned orthorexia nervosa, three articles described night eating syndrome and one article was about pica. Around one-third of the documents (34.7%) appeared in the broadsheets. The remaining articles were in the weekend supplements (49.2%), science and technology supplements (13.1%), human resources and business supplements (2.5%) and hospital guides (0.5%). In the majority of the documents, EDs were mentioned in passing (74%). These documents mainly addressed health, healthy eating, fitness, and the fashion industry. In addition, artists, celebrities, artwork, book or film characters were mentioned as affected by EDs.

There were 52 articles that addressed EDs as the main theme. Of these, 34.6% appeared in *Milliyet* between 2000 and 2007, and 64.4% appeared in *Cumhuriyet* between 2000 and 2016. Twenty-nine articles (55.8%) appeared in the broadsheets and 23 articles (44.2%) were in the supplements. The articles in the broadsheets were placed on the last page in about one-third of the documents (32.7%). The content was mainly about the fashion industry and the death of celebrities due to EDs in the West. Only 19.2% of the information related to EDs appeared in the health sections of the newspapers. Mainly, the articles included descriptions of EDs (53.8%), and the news related to the fashion industry and the celebrities with EDs in the West (23.1%). The profiles of non-celebrity individuals with EDs (11.5%), the scientific evidence (11.5%), the commentaries (3.8%) and the interviews (1.9%) were reported relatively less. There were no significant differences between the newspapers in terms of the number of articles reported and the source of information provided between 2000 and 2007 (all p values> .05). However, exemplars with EDs tended to be reported more frequently in *Milliyet* (N=8) as compared to *Cumhuriyet* (N=2) (p= .063).

For the remaining analyses, the articles with the main theme of EDs were evaluated to provide a clear picture of how the news media communicated EDs in Turkey. The content analyses yielded six categories that involved clinical characteristics, prevalence, aetiology, consequences, treatment and prevention of EDs. The intra-coder agreement for the main categories were calculated. The intra-class correlation coefficients based on a single measurement, absolute agreement and two-way mixed-effects model indicated good to excellent intra-coder agreement for the main categories. Tables 1–4 present the newspaper reporting related to each category during the study period and the comparison of *Milliyet* and *Cumhuriyet* between 2000 and 2007.

### *Clinical characteristics*

Of 52 newspaper articles that addressed EDs as the main theme, 63.5% mentioned the clinical characteristics associated with EDs. Restriction of food intake was the most frequently reported clinical symptom followed by body image disturbance, significantly low body weight, compensatory behaviours and binge eating episodes. The phrases frequently used to describe the restriction of food intake involved dieting, self-starvation and strict control over food intake. The body image disturbance consisted of domains related to preoccupation with weight and shape, intense fear of weight gain and becoming fat, disturbance in the way one's body is experienced, and negative body image. Statements related to the preoccupation with weight and shape included: 'Individuals with anorexia nervosa are extremely obsessed with food intake, weight, and shape.' The intense fear of weight gain and becoming fat can be illustrated with: 'Although she was at the lowest weight for her age and height, she was extremely afraid of gaining weight.' An example of the disturbance in the way one's body is experienced included: 'Feeling fat despite being extremely thin.' The negative body image can be illustrated with: 'I felt fat, and hated the way my body looked.'

The clinical symptoms relating to significantly low body weight consisted of phrases associated with emaciation and denial of the seriousness of low body weight. The most frequently reported compensatory behaviour was vomiting, which was followed by excessive exercise, use of laxatives and fasting. The use of diuretics, diet pills and enemas was reported in three articles. The description and characteristics of binge eating episodes and the emotions related to binge eating episodes were mentioned in 15 articles (28.8%). Of these, only three articles stated the right terminology and defined binge eating episodes as recurrent and taking place in a discrete period of time. The most frequently used phrase to identify binge eating was 'excessive eating'. The loss of control during eating, being unable to stop the urge to binge, eating fast and eating in response to emotions were the most frequently reported characteristics associated with binge eating episodes. A range of emotions including pleasure, shame, regret, rage, disgust, shame and depression following binge eating episodes was mentioned in five articles. In general, there were significantly more documents addressing the clinical characteristics of EDs in *Milliyet* between 2000 and 2007. This difference was especially pronounced for the symptoms related to the restriction of food intake.

### *Prevalence*

The content related to the prevalence of EDs appeared in 86.5% of the newspaper articles, which mainly included information related to risk groups, age of onset, comorbid situations and prevalence rates. Females or young girls were described as affected by EDs in 75% of the documents. Of these, female

**Table 5.1** Newspaper reporting on clinical characteristics of EDs

| | *Overall (2000–2016)* | | Milliyet *(2000–2007)* | | Cumhuriyet *(2000–2007)* | | $\chi^2$ |
|---|---|---|---|---|---|---|---|
| *Clinical symptoms* | *N* | *% (95% CI)* | *N* | *% (95% CI)* | *N* | *% (95% CI)* | *p value* |
| Any clinical symptom mentioned | 33 | 63.5 (49–76.4) | 15 | 83.3 (58.6–96.4) | 8 | 50 (24.7–75.3) | <.05 |
| Restriction of food intake | 23 | 44.2 (30.5–58.7) | 12 | 66.7 (41–86.7) | 5 | 31.3 (11–58.7) | <.05 |
| Body image disturbance | 20 | 38.5 (25.3–53) | 8 | 44.4 (21.5–69.2) | 4 | 25 (7.3–52.4) | .24 |
| Significantly low body weight | 19 | 36.5 (23.6–51) | 8 | 44.4 (21.5–69.2) | 6 | 37.5 (15.2–64.6) | .68 |
| Compensatory behaviours | 18 | 34.6 (22–49.1) | 10 | 55.6 (30.8–78.5) | 4 | 25 (7.3–52.4) | .07 |
| Binge eating episodes | 15 | 28.8 (17.1–43.1) | 6 | 33.3 (13.3–59) | 4 | 25 (7.3–52.4) | .71[a] |

[a]Based on Fisher's exact test.

models and celebrities with EDs were mentioned in 17.3%, and the profiles of non-celebrity women with EDs were described in 11.5%. Yet, males were identified as affected by EDs in five newspaper articles (9.6%), and the profile of a male patient with an ED was described in only one article.

Adolescence was identified as the critical period for the development of EDs in half of the articles. Three articles provided information related to childhood-onset EDs, and one described early adulthood as the critical period for the development of EDs. Pre-teens, teens or high school years were associated with the illness onset. The age range was mainly identified as between 10 and 19. Besides, two articles mentioned young adults (20s), and in three articles, the age of onset was described as between 11 and 40. Female models, and occupations associated with the overvaluation of thinness, such as stewardesses, dancers and actresses, were associated with the risk of developing EDs. The reported comorbid conditions included obesity, alcohol and substance use, sexual dysfunctions and depression. The information relating to the prevalence rates of EDs was reported in 16 articles (34.6%). It included the prevalence rates for genders and gender differences, and the prevalence rates in foreign countries and Turkey. There were significantly more articles in *Cumhuriyet* about the prevalence rates of EDs in Turkey between 2000 and 2007.

### *Aetiology*

The aetiology of EDs was discussed in 73.1% of the newspaper articles. Generally, one or two factors were mentioned as the causes of EDs without providing a comprehensive representation of the aetiology. The explanation of the biopsychosocial aetiology of EDs took place in only two newspaper articles.

Internalized thin ideal/body dissatisfaction, dieting and personality characteristics were identified as the major individual causes of EDs. Internalized thin ideal/body dissatisfaction was the most frequently reported individual cause. The statements were associated with the desire to obtain ideal body size and discontent with appearance. The representations often emphasized personal responsibility for the disturbances in eating behaviours. Example statements include: 'Anorexia is triggered by young girls' attempts to become like Barbie doll models' and 'Body dissatisfaction leads to dieting and bulimic symptoms.' Dieting was mostly discussed as a method practised by young girls to look like

**Table 5.2** Newspaper reporting on prevalence of EDs

| | *Overall (2000–2016)* | | Milliyet *(2000–2007)* | | Cumhuriyet *(2000–2007)* | | $\chi^2$ |
|---|---|---|---|---|---|---|---|
| *Prevalence* | *N* | *% (95% CI)* | *N* | *% (95% CI)* | *N* | *% (95% CI)* | *p value* |
| Any prevalence mentioned | 45 | 86.5 (74.2–94.4) | 17 | 94.4 (72.7–99.9) | 14 | 87.5 (61.7–98.4) | .59[a] |
| Females as at risk groups | 39 | 75 (61.1–86) | 16 | 88.9 (65.3–98.6) | 12 | 75 (47.6–92.7) | .39[a] |
| Adolescents as at risk groups | 26 | 50 (35.8–64.2) | 9 | 50 (26–74) | 10 | 62.5 (35.4–84.8) | .46 |
| Any mention of age of onset | 18 | 34.6 (22–49.1) | 7 | 38.9 (17.3–64.3) | 3 | 18.8 (4–45.6) | .27[a] |
| Any mention of occupations at risk | 7 | 13.5 (5.6–25.8) | 4 | 22.2 (6.4–47.6) | 2 | 12.5 (1.6–38.3) | .66[a] |
| Any mention of comorbidity | 5 | 9.6 (3.2–21) | 2 | 11.1 (1.4–34.7) | 2 | 12.5 (1.6–38.3) | 1[a] |
| High SES as a risk factor | 2 | 3.8 (0.5–13.2) | 2 | 11.1 (1.4–34.7) | 0 | 0 (0–20.6) | .49[a] |
| Gender/gender differences | 9 | 17.3 (8.2–30.3) | 2 | 11.1 (1.4–34.7) | 3 | 18.8 (4–45.6) | .65[a] |
| Prevalence in other countries | 7 | 13.5 (5.6–25.8) | 1 | 5.6 (0.1–27.3) | 3 | 18.8 (4–45.6) | .32[a] |
| Prevalence in Turkey | 7 | 13.5 (5.6–25.8) | 0 | 0 (0–18.5) | 5 | 31.2 (11–58.7) | <.05[a] |

[a]Based on Fisher's exact test.

thin models that got out of control and resulted in EDs. Perfectionism and self-discipline were reported as the underlying personality characteristics.

The most frequently reported societal cause was the fashion and media industry's influence on thin idealization, which was followed by family and peer influence and the ideal beauty norms in society. Statements often represented individuals with EDs as the victims of societal pressures. An example statement associated with the influence of fashion and media industry can be summarized as: 'Size zero models are bad role models as they trigger eating disorders such as anorexia and bulimia in young girls.' The family influence was represented as conflicted relationships, lack of affection and involvement, and maladaptive upbringing. Being teased by peers was mentioned as the peer influence. The statements relating to the ideal beauty norms emphasized the societal pressure to look young, thin and attractive as the underlying causes of EDs in women.

The biological causes of EDs were the least mentioned causes appearing in five newspaper articles. The role of hormones, lack of minerals, neurobiological abnormalities, genes and infections were mentioned as the biological determinants of EDs. There were no significant differences between the newspapers regarding the representations of aetiological factors between 2000 and 2007.

### Consequences

The physical, psychosocial and fatal impact and the long-term outcome/course were described as the consequences of EDs. The physical impact was the most frequently mentioned consequence and described as general harm to body and health, emaciation, fatigue and internal organ problems. The psychosocial consequences were associated with negative affect and poor relationships with peers and family. Death and suicide as the fatal impact of EDs were mentioned in 16 articles (30.8%). The articles mostly included statements related to chronicity and described EDs as serious and chronic conditions, difficult to treat and resistant to medication treatment. The information relating to recovery from EDs was found in statistics indicating recovery rates between 30% and 40%. The percentage of documents addressing the physical consequences associated with EDs was significantly more in *Milliyet* between 2000 and 2007.

**Table 5.3** Newspaper reporting on aetiology of EDs

| | *Overall (2000–2016)* | | Milliyet *(2000–2007)* | | Cumhuriyet *(2000–2007)* | | $\chi^2$ *p value* |
|---|---|---|---|---|---|---|---|
| *Aetiology* | *N* | *% (95% CI)* | *N* | *% (95% CI)* | *N* | *% (95% CI)* | |
| Any aetiology mentioned | 38 | 73.1 (59–84.4) | 13 | 72.2 (46.5–90.3) | 13 | 81.3 (54.4–96) | .69[a] |
| Any individual factor mentioned | 30 | 57.7 (43.2–71.3) | 11 | 61.1 (35.7–82.7) | 11 | 68.8 (41.3–89) | .73 |
| Internalized thin ideal/body dissatisfaction | 17 | 32.7 (20.3–47.1) | 6 | 33.3 (13.3–59) | 8 | 50 (24.7–75.3) | .32 |
| Dieting | 13 | 25 (14–38.9) | 3 | 16.7 (3.6–41.4) | 5 | 31.3 (11–58.7) | .43[a] |
| Personality | 8 | 15.4 (6.9–28.1) | 2 | 11.1 (1.4–34.7) | 3 | 18.8 (4–45.6) | .65[a] |
| Any societal factor mentioned | 25 | 48.1 (34–62.4) | 7 | 38.9 (17.3–64.3) | 9 | 56.3 (29.9–80.2) | .31 |
| Fashion/media influence | 13 | 25 (14–38.9) | 4 | 22.2 (6.4–47.6) | 5 | 31.3 (11–58.7) | .70[a] |
| Family/peers influence | 10 | 19.2 (9.6–32.5) | 3 | 16.7 (3.6–41.4) | 4 | 25 (7.3–52.4) | .68[a] |
| Ideal beauty norms | 7 | 13.5 (5.6–25.8) | 0 | 0 (0–18.5) | 3 | 18.8 (4–45.6) | .09[a] |
| Any biological factor mentioned | 5 | 9.6 (3.2–21) | 0 | 0 (0–18.5) | 3 | 18.8 (4–45.6) | .09[a] |

[a]Based on Fisher's exact test.

### *Treatment and prevention*

The representations associated with treatment experts appeared in seven articles, and psychologists were mentioned as experts in six of them. Additionally, three articles identified psychiatrists and two articles identified experts in dietetics and exercise as treatment facilitators. The most frequently described treatment modality included psychological treatment, appearing in six articles. This was followed by the medical treatment mentioned in three articles. Dietetic treatment, inpatient treatment and treatment centres were mentioned in one article each. The prevention strategies included advice for parents, individual measures and regulations in the fashion and media industry. Avoiding criticisms based on food and weight, facilitating a balanced diet and easy access to healthy food, becoming role models in terms of eating habits and providing an environment for expressing emotional needs were the parental strategies. The fashion and media industry regulations emphasized the importance of healthy-looking models and using the right messages to counteract thin idealization and internalization. The individual measures included avoiding strict dieting, eating a healthy and balanced diet and coping with emotions rather than using food for emotion regulation. No significant differences were observed between the newspapers regarding the percentage of documents related to the treatment and prevention of EDs between 2000 and 2007.

## Discussion

The current study investigated the representations associated with EDs in two Turkish broadsheet newspapers. The results indicated that the Turkish media coverage was more limited in terms of the number of articles about EDs than studies conducted in Western and Eastern industrialized countries (Shepherd & Seale, 2010; Sun et al., 2020). The representations related to EDs were centred on the media and fashion industry. Less than one-fifth of the documents with the main theme of EDs appeared in the newspapers' health sections. The sensationalist content on the last page of the broadsheets, which mainly included news related to the fashion industry and the death of celebrities due to EDs, accounted for around one-third of the articles. These results are consistent with previous research that demonstrated a connection between the entertainment industry and the newspaper representations of EDs (Levitt, 1997; O'Hara &

**Table 5.4** Newspaper reporting on consequences, treatment and prevention of EDs

| | *Overall (2000–2016)* | | Milliyet *(2000–2007)* | | Cumhuriyet *(2000–2007)* | | $\chi^2$ *p value* |
|---|---|---|---|---|---|---|---|
| | *N* | *% (95% CI)* | *N* | *% (95% CI)* | *N* | *% (95% CI)* | |
| *Consequences* | | | | | | | |
| Any consequence mentioned | 34 | 65.4 (50.9–78) | 14 | 77.8 (52.4–93.6) | 10 | 62.5 (35.4–84.8) | .46[a] |
| Physical | 22 | 42.3 (28.7–56.8) | 12 | 66.7 (41–86.7) | 5 | 31.3 (11–58.7) | <.05 |
| Psychosocial | 17 | 32.7 (20.3–47.1) | 9 | 50 (26–74) | 5 | 31.3 (11–58.7) | .27 |
| Fatal | 16 | 30.8 (18.7–45.1) | 3 | 16.7 (3.6–41.4) | 7 | 43.8 (19.8–70.1) | .13[a] |
| Long-term course | 14 | 26.9 (15.6–41) | 5 | 27.8 (9.7–53.5) | 4 | 25 (7.3–52.4) | 1[a] |
| *Treatment* | | | | | | | |
| Any mention of treatment | 15 | 28.8 (17.1–43.1) | 7 | 38.9 (17.3–64.3) | 3 | 18.8 (4–45.6) | .27[a] |
| Any mention of experts | 7 | 13.5 (5.6–25.8) | 5 | 27.8 (9.7–53.5) | 1 | 6.3 (0.2–30.2) | .18[a] |
| Any mention of treatment modality | 10 | 19.2 (9.6–32.5) | 3 | 16.7 (3.6–41.4) | 2 | 12.5 (1.6–38.3) | 1[a] |
| *Prevention* | | | | | | | |
| Any mention of prevention strategies | 12 | 23.1 (12.5–36.8) | 4 | 22.2 (6.4–47.6) | 5 | 31.3 (11–58.7) | .70[a] |
| Parental advice | 7 | 13.5 (5.6–25.8) | 1 | 5.6 (0.1–27.3) | 3 | 18.8 (4–45.6) | .32[a] |
| Fashion and media regulation | 5 | 9.6 (3.2–21) | 2 | 11.1 (1.4–34.7) | 2 | 12.5 (1.6–38.3) | 1[a] |
| Individual measures | 3 | 5.8 (1.2–15.9) | 1 | 5.6 (0.1–27.3) | 1 | 6.3 (0.2–30.2) | 1[a] |

[a]Based on Fisher's exact test.

Smith, 2007). The frequent representation of famous people with EDs may influence the public perception to consider that EDs are associated with a specific segment of the population and so are of little concern for ordinary people.

The news media coverage of EDs in Turkish newspapers was mainly about anorexia nervosa and bulimia nervosa. Any mention of binge eating disorder appeared in only 2.5% of the documents. Furthermore, the representations generally lacked detail and did not elaborate further than describing binge eating disorder as a disorder characterized by binges in the absence of vomiting. These findings are similar to a previous study conducted on Chinese media coverage of EDs (Sun et al., 2020), which argued that China's news media was slower in integrating newer information and classifications about EDs into its agenda than the Western news media. The current results indicated a similar pattern, highlighting the need to provide information about EDs other than anorexia nervosa and bulimia nervosa in Turkish news media to facilitate public knowledge of these conditions.

### *Clinical characteristics*

The clinical characteristics of eating disorders appeared in more than half of the documents and the descriptions were generally in accordance with the scientific reporting. Yet, it is noteworthy to mention that the right terminology to describe binge eating in Turkish (i.e., tıkınırcasına yeme) and the clinical characteristics of binge eating episodes as recurrent and taking place in a discrete period of time were scarcely described. Describing binge eating episodes as 'excessive eating' was the common terminology preferred, which might mislead the public perception about the clinical significance and severe consequences of this behaviour.

### *Prevalence*

The findings revealed that Turkish newspapers mainly described women as affected by or at risk of developing EDs and identified adolescence as the critical period for their onset. The comorbid conditions were reported as obesity, alcohol and substance use, sexual dysfunction and depression. Although the information provided was in line with the literature, the frequent representations of women and Western celebrities instead of males and individuals from diverse backgrounds may contribute to the misconception that EDs are illnesses of wealthy Western women. Furthermore, associating EDs with celebrities or communicating EDs as problems primarily of the West may contribute to the misconception that they impact only certain cultures. Therefore, similar to the suggestions reported in the previous literature (O'Hara & Smith, 2007; Shepherd & Seale, 2010), the findings of the current study demonstrated the need to portray people from various backgrounds to communicate that EDs may affect anyone regardless of culture, gender or background.

### *Aetiology*

Similar to the previous studies, individual and societal factors were frequently reported as the causes of EDs, whereas biological factors were mentioned less frequently (Mondini et al., 1996; O'Hara & Smith, 2007; Shepherd & Seale, 2010; Sun et al., 2020). Only two articles mentioned that EDs had a biopsychosocial aetiology and provided a comprehensive overview of the causes of EDs. In general, the tendency was to report one or two causal factors per article without providing a detailed account of the aetiology. The reporting style relating to individual factors emphasized self-responsibility for the disordered eating behaviours, whereas individuals with EDs were represented as victims when societal factors were presented. Biological aetiology was presented neutrally. Previous studies indicated that perceptions of self-responsibility and sociocultural aetiology were associated with the stigma towards EDs (Ebneter et al., 2011; Roehrig & McLean, 2010). Thus, the Turkish media coverage might perpetuate the stigma towards EDs by increasing the public perception of personal responsibility and victimization. Therefore, changing the stigmatizing style of reporting and increasing the inclusion of biological evidence in descriptions of EDs in newspaper reporting may be required.

### *Consequences, treatment and prevention*

The physical, psychosocial and fatal impacts associated with EDs were presented in more than half of the documents. The frequent mention of the consequences of EDs was similar to two previous studies conducted in the UK and

China (Shepherd & Seale, 2010; Sun et al., 2020) but dissimilar to two other studies conducted in Italy and the USA (Mondini et al., 1996; O'Hara & Smith, 2007). The treatment and prevention of EDs were the least mentioned themes. The most frequently described experts and treatment modalities included psychologists and psychological treatment respectively. However, no details were provided related to the type and efficacy of the treatment approaches. The experts in dietetics and exercise were mentioned as treatment providers almost as frequently as the psychiatrists. The National Institute for Health and Care Excellence (2017) emphasizes that dietary counselling should not be provided as the only treatment for EDs. Thus, it can be inferred that although EDs were represented as serious illnesses with medical complications, the need for medical treatment including hospitalization was neglected in newspaper representations. The prevention strategies were mostly in the form of guidance to families to detect EDs in their children. The individual measures to prevent EDs tended to emphasize a strong connection between strict dieting, healthy eating, emotion regulation and EDs. Other strategies reported in the literature such as media literacy, resisting sociocultural pressures and improving body/self-esteem were neglected (Ciao et al., 2014).

### *Comparison between the newspapers*

*Milliyet* reported more frequently on the clinical symptoms and adverse physical consequences of EDs, whereas the prevalence rates in Turkey were mentioned more frequently in *Cumhuriyet.* In addition, albeit at a tendency level, a significantly higher number of exemplars with EDs were represented in *Milliyet.* As argued previously by Shepherd and Seale (2010), these findings might be associated with the agenda of the newspapers. *Milliyet* follows a mainstream centrist agenda, whereas *Cumhuriyet* is identified with a leftist thought agenda. Thus, the higher number of reports about the clinical characteristics of EDs and their serious consequences could be associated with the populist agenda of *Milliyet,* whereas the higher number of reports about the prevalence rates of EDs in Turkey could be associated with the public health agenda of *Cumhuriyet.* However, further research in a larger sample of newspapers from diverse agendas is required to determine whether these findings can be generalized.

## Conclusion

This was the first study to examine the media coverage of EDs in Turkish newspapers. The results demonstrated limited coverage in terms of the number of articles about EDs in Turkish news media compared with previous studies. The media coverage mainly addressed anorexia nervosa and bulimia nervosa and tended to associate EDs with the media and the fashion industry. The clinical characteristics and adverse consequences were reported frequently, but treatment and prevention of EDs were often neglected. Reporting guidelines need to address strategies to convey the complex aetiology of EDs without using stigmatizing language and to mention individuals with EDs from diverse backgrounds. Further studies on the representations of EDs in other media sources, including the internet, are required.

## Acknowledgements

The author would like to thank librarian Hayri Özkan for his generous support in retrieving the newspaper articles from the archive of Prof. Dr Fuat Sezgin Library at Bursa Uludag University.

## References

ABBYY Production LLC. (2013). *ABBYY FineReader user's guide* (version 12) [Computer Software]. https://www.abbyy.com/media/20162/guide_english.pdf

Aci, O.S., Ciydem, E., Bilgin, H., Ozaslan, Z., & Tek, S. (2020). Turkish newspaper articles mentioning people with mental illness: a retrospective study. *International Journal of Social Psychiatry* 66(3): 215–24. https://doi.org/10.1177/0020764019894609

Anderson, R., Gratwick-Sarll, K., Bentley, C., Harrison, C., & Mond, J. (2016). Adolescents' perception of the severity of binge eating disorder: a population-based study. *Journal of Mental Health* 25(1): 16–22. https://doi.org/10.3109/09638237.2015.1057329

Angermeyer, M.C., & Dietrich, S. (2006). Public beliefs about and attitudes towards people with mental illness: a review of population studies. *Acta Psychiatrica Scandinavica* 113(3): 163–79. https://doi.org/10.1111/j.1600-0447.2005.00699.x

Angermeyer, M.C., Millier, A., Remuzat, C., Refai, T., & Toumi, M. (2013). Attitudes and beliefs of the French public about schizophrenia and major depression: results from a vignette-based population survey. *BMC Psychiatry* 13(1): 313. https://doi.org/10.1186/1471-244X-13-313

Arcelus, J., Mitchell, A.J., Wales, J., & Nielsen, S. (2011). Mortality rates in patients with anorexia nervosa and other eating disorders: a meta-analysis of 36 studies. *Archives of General Psychiatry* 68(7): 724–31. https://doi.org/10.1001/archgenpsychiatry.2011.74

Blodgett Salafia, E.H., Jones, M.E., Haugen, E.C., & Schaefer, M.K. (2015). Perceptions of the causes of eating disorders: a comparison of individuals with and without eating disorders. *Journal of Eating Disorders* 3: 32–32. https://doi.org/10.1186/s40337-015-0069-8

Boke, O., Aker, S., Alptekin Aker, A., Sarisoy, G., & Sahin, A.R. (2007). Schizophrenia in Turkish newspapers. *Social Psychiatry and Psychiatric Epidemiology* 42(6): 457–61. https://doi.org/10.1007/s00127-007-0198-8

Cheng, Z.H., Perko, V.L., Fuller-Marashi, L., Gau, J.M., & Stice, E. (2019). Ethnic differences in eating disorder prevalence, risk factors, and predictive effects of risk factors among young women. *Eating Behaviours* 32: 23–30. https://doi.org/10.1016/j.eatbeh.2018.11.004

Ciao, A.C., Loth, K., & Neumark-Sztainer, D. (2014). Preventing eating disorder pathology: common and unique features of successful eating disorders prevention programs. *Current Psychiatry Reports* 16(7): 453. https://doi.org/10.1007/s11920-014-0453-0

Corrigan, P.W., Powell, K.J., & Michaels, P.J. (2013). The effects of news stories on the stigma of mental illness. *Journal of Nervous and Mental Disease* 201(3): 179–82. https://doi.org/10.1097/NMD.0b013e3182848c24

Crisafulli, M.A., Von Holle, A., & Bulik, C.M. (2008). Attitudes towards anorexia nervosa: the impact of framing on blame and stigma. *International Journal of Eating Disorders* 41(4): 333–39. https://doi.org/10.1002/eat.20507

Crisp, A.H., Gelder, M.G., Rix, S., Meltzer, H.I., & Rowlands, O.J. (2000). Stigmatisation of people with mental illnesses. *British Journal of Psychiatry* 177(1): 4–7. https://doi.org/10.1192/bjp.177.1.4

Dey, M., Castro, R.P., Jorm, A.F., Marti, L., Schaub, M.P., & Mackinnon, A. (2020). Stigmatizing attitudes of Swiss youth towards peers with mental disorders. *PloS One* 15(7): e0235034. https://doi.org/10.1371/journal.pone.0235034

Dryer, R., Uesaka, Y., Manalo, E., & Tyson, G. (2015). Cross-cultural examination of beliefs about the causes of bulimia nervosa among Australian and Japanese females. *International Journal of Eating Disorders* 48(2): 176–86. https://doi.org/10.1002/eat.22269

Ebneter, D.S., & Latner, J.D. (2013). Stigmatizing attitudes differ across mental health disorders: a comparison of stigma across eating disorders, obesity, and major depressive disorder. *Journal of Nervous and Mental Disease* 201(4): 281–85. https://doi.org/10.1097/NMD.0b013e318288e23f

Ebneter, D.S., Latner, J.D., & O'Brien, K.S. (2011). Just world beliefs, causal beliefs, and acquaintance: associations with stigma toward eating disorders and obesity. *Personality and Individual Differences* 51(5): 618–22. https://doi.org/10.1016/j.paid.2011.05.029

Field, A.E., Cheung, L., Wolf, A.M., Herzog, D.B., Gortmaker, S.L., & Colditz, G.A. (1999). Exposure to the mass media and weight concerns among girls. *Pediatrics* 103(3): e36-e36. https://doi.org/10.1542/peds.103.3.e36

*Gazete tirajları* (n.d.). http://gazetetirajlari.com/index.aspx

Griffiths, S., Mond, J.M., Murray, S.B., & Touyz, S. (2015). The prevalence and adverse associations of stigmatization in people with eating disorders. *International Journal of Eating Disorders* 48(6): 767–74. https://doi.org/10.1002/eat.22353

Hinshaw, S.P., & Stier, A. (2008). Stigma as related to mental disorders. *Annual Review of Clinical Psychology* 4: 367–93. https://doi.org/10.1146/annurev.clinpsy.4.022007.141245

Hudson, J.I., Hiripi, E., Pope, H.G., Jr., & Kessler, R.C. (2007). The prevalence and correlates of eating disorders in the National Comorbidity Survey Replication. *Biological Psychiatry* 61(3): 348–58. https://doi.org/10.1016/j.biopsych.2006.03.040

IBM Corp. (2015). *IBM SPSS Statistics for Windows* (Version 23.0) [Computer Software]. Armonk, NY: IBM Corp.

Jorm, A.F. (2000). Mental health literacy: public knowledge and beliefs about mental disorders. *British Journal of Psychiatry* 177: 396–401. https://doi.org/10.1192/bjp.177.5.396

Levitt, H.M. (1997). A semiotic understanding of eating disorders: the impact of media portrayal. *Eating Disorders* 5(3): 169–83. https://doi.org/10.1080/10640269708249223

Makino, M., Tsuboi, K., & Dennerstein, L. (2004). Prevalence of eating disorders: a comparison of Western and non-Western countries. *MedGenMed: Medscape General Medicine* 6(3): 49.

Mangweth-Matzek, B., & Hoek, H.W. (2017). Epidemiology and treatment of eating disorders in men and women of middle and older age. *Current Opinion in Psychiatry* 30(6): 446–51. https://doi.org/10.1097/YCO.0000000000000356

Mayring, P. (2014). Qualitative content analysis: theoretical foundation, basic procedures and software solution. Kalegenfurt: http://nbn-resolving.de/urn:nbn:de:0168-ssoar-395173

Mond, J.M., & Hay, P.J. (2008). Public perceptions of binge eating and its treatment. *International Journal of Eating Disorders* 41(5): 419–26. https://doi.org/10.1002/eat.20512

Mond, J.M., Hay, P.J., Rodgers, B., Owen, C., & Beumont, P.J. (2004). Beliefs of women concerning causes and risk factors for bulimia nervosa. *Australian and New Zealand Journal of Psychiatry* 38(6): 463–69. https://doi.org/10.1080/j.1440-1614.2004.01384.x

Mondini, S., Favaro, A., & Santonastaso, P. (1996). Eating disorders and the ideal of feminine beauty in Italian newspapers and magazines. *European Eating Disorders Review* 4(2): 112–20. https://doi.org/10.1002/(Sici)1099-0968(199606)4:2<112::Aid-Erv152>3.0.Co;2-6

Mulders-Jones, B., Mitchison, D., Girosi, F., & Hay, P. (2017). Socioeconomic correlates of eating disorder symptoms in an Australian population-based sample. *PloS One* 12(1): e0170603-e0170603. https://doi.org/10.1371/journal.pone.0170603

Murray, S., Touyz, S., & Beaumont, P. (1990). Knowledge about eating disorders in the community. *International Journal of Eating Disorders* 9(1): 87–93. https://doi.org/10.1002/1098-108X(199001)9:1<87::AID-EAT2260090110>3.0.CO;2-2

National Institute for Health and Care Excellence. (2017). *Eating disorders: recognition and treatment* (Nice guideline [NG69]). https://www.nice.org.uk/guidance/ng69

O'Hara, S.K., & Smith, K.C. (2007). Presentation of eating disorders in the news media: what are the implications for patient diagnosis and treatment? *Patient Education and Counseling* 68(1): 43–51. https://doi.org/10.1016/j.pec.2007.04.006

Parcesepe, A.M., & Cabassa, L.J. (2013). Public stigma of mental illness in the United States: a systematic literature review. *Administration and Policy in Mental Health* 40(5): 384–99. https://doi.org/10.1007/s10488-012-0430-z

Reas, D.L. (2017). Public and healthcare professionals' knowledge and attitudes toward binge eating disorder: a narrative review. *Nutrients* 9(11): 1267. https://doi.org/10.3390/nu9111267

Roehrig, J.P., & McLean, C.P. (2010). A comparison of stigma toward eating disorders versus depression. *International Journal of Eating Disorders* 43(7): 671–74. https://doi.org/10.1002/eat.20760

Shepherd, E., & Seale, C. (2010). Eating disorders in the media: the changing nature of UK newspaper reports. *European Eating Disorders Review* 18(6): 486–95. https://doi.org/10.1002/erv.1006

Speerforck, S., Schomerus, G., Matschinger, H., & Angermeyer, M.C. (2017). Treatment recommendations for schizophrenia, major depression and alcohol dependence and stigmatizing attitudes of the public: results from a German population survey. *European Archives of Psychiatry and Clinical Neuroscience* 267(4): 341–50. https://doi.org/10.1007/s00406-016-0755-9

Stewart, M.C., Keel, P.K., & Schiavo, R.S. (2006). Stigmatization of anorexia nervosa. *International Journal of Eating Disorders* 39(4): 320-25. https://doi.org/10.1002/eat.20262

Striegel-Moore, R.H., & Bulik, C.M. (2007). Risk factors for eating disorders. *American Psychologist* 62(3): 181–98. https://doi.org/10.1037/0003-066x.62.3.181

Sun, S., He, J., Fan, X., Chen, Y., & Lu, X. (2020). Chinese media coverage of eating disorders: disorder representations and patient profiles. *International Journal of Eating Disorders* 53(1): 113–22. https://doi.org/10.1002/eat.23154

van Hoeken, D., & Hoek, H.W. (2020). Review of the burden of eating disorders: mortality, disability, costs, quality of life, and family burden. *Current Opinion in Psychiatry* 33(6): 521–27. https://doi.org/10.1097/yco.0000000000000641

Wonderlich, S., Mitchell, J.E., Crosby, R.D., Myers, T.C., Kadlec, K., LaHaise, K., Swan-Kremeier, L., Dokken, J., Lange, M., Dinkel, J., Jorgensen, M., & Schander, L. (2012). Minimizing and treating chronicity in the eating disorders: a clinical overview. *International Journal of Eating Disorders* 45(4): 467–75. https://doi.org/10.1002/eat.20978

Young, M.E., Norman, G.R., & Humphreys, K.R. (2008). Medicine in the popular press: the influence of the media on perceptions of disease. *PloS One* 3(10): e3552-e3552. https://doi.org/10.1371/journal.pone.0003552

# 6 Experiencing Newspaper Representations of Eating Disorders: An Interpretative Phenomenological Study

*Laura A. Cariola and Billy Lee*

## Introduction

Eating disorders (EDs) are prevalent but not well-understood mental health disorders. Although there has been increased concern for how newspaper reporting on EDs impacts public misunderstanding, leading to stigmatizing and discriminatory attitudes towards those affected (O'Hara & Clegg Smith, 2007), the impact of these discourses on the individuals affected has been largely neglected. To address this gap in empirical research, this study focused on exploring how individuals with EDs relate to media reports about EDs and aimed to discover more credible and constructive discourses that are employed by the individuals themselves.

As mentioned in the introduction to this edited volume, Goffman (1963) has described the process whereby stigmatized individuals are discredited in our minds from being whole to tainted persons, which creates a social separation between 'them' and 'us'. Research indicates that both lay people and health professionals may hold stigmatizing attitudes and erroneous beliefs about individuals with EDs (Crisp, 2005). For example, individuals with EDs are perceived as difficult to communicate and empathize with, and their illness as largely self-inflicted, with vanity and narcissism as the root cause. Finally, perceptions

Laura A. Cariola and Billy Lee, 'Chapter 6: Experiencing Newspaper Representations of Eating Disorders: An Interpretative Phenomenological Study' in: *Eating Disorders in Public Discourse: Exploring Media Representations and Lived Experiences*. University of Exeter Press (2023).  DOI: 10.47788/XATI1798 of the treatment of EDs and recovery are often overestimated (Crisp et al., 2000; Crisp, 2005). There is evidence that individuals with a diagnosis of anorexia nervosa are perceived as having voluntary control over their disordered eating behaviour (Roehrig & McLean, 2010). Those affected by an ED conversely perceive that other people, and the public in general, fail to recognize the legitimacy of their difficulties as a mental health condition. Instead, it is seen as a personal choice along with a simplistic view of treatment as regaining the appetite and 'eating more' (Dimitropoulos et al., 2015). The lack of public understanding and support due to such perceptions has been associated with sufferers' experiences of shame, low self-esteem, secrecy and denial. These impede help-seeking from both professional services and family and friends due to the reluctance to self-disclose (Ali et al., 2015). Men with EDs may experience further self-stigma in suffering from a condition regarded stereotypically as a female disorder. This serves to diminish further their willingness to engage in help-seeking behaviours that are already inconsistent with stereotypes of traditional masculinity, such as physical self-reliance (Griffiths et al., 2015).

Research has identified the news media as a sociocultural factor in the development of body dissatisfaction in the West (e.g., Prosava, Posavac & Weigel, 2001). The emphasis in the fashion industry and news media, including newspapers, on the thin body ideal of feminine beauty has been associated with increased body shape manipulation and cultural conformity. The allure of visual representations depicting ideals of physical beauty is further amplified by increased access to plastic surgery (Derenne & Beresin, 2006). A growing body of research has identified a robust link between the internalization of the thin body ideal, body dissatisfaction and the development of disordered eating behaviour and beliefs (Grabe, Ward & Hyde, 2008).

Despite the role of the media and related discourses in the propagation of stereotypes of EDs and the thin body ideal, only a few studies have directly addressed how EDs are presented in newspapers. An early study of 347 Italian newspapers and magazines (Mondini, Favaro & Santonastaso, 1996) on EDs found that news stories tended to emphasize sociocultural elements, such as the fashion industry, and stereotypes of disordered family dynamics (e.g., strict parents, rejecting mothers or absent fathers). With a focus on English-language newspapers, O'Hara and Clegg Smith (2017) studied 210 the US articles, finding that the majority were focused on celebrities in the arts and entertainment industry, and on young white women. These articles also often conflated and failed to distinguish between 'extreme dieting' versus eating disordered behaviour. The EDs were represented principally as a female issue and their aetiology as predominantly due to family and self-esteem issues. The consideration of genetic or biological determinants of EDs was nearly absent. Side-effects of treatment were largely under-reported, and treatment outcomes were over-optimistic in comparison to medical literature. A similar trend was identified in a study that explored 205 the UK newspaper articles (Shepard & Seale, 2010). They found the UK newspaper stories are predominately driven by a populist agenda with a voyeuristic and sensationalist focus on harrowing and lucid accounts of clinical complications and hospitalizations. Gulec's (this volume) analysis of 199 Turkish newspaper articles showed that representations of EDs related predominantly to sensationalist coverage of the fashion industry and celebrity deaths due to EDs. There was also increased focus on women and Western celebrities rather than men and individuals from diverse backgrounds, contributing to the misconception that EDs only affect certain populations and cultures. Sun and colleagues (2019) analysed 292 Chinese articles, identifying that the majority focused on anorexia nervosa and bulimia nervosa that affected women and young people. Concerning the causes of EDs, the majority of articles reported personal and environmental factors of EDs with only a minority of articles mentioning biological/genetic factors. Descriptions of the aetiology provided mainly superficial information about psychological and medical treatment and clinical complications associated with EDs.

On the question of stigmatization, studies of the UK newspapers have produced mixed findings: one study demonstrated a stigmatizing of EDs (Rhydderch et al., 2016), while other studies have found no evidence of stigmatization (Goulden, 2011; Bowen, Lovell & Waller, 2020; Bowen & Waller, this volume).

While newspaper representations of EDs have received some scholarly attention, little is known about how individuals diagnosed with an ED make sense of these representations and any impacts on their lived experience. The study reported in this chapter employed Interpretative Phenomenological Analysis (IPA) (Smith, Flowers & Larkin, 2009) to understand the personal lifeworlds of individuals affected by EDs, in particular, how they make sense of newspaper representations. The hermeneutic phenomenological philosopher Hans Georg Gadamer (2004) devised a systematic ontology of human being as the 'being-of-understanding' with discourse central to our understanding and experiencing of the world and ourselves. This discoursal constitution of our very lived experience implies that we cannot escape being changed by what we see, hear and read (Gadamer, 2004). The influence of Gadamer's hermeneutics on the development of IPA has been to recognize that as the being-of-understanding, we are both constituting of, and constituted by, the texts of our social milieu and culture (Smith, Flowers & Larkin, 2009). Through a hermeneutic phenomenological understanding of our eating disordered participants' sense-makings, we further sought to discover more truthful ways in which newspapers might disclose the 'nature' of EDs. Commensurate with the method of IPA, we regarded our study participants as experts of their own lived experience, facilitating as much as possible 'the individual to speak with authenticity' (Pathway, 2017, p. 10). Here our understanding of authenticity is not in terms of a 'naïve humanism'. Rather it is a recognition of the pervasive forces of 'everydayness', including everyday discourse, which pervade our enculturated being-in-the-world (Heidegger, 1962). The perpetual tide of text and language carries us forward, but language is also what we struggle against, in order to speak ourselves, rather than be spoken by it. The involvement of individuals' lived experiences of mental health in mental health research is beginning to foster greater social inclusion and to be regarded as indispensable to developing service provision. This represents a radical re-evaluation of sociocultural attitudes and beliefs about illness and health (NHS, 2018; Rethink Mental Illness, 2017).

## Method

This qualitative study adopted an interpretative phenomenological approach that focused on exploring the meaning-making of individuals self-identified as recovering from or suffering from an ED. Smith, Flowers and Larkin (2009) described IPA as a methodology that draws theoretical influences from phenomenology (study of experience), hermeneutics (study of interpretation) and ideography (study of individuals and specifics) in order to disclose individual lived experience of existential import. IPA involves close interpretative engagement between the researcher and participants where the researcher is required to be self-reflective and to be able to bracket their fore-understandings and impact on the knowledge co-created. Smith and Osborne (2003) refer to a process of double hermeneutics, whereby the researcher tries to glimpse an insider perspective through empathically voicing participants' experiences from their personal accounts, while sensitively interpreting, interrogating and understanding their lived experience using external theories and frameworks. As such, IPA recognizes the double role of the researcher as a co-participant in the disclosive dialogue, and as a curator of the unfolding phenomenon.

## *Participants and data*

The research was granted ethical approval by the School of Health in Social Science Research Ethics Committee. In total, five participants who self-identified as suffering or recovering from a diagnosed ED voluntarily participated in this study. They were four women and one man, ranging in age from 21 to 40 years, all of white ethnicity. The participants were all diagnosed with anorexia nervosa. The inclusion criteria were that the participants were (1) aged 18 years or above, (2) diagnosed with an ED and (3) proficient English speakers. Recruitment was through a flyer with a call for participation that was disseminated to mental health charities, self-help groups and mental health support services in the UK, who forwarded the flyer to their networks. The flyer was also posted on social media sites. Potential participants were able to contact the researchers to express interest or ask questions about participating in the interview for the study.

## *Procedure*

A semi-structured interview schedule was prepared. Prior to the interviews, participants were given information about the study and a consent form. They were also given the opportunity to ask questions about the study before beginning the interview. Five semi-structured interviews were conducted on Skype, and digitally recorded and transcribed. The interviews lasted between 27 and 51 minutes. At the beginning of the interviews, participants were asked demographic questions. During the interview, they were asked for their reflections on (1) how EDs are portrayed and written about in the UK news media, (2) how newspaper portrayals relate to their experiences of EDs and (3) how newspaper portrayals may inform and misinform public understanding of their ED. Probes were used to facilitate participants to elaborate on specific experiences, or if their response was unclear. The interviewer remained mindful during the interview of the hermeneutic stance, by being curious and watchful of the speaker's experiential process, and by focusing attention on the participants' own voicing, bracketing where necessary personal concerns and preconceptions (Smith, Flowers & Larkin, 2009).

### *Ethics*

The research team comprised two scientist-practitioners: the first author conducted the interviews, and both were involved in the analysis of the interview transcripts. Participants were provided with information about the purpose of the study, informed about their ethical rights to withdraw and given the opportunity to ask questions about the study. Participants were also informed that the study would be confidential, and that all data would be anonymized. All participants provided informed consent and consented for the interviews to be digitally recorded. The study received ethical approval from the School of Health in Social Science's Ethics Committee at the University of Edinburgh.

### *Analysis*

The researchers adopted the methodology and philosophical stance of IPA, as outlined by Smith, Flowers and Larkin (2009). All interviews were transcribed and the transcripts read and re-read by the researchers to actively immerse themselves in the data. The engagement with the individual lifeworlds allowed distinctive voices of each participant and their feeling tone to shine through. The descriptive, linguistic and conceptual content of all the transcripts was noted. Detailed notes and comments accompanied the conceptual clustering and surfacing of intra-case themes, staying close to participant wording and to recollect possible meanings. In this stage, each transcript was analysed separately to maintain an idiographic and hermeneutic focus on the lifeworld (Smith, Flowers & Larkin, 2009). Connections across the individual emergent themes were then derived by grouping according to conceptual similarities. At this stage, some emergent themes that had a weaker evidence base were discarded. The process was repeated across the individual theme tables in a cross-case analysis to identify overarching themes between participants' accounts. This iterative and inductive process led to the development of the superordinate and sub-theme labels.

## Results

The analysis identified five superordinate themes that described how individuals affected by a ED make sense of newspaper representations in relation to their lived experience: (1) reification of the ED identity, (2) loneliness and incommunicado, (3) misunderstood by significant others, (4) never feeling sufficient and (5) perverse and exacerbating medicalization. The superordinate and subordinate themes are outlined below.

### *Theme 1: Reification of the ED identity*

This theme reflects participants' experiences of newspaper reporting as sensationalizing and drawing on shock value, often with images and stories focused on bodily appearance, physical size and weight. Participants felt their actual lived experiences were trivialized by stereotypical and oversimplified accounts. They expressed moral reactions, frustrations, and indignation towards a reification of what they saw as a false ED identity.

**Sub-theme 1: Huge emphasis on appearance.** Participants perceived reporting of EDs as narrowly focused on physical appearance, especially of white adolescent girls with anorexia nervosa, as victims of model culture. Beatrice states:

> I remember thinking in the press previously it was always, it's also the media with the size zero model thing. Now, to be honest with you, my eating disorder is not, for me, was not coming from the model culture. My eating disorder didn't evolve from seeing thin models. That's not part of the pathology. But in the public view of an eating disorder, they kind of equate the eating disorder to individuals with the thin models. And then they say one causes the other, which is not true, but you can see that in the media.

She takes issue with the media's preoccupation with the 'size zero model thing' and she denies it is for her a 'part of the pathology'. However, the public 'equates', as she puts it, EDs with 'thin models'. Moreover, they believe 'one causes the other'. Thus, Beatrice expresses annoyance that not only are the public misinformed by a powerful stereotype, they further draw the false conclusion that all eating disordered individuals have been similarly afflicted by 'thin model culture'. The emphasis on visual appearance and body image implicates fashion and personal vanity, 'which is not true'. For the participants, this reframing of EDs, as essentially a problem with body dissatisfaction and over-dieting, minimizes the serious psychological dimensions, mental health facets and potential medical complications that go beyond food and physical appearance.

**Sub-theme 2: Shock, sensation and stereotypes.** Some participants experienced sensationalism about EDs as seeking principally to shock readers, employing depictions of EDs at their most visually extreme, notably anorexia nervosa. Ophelia states:

> There's been quite a few cases in the media that they are shock stories. But, that's only like [...] it happens all the time. The ones that are sticking in my mind are basically where people have been failed by health services or by their treatment teams and they've died because there have been, well, real questions raised about the care that they received. When you read how those stories are written, they obviously draw on all of the, like, shock factor things that impact on the reader. Usually, they'll draw on what that person was eating, how much exercise that person was engaging in, or how they resisted treatment or how they lied about their weight, or basically how they were not, like, monitored.

**Sub-theme 3: Censorship, frustration and annoyance.** Two participants spoke of their activism to raise awareness of EDs. They expressed frustration and indignation towards reductionistic narratives, and newspaper censorship of actual lived experience. Beatrice recalls remonstrating with a journalist:

> They wanted to know how much weight I'd lost. I had to say 'it's not just about that. I don't want to talk about that. I want to talk about my life and the life I have created. Yes, maybe the life I lost, but more the life I have created' and they then said 'have you got any good pictures?' and I said 'yeah, no, no'.

John expressed a similar frustration:

> Every time, every time you try to get everything across, quite a lot of the times when it goes to the editor, it seems when it's published, it seems to be they focused upon the eating side of things and the 'BMI' rather than focusing upon everything else that we've spoken about, about what actually led you to the eating disorder.

For both participants, there is frustration towards journalists who misappropriate what they are trying to 'get across' or 'what it is about' by reducing everything to the eating side, weight loss or BMI (Body Mass Index). There is annoyance towards what they perceive to be censorship, through a selective erasure of the parts of their lived experience that do not fit the stereotype, as when Beatrice remonstrates with her interviewer that she wished to talk more about the life she created than the life she lost. John's experience was of disregard of his own insights into his ED. His sharing of his experience losing his mum and eating as a way of coping with his grief was painfully undermined by the editorial 'cutting and sensationalizing' which is 'the wrong thing to put out to people'.

### *Theme 2: Loneliness and incommunicado*

This theme reflects the extreme loneliness and incommunicability of participants' experiences. There is a sense of being shut down and muted by other people's assumptions and beliefs. These include that the ED is a matter of choice that can be easily overcome—if only the person would simply eat more.

**Sub-theme 1: The invalidated voice.** Some participants described the difficulty in communicating as their own voice being crowded out or shut down by others' assumptions and stereotypes:

> I would say probably over the past two and a half years, I definitely fell into a relapse at some point last year and have been doing a lot better since. And it was really obvious, because I had lost a lot of weight. It was really not good. And I've gained a lot of weight back now. So obviously, from the outside, it looks like I'm doing absolutely fine. I've not gained all of the weight back, but I definitely look a lot better than I did weight-wise. But so someone I work with, my boss, actually, took it upon herself to say 'Oh it's so great to see you looking so well. You know there was a time when I thought, last year, you were just so pale you were just going to drop dead. Now, you just look like you got so much life back, it's so nice to see' And inside I'm like 'God I'm going back into treatment. I'm really having a difficult time right now' How like, how can I say that? (Ophelia)

Ophelia's boss knew about her ED but simply assumed that her increased bodily weight indicated she had recovered, at a time when she was in fact relapsing and going back into treatment. This invalidates her own voice such that the actuality of her situation is taken over by her boss's assumption about body weight and wellness. The weight of other people's assumptions incurs a double loss:

> 'God, I really must be fine then if that's what she thinks or if that what it looks like, then I don't have a problem, so I really shouldn't go back into treatment, oh, I'm fine, really' Which is obviously [...] if I think about that from an outside point-of-view that's really damaging, but it does kind of play with what I would call the eating-disorder voice of 'oh, well, you must be fine. You don't have a problem. You're absolutely fine. There's nothing wrong with you. It's fine that you're engaging in all these behaviours. You're fine!' (Ophelia)

Not only does Ophelia lose her voice, we see in the above extract how it is even more damaging that her actual experience is taken over by what she calls the 'eating-disorder voice'. We see the insistent refrain of 'You're fine', 'really fine', 'absolutely fine', 'must be fine', voiced no fewer than five times in the short extract. This then casts self-doubt on her original instinct to seek help, as when the ED voice, as judge and jury, proclaims she doesn't have a problem and there's nothing wrong with her. What is 'really damaging' then is that the instinct to seek help and self-care is attacked and undermined.

**Sub-theme 2: People see ED as a choice.** Participants experienced reactions from others suggesting that their eating difficulties and behaviour were matter of choice. Claudia states:

> Like, I think people see it as choice, and it's not something that you choose. People are like 'Oh for God's sake, she should just bloody eat'. But it's not, it's not, you don't choose to be this way. It's something that's distressing that happens to you as a result of a lot of factors. But you don't, it's not a choice that you make. It's like [...] at the end of the day it's an illness, in the same way that anything else, cancer or something, is an illness. And at the end of the day it is life threatening in a lot of situations as well [...] you don't choose to be that, you don't choose to put yourself in that position. It's not a choice.

There is a quality of exasperation for Claudia as she reiterates eight times her negation that her illness is a choice. As people have expressed their exasperation towards her, she expresses her exasperation at the fallacy that she chooses her illness. Her comparison with cancer is stark: it is life-threatening, it is distressing and you don't put yourself in that position. Participants' suffering is compounded by this invalidation, which adds an additional torment that is both medically exacerbating and psychologically undermining.

**Sub-theme 3: Isolation.** Three participants described extreme isolation with their ED, being unable to communicate with family and friends, who likewise did not know how to help. Ophelia depicts the following:

> My mum didn't know anything really. She knew that I was not well. She knew that I wasn't eating. She knew that I had lost a lot of weight. She obviously connected the dots and thought I had an eating disorder. She marched me to the doctors. They confirmed 'she has an eating disorder'. There was no conversation that happened about any of that. I got an emergency [...] well, I had a couple of short hospital stays in general wards, and then I got an emergency admission to an inpatient unit for a year and didn't let anyone visit me. My family did not know how to deal with that.

Both extracts convey extreme isolation, which feels all the more desperate given that their families do not know how to help. The not knowing is harmful in both extracts, amplifying the suffering on all sides. The initial separations from family are violent and severe. For Ophelia, 'for a year they didn't let anyone visit me', while Beatrice was '10 years in hospital most of the time' after disowning her parents. We learn that she found herself alone, tied to a bed in France, and sectioned in an 'ancient loony bin'. The account is terrifying as we learn that 'that's not the worst of it'. It attests to what the extreme incarceration and being incommunicado wrought psychologically on patients already suffering from a debilitating illness.

### *Theme 3: Misunderstood by significant others*

This theme captures participants' experiences of being misunderstood by and unintelligible to crucial people in their lives, including family, close friends and medical professionals. There were divisions in their lifeworlds that are difficult to express with ordinary language.

**Sub-theme 1: Unintelligibility.** Participants articulated the anguish alongside the disorder of being utterly unintelligible to the closest people in their lives. Ophelia recalls the run-up to her sister's birthday party:

> My mum ended up yelling at me really shouting at me. You know I'm a grown adult, and I was staying at her house a couple of nights to do these things for my sister's birthday. She just yelled, she shouted, she couldn't cope with seeing me like that. She was yelling at me to get out of the house, to not come back, that I was going to die, all of these things.

The juxtaposition of the angry outburst with her original intention to assist preparations for her sister's birthday party evokes a shocking image. The severity of the incident is underscored by her contrast between 'the yelling' with being a 'grown adult'. She recalls rationalizing to herself: 'I was full-time lecturing, I was working on my PhD, I was working as a therapist, and I'm not actually going to die. I am okay. I'm getting on with my life.' We gain a sense from Ophelia's experience of deep divisions in her relational lifeworld, her mother unable to cope, and how these might undermine a young adult's developing self-concept.

**Sub-theme 2: People don't know what to say.** People not knowing how to talk and to be alongside the ED was experienced by some participants. John explains the harm therein:

> Like family and friends don't know what to say to you because I think they as well, I think, they probably think that mentioning things, obviously it can cause you to eat and things like that. They feel that they're obviously going to pull you back into an eating disorder. So a lot of people don't know what to say to you because they don't know what to say as the right thing or the wrong thing, and I feel that can be quite a harmful thing as well.

He explains how it is a harmful thing that 'people just don't know how to approach' his ED. This not knowing does not lead to curiosity and further engagement and understanding. Rather, there is an edginess around mentioning things and fear of 'pulling you back' and 'cause you to eat and things like that'. He says people don't know 'the right thing or the wrong thing' to say and this existential wariness undermines his relationships. In another part of the interview, he attributes this kind of not knowing to the misleading stereotypes by the news media.

**Sub-theme 3: Shrouded in secrecy.** The role of secrecy was a core aspect of the experience for a number of participants. John states:

> Eating disorders, for me, I think are shrouded in secrecy and I think the biggest part of recovering is kicking back that secrecy.

John was in denial about his eating problems at the beginning stages because his eating problems did not fit with being a man. He also hid his problems from 'public society' because of the stigma of a 'female illness'. He is disgruntled at the misrepresentation and his activism seeks to speak out in public alongside other men as 'with Christopher Eccleston and quite a few others, I think it's made a lot of difference'.

### *Theme 4: Never feeling sufficient*

This theme reflects participants' experiences of their self-identity—as not enough, of falling short, of self-judgement and comparing the self, and of a need to conform and to resist conformity. There are self-referential emotions associated with failures and achievements positioned as self-ideals, stereotypes and 'the ED identity' that come together in the mix.

**Sub-theme 1: Comparing, competing, judging and resisting.** Participants would judge their illness competitively against others and media ideals. Ophelia aspired to an ideal of anorexia:

> However like one of the reasons that I watched it, probably five times, was to compare myself to everybody that was on that show, and basically make myself feel like I wasn't sick enough or wasn't doing eating disorder correctly because I wasn't fasting for 10 days straight [...] or because my blood work wasn't hitting the floor every week.

She is referring to an ED documentary and her comparison leads her to doubt the severity of her illness as 'not being sick enough'. She develops a thought pattern wherein an imagined eating-disorder-ideal becomes significant. This sustains her dysfunctional eating behaviour through reimagining it as a skill requiring discipline, comparison and competency to execute 'correctly'. Not being 'enough' was a recurring theme in Ophelia's interview. She dwelt on her conflicted relationship with her mother, and struggled to resist an infantilizing dynamic that undermined her identity achievement and an adult–adult relationship with her mother. The recurring self-talk in her interview seemed important to shore up the belief she is an adult, sufficient to herself, and not a child after all.

**Sub-theme 2: Fear of not fitting the stereotype.** Participants described the fear and embarrassment of deviating from the eating disorder stereotype. John articulates his stigma as a man:

> At first, the very early stages of my eating disorder, I didn't believe I actually had an eating disorder. Then farther on down the line, I knew I had an eating disorder and I felt I had to hide it from public society because I felt a fear of what people would think of me. Especially as a male with an eating disorder, I feel there's this kind of stigma around it as well.

Ophelia is embarrassed at being older:

> You never see a diverse range of ethnicities that are, like, written about or even spoken about. You don't see them represented, so I'm trying to think [...] God, what if I was someone who wasn't white? How would I feel about approaching treatment? Would I just feel like I don't fit the mould of those affected? And like I said, I'm getting older now and I think 'God, I'm actually like a little embarrassed that this is still a problem.' And I don't see people of like different eating disorder, I don't see a lot of diversity represented at all, I think.

Both participants experience secondary emotions around not fitting the media stereotype of their illness. John fears what people will think of him because he is male, while Ophelia is embarrassed at being older and no longer fitting the mould of the 'white teenager affected by anorexia nervosa'. They perceive themselves as policed by specific manifestations of this illness validated by the media. A valid manifestation being 'female white teenager with anorexia nervosa'.

**Sub-theme 3: Need for identity.** Participants expressed concerns around not fitting the images of people with EDs and their need for identity.

> I was never going to be sufficiently anorexic. I don't even know if I really wanted to be, but I wanted to be sufficient at something. And I had so much pain that this is a way of concealing it or dealing with it very bad, very bad. But I was always trying to fit in, I guess, maybe, but realising that I was a misfit, on the websites and in the media I found, in the early days of my illness, I found other misfits. And we had a little competition with ourselves, who could do the worst damage really. It's terrible. (Beatrice)

Beatrice could not relate her own experience and sense of self to public images of EDs. A number of segments stand out from this short extract. She experiences herself as insufficient and ambivalent towards the anorexic identity. However, she is aware of herself as needing to be 'sufficient at something' and as always trying to fit in. She began to access pro-ana webpages and found there a sense of identity with 'other misfits'. However, this community exacerbated her eating difficulties through a competitive cycle of self-harm. This sub-theme displays an inner existential need of being and belonging, which for some participants found expression through being with others who also embodied their angst through severe control of ingestion.

### *Theme 5: Perverse and exacerbating medicalization*

This superordinate theme reflected participants' experiences of a lack of appropriate medical support for their ED and their beliefs in not deserving treatment once referred to an ED treatment programme.

**Sub-theme 1: Medical ignorance and ineptitude.** Some participants experienced inept care or a reductionistic approach to EDs. John states:

> I find that, especially with general practitioners, yeah. I think there's a real lack of understanding with that. And I think that the way they relate to eating disorders, I think it's probably not helping them either because there are certainly GPs that I've struggled quite a lot with actually speaking to them. I was pushed away constantly when I actually went to speak to them because they kept focusing and saying 'Oh, it's just grief you are suffering with, it will get better'. They gave me antidepressants and I kept losing weight, losing weight, losing weight all the time. That actually caused me, obviously, to have the heart attack before I was actually getting any help. I just feel there's a lack of understanding with the GPs.

John's GP explained away his weight loss as 'just grief' from the death of his mother. He 'struggled quite a lot with actually speaking to them' and was pushed away constantly and prescribed antidepressants. He reiterates in the extract 'losing weight, losing weight, losing weight', as if hitting a wall, and he had a heart attack before his difficulties were acknowledged and he received specialist treatment. John is now an activist advocating a focus on recovery and 'seeing the whole person' and their underlying issues, rather than 'just getting them fattened up and sent straight back into the community'.

**Sub-theme 2: Difficulty accessing treatment.** Participants described their difficulties in accessing specialized ED treatment and complex emotions once referred. Beatrice states:

> I remember every admission, I would always think I wasn't ill enough to be there, didn't deserve to be there. I think some of those stereotypes, those questions or those feelings were perpetuated by the policy, the admission policy. Whereby you couldn't get in until you were about to die. And then, even then I would be admitted in a wheelchair, but I just, I felt I didn't deserve to be in a wheelchair. They gave me one of those beds that are really soft, I can't remember, it's the air beds because I had so many bedsores. I had chucked it off, I wouldn't lie on it because I didn't think I deserved it.

She laments the reductionistic criteria to qualify for specialized treatment set forth by the admissions policy, requiring patients to be 'about to die'. Even though 'admitted in a wheelchair', she felt undeserving of treatment, although she had met the BMI threshold. In the extract, while critically ill, Beatrice is struggling with questions of deserving treatment, while discounting her physical ailments such as 'bedsores'. They do not come within the scope of the admissions criteria and therefore do not count or cast doubt on her 'deserving', a word she repeats three times. Her narrative reflects harmful perfectionism which appears to be the result of unhelpful stereotypes based on medical and cultural ideals that centre around the thin body stereotype.

**Sub-theme 3: Need for authenticity.** A pervasive theme in the background for all the participants was a tacit need for their own voices to be heard. For example, Beatrice feels healthcare practitioners need to engage with patients as equal partners, sharing in decision-making about their mental healthcare and treatment design and planning:

> I think the structure of treatment programmes should be created around the individual stories. I spoke to someone at the [mental health organization] about that, and they said 'This is what we need to change, not necessarily trying to find data or statistics or evidence, etc. We just need to listen to the people who get well and hear what they have to say about what treatments there should be.' (Beatrice)

Her final and successful treatment programme offered her a space to identify and work with her strengths and weaknesses, as well as to identify her unique values, life choices and decisions. Within this therapeutic frame, she was released from the limiting binary of conforming versus not conforming, instead developing her own sense-making that ultimately allowed her to understand her needs and purposes beyond the narrow confines of the ED identity.

## Discussion

While representations of EDs have received some scholarly attention, this study is the first to examine how affected individuals make sense of ED discourses as reported in newspapers. The study also sought to understand the impact of newspaper reports on their lived experience of their disorder. Using an experience-near, semi-structured interview, and detailed IPA of the transcripts, we identified five themes: reification of the ED identity; loneliness and incommunicado; misunderstood by significant others; never feeling sufficient; and perverse and exacerbating medicalization. These themes indicate a fracture between newspaper discourses and self-experiences, which was a significant source of existential trouble for the participants.

Participants perceived that newspaper representations reinforced cultural myths around those affected in several ways (Mondini, Favaro & Santonastaso, 1996; O'Hara and Clegg Smith, 2017; Shepard & Seale, 2010). They sensationalized eating difficulties, recycling clichés and oversimplified narratives that focused predominantly on physical appearance and white young women. These narratives were reinforced by imagery that reduced EDs to a single dimension, such as weight loss. Such a reductionism contributed to a public understanding of EDs that could be harmful to social relationships. For instance, participants in this study experienced simplistic beliefs and over-generalized assumptions that did not permit a communicative space with others to share their actual experience, leading to a sense of loneliness from family, friends, medical professionals and other significant people. Their experience of EDs was not only incommunicable, but unintelligible even to close family and friends. Some participants sensed that others judged their ED to be a matter of choice, and thus resisted acknowledging the mental health problem. Previous research has linked such perceptions to self-stigma, including shame, secrecy and low self-esteem, which impede disclosure and help-seeking behaviour, particularly by men (Ali et al., 2015; Griffiths et al., 2015). The sense that others find it 'difficult to say anything' resonates with some previous findings that those with EDs are hard to talk to and to empathize with (Crisp et al., 2000; Crisp, 2005).

A conflict between public discourse and self-experience may manifest in seemingly paradoxical ways (Butt & Langdridge, 2003). In this study, some participants reflected a competitiveness to embody and to conform to the 'ED identity', meanwhile experiencing anxiety deviating from or failing to achieve the stereotype. In EDs, the distorted perception of the body is central. While some psychological literature has indicated that EDs may be understood as a bodily manifestation of 'taking back control' (Carr, 2005), this was not specifically expressed by the participants.

This study identifies a dynamic between newspaper and medical discourses that works to reinforce public misperceptions and lack of information about EDs (see also Lyons, McAndrews & Warne, this volume). Both the medical setting and newspaper context are consistent with the standardized nosology, which appears to break down personal lived experience and the attempts at sense-making. A need for authenticity and voice emerged as a strong theme of the study. For example, one participant described her use of art to develop creative self-expression, which then became her own path to obtain better self-understanding, a sense of identity, and authenticity. The same participant provided a powerful account of finding her voice in a treatment that emphasized a patient-centred stance. This individualized approach to treatment acknowledged her whole person, allowing her to clarify her self-stigmatizing beliefs.

We posit the following recommendations for ethical reporting: (a) journalistic practice characterized by integrity and accountability, (b) including reports on individuals' resilience and recovery, (c) reporting EDs within their emotional context, (d) including a diversity of people affected and (e) staying informed about mental health research. These would facilitate increased public understanding, thus enabling families, peers and the broader community to engage with those suffering. Journalists are well placed to educate the public and enhance lives by promoting empathy and avoiding sensationalism (Aitamurto & Varma, 2018).

This study's main limitation concerned the self-selection of the participants, who were a sample of highly articulate individuals with some experience of mental health activism. Their recovery experiences may also not be typical or generalizable to other individuals with an ED diagnosis. In IPA, the researchers' subjectivity is an integral part of the research process. Both the authors are scientist-practitioners and the study was conducted from a mental health perspective, which emphasized an empathic stance to mitigate a misappropriation of participants' voices or their narratives. Attention was also given to the risk of creating new stereotypes and clichés about EDs. While the phenomenological methodology employed in this study is not immune to the risks of misappropriation, it builds in methodological structures to attempt to mitigate these risks where possible.

## Conclusion

This study adopted an interpretative phenomenological stance to disclose how individuals with an ED make sense of newspaper discourses in relation to their lived experience. The results may inform journalistic standards and guidelines for mental health reporting. Qualitative methods such as IPA, which seek to give voice to suffering, instead of exacerbating it, may offer a model for ethical reporting and the inclusion of mental health difference in the diverse community.

## Acknowledgements

We would like to thank the participants of this study for sharing their experiences.

## References

Aitamurto, T., & Varma, A. (2018). The constructive role of journalism. *Journalism Practice* 12(6): 695–713. https://doi.org/10.1080/17512786.2018.1473041

Ali, K., Farrer, L., Fassnacht, D.B., Gulliver, A., Bauer, S., & Griffiths, K.M. (2016). Perceived barrier and facilitators towards help-seeking for eating disorders: a systematic review. *International Journal of Eating Disorders* 50(1): 9–21. https://doi.org/10.1002/eat.22598

Bowen, M., Lovell, A., & Waller, R. (2020). Stigma: the representation of anorexia nervosa in UK newspaper Twitter feeds. *Journal of Mental Health* 15: 1–8. https://doi.org/10.1080/09638237.2020.1793128

Butt, T., & Langdridge, D. (2003). The construction of self: the public reach into the public sphere. *Sociology* 37(3): 477–92. https://doi.org/10.1177/00380385030373005

Carr, A. (2005). *The Handbook of Child and Adolescent Clinical Psychology: A Contextual Approach*. London: Routledge.

Crisp, A. (2005). Stigmatization of and discrimination against people with eating disorders including a report of two nationwide surveys. *European Eating Disorders Review* 13(3): 147–52. https://doi.org/10.1002/erv.648

Crisp, A.H., Gelder, M.G., Rix, S., Meltzer, H.I., & Rowlands, O.J. (2000). Stigmatisation of people with mental illnesses. *British Journal of Psychiatry* 177: 4–7.

Derenne, J.L., & Beresin, E.V. (2006). Body image, media, and eating disorders. *Academic Psychiatry* 30(3): 257–61. https://doi.org/10.1192/bjp.177.1.4

Dimitropoulos, G., Herschman, J., Toulaney, A., & Steinegger, C. (2015). A qualitative study on the challenges associated with accepting familial support from the perspective of transition-age youth with eating disorders. *Eating Disorders* 24(3): 1–17. https://doi.org/10.1080/10640266.2015.1064276

Gadamer, H.-G. (2004). *Truth and Method*. London: Continuum. (Original work published 1960.)

Goffman, E. (1963). *Stigma: Notes on the Management of Spoiled Identity*. Englewood Cliffs, NJ: Prentice Hall.

Goulden, R., Corker, E., Evans-Lacko, S., Rose, D., Thornicroft, G., & Henderson, C. (2011). Newspaper coverage of mental illness in the UK, 1992-2008. *BMC Public Health* 11: 796. https://doi.org/10.1186/1471-2458-11-796

Grabe, S., Ward, L.M., & Hyde, J.S. (2008). The role of the media in body image concerns among women: a meta-analysis of experimental and correlational studies. *Psychological Bulletin* 134(3): 460–76. https://doi.org/10.1037/0033-2909.134.3.460

Griffiths, S. Mond, J.M., Li, Z., Gunatilake, S., Murray, Sheffield, J., & Touz, S. (2015). Self-stigma of seeking treatment and being male predict an increased likelihood of having an undiagnosed eating disorder. *International Journal of Eating Disorders* 48(6): 775–78. https://doi.org/10.1002/eat.22413

Heidegger, M. (1962). *Being and Time*. Oxford: Blackwell.

Mondini, S., Favaro, A., & Santonastaso, P. (1996). Eating disorders and the ideal of feminine beauty in Italian newspapers and magazines. *European Eating Disorders Review* 4(2): 112–20. https://doi.org/10.1002/(sici)1099-0968(199606)4:2<112::aid-erv152>3.0.co;2-6

NHS (2018). Mental health improvement. Chapter 1. Retrieved from https://improvement.nhs.uk/documents/3450/NHS_Mental_Health_Improvement_Chpter_1.pdf

O'Hara, S.K., & Clegg Smith, K. (2017). Presentation of eating disorders in the news media: what are the implications for patient diagnosis and treatment? *Patient Education and Counselling* 68(1): 43–51. https://doi.org/10.1016/j.pec.2007.04.006

Pathway (2017). Experts by experience: involvement handbook. London: Pathway. Retrieved from https://www.pathway.org.uk/wp-content/uploads/2013/05/EbE-Involvement-Handbook.pdf

Posavac, H.D., Posavac, S.S., & Weigel, R.G. (2001). Reducing the impact of media images on women at risk for body image disturbance: three targeted interventions. *Journal of Social and Clinical Psychology* 20(3): 324–40. https://doi.org/10.1521/jscp.20.3.324.22308

Rethink Mental Illness (2017). Progress through partnership: involvement of people with lived experience of mental illness in CCG commissioning. London: Rethink Mental Illness.

Roehrig, J.P., & McLean C.P. (2010). A comparison of stigma towards eating disorders versus depression. *International Journal of Eating Disorders* 43(7): 671–74. https://doi.org/10.1002/eat.20760

Rhydderch, D., Krooupa, A.M., Shefer, G., Goulden, R., Williams, P., Thornicroft, A., Rose, D., Thornicroft, G., & Henderson, C. (2016). Changes in newspaper coverage of mental illness from 2008 to 2014 in England. *Acta Psychiatrica Scandinavica* 134(S446): 45–52. https://doi.org/10.1111/acps.12606

Shepard, E., & Seale, C. (2010). Eating disorders in the media: the changing nature of UK newspaper reports. *European Eating Disorders Review* 18(6): 486–95. https://doi.org/10.1002/erv.1006

Sun, S., He, J., & Fan, X. (2019). Chinese media coverage of eating disorders: disorder representations and patient profiles. *International Journal of Eating Disorders* 53(1): 113–22. https://doi.org/10.1002/eat.23154

Smith, J.A., Flowers, P., & Larkin, M. (2009). *Interpretative Phenomenological Analysis: Theory, Method and Research*. London: Sage.

Smith, J.A., & Osborne, M. (2003). Interpretative phenomenological analysis. In J.A. Smith (ed.), *Qualitative Psychology: A Practical Guide to Methods* (pp. 51–80). London: Sage.

# 7 Narrative Experiences of Social Media and the Internet from Men with Eating Disorders

*Gareth Lyons, Sue McAndrew and Tony Warne*

## Introduction

This chapter is based on a wider PhD research project which examined the lived experiences of men with eating disorders (EDs). In total, seven men diagnosed with anorexia nervosa were interviewed about their experiences of living with the illness. The range of topics covered furthered the limited research on men's lived experiences of anorexia, highlighting a range of issues outside of the clinical environment. Such issues could be developed by future research regarding the wider effects of the illness, which may in turn help people cope better with, combat and defeat the illness. In relation to this book, this chapter specifically examines experiences the men shared in relation to their encounters with the media and digital information providers.

## Background

Male anorexia, specifically charting lived experiences, is an area of limited research (Lyons et al., 2019). When reviewing the literature, Jones and Morgan (2010) examined seventy-seven research studies focusing on male anorexia, but not one explored lived experience. This was reiterated by Räisänen and Hunt (2014, p. 6) who stated that 'men with EDs are under-diagnosed, undertreated

Gareth Lyons, Sue McAndrew and Tony Warne, 'Chapter 7: Narrative Experiences of Social Media and the Internet from Men with Eating Disorders' in: *Eating Disorders in Public Discourse: Exploring Media Representations and Lived Experiences*. University of Exeter Press (2023). © Gareth Lyons et al. DOI: 10.47788/DBCF4677 and under-researched'. This lack of research on men's experiences of EDs perpetuates the notion of EDs being a female illness.

Our own literature review focused on male-specific studies that were published between 2000 and 2016. We did not find a single study which examined lived experiences outside of the clinical environment. However, two studies focused on lived experiences relating to clinical settings; one taking account of services users' experiences of specialist eating disorder services (Robinson et al., 2012), the other exploring help-seeking behaviour and initial contact with primary care services (Räisänen & Hunt, 2014). While a further study (Button & Warren, 2001) explored people's lived experiences of eating disorders, the sample was made up of thirty-five women and one man, with findings anonymized.

Academia ignores men with EDs, thus helping to maintain the common myth of it being a female illness and perpetuating the stigma associated with men who have the same diagnosis (King, 2013). Globally, anorexia has traditionally been shown as 90% female and 10% male, and until recently this was the accepted status quo. This was reinforced by official statistics for those undergoing hospital treatment in the UK. NHS Digital (2013, 2020), for instance, shows a greater disparity than the 90% women 10% men split; figures indicating 93/7 in 2012–2013 and 94/6 in 2019–2020. The problem with official statistics is that they do not take into account the numbers of males and females who do not come to the attention of health services, or those who are not deemed severe enough to warrant hospital care. For men, this is considered a restricting factor, with many being undiagnosed for a myriad of reasons; ranging from mental health, social, cultural and masculinity stigma, to lack of knowledge of the illness in men on the part of health professionals and the general public (Ousley et al., 2008; MacCaughelty et al., 2016). Additionally, the DSM-IV (American Psychiatric Association [APA], 1994) was not kind in its classification of EDs, making it difficult for men to be diagnosed (Freeman, 2005; Attia & Roberto, 2009). For example, symptoms of amenorrhoea were central to the diagnosis, making it difficult to diagnose men as having anorexia (Freeman, 2005). Despite DSM-5 (APA, 2013) changing classification criteria for eating disorders, and although Marsh (2017) found more men were being treated for EDs, it remains unclear if the classification change has benefited men who seek help.

While the official statistic of a 90:10 split between women and men having an ED continues to dominate service provison, these figures have been challenged (Knowles, 2011; Marsh, 2017; Skolnick, 2014), with each of these studies showing large statistical increases in male inpatient numbers since the millenium. However, more recently it has been suggested that the ratio of women to men experiencing an ED is 75% to 25% respectively, challenging the previous split (Hudson et al., 2007; Skolnick, 2014). This may result in more funding and research into male EDs and greater awareness of the illness.

### *Media as a capital disseminator and eating disorders*

Media is now considered to be a major source of communication worldwide. Communication is based around a simple structure—the sender, the message and the receiver. While the sender codes the message and the meaning they want the receiver to derive from it, the receiver decodes and interprets the message themselves. This allows the message to be interpreted differently depending upon the receiver's frame of reference (Hall, 1999). An example of interpretation is offered by Norris et al. (2003), who wrote about different interpretations of 9/11; for some, those responsible were terrorists and murderers, while others believed them to be martyrs and freedom fighters.

Traditionally, the media—images seen on TV, in newspapers, advertisements and so on—has been blamed as a creator of EDs. While this view has been challenged and shown to be largely incorrect (Stice et al., 2001), the media is now regarded as being a potential trigger for developing an ED in those predisposed to the illness (Tyre, 2005).

Media is one of the main highways for the spread of capital. In our current world, thoughts, ideas and opinions can spread quickly, but those thoughts, ideas and opinions are still largely controlled by those who own media distribution channels. For example, Becker et al.'s (2002) study of media effectiveness in spreading capital in the area of EDs found that after the advent of television on the Fijian islands, there was a change in eating habits and body dissatisfaction. Other studies (Tong et al., 2005; Younis & Ali, 2012; Musaiger et al., 2014) have indicated that the spread of Western culture through media has brought about increased cases of EDs, with it having greater influence on male adolescents than on their female counterparts (Toro et al., 2005). Agliata and Tantleff-Dunn (2004) showed how media portrayals of the ideal male body lead to dissatisfaction in men, showing men have similar worries to women when exposed to such images. McCabe and McGreevy (2011) found a major influence for men to lose weight were messages in the media, while the main factor for men to build muscle mass came from their peers, highlighting the importance of sociocultural influences on adult male behaviour in changing their body image. These findings were reiterated by Morgan and Arcelus (2009), who found external influences such as the media and social clubs were important to men, and may have a direct bearing on their self-image.

However, while media can potentially have a negative effect on people, it is dependent upon the framing of the message and how it is interpreted. Regarding EDs, Cooperman (2000) highlighted the importance of health promotion. Her study, focusing on males with EDs, found that a local media article highlighting the existence of male EDs resulted in a rise in referrals to services in that particular area. Raising awareness of male EDs may also lead to a reduction in stigma (Morris, 2006). The media's portrayal of EDs, while improving over time, still has the potential to create a barrier for sufferers (Beat, 2011a; Beat, 2011b). Cooperman's (2000) study indicated that there were still many barriers to overcome, particularly for men, but the lack of change since her study remains evident today (Lyons et al., 2019).

## Literature Review

Our literature review was designed to look specifically for published academic research with a focus on men who experienced EDs. Searching for studies published from January 2000 to December 2016, 61 studies were found. Of those identified, 17 were qualitative, 13 of these being case studies, with 10 focusing on a single male. There was a dearth of studies looking at the lived experiences of men with anorexia per se, with only three focusing on lived experiences relating to clinical environments (Button & Warren, 2001; Räisänen & Hunt, 2014; Robinson et al., 2012).

The number of published studies (Figure 7.1) was consistent over the sixteen-year period, the exceptions being 2012 and 2014, when there were spikes in publications related to the topic. Cooperman (2000) called for greater research into male EDs, but this appeared to go unheeded, with both Mitchison et al. (2013) and Räisänen and Hunt (2014) calling for the same action thirteen and fourteen years later.

Over half the research identified came from the USA (22 studies) and the UK (10 studies). However, apart from single case studies from China, Iraq and the UAE, the remaining studies came from countries which are European or

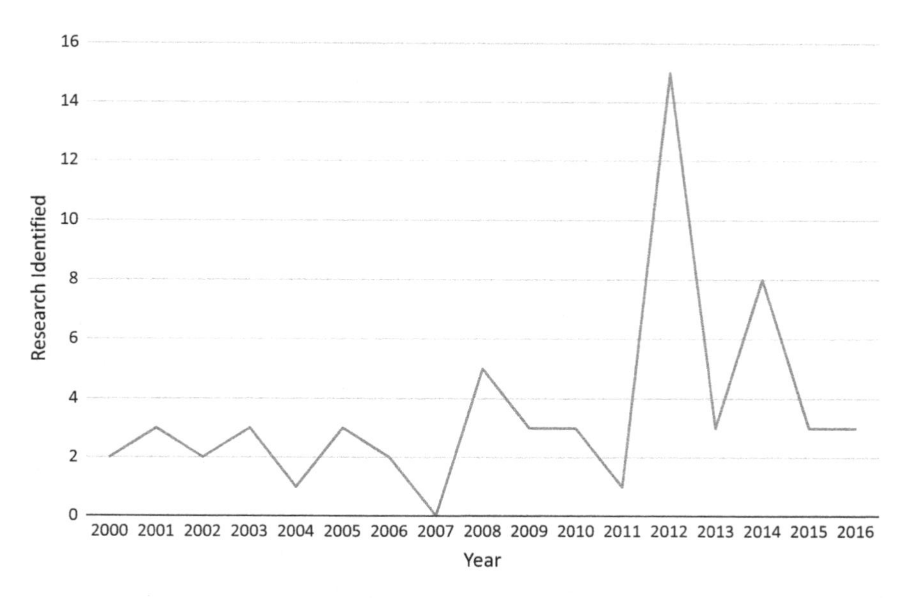


**Figure 7.1** Research studies: with a focus on male anorexia (January 2000–December 2016)

Western facing. Anorexia has traditionally been thought of as a 'Western' illness, and consequentially academics have cited Western culture for the growth of EDs outside of the Western world (Becker et al., 2002; Musaiger et al., 2014; Tong et al., 2005; Younis & Ali, 2012).

## Methodology

This research was based on an interpretivist philosophy, the researchers trying to remain as objective as possible, while recognizing the collecting of lived experiences may be affected by our prior experiences; specifically, with one of the researchers having experienced anorexia first-hand. From the outset, the researchers accepted their own positions in relation to male EDs and the temporal telling of the participants' stories and experience. Using this self-knowledge, and paying attention to the way in which participants told their stories, ensured trustworthiness and authenticity when analysing data and presenting findings. Foregrounding participants' experiences over our own was achieved by being open with each other about our interpretations of the interviews and erring on the side of caution in our conclusions, evidencing them within the context of available academic literature.

The men's stories and experiences were gathered using narrative inquiry. Narrative interview techniques work on the principle of allowing participants to tell their stories with the minimum of restrictions (Etherington, 2011), these being only standard ethical flags. Story telling allowed the men to organize and contextualize their experience, make sense of life events and share associated emotions, thoughts and beliefs (Fraser, 2004). Using narrative in this study facilitated men who had direct experience of EDs to express and contextualize their own stories in their own words.

## *Research structure*

Of the eight men interviewed, six asked for a telephone interview (the reason given for this was that it cut down on travel), one local man preferred a face-to-face interview, and one would only do his via email. The average interview length was one hour and twenty minutes. The technique allowed the men to control the discourse and attribute their own meanings when articulating their experiences (Gephart, 1999).

While the email interview was not as successful as the face-to-face and telephone interviews, in terms of the given themes being reduced to short one-sentence answers, it did offer benefit to the participant. It gave the participant a greater level of anonymity, and the ability to reflect and edit what he shared. While this approach did require the researcher to ask a lot of follow-up questions and came at the cost of spontaneity, it does protect the participant and may be more of an ethical consideration when dealing with vulnerable people with mental health issues.

## *Ethical considerations*

The study was guided by the Declaration of Helsinki's (WHO, 2013) policy on research involving human participants, the code of the Association of Internet Researchers (Ess, 2002) and Markham and Buchanan's (2012) recommendations to the Association of Internet Researchers for dealing with online communications. The UK Data Protection Act was observed in relation to storing information and anonymity, the latter only being broken in extreme circumstances such as a threat or danger to the participant/someone else. Ethical approval was granted by the University of Salford, and Beat, whose website advertised the study.

### *Research sample*

Inclusion criteria to take part in the study was deliberately simple:

1) Male
2) Over eighteen
3) Have been diagnosed or self-diagnosed with anorexia or an atypical form such as eating disorders not otherwise specified (EDNOS) (APA, 2013)
4) Able to speak English

Theoretical Sampling was the main approach taken to try to recruit participants. Two UK eating disorder charities were canvased for help; Beat (the UK's largest eating disorder charity) and Men Get Eating Disorders Too (MENGET) (at the time of the study the UK's only male-specific eating disorders charity). Both charities agreed to share the study details and Beat advertised it on their website's research section, social media and contacted people on a database of potential participants. There was no evidence of MENGET advertising the study. All participants referred to Beat as the source for their participation.

## Findings

### *Media portrayals of male EDs*

All participants were asked about their thoughts on media portrayals of EDs. While some of them had direct experience of working with media by sharing their experiences, others had indirect interactions, such as at conferences. In 2011, Beat issued a set of guidelines to the media, requesting them not to use lowest weight, BMI, actual food intake and shocking imagery in their reports. The guidelines were not intended to impose on media freedom, but rather help journalists resolve reporting dilemmas, reduce stigma associated with EDs and improve public understanding of these complex disorders (Beat, 2011a; Beat, 2011b). However, study participants shared stories of how encounters with media showed no evidence of the guidelines being heeded.

When asked about male portrayals of EDs in the media, Henry perhaps summed up the feelings of all of the men: 'If they're portrayed at all! I just don't see it, I really really don't.' He did add that when he had seen male portrayals

**Table 7.1** Demographic breakdown of the men interviewed

| | *Stephen* | *Alan* | *Richard* | *Henry* | *Russell* | *Kevin* | *Michael* |
|---|---|---|---|---|---|---|---|
| Age | 23 | 24 | 25 | 27 | 31 | 34 | 34 |
| Believed onset | 14 | 17 | 17 | 16 | 27 | 15 | 15 |
| Ethnicity | White | White | White | White | White | White | White |
| Sexuality | Hetero | Gay | Gay | Hetero | Hetero | Bisexual | Hetero |
| Classification | Anorexia | Anorexia | Anorexia | Anorexia | Anorexia | Anorexia | Anorexia |
| ED behaviours | | | | | | | |
| Food restriction | Yes | Yes | Yes | Yes | Yes | Yes | Yes |
| Vomiting | | Yes | Yes | | | Yes | |
| Laxative use | | Yes | Yes | Yes | | | |
| Excessive exercise | | Yes | Yes | Yes | Yes | Yes | Yes |
| Diet pills | | Yes | | | | | |
| Amphetamines | | Yes | | | | | |

of EDs, they seemed to only involve young men and sport, and were simplified into a good news story of anguish with a happy ending, the ED being equated to a 'tap which can be turned on and off'.

Stephen believed portrayals of men with EDs were 'pretty much non-existent'. He talked of seeing images of super skinny or bulked up men. This was echoed by Russell, who reiterated stories of the 'masculine chap down the gym desperate for a body, a super body'. Stephen felt that despite the work of the ED charities, the media remain uninterested in EDs in men.

As with Henry and Stephen, Kevin highlighted a lack of representation of men with EDs in the media. Kevin stated, 'I can't think off the top of my head of ever seeing a fictional representation of a man with an eating disorder.' Richard did cite a fictional case of EDs in the UK media via the soap-opera *Hollyoaks*. However, Kevin's point is valid, as researchers often concentrate on non-fictional stories, while many people's sources of capital are from fictional sources, such as soap-operas, reality TV, films and so on.

Richard felt the media all too often focus on the story and not how the person within the story may be affected. He cited a BBC journalist speaking at a parliamentary conference, whom he quoted as saying that she was 'not interested about the person in a story'. Richard said:

> There was quite a few angry people in the [Scottish] parliament conference on that day, including myself, but she writes articles on people with health issues. They involve people, not celebrities, normal people going about their daily lives, who have told their stories for no money [...] ruining people's reputations for putting it out there, but the actual eating disorder itself they sensationalise it. It's all about the bones showing.

### *The 16-year-old girl sitting in the corner shaking at the thought of a lettuce leaf*

One of the main stereotypical pictures of anorexia that several of the men referred to in various guises was of a teenage girl picking at food. This stereotypical picture is unhelpful to people who do not fit this image. Russell referred to this image, stating: 'I'm not the 16-year-old [girl] sitting in the corner shaking at the thought of a lettuce leaf.'

Kevin shared what he believed to be a stereotypical view of anorexia: 'an issue of teenage girls who've read too many copies of *Heat* magazine'. This, he believed, was not helpful as it is a label that does not fit many women, let alone men, serving only to stigmatize and shame those who do not fit the stereotype. Kevin said: 'I think it certainly made it harder for me. Feeling quite ashamed about having it [ED] and not wanting to talk about it. Part of that, maybe not consciously, but unconsciously, was shame of being a thirty-year-old bloke with a teenage girls' disease.'

Alan believed media portrayals of EDs in general are negative and patronizing, with a focus on bad choices and shocking the audience with images of severe weight loss. Alan said: 'they do need to portray not just dumb little girls who want to sit in a small skirt and want to look like Giselle, to over simplify it, people don't yet know enough about how detailed it is.' Alan believed society largely ignore all mental health issues, and particularly EDs: 'It's a very British stiff upper lip, like kind of ignoring it, [as if] it doesn't quite exist.'

The men who had experienced group treatment were at pains to state that the stereotype they had witnessed in the media—young, female teenagers—was harmful to many more people than just themselves, citing older women as being commonly marginalized. Henry felt that only 10–15% of the people he had met with an ED fitted the traditional stereotype.

### *Working with the media*

The main issue for the men who directly shared their story with media outlets was the lack of knowledge or adherence to Beat's (2011a, 2011b) guidelines. Collectively the men could understand the need to sensationalize in order for the story to meet the needs of the media outlet, i.e., people buying papers, watching TV, and so on; however, there was a feeling that at times they were overlooked as individuals with feelings and emotions.

Michael had tried to improve the awareness of male EDs by sharing his story; writing a book, as well as giving interviews about his experiences. While it was clear he had given multiple interviews, he spoke of a negative experience when working with a magazine who asked him for any photographs of when he was ill. Michael said: 'That annoys the hell out of me because they're not particularly interested when I say "no I haven't but do you want to hear why I haven't?"' What he was asked for was not in keeping with Beat's guidelines.

Richard had multiple experiences similar to Michael, stating that he was asked by one journalist for a picture of him at his 'most ill'. He responded by saying, 'When I was ill the last thing I wanted to do was sit and take a picture of myself in a hospital bed thinking the *Daily Mirror* might need this.' Richard was rejected by another media outlet because the images he did send with his story were 'not revealing enough'. He interpreted this as them not being shocking enough to sell his story to their audience, which he believed could reinforce the negative stereotypes of EDs. In another interview, Richard told of how the journalist did not ask about his feelings or what he believed were the triggers to his ED, but focused on weight, making statements such as 'so you were this weight and that weight' and 'oh my god that's such a lot of weight you've lost'. Richard did not know if the journalist was fishing for information, had a lack of understanding about anorexia, or if this was just a normal human reaction to his story.

The most graphic experience Richard shared was about a sensationalist headline being used by a media outlet. This referred to his pre-anorexia obesity and his closeness to death from the illness and its complications. The headline left Richard 'fuming'. Richard reflected upon his experiences of the media by saying: 'My experience I was telling was personal to me. They [the media] didn't care about that, they wanted a headline grabbing story to glamorize pictures of my bones sticking out. I wasn't prepared to do it and I still won't do it.'

Alan gave an interview for a national media source which had been set up by Beat. Alan stated the interviewer was not aware of and/or ignored the media guidelines published by Beat. Alan stated: 'This guy started asking me about what exact weight did I get down to, and I refused to do it, but he kicked off. I should have had an apology about that—I was like Beat should have told you about this, I'm not going to discuss it.'

Alan believed he had not been protected by Beat, who had set the interview up, and although he understood that the journalist could have simply ignored Beat's guidelines, he was unhappy that he never received an apology. Such disrespect could compromise the mental health of a more vulnerable person.

## *Male anorexia on the internet*

### *Eating disorder charities, their websites and interactions*

At the time of the interviews (2015), there were more charities in the UK but the participants, with the exception of Richard, only spoke of Beat and MENGET; the two UK charities with the largest profile and most media coverage. The lack of discussion about other charities could indicate potential issues. Firstly, they are small and do not get the same attention as the larger charities. Secondly, they do not have the same fiscal resources as the larger charities, as they cannot access mainstream media and funding. Richard, who volunteered for various charities before setting up his own charity, felt the poor relationship between Beat and MENGET was not helping people with EDs. He stated: 'I can't be bothered with that and a lot of the organization's people can't be bothered with that, you come in to help people, not get involved with politics.' Richard may be naïve to think the two charities would work well with each other, given they are both competing for funding, and MENGET was started by the former high-profile Beat activist, Sam Thomas.

Richard's opinion about friction between the charities is valid and has been noted within the public domain. In 2014, Beat commissioned a video advert to highlight the problems men have in talking about EDs. The advert was shocking, showing a man in a pub, vomiting his testicles onto the table in front of his friends. At previews the video shocked people and was pulled before it went 'live'. However, Sam Thomas (2014), the founder of MENGET, commented:

> We need to stop this atrocious video before it causes real and very serious damage. I will not stand for it and nor will I tolerate this ignorance against male eating disorders or masculinity. Beat have clearly lost their way on this one, prioritising the 'brand' over the cause and people affected.

Sam Thomas was not the only one shocked by this; Michael commented on the video during his interview. However, Thomas's words about Beat 'losing its way' and the charity's focus on 'brand' clearly demonstrates the tensions Richard alluded to. The focus on brand which Sam Thomas alluded to was echoed in participants' interviews. There was a feeling among the men that the appearance of Beat's website was female-focused. While the men accepted this as fair, due to EDs being more prominent among women, since the interviews, Beat's website has been redesigned and is now more neutral in appearance.

One area where the men felt let down related to the corporate nature of Beat's website and their verbal/written interactions with the charity. Russell spoke of asking the charity for a Beat-branded vest to wear when taking part in a fun run. After being told to ask for a vest via email, Richard said:

> Three weeks later they sent me a reply back saying if I make a donation they will supply one … I always feel they are actually doing you a favour by

> talking to you and you don't feel that supported … I've always felt with Beat that they are more of a business brand than a charity.

Russell went on to say: 'I will bend over backwards to help raise money for them, but I just don't feel quite as connected to them because I don't trust them as much as I do someone like MENGET.'

This corporate nature is partially due to the size of the charity and its success over time. In order to operate, it needs to take a business-like approach, having to pay full-time staff and large administration costs. This can be a major cause of public distrust in charities; the charity having to raise lots of money to be economically viable, before it can support those it aims to support (Charity Commission, 2016). Richard referred to Beat as a 'money whore'.

The men felt more kinship with MENGET because it was male-specific. However, they commented on its size and location (Brighton, south-east the UK) being remote from them and therefore, as with Beat, it was only able to provide internet information rather than support. Richard believed MENGET centred too much on its founder, the public face in media interviews, removing opportunities from other volunteers such as himself. While Russell believed Beat was 'faceless' and 'too large', Kevin suggested MENGET was 'too small' to be worth interacting with. Richard felt MENGET was in some ways a self-promotion tool for the founder. These comments are interesting and highlight the complexity of how charitable organizations raise the profile of who or what they represent, while at the same time meeting the needs of the diverse population they are set up to serve.

Generally, the men were pleased that some charities are trying to raise awareness of EDs, but they were also critical of the work they did for men. One man was so disappointed at the lack of coverage in his geographical area that he set up his own charity and website. Living in the north-west of England, Henry expressed similar concerns. Talking about Beat, he stated: 'major issue is that it's so South-East central [Beat is located in Norwich]. I don't think that there's any reach.' Since the study ended, the charities have been able to provide better full-time outreach, including Beat opening an office in Scotland. But it perhaps shows the limitations; while websites and digital communication offer potential for global reach in providing general information, there is less focus on more interpersonal interactions which are often beneficial for health. Although charities do offer, where possible, local drop-in groups, the men who took part in this study felt they were not helpful due to a focus on women.

## *Social media*

As previously discussed, the men who responded to the study advertisements were signposted by the charity Beat. The largest uptake was after the charity advertised the study on social media, with the men citing Beat's Facebook page as their source of recruitment, rather than the charity's website or potential participant database. However, when asked about media portrayals and eating disorder charities, at no point did the men talk about their use of social media. This was surprising, considering many of them had seen and acted upon a post on social media to take part in the study. All interviewees made limited mention of Facebook and/or Twitter, usually with negative connotations. Michael spoke of Facebook, stating:

> When I see people on Facebook that I was at university with and they are all going to each other's weddings and talking about what happened back in university and I'm like that really doesn't mean anything to me as I wasn't there. Physically I was there, but mentally I was off in anorexia land, a bit just passing by to be honest.

As a naturally shy person, Michael recognized, with hindsight, that his anorexia and his behaviours prevented him from integrating with the other people at university. He was concentrating on food restriction and exercising; as such, even though he was present, he missed out on living. A situation Bowen and Waller (see this volume) could empathize with.

Russell was the only man to mention Twitter. He used this as an aid to find information about losing weight, finding and downloading a fitness-tracking app (MyFitnessPal), which he initially used as a tool to lose weight and get fit. Unfortunately, his usage of the app morphed into misuse, and he was able to compete against the app's goals to lose unhealthy amounts of weight, whilst ignoring inbuilt app warnings. Russell rationalized that every calorie he saved from food or burnt through exercise was a positive:

> By the time you add that all up [calories] at the end of the week you're thinking that's one and half days of food that I haven't eaten, but your brain is saying that's brilliant; because it has set this limit and you're underneath it.

Russell's behaviours focused around the app could not continue indefinitely. He stated:

> My entire life was revolving around mass exercise to do this app and it got more and more nuts, and it got to the point where I just literally said I've got to stop because my body can't. I was doing an hour's row every day and my body was just going I can't row for an hour everyday anymore; I don't have the strength or the muscle to do it.

It could be suggested that Russell's rigidity and his need to abide by rules would predispose the app to becoming an instrument by which he could exercise his control, but one that ultimately had the potential to control him. Given research on perfectionism (Treasure, 2005) and rigidity (Murray et al., 2014) in relation to anorexia, it is not surpsing that a weight managment app could be misused in such a way by those predisposed to anorexia (see Eikey et al., this volume).

### *Internet forums/blogging*

As with social media, it was perhaps surprising that the men did not readily engage in using forums. Only Henry and Richard spoke about using forums and blogging, although one of the other men did publish his experiences in book form. Henry shared that he had been quite active in blogging and on forums, but this was related to general mental health. However, Henry stepped away from this because he feared for his own health:

> The communities were quite toxic, it felt dangerous … I think that you can spend time with people, people with mental illnesses and it can become, I'm trying to think the right words, draining and distracting to your own health.

Henry's comments demonstrate how, when at a low point in his life, other people's problems affected him. As a way of protecting himself, Henry spoke of keeping his distance and his privacy in order to feel safe and comfortable. Richard had mixed experiences with forums. He spoke positively about being able to use the MENGET forum anonymously until he felt confident enough about being open with his name. He was also able to use it to gain information and support that he was not able to get from the health services. However, he also used pro-anorexia forums (described in the next section) which enabled him to implement behaviours which later became damaging to his health.

### *Pro-anorexia and thinspiration websites/forums*

Richard was the only man to share his experiences of using pro-anorexia or thinspiration websites and forums. Upon deciding to lose weight and a friend recommending websites, Richard found that he started to lose weight. Richard's narrative demonstrates how this became insidious, stating: 'Little did I know at that time that they were thinspiration websites and full of internet trolls … they were encouraging really extreme diets.' Reflecting upon Richard's statement, it is difficult not to think, 'How could you not see it was a pro-anorexia site?' However, when considering his vulnerability, lack of confidence and his desperation to lose weight, coupled with lack of knowledge about anorexia in men and pro-anorexia websites, it is easy to understand how someone could be sucked into a site, especially if it is well designed, before they realize what it is.

In contrast, Richard could have been 'so desperate to lose the weight' that he unconsciously ignored any danger signals, or perhaps there was cognitive dissonance. Richard's descriptions of the imagery (danger signs) he saw, which was promoted by the site, included a skeletal male physique. This was reinforced with images 'of young boys and young adolescent males with their hip-bones sticking out'. He added that slogans were used such as 'eating is cheating', and animations would change letters and words to reinforce messages. For example, the word 'eat' would change into 'fat' with the letters 'e' and 'f' changing.

As Richard lost weight, he became 'quite euphoric' and 'thought this is quite good'. He also received positive affirmation from other users on the sites and acquiesced to more and more extreme measures to lose weight, partially because he was losing weight and partially because he was pleasing his 'friends' on the sites. Richard stated:

> I thought that people in the on-line chat rooms were genuine friends at the time, but then they started getting nasty. The more weight I lost it wasn't good enough for them and they wanted more, and they wanted double and they wanted it quicker and they were egging me on.

Worryingly, and at the time of writing this chapter (2020), a simple search of the internet using the words 'pro anorexia' found several sites offering thinspiration tips presented as respectable ways of losing weight. The tips are written in a way that portrays the advice as originating via the NHS. It is understandable how someone who is already vulnerable can take on board some of the tips without question.

### *Ignorance isn't bliss: the need for greater awareness*

One of the most interesting outcomes of our study was that only two of the men interviewed (Kevin and Russell) recognized their symptoms before diagnosis; both were in their late twenties when seeking help. The other men spoke of shock when being diagnosed with anorexia, a phenomenon both Cooperman (2000) and Paterson (2007) identified. This lack of knowledge about EDs in men is worrying. The narratives of the five men who did not recognize their symptoms told, to a greater or lesser degree, the same story; a reduction of, a preoccupation with, and ways to avoid food, a marked increase in exercise, being overweight and lacking confidence. In hindsight, it is surprising the men did not recognize the signs of an ED; however, it is likely they did not consider it as they had probably never heard of, read about or seen a man diagnosed with an ED.

Michael eloquently illustrated this when he said:

> I was getting worse, so I knew something wasn't quite right. I could see the weight going down and I had it; there were all these posters up around university, and I don't think anyone believes me when I say this, and it was all about meningitis and there were all these symptoms; 'are you feeling really tired? Is your skin looking terribly?' And I was getting quite worried that I had meningitis or something … and within five minutes the doctor was mentioning the word anorexia which was the first time it had ever occurred to me.

When speaking of his diagnosis, Stephen said: 'I was very upset, but in some ways relieved as it finally made everything make sense.' Henry, seeking treatment during his first year at university, said, 'I didn't know what was wrong with me, there was no kind of … I was just in a state. I don't think I consciously like went [to the GP] because I was worried about eating disorders.'

Richard woke in a hospital room after collapsing in his room at university; he said the last thing he remembered before collapsing was vomiting and passing blood in his urine. He was diagnosed with gall bladder and pancreatic problems caused by his weight loss through anorexia. This, he said, was the first time he had ever thought about anorexia. Russell perhaps spoke for many of the men, saying that before he experienced anorexia, he had 'never even thought about it. I will hold my hands up and say that to me anorexia was the 16-year-old skinny girl', indicating how much needs to be done to build awareness of male EDs.

The lack of experience and survivor stories was an issue raised during the interviews. The men felt this was harmful, as stories about eating disorders focused solely on the positives and recovery, without recognizing the negative experiences people go through. There was consensus that if these stories were shared, they might help people feel less isolated when/if they encounter negative experiences.

## Discussion

### *Media portrayals*

The fact that most of the men did not recognize their symptoms would suggest a lack of information about anorexia in men in the public consciousness. The men felt there were few well-publicized examples of males with EDs. Although there are some high-profile men who have said they have had an eating order—Elton John (bulimia, singer), John Prescott (bulimia, the UK politician), David Coulthard (bulimia, racing driver), Andrew Flintoff (bulimia, cricketer), Christopher Eccleston (anorexia, actor)—there is a natural scepticism, as often these claims are associated with a book, TV programme, film or record launch. Those of the men who had worked with media agencies to improve knowledge all had negative experiences, with sensationalism and stereotypes being the main issues. They called for greater understanding and an approach which saw them as humans rather than media sensationalized stories. However, Cooperman (2000) affirmed that local media stories in the geographical area where she was studying did show an increase in men coming forward.

### *Seeing the other side*

But would removing sensationalism and stereotypes actually help men? With the growth of the internet, sensationalism and clickbait allow stories to stand out, attract readers, webpage clicks and advertising. In the UK, the Trinity Mirror group evaluated their journalists' performance based upon how many webpage clicks their stories received (Frampton, 2015). Under these conditions, there is a legitimate argument to suggest that if the ED community insisted upon stories being presented that lack sensationalism, the number of views would drop, potentially leading to them not being covered in the future. This could subsequently lead to eating disorders taking a backseat in being recognized as genuine illnesses that people need help to address. Michael suggested that when he refused to share images of himself at his most ill, media outlets were less interested in his story. It is an interesting paradox: a requirement for sensationalized stories that will reach the masses versus factual and informative communication that addresses the needs of the few.

## Conclusion

One of the main areas where media, social media and digital technology can be used is in raising awareness that EDs can affect anyone at any age. Only two of the men interviewed had any inclination before their diagnosis that the symptoms they were experiencing could be an ED. However, with hindsight, six of the seven men acknowledged that the onset of their ED occurred between the ages of 14 and 17. This is one demographic that could be easily targeted through use of media in schools.

The men participating in this study were all familiar with the promotion of male EDs or at the very least aware of what was going on in the field. The fact that they all came forward to take part indicated a willingness to share their experiences and to improve wider knowledge, which we were thankful for. The men could be considered 'a sample of activists' due to the lack of breadth in our advertising, which was solely through ED charities, and that would be a valid comment. The stories the men shared, specifically in relation to media, indicate that there is a tremendous amount of work needed to increase the awareness of anorexia and EDs in men. Funding for a larger qualitative study of men's experiences with EDs, to continue to inform policy and health and education practice, would be welcome.

## References

Agliata, D., & Tantleff-Dunn, S. (2004). The impact of media exposure on males' body image. *Journal of Social and Clinical Psychology* 23(1): 7–22. https://doi.org/10.1521/jscp.23.1.7.26988

American Psychiatric Association (1994). *Diagnostic and Statistical Manual of Mental Disorders* (DSM-IV). Washington, DC: American Psychiatric Association.

American Psychiatric Association (2013). *Diagnostic and Statistical Manual of Mental Disorders* (DSM-5). Washington, DC: American Psychiatric Association.

Beat. (2011a). Media guidelines for reporting eating disorders. Norwich.

Beat. (2011b). Warning. This picture can seriously damage your health. Norwich.

Becker, A.E, Burwell, R.A., Gilman S.E., Herzog, D.B., & Hamburg, P. (2002). Eating behaviours and attitudes following prolonged exposure to television among ethnic Fijian adolescent girls. *British Journal of Psychiatry* 180: 509–14. https://doi.org/10.1192/bjp.180.6.509

Button, E.J., & Warren, R.L. (2001) Living with anorexia nervosa: the experience of a cohort of sufferers from anorexia nervosa 7.5 years after initial presentation to a specialized eating disorders service. *European Eating Disorders Review* 9(2): 74–96. https://doi.org/10.1002/erv.400

Charity Commission (2016). Public trust and confidence in charities. London: Charity Commission.

Cooperman, J. (2000) Eating disorders in the United Kingdom: review of the provision of health care services for men with eating disorders. Report. Norwich: UK Eating Disorders Association.

Ess, C. (2002) Eating disorder charities. Report. Association of Internet Researchers.

Etherington, K. (2011). Narrative approaches to case studies. Retrieved from: https://www.keele.ac.uk/media/keeleuniversity/facnatsci/schpsych/documents/counselling/conference/5thannual/NarrativeApproachestoCaseStudies.pdf

Frampton, B. (2015). Clickbait: the changing face of online journalism. Retrieved from: https://www.bbc.co.uk/news/uk-wales-34213693

Fraser, H. (2004). Doing narrative research: analysing personal stories line by line. *Qualitative Social Work* 3(2): 179–201. https://doi.org/10.1177/1473325004043383

Freeman, A.C. (2005). Eating disorders in males: a review. *South African Psychiatry Review* 8(2): 58–64. https://doi.org/10.4314/ajpsy.v8i2.30185

Gephart, R. (1999). Paradigms and research methods. *Research Methods Forum* 4.

Griffiths, S., Murray, S.B., & Touyz, S. (2013). Disordered eating and the muscular ideal. *Journal of Eating Disorders* 1: 15. https://doi.org/10.1186/2050-2974-1-15

Hall, S. (1999). Encoding, decoding. In S. During (ed.), *The Cultural Studies Reader* (pp. 507–17). London: Routledge.

Hudson, J.I., Hiripi, E., Pope Jr., H.G., & Kessler, R.C. (2007). The prevalence and correlates of eating disorders in the national comorbidity survey peplication. *Biological Psychiatry* 61(3): 348–58. https://doi.org/10.1016/j.biopsych.2006.03.040

Jones, W.R. & Morgan, J.F. (2010). Eating disorders in men: a review of the literature. *Journal of Public Mental Health* 9(2): 23–31. https://doi.org/10.5042/jpmh.2010.0326

Josselson, R., & Lieblich, A. (eds) (1995). *Interpreting Experience: The Narrative Study of Lives*. London: Sage.

King, D. (2013). Thickening thin narratives: a feminist narrative conceptualization of male anorexia nervosa. *Narrative Works: Issues, Investigations, & Interventions* 3(1): 31–54. https://doi.org/10.7202/1062053ar

Knowles, R. (2011). Rise in men suffering from eating disorders, say GPs. Retrieved from: http://www.bbc.co.uk/newsbeat/14051772

Lacan, J. (2003). *Lacan. Ecrits: A Selection.* (Translated by Alan Sheridan.) London: Routledge.

Lyons, G., McAndrew, S., & Warne, T. (2019). Disappearing in a female world: men's experiences of having an eating disorder [ED] and how it impacts their lives. *Issues in Mental Health Nursing* 40(7): 557–66. https://doi.org/10.1080/01612840.2019.1576815

MacCaughelty, C., Wagner, R., & Rufino, K. (2016). Does being overweight or male increase a patient's risk of not being referred for an eating disorder consult? *International Journal of Eating Disorders* 49(10): 963–66. https://doi.org/10.1002/eat.22556

Marsh, S. (2017). Eating disorders in men rise by 70% in NHS figures. Retrieved from: https://www.theguardian.com/society/2017/jul/31/eating-disorders-in-men-rise-by-70-in-nhs-figures [Accessed 1 August 2017].

Markham, A., & Buchanan, E. (2012). Ethical decision-making and Internet research: recommendations from the AoIR ethics working committee (Version 2.0). Recommendations. Retrieved from: http://www.aoir.org/reports/ethics2.pdf. AoIR Ethics Committee.

McCabe, M.P., & McGreevy, S.J. (2011). Role of media and peers on body change strategies among adult men: is body size important? *European Eating Disorders Review* 19(5): 438–46. https://doi.org/10.1002/erv.1063

Mitchison, D., Mond, J., Slewa-Younan, S., & Hay, P. (2013). Sex differences in health-related quality of life impairment associated with eating disorder features: a general population study. *International Journal of Eating Disorders* 46(4): 375–80. https://doi.org/10.1002/eat.22097

Morgan, J.F., & Arcelus, J. (2009). Body image in gay and straight men: a qualitative study. *European Eating Disorders Review* 17: 435–43. https://doi.org/10.1002/erv.955

Morris, G. (2006). *Mental Health Issues and the Media: An Introduction for Health Professionals*. London: Routledge.

Murray, S.B., Griffiths, S., Rieger, E., & Touyz, S. (2014). A comparison of compulsive exercise in male and female presentations of anorexia nervosa: what is the difference? *Advances in Eating Disorders: Theory, Research and Practice* 2(1): 1–6. https://doi.org/10.1080/21662630.2013.839189

Musaiger, A.O, Al-Mannai, M., & Al-Lalla, O. (2014). Risk of disordered eating attitudes among male adolescents in five Emirates of the United Arab Emirates. *International Journal of Eating Disorders* 47: 898–900. https://doi.org/10.1002/eat.22256

NHS Digital (2013). Hospital episode statistics, admitted patient care, England: 2012–13 [NS]. Retrieved from: http://content.digital.nhs.uk/catalogue/PUB12566

NHS Digital (2020). Hospital episode statistics, admitted patient care, England: 2019–20 [NS]. Retrieved from: https://digital.nhs.uk/data-and-information/publications/statistical/hospital-admitted-patient-care-activity/2019-20

Norris, P., Kern, M., & Just, M. (2003). Introduction: framing terrorism. In P. Norris, M. Kern, & M. Just (eds), *Framing Terrorism: The News Media, Government, and the Public* (pp. 3–27). London: Routledge.

Ousley, L., Cordero, E.D., & White, S. (2008). Eating disorders and body image of undergraduate men. *Journal of American College Health* 56(6): 617–22. https://doi.org/10.3200/jach.56.6.617-622

Paterson, A. (2007). Men's Health Forum. [online]. Retrieved from: http://www.malehealth.co.uk/userpage1.cfm?item_id=1619

Räisänen, U., & Hunt, K. (2014). The role of gendered constructions of eating disorders in delayed help-seeking in men: a qualitative interview study. *BMJ Open* 4(4). https://doi.org/10.1136/bmjopen-2013-004342

Robinson, K.J., Mountford, V.A, & Sperlinger, D.J. (2012). Being men with eating disorders: perspectives of male eating disorder service-users. *Journal of Health Psychology* 18(2): 176–86. https://doi.org/10.1177/1359105312440298

Skolnick, A. (2014). Male anorexia negatively affects treatment for endocrine conditions. Retrieved from: http://media.aace.com/press-release/male-anorexia-negatively-affects-treatment-endocrine-conditions.

Soban, C. (2006). What about the boys? Addressing issues of masculinity within male anorexia nervosa in a feminist theraputic environment. *Journal of Men's Health* 5(3): 251–67. https://doi.org/10.3149/jmh.0503.251

Stice, E., Spangler, D., & Agras, S.W. (2001). Exposure to media-portrayed thin-ideal images adversely affects vulnerable girls: a longitudinal experiment. *Journal of Social and Clinical Psychology* 20(3): 270–88. https://doi.org/10.1521/jscp.20.3.270.22309

Tong, J., Miao, S.J., Wang, J. et al. (2005). Five cases of male eating disorders in central China. *International Journal of Eating Disorders* 37(1): 72–75. https://doi.org/10.1002/eat.20061

Toro, J., Castro, J., Gila, A., & Pombo, C. (2005). Assessment of sociocultural influences on the body shape model in adolescent males with anorexia nervosa. *European Eating Disorders Review* 13: 351–59. https://doi.org/10.1002/erv.650

Treasure, J. (2005). *Anorexia Nervosa: A Survival Guide for Families, Friends and Sufferers*. Hove: Routledge.

Tyre, P. (2005). Fighting anorexia: no one to blame. *Newsweek*. December 5.

World Health Organization (2013). Standards and operational guidance for ethics review of health-related research with human participants. Geneva: WHO.

Younis, M.S., & Ali, L.D. (2012). Adolescent male with anorexia nervosa: a case report from Iraq. *Child and Adolescent Psychiatry and Mental Health* 6(1): 5. https://doi.org/10.1186/1753-2000-6-5

# Part II

# Participatory Media and User-Generated Discourse

# Online Negative Enabling Support Group (ONESG) Theory: Understanding Online Extreme Community Communication Promoting Negative Health Behaviours

*Stephen M. Haas, Nancy A. Jennings and Pamara F. Chang*

## Introduction

Online communication impacts individuals and societies across geographic and temporal boundaries. Approximately four billion people are using the internet worldwide, and in recent years, increases in smartphone ownership have been a driving force in people gaining access to the internet globally (Internet World Stats, 2020). The wide spectrum of diverse users and contexts has prompted scholars from various fields to explore how, why and to what end the internet is used, and studies indicate both positive and negative impact of internet use (Kraut et al., 2002).

Online access to health information has been predominantly viewed as beneficial (Pew Research Center, 2018). Surveys indicate that 80% (93 million) of US Internet users have searched for health-related topics online (Pew Research Center, 2013), and 'estimates indicate that approximately 1 in 5 Internet users in the United States have gone online *to find others with health concerns similar to their own*' (DeAndrea, 2015, p. 147, emphasis added). Online health communities

Stephen M. Haas, Nancy A. Jennings and Pamara F. Chang, 'Chapter 8: Online Negative Enabling Support Group (ONESG) Theory: Understanding Online Extreme Community Communication Promoting Negative Health Behaviours' in: *Eating Disorders in Public Discourse: Exploring Media Representations and Lived Experiences*. University of Exeter Press (2023). 
DOI: 10.47788/PISN2308

offer features and affordances of online interactions that enable people to access others with common health interests, conditions and diseases that foster people's ability to seek advice, express problems and concerns, and to receive feedback and social support from others 24/7—anywhere, anytime. Social media platforms have allowed online users to access diverse social networks to establish and maintain connections that increase perceptions of social support, increase self-esteem and increase a greater sense of wellbeing (Ellison et al., 2007).

Despite benefits, increasing evidence suggests the internet also may be used for negative purposes that consequently may have undesirable or harmful implications, and negative views of the internet have increased (Pew Research Center, 2018). Research has begun to shed light on negative aspects of some online communities—such as flaming, bullying, negative stereotyping (Hinduja & Patchin, 2010), and lack of health information credibility (Wright & Bell, 2003). In addition, hate groups, political extremist groups, and terrorist recruitment communities are increasing their presence online (e.g., McNamee et al., 2010; Torress Soriano, 2012), yet investigation of online extreme communities has received less scholarly attention.

In 2011, Haas, Irr, Jennings and Wagner developed Online Negative Enabling Support Group (ONESG) theory through analysing the communicative message exchanges of members of the online pro-anorexia movement. ONESG theory highlights six primary communication characteristics utilized to promote negative health behaviours and create a sense of community among its online members. The characteristics of ONESG theory offer deeper understanding of the communication that is exchanged in online groups that promote negative health behaviours. Yet, due to space limitations, the original model's conceptualization was limited to one paragraph (p. 51). The goals of this chapter are: (1) to add to the literature through further conceptual development and elaborate the key theoretical propositions of the six ONESG communication characteristics, and (2) to encourage heuristic application of ONESG theory to multiple types of online extreme communities that promote negative health behaviours. We begin with background literature and then move to conceptualization of ONESG theory.

## *Online extreme communities*

Online extreme communities consist of groups where 'views considered extreme or unacceptable to the mainstream can be expressed relatively freely, with online communities often formed by those who share similar opinions' (Bell, 2007, p. 449). In other words, online, groups of like-minded individuals can exchange ideas, opinions and beliefs viewed as negative, taboo or potentially harmful offline and receive positive validation that magnifies acceptance of the ideas among the online group members. The internet promotes the ability to create and manage one's messages through synchronous or asynchronous interactions, which can allow individuals to manipulate and manage their meanings, as well as manipulate their identity and self-presentation, more easily than in offline face-to-face (FTF) encounters (Attrill, 2015). Information manipulation theory (McCornack, 1992), based on Grice's four maxims, posits that it is common in conversations to manipulate: (1) quantity (how much information), (2) quality (how truthful), (3) relevance (is it on topic?) and (4) clarity (how ambiguous?) of the information we reveal to others, depending on many factors, such as potential risk of damage to relationships, risk of embarrassment and creation of a negative self-image. Walther (1996) proposed that the internet allows even greater opportunity for information manipulation. Feelings of freedom from social norms and constraints that often prevent the expression of extreme ideas in everyday FTF encounters often are not present.

According to Brown and Levinson's politeness theory (1987), when people interact FTF, there are common expectations and social norms for behaviour, topic appropriateness and for individuals to aid each other in maintaining a positive image or 'face'. This mutual 'face work' is accomplished by avoiding negative self or other criticism, and avoiding negative or extreme topics in general that might result in conflict and potential for 'loss of face' by one or both parties (Sifanou, 2012). Walther (1996) highlights that, online, the ability to seek out 'like-minded individuals' (i.e., people who share common ideals, beliefs, values, experiences and goals) circumvents common interaction norms and creates the potential for extreme ideas to flourish, be perpetuated and expanded upon, and even spiral out of control. He also argued that message senders and receivers are more likely to idealize others online, allowing for what he termed an 'Intensification Feedback Loop' (p. 27)—where like-minded individuals receive positive feedback about their extreme ideas, creating the potential for those ideas to expand and become even more toxic. Walther (1996) proposed that while the internet is a place of 'reduced cues' (i.e., lacking important nonverbal visual and tonal properties of FTF interactions), people may actually engage in more 'hyperpersonal' communication online; that is, they may provide more personal and deeper self-disclosure than in FTF encounters. The internet allows for freedom of expression of people's innermost thoughts with potentially low personal risk or fear of retribution.

### *Online negative health behaviour promotion*

Online negative health behaviour promotion is thriving, and there is an increasing need to understand the communication exchanged in online extreme communities that promote negative health behaviours (Bell, 2007). The internet circumvents many barriers to the development of community such as physical location and temporal constraints. The pro-anorexia movement is one online community where individuals promote anorexic health behaviours (also see Lueders, this volume). Scholars have studied this context and illuminated communication exchanged in this extreme community where radical views of health are expressed that the larger 'non-community members' (e.g., caregivers, physicians, family) likely judge to be harmful. Through analysis of the communication characteristics and strategies of online messages exchanged on pro-anorexia public websites and forums, Haas et al. (2011) developed a grounded Online Negative Enabling Support Group (ONESG) model. While the model emerged from online health communication messages exchanged with the purpose of offering social support in promotion of anorexic behaviours (young women aged 13–26), we propose that the characteristics discovered have the potential to advance understanding of other online communities that promote negative health behaviours (e.g., self-injury, drugs or alcohol promotion, violence and so on). Also, we theorize that these communication characteristics and strategies may be fundamental to understanding the creation and growth of many other types of extreme ONESGs beyond anorexia (e.g., hate groups, terrorist groups and so on). Haas et al.'s (2011) original explanation of the ONESG model was underdeveloped (p. 51). The goal here is to further conceptualize the core communication principles and offer propositions that clearly delineate ONESG theory. We also theorize about areas beyond pro-anorexia where the theory has potential for application in other types of online extreme communities. Finally, we discuss implications and suggestions for future research on ONESGs.

## Online Negative Enabling Support Group (ONESG) Theory: Conceptualizations and Theoretical Propositions

ONESG theory (Haas et al., 2011) emerged from research examining public pro-anorexia websites, blogs and online forums (*N* = 1,200 messages). The pro-anorexia (or pro-ana) online movement involves those who advocate that anorexia is not a mental health condition, but rather a 'lifestyle choice' (see Lueders, this volume; Mulveen & Hepworth, 2006). Thriving on an anti-recovery theme, pro-ana movement members exchange online advice, counselling and support in maintaining the choice to be anorexic (Schmidt & Treasure, 2006), and vehemently denounce a victim mentality that they are mentally ill or unsound (see Cariola, this volume; Shade, 2003). Pro-ana members' families often experience distress and frustration from dealing with difficult health behaviours, feelings of shame, loss and social isolation, as well as feelings of guilt (Treasure et al., 2001). With these types of tensions and reduced support expectations from those close to them, pro-anas may seek like-minded individuals online to socialize and interact with those who support their 'lifestyle choice.'

Six core communication characteristics emerged from Haas et al.'s (2011) grounded thematic analysis that may be useful beyond the pro-anorexia context to explain the communication employed in other types of online negative enabling groups that co-construct and support extreme online communities. The six communication characteristics which function together to form ONESG theory are: (1) exchange of mediated anonymous disclosures, (2) co-construction of negative health behaviours as positive behaviours, (3) expression of tips and techniques to enact negative behaviours, (4) uncontested self or other negative expressions, (5) expression of cohesion and group encouragement and (6) reconstructing mediated weak ties into strong tie support. In the following sections, each online communication characteristic is explained and further conceptualized. Application to other types of online groups that ONESG theory may aid in conceptualizing and furthering understanding of communication exchanges are theorized.

### *Exchange of mediated anonymous disclosures*

One of the primary communication features of online venues is anonymity. Anonymity is defined as 'the inability of others to identify an individual or for others to identify one's self. This may be within a large social context, such as a crowd, or in a smaller context, such as two-person communication over the Internet' (Christopherson, 2007, p. 3040). More specifically, anonymity exists on a continuum/spectrum, and two types of anonymity most relevant to computer-mediated communication research are discursive and visual anonymity (Qian & Scott, 2007). Discursive anonymity refers to messages that cannot be linked to a specific source (Qian & Scott, 2007). Individuals online can specifically manage their level of discursive anonymity through the use of identity management cues (i.e., person's name, age, location, school, employer and so on) or information identified on profiles (Viégas, 2005). Visual anonymity refers to the extent to which people can see and/or hear the individual online, often managed through their display of pictures, icons, videos and the like (Qian & Scott, 2007). Anonymity online has been found to result in decreased inhibitions (Suler, 2004), increased intimate levels of self-disclosure (Bargh et al., 2002), deindividuation (Christopherson, 2007) and increased levels of embarrassing or stigmatizing self-disclosures (Rains, 2014), especially in online health contexts and support groups (e.g., Andalibi et al., 2016; DeAndrea, 2015; De Choudhury & Kıcıman, 2017; Leavitt, 2015).

Anonymity can be a mechanism that influences social interactions online and further drives uninhibited self-expression and disclosures (Wright & Miller, 2010), all of which are illuminated within an ONESG. Individuals have the ability to deindividuate (Christopherson, 2007) by altering their degree of anonymity when they engage with others online, and often, this may increase online what is perceived as inappropriate or uncharacteristic behaviours in FTF contexts (Eastwick & Gardner, 2009). These behaviours can be attributed to cyberdisinhibition, which posits that, due to anonymity, individuals have the freedom to join and leave online communities when they want. This may lead individuals to behave in ways that contradict normative behaviours. Within an ONESG, cyberdisinhibition is prevalent and is demonstrated through the expression of extreme health-related ideas, opinions and values that individuals feel they could not express offline for fear of negative judgement, stigmatization and social sanctions. In addition, the social identity and deindividuation effects (SIDE) model helps explain the effects of collective cyberdisinhibition. SIDE proposes that individuals who interact anonymously exhibit deindividuation behaviour that may be inconsistent with their offline social and group identity (Lea & Spears, 1992; Spears et al., 2002). SIDE posits that online anonymity reduces accountability and leads to deindividuation and depersonalization in computer-mediated communication. Therefore, individuals can be socially influenced online to express common group attitudes and consequently adopt and partake in negative health behaviours (e.g., self-injury encouragement sites) (Whitlock, 2010).

The potential for ONESGs to perpetuate extreme ideas underscores Walther's (1996) notion of an 'Intensification Feedback Loop' by expressing extreme ideas through computer-mediated communication channels where users are able to find support and expand the reach of these ideas through the validation of online feedback. The interplay of anonymity, cyberdisinhibition, deindividuation and receipt of social validation within ONESGs functions to intensify extreme ideas and behaviour promotion within the community. These dynamics may be applicable to various intensive online communities. For example, the exchange of mediated anonymous disclosures enables 'toxic technocultures' where subcultures are created online and focus on the implicit or explicit harassment of individuals; these toxic technocultures, fostered by anonymity, thrive in online platforms like 4chan, 8chan and Reddit (Massanari, 2015). Features of these platforms that enable anonymity (e.g., throwaway accounts) (Leavitt, 2015) can further drive individuals to engage in and encourage negative health enabling behaviours ranging from self-injury and cutting behaviours (Whitlock, 2010) to suicidal ideation and live stream suicides (De Choudhury & Kıcıman, 2017; Westerlund et al., 2015). Therefore, online anonymity is a key foundational component to the emergence of ONESGs.

Proposition 1: Exchange of mediated anonymous disclosures—ONESG members utilize online anonymity (the ability to engage in unidentifiable communication in the online environment) to express and support enactment of extreme negative health behaviours.

### *Co-construction of negative health behaviours as positive behaviours*

Another central communication characteristic of ONESGs is the desire to reconstruct negative and potentially harmful health behaviours into positive behaviours worthy of enactment. Through the exchange of online messages, these groups promote negative health behaviours in a way that normalizes the behaviours into perceived positive actions. In other contexts, extreme anti-abortion ONESGs may rationalize encouragement of members to murder physicians who perform abortion procedures by applying Machiavellian principles that the ends (which they judge as positive) justify the means (even if negative behaviours are enacted to achieve the group's goals). ONESGs reframe negative, dangerous and even deadly behaviours into positive behaviours to be enacted.

Several seminal linguistic theories are foundational to the communicative social construction of ONESGs. For instance, linguistic determinism theory (Wittgenstein, 1922) asserts that language not only reflects and shapes reality, but also constrains human perceptions. Similarly, Benjamin Lee Whorf, co-creator of the Sapir-Whorf Hypothesis, was an early sociolinguist who recognized that language and symbol use (e.g., labels) shape perception (Carroll, 1956). The linguistic referents and labels that we assign to objects, people, places and so on have the power to influence co-construction and change how people perceive the world (Berger & Luckman, 1967). At the turn of the century, as an example of linguistic determinism, the word 'cripple' was commonplace to describe people with physical impairments. Over time, linguistic labels to describe persons with disabilities have evolved in Western societies to terms such as 'handicapped', 'handi-capable' and more recently 'physically challenged'. In extreme online communities, such as ONESGs, the expression and linguistic reframing of negative health behaviours to possess positive characteristics and connotations establishes newly constructed norms within these groups that encourage the continued exchange of these negative ideas. Over time, group members cease to perceive the negative health behaviours as having potential harm and instead view them positively.

This communication process likely extends to other types of online groups. For instance, individuals on pro-suicide sites exchange messages that encourage others to commit suicide by telling others that death will free them from their worldly concerns and personal pain (Padmanathan et al., 2018); thus suicide, a taboo FTF conversation topic, is socially reconstructed from physical death into a 'release from pain'. Furthermore, pro-suicide online communities may be attractive to those contemplating suicide because these communities transform suicidal planning from a solitary, lonely process into a shared and normalized behaviour, consequently co-constructing these extreme negative health behaviours into positive ones, so much so that there are online suicide pacts and group 'live' suicides (Aboujaoude, 2016).

Proposition 2: Co-construction of negative health behaviours as positive behaviours—ONESG members communicate online to co-construct negative health behaviours to be perceived as positively valenced and worthy of enactment.

### *Expression of tips and techniques to enact negative health behaviours*

ONESGs also use the internet to exchange tips and techniques for enacting the negative health behaviours they promote. ONESG community members provide advice and instructions that promote 'best practices' for engaging in negative health behaviours. Because the behaviours have been reconstructed positively, messages are exchanged to aid group members in successfully enacting now positively perceived health behaviours. Uses and gratifications theory (UGT; Blumler & Katz, 1974) has been widely applied to explain the psychological functions of how and why people engage with media (Klapper, 1963). With the increasing utilization of technology in communication processes, UGT has been applied to information and communication technologies (including the internet) and getting information has been identified as a primary and frequent function of media consumption across platforms (Papacharissi & Rubin, 2000; Haridakis & Hanson, 2009). As such, ONESGs constitute a key communicative function by providing tips and techniques in fulfilling an informative need through mediated online communication.

More recently, scholars have used UGT to explore not only the motives of use of the internet as a consumer, but also as a content creator. Attention has been given to the motives expressed by bloggers (Hollenbaugh, 2011) and creators of personal home pages (Papacharissi, 2002) to better understand why they share content with others. Once again, providing information was a leading reason why content producers created home pages and blogs. Hollenbaugh (2011) discovered that bloggers attributed an altruistic component to the motive of providing information. Specifically, bloggers want to share information to motivate, support and encourage others, and preferred blogs as a means to reach many people at once rather than through individual communication acts (Hollenbaugh, 2011). Moreover, bloggers expressed that blogging provides a means for archiving and organizing thoughts and feelings for further reflection (Hollenbaugh, 2011). Through the lens of ONESG theory and UGT, these websites and blogs can provide a means to inform and motivate as well as archive tips and techniques for future use.

In extending ONESG theory to other online contexts and phenomena, self-injury websites (e.g., self-cutting) are a prime example of negative health behaviour promotion through online sites, offering instruction and advice to individuals about ways to physically harm one's body in locations that can be obscured (Miguel et al., 2017). Pro-suicide online communities provide methods to successfully commit suicide in obscure and original ways (e.g., suicide by inhaling helium or ether) (Aboujaoude, 2016). These kinds of ONESGs regularly post advice, and even step-by-step instructions, for enacting negative health behaviours through online group message exchanges and subsequently archive this information for future reference.

Proposition 3: Expression of tips and techniques to enact negative health behaviours—ONESG members communicate online to exchange tips and techniques that give advice on enactment of negative health behaviours.

### *Uncontested self or other negative expressions*

One particularly salient communication characteristic of pro-anorexia online message exchanges is a high volume of self-critical or other-critical statements that go unchallenged by members of the community. Establishment of an 'in-group' versus 'out-groups' has long been a key feature defining group membership (Blanton et al., 2000). Groups develop unique 'in-group cultures' made up of common beliefs, practices and norms. They may even create specialized language and unique speech codes (Philipsen, 1974).

One prominent communication feature of ONESGs is the exchange of self and other-directed messages which are not challenged or corrected by group members. In traditional FTF support groups, expressions of low esteem are contradicted and replaced with positive reframing and personal empowerment messages (Chesler & Chesney, 1988; Lehardy & Fower, 2018). Importantly, in ONESGs, there is a lack of challenge or correction of negative self or other-directed messages around the negative health behaviour within these online communities, which is a defining communication characteristic. Other types of ONESGs may vary in the amount and degree of self-directed negative expression, and yet uncontested negative 'other-directed' expressions (i.e., negative out-group messages) are a common feature of ONESGs.

In online hate groups, for example, a central focus is 'other-directed' negative message postings which attack other racial or ethnic groups (de Koster & Houtman, 2008). Importantly, in ONESGs, these types of negative expressions are not challenged or corrected by members of these extreme online communities; instead, through lack of objection, the messages are validated and legitimated. This further perpetuates the expression of negative self or other messages. This appears to be an important communication characteristic of ONESGs because, as stated previously, in other types of online support groups, the norm is to challenge individuals when they post self- or other-targeted negative comments. The lack of challenge from other members within ONESGs is likely interpreted as agreement, support and encouragement to continue to express and expand upon the extreme messages.

Proposition 4: Uncontested self or other negative expressions—ONESG members' self- and other-directed negative expressions related to the negative health behaviour go unchallenged by group members.

### *Expression of cohesion and group encouragement*

Another key feature of in-groups is communication to establish common bonds among members to encourage the group's shared ideas and goals. Ren et al. (2007) submit that people develop attachment to online communities through two different mechanisms: (1) common identity (through a commitment to the group's goals or purpose) and (2) common bonding (through social or emotional attachments to individuals within the online community). Within ONESGs, both approaches play a role in the cohesiveness and bonding within the group.

Common identity serves as a mechanism to find and join the ONESG with a shared purpose and also functions as a means to maintain cohesion within the group. ONESG members experience three principles of common identity attributed by Ren et al. (2007): (1) a shared identity through the health condition lived by the members (social categorization), (2) maintenance of the shared goal of the community, in this case shared negative health practices that lead to outcomes (interdependence) and (3) comparison to the out-group (those not supporting or engaging in the negative health behaviour) which further strengthens the in-group commitment (intergroup comparisons). Group encouragement of negative health behaviours and choices helps to build self-esteem and empowerment that is necessary to maintain and normalize the negative behaviours. In traditional FTF support groups, this type of encouragement and empowerment contributes to an increased sense of personal agency and control toward achieving positive coping (Ussher et al., 2006). In the case of ONESGs, the empowerment encourages control over negative health behaviours for success as a community member and to cope with the out-group that discourages the behaviours.

As group members encourage one another, their feelings of social and emotional attachment to particular members may grow, fulfilling the common bond mechanism within online communities (also see Mincey, this volume). Ren et al. (2007) identify three causes of common bonding: (1) social interaction, (2) personal information (self-disclosure) and (3) personal attraction through similarity. The social interaction and bonding to particular members leads to a sense of community rather than the isolation individuals may feel in their FTF experiences. Research on virtual environments suggests that a higher sense of accord and unity may be experienced when participants feel a higher sense of 'co-presence' in being with others online (Slater et al., 2000). This co-presence and bonding can lead to what support group participants call a 'family', such as a 'cancer family' created in FTF support groups for cancer patients (Ussher et al., 2006). The family metaphor is formed through individual friendships within the group as well as a sense of caring during group meetings and interactions 'where the sharing of emotions and mutual experiences serves to unite people as they get to know intimate details of each other's lives' (Ussher et al., 2006, p. 2568). Group members feel affection and cared for within the online community, which is further enhanced through a sense of being with others that share similar experiences. In-group affection and bonding messages serve to heighten ONESG members' feelings of mutual understanding, camaraderie and closeness to one another (e.g., 'We're here for you').

Exchanging online messages that promote in-group bonding and connection is another important communication characteristic of ONESGs. Finding caring others to support negative health behaviour enactment is particularly difficult in FTF interactions where the behaviours may be stigmatized and may result in relational risk, censure or damage. Therefore, the online affordances of ONESG group encouragement and co-presence enable social interactions with similar individuals that cannot be easily replicated offline.

Proposition 5: Expression of cohesion and group encouragement—ONESG members exchange messages of community connectedness and caring that support enactment of negative health behaviours.

### *Reconstructing mediated weak ties into strong tie support*

Over time, ONESG members may gradually feel closer to other members online—their 'online family'—than they do to their own biological family or friends. This leads to the final ONESG communication characteristic—reconstructing mediated weak ties into strong tie support. The internet has been theorized to establish weak tie relationships between people (Walther & Boyd, 2002; Wright et al., 2010). Weak ties lack the close connection of strong bonds that are usually formed in FTF relationships (e.g., family, friends) (Haythornewaite, 2011; Walther & Bond, 2002). However, Wright and Miller (2010) explain that online weak ties provide several benefits to internet users:

> (1) greater utility related to increased situational similarity—i.e., experiential similarity rather than demographic or interpersonal similarity; (2) greater objectivity resulting from less emotional attachment; (3) greater security stemming from the reduced interpersonal risk of weak ties; and (4) greater interpersonal comfort associated with reduced social complications and less stringent role obligations relevant to reciprocity failure. (p. 504)

In other words, online weak tie connections allow access to like-minded individuals and freedom to express ideas under few social constraints or fear of threat to one's offline strong tie relationships, as well as low expectations for equity in reciprocity of support. What is different with ONESGs is the potential for online weak tie interactions to take on more psychological valence and feelings of connection than to offline strong tie relationships, especially if the common interest receives negative social judgement and stigma in one's offline strong tie networks. ONESG group members share an experience that is different than that of their friends and family, which members indicate changes their interactions and relationships with family and friends offline (Adamsen, 2002). As such, the weak ties that brought members together may become psychological strong ties when members experience situational similarity, acceptance of shared goals and beliefs, and increased comfort of finding a 'safe space' to express opinions, concerns and information that are not accepted or validated by out-group members (e.g., 'My family and friends just don't understand'). This is further evidenced in the online environment through Walther's (1996) hyperpersonal theory, which suggests people may express even deeper thoughts and intimate feelings, and in more detail, online than they often do in everyday FTF communication. As such, the ONESG becomes a pure bonding group 'where social and ideological homogeneity overlaps, deepening networks among people sharing similar backgrounds and beliefs' (Norris, 2002, p. 5) to form an online extreme community. Today, the internet allows for direct connection to like-minded individuals and encourages weak ties to develop into strong ties, particularly within ONESG communities where strength is gathered through unity and opposition to contradictory outside beliefs opposing the negative health behaviour.

Proposition 6: Reconstructing mediated weak ties into strong tie support—ONESG members' communication reconstructs online weak tie relationships into perceived strong ties.

## Theoretical Implications and Future Research

ONESG theory emerged inductively from examining online message exchanges between members of the online pro-anorexic movement. We theorize that the six communication characteristics summarized in the list below, together, likely apply beyond the pro-anorexia context and hold heuristic potential for exploring other types of ONESGs that promote negative health behaviours. As global online connectivity continues to grow, research on the communication within extreme online communities is exigent. While the six communication characteristics may be present in various ONESG contexts, the specific ways these manifest may differ and there may be different interrelationships between the characteristics within an online extreme community. For example, some ONESG groups may rely more on in-group than out-group dynamics, while others may focus primarily on tips to enable negative health behaviours. Utilizing ONESG theory as a framework may increase understanding of the specific ONESG mechanisms that carry more weight than others and help to illuminate different communication dynamics, online relationships within the community, leadership trends, contribution to negative outcomes and even a deeper understanding of the context itself. We seek to encourage future investigations of a diverse range of ONESGs to explore the applicability of the ONESG theory in other online contexts.

## ONESG THEORY COMMUNICATION PROPOSITIONS

1. Exchange of mediated anonymous disclosures

   Proposition 1: ONESG members utilize online anonymity (the ability to engage in unidentifiable communication in the online environment) to express and support enactment of extreme negative health behaviours.

2. Co-construction of negative health behaviours as positive behaviours

   Proposition 2: ONESG members communicate online to co-construct negative health behaviours to be perceived as positively valenced and worthy of enactment.

3. Expression of tips and techniques to enact negative health behaviours

   Proposition 3: ONESG members communicate online to exchange tips and techniques that give advice on enactment of negative health behaviours.

4. Uncontested self or other negative expressions

   Proposition 4: ONESG members' self- and other-directed negative expressions related to the health behaviour go unchallenged by group members.

5. Expression of cohesion and group encouragement

   Proposition 5: ONESG members exchange messages of community connectedness and caring that support enactment of negative health behaviours.

6. Reconstructing mediated weak ties into strong tie support

   Proposition 6: ONESG members' communication reconstructs online weak tie relationships into perceived strong ties.

To date, several studies have utilized the ONESG grounded model (Haas et al., 2011) as an impetus for undertaking additional pro-anorexia online research, and to illuminate their findings (see Chang & Bazarova, 2015; Yeshua-Katz & Martins, 2013). For example, Chang and Bazarova (2015) used the model as an explanatory theoretical framework to further explore pro-anorexic online message exchanges. They used linguistic analysis to analyse 'disclosure-response patterns' in 22,000 message exchanges in a pro-anorexia online community. Their findings provide further evidence of the six ONESG communication characteristics and lend quantitative support to the explanatory strength of ONESG theory in that context. Throughout this chapter, we have hypothesized that multiple types of ONESGs may exist (e.g., self-cutting ONESGs, pro-suicide ONESGs). Online suicide promotion has increased over the past decade (Biddle et al., 2016), and Scherr and Reinemann (2016) found in a two-wave survey that increased thoughts of 'individual suicidality increases the odds of using health forums or support groups online' (p. 85) which may have positive or negative influences. Suicide rates rose 28% between 2003 and 2018 in the USA (NIMH, 2018), and an increase in self-injury ONESG communities may be a contributing factor. We seek to encourage researchers to further explore the communication exchanged in these types of online extreme communities in order to test and expand ONESG theory through future computer-mediated communication research.

In advancing online theory, several of the emergent ONESG communication characteristics are in line with previous theories of group alignment and identity (Tajfel & Turner, 1979; Swann et al., 2012) and psychological kinship (McNamara & Henrich, 2017) that may be foundational to group formation and maintenance. For instance, promotion of intergroup cohesion and psychological connection among members has been recognized as a primary characteristic of group membership tied to willingness to self-sacrifice for the group (Whitehouse, 2018). Initiation rituals (e.g., military, fraternities) and shared personal experiences also form the basis for in-group bonding (Swann et al., 2012). An important difference from traditional in-group theory is that ONESGs are composed of an online community of strangers who interact anonymously via the internet to promote negative health behaviour, and likely will never meet in person.

Moreover, as new online communication tools and new social media sites emerge, more research will be required to understand the potential for ONESGs to develop and flourish. For instance, Tumblr (launched in 2007) became a new home for pro-anas to express their online 'thinspiration' messages, and social media platforms have an extensive reach that draws eating disorder and self-harm bloggers (Cavazos-Rehg et al., 2020; Miguel et al., 2017)—perfect for ONESGs to flourish. As new communication tools (e.g., SMS apps, websites and so on) are developed, it will be important for researchers to explore how these are utilized to form ONESGs. Increasing understanding of the communication strategies that allow extreme online communities to flourish also may be informative in developing health communication interventions for those who engage in negative health behaviours or suffer from mental health problems. Many people are unaware that ONESGs exist. With pro-anorexics, for instance, physicians and parents who become aware of a child's online pro-ana ONESG interactions may be able to more closely monitor and intervene in the child's online activity, and thus create opportunities to encourage more positive health behaviours. Therefore, understanding the communication within ONESGs may have the potential to be used to develop positive health interventions to combat the promotion of negative health behaviours online.

Finally, continuing to investigate and extend ONESG theory may have potential to add to critical cultural theory in understanding how the internet is being used by subculture groups who may promote other negative behaviours (e.g., bullying teenagers) or subversive groups (e.g., hate groups) that may seek larger cultural and political change (McNamee et al., 2010). In every society, there exists the dominant hegemonic culture, and minority subculture groups which the dominant culture seeks to control either through subordination or co-optation (Gramsci, 1971; Habermas, 1989). Guerrilla warfare and terrorism are labels that the dominant group applies to the strategies and tactics used by violent subversive groups who challenge and attack the dominant culture. The internet has become a pivotal tool for recruitment and training by radical subversive groups (and paradoxically also exposes terrorist groups to potential discovery by the dominant culture; Torres Soriano, 2012). Thus, terrorist groups that seek to physically harm others (i.e., an other-directed negative health behaviour) may be another example of online extreme communities that operate as extreme ONESGs. Understanding the communication strategies and tactics of such groups may provide the key to exposing online extreme communities. Future research should explore applications of ONESG theory in various types of extreme online groups.

## Conclusion

The internet will continue to be utilized by individuals and groups for both positive and negative purposes. ONESG theory has much potential for expanding our understanding of how ONESG communities develop and utilize the internet to encourage negative health behaviours. As the world continues to move towards an integrated, global information-based society, it will become even more important to understand how online groups communicate and promote negative health behaviours via the internet that impact the offline world. We suspect that ONESG theory underpins the online communication used by these groups, and we call for future research to explore this ever-expanding area of ONESG computer-mediated communication.

## References

Aboujaoude, E. (2016). Rising suicide rates: an under-recognized role for the Internet. *World Psychiatry* 15: 225–27. https://doi.org/10.1002/wps.20344

Adamsen, L. (2002). From victim to agent: the clinical and social significance of self-helpgroup participation for people with life threatening diseases. *Scandinavian Journal of Caring Sciences* 16(3): 224–31. https://doi.org/10.1046/j.1471-6712.2002.00060.x

Andalibi, N., Haimson, O.L., De Choudhury, M., & Forte, A. (2016, May). Understanding social media disclosures of sexual abuse through the lenses of support seeking and anonymity. In *Proceedings of the 2016 CHI Conference on Human Factors in Computing Systems* (pp. 3906–18). New York: ACM.

Attrill, A. (2015). *The Manipulation of Online Self-Presentation: Create, Edit, Re-edit and Present.* New York: Palgrave Macmillan.

Bargh, J.A., McKenna, K.Y., & Fitzsimons, G.M. (2002). Can you see the real me? Activation and expression of the true self on the Internet. *Journal of Social Issues* 58(1): 33–48. https://doi.org/10.1111/1540-4560.00247

Bell, V. (2007). Online information, extreme communities and Internet therapy: is the Internet good for our mental health? *Journal of Mental Health* 16(4): 445–57. https://doi.org/10.1080/09638230701482378

Berger, P.L., & Luckman, T. (1967). *The Social Construction of Reality: A Treatise in the Sociology of Knowledge.* London: Penguin.

Biddle, L., Derges, J., Mars, B., Heron, J., Donovan, J.L., Potokar, J., … & Gunnell, D. (2016). Suicide and the Internet: changes in the accessibility of suicide-related information between 2007 and 2014. *Journal of Affective Disorders* 190: 370–75. https://doi.org/10.1016/j.jad.2015.10.028

Blanton, H., Crocker, J., & Miller, D.T. (2000). The effects of in-group versus out-group social comparison on self-esteem in the context of a negative stereotype. *Journal of Experiential Social Psychology* 36: 519–30. https://doi.org/10.1006/jesp.2000.1425

Blumler, J.G., & Katz, E. (1974). *The Uses of Mass Communications: Current Perspectives on Gratifications Research.* London: Sage.

Brown, P., & Levinson, S.C. (1987). *Politeness: Some Universals in Language Usage*. Cambridge: Cambridge University Press.

Carroll, J.B. (1956). *Language, Thought and Reality: Selected Writings of Benjamin Lee Whorf*. Cambridge, MA: MIT Press.

Cavazos-Rehg, P.A., Fitsimmons-Craft, E.E., Krauss, M.J., Anako, N., Xu, C., Kasson, E., Costello, S.J., & Wilfley, D.E. (2020). Examining self-reported advantages and disadvantages of socially networking about body image and eating disorders. *The Journal of International Eating Disorders* 53: 852–62. https://doi.org/10.1002/eat.23282

Chang, P.F., & Bazarova, N.N. (2015). Managing stigma: exploring disclosure-response communication patterns in pro-anorexic websites. *Health Communication* 31(2): 217–29. https://doi.org/10.1080/10410236.2014.946218

Chesler, M., & Chesney, B.K. (1988). Self-help groups: empowerment attitudes and behaviours in disabled or chronically ill persons. In H.E. Yuker (ed.), *Attitudes Toward Persons with Disabilities* (pp. 230–45). New York: Springer.

Christopherson, K.M. (2007). The positive and negative implications of anonymity in Internet social interactions: on the Internet, nobody knows you're a dog. *Computers in Human Behaviour* 23: 3038–56. https://doi.org/10.1016/j.chb.2006.09.001 http://dx.doi.org/10.1016/j.chb.2006.09.001

DeAndrea, D.C. (2015). Testing the proclaimed affordances of online support groups in a nationally representative sample of adults seeking mental health assistance. *Journal of Health Communication* 20: 147–56. https://doi.org/10.1080/10810730.2014.914606

De Choudhury, M., & Kıcıman, E. (2017). The language of social support in social media and its effect on suicidal ideation risk. In *Proceedings of the International AAAI Conference on Weblogs and Social Media. International AAAI Conference on Weblogs and Social Media* (Vol. 2017, p. 32). NIH Public Access.

de Koster, W., & Houtman, D. (2008). Stormfront is like a second home to me: on virtual community formation by right-wing extremists. *Information, Community, & Society* 11: 1155–76. https://doi.org/10.1080/13691180802266665

Eastwick, P.W., & Gardner, W.L. (2009). Is it a game? Evidence for social influence in the virtual world. *Social Influence* 4(1): 18–32. https://doi.org/10.1080/15534510802254087

Ellison, N.B., Steinfield, C., & Lampe, C. (2007). The benefits of Facebook friends: social capital and college students use of online social network sites. *Journal of Computer-Mediated Communication* 12(4): 1143–68. https://doi.org/10.1111/j.1083-6101.2007.00367.x

Gramsci, A. (1971). *Selections from the Prison Notebooks* (Q. Hoare & G.N. Smith, trans). New York: International Publishers.

Haas, S.M., Irr, M.E., Jennings, N., & Wagner, L. (2011). Communicating thin: a grounded model of Online Negative Enabling Support Groups (ONESGs) in the pro-anorexia movement. *New Media & Society* 13: 40–57. https://doi.org/10.1177/1461444810363910

Habermas, J. (1989). *The Structural Transformation of the Public Sphere* (T. Burger & F. Lawrence, trans). Boston, MA: MIT Press.

Haridakis, P., & Hanson, G. (2009). Social interaction and co-viewing with YouTube: blending mass communication reception and social connection. *Journal of Broadcasting & Electronic Media* 53(2): 317–35. https://doi.org/10.1080/08838150902908270

Haythornewaite, C. (2011). Strong, weak, and latent ties and the impact of new media. *The Information Society* 18: 385–401. https://doi.org/10.1080/01972240290108195

Hinduja, S., & Patchin, J.W. (2010). Bullying, cyberbullying, and suicide. *Archives of Suicide Research* 14: 206–21. doi:10.1080/13811118.2010.494133

Hollenbaugh, E.E. (2011). Motives for maintaining personal journal blogs. *Cyberpsychology, Behaviour, and Social Networking* 14: 13–20. https://doi.org/10.1089/cyber.2009.0403

Internet World Stats (2020). Usage and population statistics. Retrieved from: https://www.internetworldstats.com/stats.htm

Klapper, J.T. (1963). Mass communication research: an old road resurveyed. *Public Opinion Quarterly* 27(4): 515–27. https://doi.org/10.1086/267201

Kraut, R., Kiesler, S., Boneva, B., Cummings, J., Helgeson, V., & Crawford, A. (2002). Internet paradox revisited. *Journal of Social Issues* 58: 49–74. https://doi.org/10.1111/1540-4560.00248

Lea, M., & Spears R. (1992). Paralanguage and social perception in computer-mediated communication. *Journal of Organizational Computing* 2: 321–41. https://doi.org/10.1080/10919399209540190

Leavitt, A. (2015). This is a throwaway account: temporary technical identities and perceptions of anonymity in a massive online community. In *Proceedings of the 18th ACM Conference on Computer Supported Cooperative Work & Social Computing* (pp. 317–327). New York: ACM.

Lehardy, E.N., & Fowers, B.J. (2018). Ultimate (evolutionary) explanations for the attraction and benefits of chronic illness support groups: attachment, belonging, and collective identity. *Current Psychology: A Journal for Diverse Perspectives on Diverse Psychological Issues*. Published online, 13 April 2018. https://doi.org/10.1007/s12144-018-9841-7

Massanari, A. (2017). #Gamergate and The Fappening: how Reddit's algorithm, governance, and culture support toxic technocultures. *New Media & Society* 19(3): 329–46. https://doi.org/10.1177/1461444815608807

McCornack, S.A. (1992). Information Manipulation Theory. *Communication Monographs* 59: 1–16. https://doi.org/10.1080/03637759209376245

McNamara, R.A., & Henrich, J. (2017). Kin and kinship psychology both influence cooperative coordination in Yasawa, Fiji. *Evolution and Human Behaviour* 38: 197–207. https://doi.org/10.1016/j.evolhumbehav.2016.09.004

McNamee, L.G., Peterson, B.L., & Peña, J. (2010). A call to educate, participate, invoke, and indict: understanding the communication of online hate groups. *Communication Monographs* 77: 257–80. https://doi.org/10.1080/03637751003758227

Miguel, E.M., Chou, T., Golik, A., Cornacchio, D., Sanchez, A.L., DeSerisy, M., & Comer, J.S. (2017). Examining the scope and patterns of deliberate self-injurious cutting content in popular social media. *Depression & Anxiety* 34: 786–93. https://doi.org/10.1002/da.22668

Mulveen, A.R., & Hepworth, J. (2006). An interpretative phenomenological analysis of participation in a pro-anorexia internet site and its relationship with disordered eating. *Journal of Health Psychology* 11(2): 283–96. https://doi.org/10.1177/1359105306061187

Norris, P. (2002). The bridging and bonding role of online communities. *Harvard International Journal of Press/Politics* 7(3): 3–13. https://doi.org/10.1177/1081180x0200700301

NIMH (National Institutes of Mental Health) (2018). Suicide. Retrieved at: https://www.nimh.nih.gov/health/statistics/suicide.shtml

Padmanathan, P., Biddle, L., Carroll, R., Derges, J., Potokar, J., & Gunnell, D. (2018). Suicide and self-harm related Internet use: a cross-sectional study and clinician focus groups. *Crisis: The Journal of Crisis Intervention and Suicide Prevention* (online first, May). https://doi.org/10.1027/0227-5910/a000522

Papacharissi, Z. (2002). The self online: the utility of personal home pages. *Journal of Broadcasting & Electronic Media* 46(3): 346–68. https://doi.org/10.1207/s15506878jobem4603_3

Papacharissi, Z., & Rubin, A.M. (2000). Predictors of Internet use. *Journal of Broadcasting & Electronic Media* 44(2): 175–96. doi:10.1207/s15506878jobem4402_2

Pew Research Center (January 2013). Health Online 2013. Available at: http://www.pewinternet.org/files/old-media//Files/Reports/PIP_HealthOnline.pdf

Pew Research Center (April 2018). Declining majority of online adults say the Internet has been good for society. Retrieved from: http://assets.pewresearch.org/wp-content/uploads/sites/14/2018/04/27165144/PI_2018.04.30_Internet-Good-Bad_FINAL.pdf

Philipsen, G. (1974). A theory of speech codes. In G. Philipsen & T. L. Albrecht (eds), *Developing Communication Theories* (pp. 119–56). New York: State University of NY Press.

Qian, H., & Scott, C.R. (2007). Anonymity and self-disclosure on weblogs. *Journal of Computer-Mediated Communication* 12(4): 1428–51. https://doi.org/10.1111/j.1083-6101.2007.00380.x

Rains, S.A. (2014). The implications of stigma and anonymity for self-disclosure in health blogs. *Health Communication* 29(1): 23–31. https://doi.org/10.1080/10410236.2012.714861

Ren, Y., Kraut, R., & Kiesler, S. (2007). Applying common identity and bond theory to design of online communities. *Organization Studies* 28(3): 377–408. https://doi.org/10.1177/0170840607076007

Scherr, S., & Reinemann, C. (2016). First do no harm: cross-sectional and longitudinal evidence for the impact of individual suicidality on the use of online health forums and support groups. *Computers in Human Behaviour* 61: 80–88. https://doi.org/10.1016/j.chb.2016.03.009

Schmidt, U., & Treasure, J. (2006). Anorexia nervosa—valued and visible: a cognitive- interpersonal maintenance model and its implications for research and practice. *British Journal of Clinical Psychology* 45: 343–66. https://doi.org/10.1348/014466505x53902

Shade, L.R. (2003). Weborexics: the ethical issues surrounding pro-ana websites. *ACM SIGCAS Computers and Society* 32(7): 2. https://doi.org/10.1145/968358.968361

Sifanou, M. (2012). Disagreements, face and politeness. *Journal of Pragmatics* 44: 1554–64. https://doi.org/10.1016/j.pragma.2012.03.009

Slater, M., Sadagic, A., Usoh, M., & Schroeder, R. (2000). Small-group behaviour in a virtual and real environment: a comparative study. *Presence: Teleoperators and Virtual Environments* 9(1): 37–51. https://doi.org/10.1162/105474600566600

Spears, R., Postmes, T., Lea, M., & Wolbert, A. (2002). When are net effects gross products? The power of influence and the influence of power in computer-mediated communication. *Journal of Social Issues* 58(1): 91–107. https://doi.org/10.1111/1540-4560.00250

Suler, J. (2004). The online disinhibition effect. *Cyberpsychology & Behaviour* 7(3): 321–26. https://doi.org/10.1089/1094931041291295

Swann, W.B., Jensen, J., Gómez, A., Whitehouse, H., & and Bastian, B. (2012). When group membership gets personal: a theory of identity fusion. *Psychological Review* 119: 441–56. https://doi.org/10.1037/a0028589

Tajfel, H., & Turner, J.C. (1979). An integrative theory of intergroup conflict. In W.G. Austin & S. Worchel (eds), *The Social Psychology of Intergroup Relations* (pp. 33– 47). Pacific Grove, CA: Brooks-Cole.

Torress Soriano, M.R. (2012). The vulnerabilities of online terrorism. *Studies in Conflict & Terrorism* 35: 263–77. https://doi.org/10.1080/1057610x.2012.656345

Treasure, J., Murphy, T., Szmukler, G., Todd, G., Gavan, K., & Joyce, J. (2001). The experience of caregiving for severe mental illness: a comparison between anorexia nervosa and psychosis. *Social Psychiatry Psychiatric Epidemiology* 36: 343–47. https://doi.org/10.1007/s001270170039

Ussher, J., Kirsten, L., Butow, P., & Sandoval, M. (2006). What do cancer support groups provide which other supportive relationships do not? The experience of peer support groups for people with cancer. *Social Science & Medicine* 62(10): 2565–76. https://doi.org/10.1016/j.socscimed.2005.10.034

Viégas, F.B. (2005). Bloggers expectations of privacy and accountability: an initial survey. *Journal of Computer-Mediated Communication* 10(3). https://doi.org/10.1111/j.1083-6101.2005.tb00260.x

Walther, J.B. (1996). Computer-mediated communication: impersonal, interpersonal, and hyperpersonal interaction. *Communication Research* 23(1): 3–43. https://doi.org/10.1177/009365096023001001

Walther, J.B., & Boyd, S. (2002). Attraction to computer-mediated social support. In C.A. Lin & D. Atkin (eds), *Communication Technology and Society: Audience Adoption and Uses* (pp. 153–88). Cresskill, NJ: Hampton Press.

Westerlund, M., Hadlaczky, G., & Wasserman, D. (2015). Case study of posts before and after a suicide on a Swedish internet forum. *The British Journal of Psychiatry* 207(6): 476–82. https://doi.org/10.1192/bjp.bp.114.154484

Wittgenstein, L. (1922). *Tractatus Logico-Philosophicus.* London: Routledge and Kegan Paul.

Whitehouse, H. (2018). Dying for the group: towards a general theory of extreme self sacrifice. *Behavioural and Brain Sciences* 41: 192. https://doi.org/10.1017/s0140525x18000249

Whitlock, J. (2010). Self-injurious behaviour in adolescents. *PLoS Medicine* 7(5): e1000240. ttps://doi.org/10.1371/journal.pmed.1000240

Wright, K.B., Bains, S., & Banas, J. (2010). Weak-tie support network preference and perceived life stress among participants in health-related, computer-mediated support groups. *Journal of Computer-Mediated Communication* 15(4): 606–24. https://doi.org/10.1111/j.1083-6101.2009.01505.x

Wright, K.B., & Bell, S.B. (2003). Health-related support groups on the Internet: linking empirical findings to social support and computer-mediated communication theory. *Journal of Health Psychology* 8: 37–52. https://doi.org/10.1177/1359105303008001429

Wright, K.B., & Miller, C.H. (2010). A measure of weak tie/strong tie network preference. *Communication Monographs* 77(4): 500–517. https://doi.org/10.1080/03637751.2010.502538

Yeshua-Katz, D., & Martins, N. (2013). Communicating stigma: the pro-ana paradox. *Health Communication* 28(5): 499–508. https://doi.org/10.1080/10410236.2012.699889

# Eating Disorder Discourse in a Diet and Fitness App Community: Understanding User Needs Through Exploratory Mixed Methods

*Elizabeth V. Eikey, Oliver Golden, Zhuoxi Chen and Qiuer Chen*

## Introduction

In addition to 'general-purpose' social media, as well as both general and eating disorder-specific online forums, eating disorder discourse can also be found across mobile applications (apps) that track food, physical activity and weight (i.e., diet and fitness apps, calorie counters, weight loss apps and so on) and their subsequent online communities. Such diet and fitness apps have become increasingly popular (Krebs & Duncan, 2015). Many of these apps also have an associated online community for users to provide social support and connect to one another. Although past research has focused heavily on pro-eating disorder online communities, such as those described in Chapters 7, 8 and 11, extant literature suggests that the line between 'healthy' eating and exercise content and disordered content is continuously becoming less distinct (Stover, 2014; Tiggemann & Zaccardo, 2015). Although some online communities have the potential to be therapeutic and provide essential social support for people with or at risk of eating disorders (Bowler et al., 2012; Keski-Rahkonen & Tozzi, 2005; Whitlock,

Elizabeth V. Eikey, Oliver Golden, Zhuoxi Chen and Qiuer Chen, 'Chapter 9: Eating Disorder Discourse in a Diet and Fitness App Community: Understanding User Needs Through Exploratory Mixed Methods' in: *Eating Disorders in Public Discourse: Exploring Media Representations and Lived Experiences*. University of Exeter Press (2023). © Elizabeth V. Eikey et al. DOI: 10.47788/DCZA4511

Powers & Eckenrode, 2006) (echoed in Chapter 10), research has shown that online weight loss, diet and fitness communities can negatively affect users by promoting eating disorders (Stover, 2014; Tiggemann & Zaccardo, 2015).

While dieting and weight control methods are closely linked to eating disorders (Ackard, Croll & Kearney-Cooke, 2002; Neumark-Sztainer et al., 2006; Shisslak, Crago & Estes, 1995), most diet and fitness apps do not focus on how to support eating disorder-related needs, which can lead to unintended negative consequences for users, such as triggering or exacerbating eating disorder-related behaviours and symptoms (Eikey, 2021; Eikey et al., 2017; Eikey & Reddy, 2017; Honary et al., 2019; Levinson et al., 2017; Simpson & Mazzeo, 2017). Instead, many diet and fitness apps focus on the tangible mechanics of weight loss, food and exercise tracking but do not integrate elements of mental health support well. Unfortunately, because dieting is often normalized, eating disorder-related behaviours may go unnoticed, being viewed as a 'normal' part of dieting. Although dieting may include healthy behaviours, often people view unhealthy weight control methods as part of dieting (Ackard et al., 2002).

Due to the connection between dieting and eating disorders, diet and fitness app designers and developers should consider ways to better support users with or at risk of eating disorders in order to mitigate adverse consequences. This chapter bridges research on eating disorder discourse in online communities and diet and fitness apps. Specifically, it explores using an online diet and fitness app community in order to begin to understand these users' needs. While researchers have sought to understand how people discuss diet and fitness apps within online eating disorder communities (e.g., McCaig et al., 2020), few studies have focused on how people discuss eating disorders within online diet and fitness app communities (e.g., Eikey et al., 2017). These communities provide a window into the experiences of diet and fitness app users with eating disorders and thus are a rich environment for a language-based research study.

We build on prior research by conducting a computational and qualitative analysis of eating disorder-related posts from diet and fitness app users to better understand how to support users. Our goal is to highlight the needs of users who have experiences with eating disorders by investigating their posts in an online community associated with the diet and fitness app they use; we do this by exploring frequent terms and topics as well as their goals and needs in using the app. Thus, in this chapter, we begin to shed light on the following research questions:

**RQ1.** What are the most common terms and topics in eating disorder-related posts within an online diet and fitness app community?

**RQ2a.** What types of health goals (e.g., weight loss, gain, muscle gain) do users discuss in eating disorder-related posts in an online diet and fitness app community?

**RQ2b.** What do users need in terms of reaching their health goals?

## Methods

To create our dataset, we first extracted posts from a diet and fitness app's online community.[1] We took care to obtain and present posts in a way that protected the privacy of users and ensured they were able to 'speak for themselves', as discussed in Chapter 10. In order to isolate discussions about eating disorders, we searched forum threads for eating disorder-related keywords, looking specifically at thread titles and post bodies. The keywords we used were 'eating disorder', 'anorex*', 'binge eating disorder', 'bulimia' and 'EDNOS' (short for eating disorder not otherwise specified, which was in past editions of the Diagnostic and Statistical Manual). We collected every thread returned by each keyword search, which included the original discussion posts and responses. This allowed us to understand the original thread post in the context of the response(s) it received. Data extracted included the post date, thread ID and content of the post. Posts were made at any time from 2009 to 2019. Overall, our dataset contained 27,900 posts, of which 1,941 were original discussion posts (i.e., the user's original post to start the discussion thread) and 25,959 were discussion responses. For this chapter, we focus on the original discussion posts to better understand what users who use eating disorder keywords turn to the online community for. We analysed these posts related to eating disorders using two approaches: (1) exploratory computational methods in order to characterize the dataset and (2) exploratory manual qualitative coding in order to understand what needs users talk about in relation to their health goals. These approaches complement one another because the computational methods provide a broad overview of frequent words and topics while the qualitative coding helps to provide context. BED and eating disorder keywords yielded the most posts, followed by anorexia, bulimia and EDNOS.

### *Phase 1: Exploratory computational methods*

Before analysis, we first cleaned the dataset, deleting the HTML symbols and stop words. We then used latent Dirichlet allocation (LDA) to obtain the top 30 most salient terms among all the posts and classify the posts into ten topics. Each topic returns the 30 most relevant terms, helping us understand what users are posting about. LDA is a generative statistical model for discovering the abstract 'topics' and is one of the most popular topic modelling methods. The aim of LDA is to find topics a post belongs to, based on the words in it. Words are sorted with respect to their probability score of them belonging into a topic. LDA goes through each post and randomly labels each word in the post as one of $n$ topics ($n$ is chosen beforehand). For each post $p$, it goes through each word $w$ and computes:

1. The proportion of words in post $p$ that are labelled as topic $t$.
2. The proportion of labels to topic $t$ over all posts that come from this word $w$.

Then it updates the probability of the word $w$ belonging to topic $t$. The top $x$ words are chosen from each topic to represent the topic. We set $x$ as 30 and sorted all the words in topic 1 based on their score. We applied the computational method to the overall dataset. LDA provided us with the top 30 most salient terms, the top 20 most salient terms of the 10 topics based, and the top 30 most salient terms for each keyword group (only 13 terms were provided for the keyword EDNOS due to too few overall posts in the corpus for that particular keyword). Duplicates were removed for analyses across the data, but duplicates were included for analyses that were conducted within keyword groups, so as not to compromise the analyses.

### *Phase 2: Exploratory qualitative methods*

For the manual qualitative analysis, we randomly sampled 50 posts from each keyword group except EDNOS (where we sampled 10 posts due to the low number of posts in this category). This left us with a sample of 210 posts. To obtain each sample from the keyword groups, we started with the original posts from each keyword group. We then created an additional column in Excel and used the function =rand() and applied it to every row. We then copy-pasted the numbers generated over the function =rand() to stop the function from continuing to generate random numbers and then sorted the random numbers from smallest to largest, leaving the posts randomly organized. Starting from the first post in the random order, we took the number of posts needed for each keyword and copy-pasted them into a master document for coding purposes. We repeated this for every keyword group and labelled each sample with the keyword it was selected for in the master spreadsheet.

Then each post in the sample was first screened to determine if the poster was self-disclosing a mental health experience in order to understand individuals' personal experiences and needs related to their own mental health. 'Mental health experience' referred to any specific mental illness (e.g., anorexia, binge eating disorder), symptoms and treatments of mental health challenges (e.g., bingeing, therapy, hospitalization for an eating disorder) or emotions the original poster described as abnormal or excessive (e.g., too obsessed, overwhelmed, exhilarated). Posts that did not meet this inclusion criteria were removed from the sample, leaving us with 169 posts for analysis.

Posts that met the initial inclusion criteria were then coded using an inductive approach. The main purpose of the inductive approach is to create themes in a raw data set that allows for patterns to emerge (Thomas, 2003). For the purposes of this chapter, we focused on understanding health goals (e.g., weight changes) and users' needs around these goals. We first became familiar with the dataset by independently reading through the 169 posts and taking notes. Then we came together to draft and iteratively refine a codebook. Each post was coded for the type of health goal users discussed (e.g., lose weight, gain weight, gain muscle and so on) and then grouped into themes based on how users talked about their goals. Two researchers independently coded all 169 posts, and then we came together as a group to discuss any disagreements until consensus was reached.

## Results

### *Phase 1: Exploratory computational methods*

#### *Salient terms and topics across dataset (RQ1)*

The top 30 most salient terms are presented in Figure 9.1. Terms such as 'weight' and 'eat' appeared frequently across the dataset. Using LDA, these words were

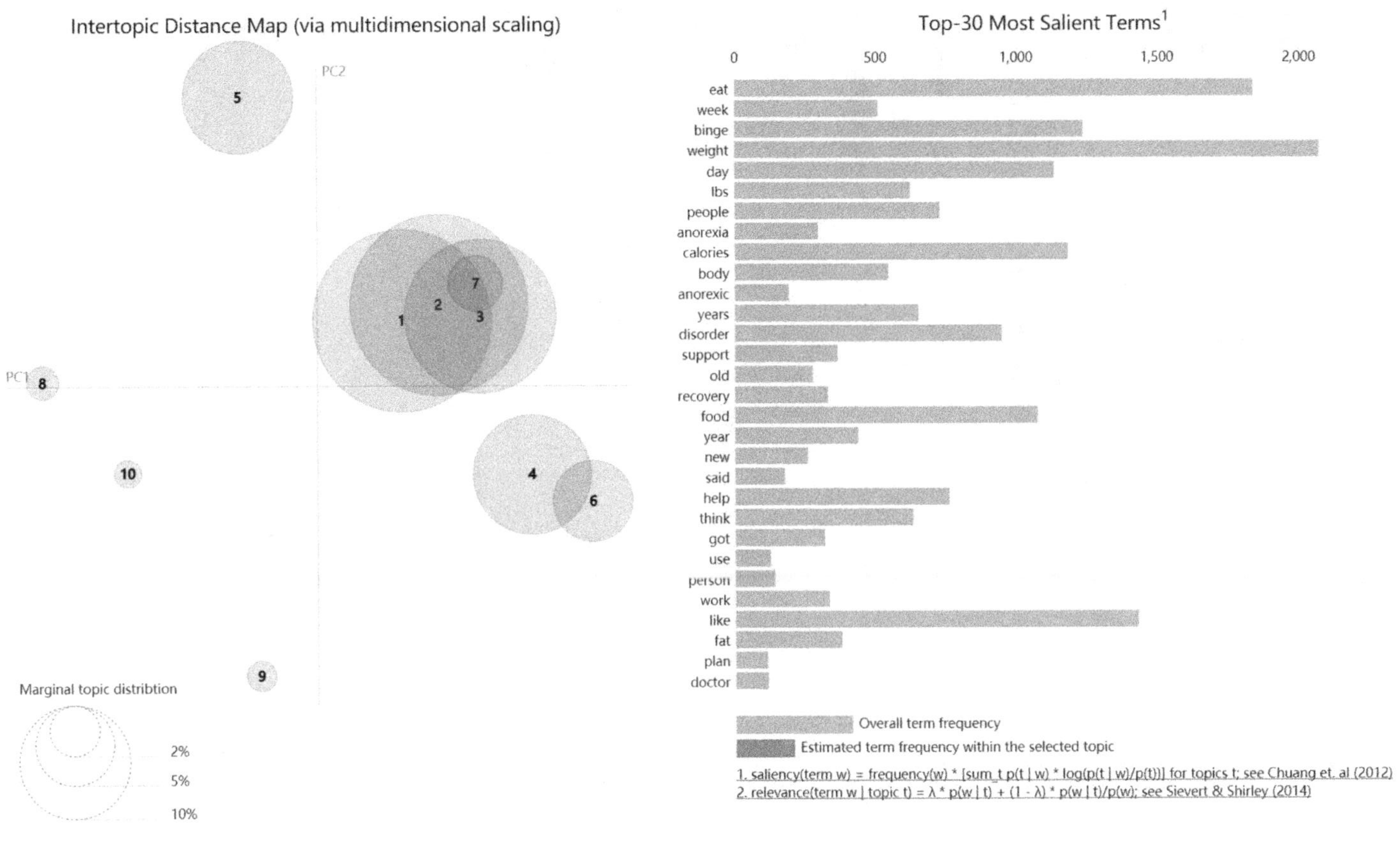


**Figure 9.1** Top 30 most salient terms of the 1,838 unique posts

grouped into topics; the top 10 topics can be seen in Table 9.1. Overall, the majority of the most frequently discussed topics gather together (e.g., #1, #2, #3, #7), accounting for 71.8% of all the tokens, as shown in Figure 9.2. Many of the posts contained similar items, and there was not a big distribution among the posts, according to the most salient words of specific topics. Topic 1 seemed to focus on people disclosing a disorder through a personal narrative history and looking for support and friends. Topic 2 seemed to focus on aspects related to one's body and working out. Topic 3 seemed to focus on one's family, and topic 7 seemed to focus on informational aspects like reading and research. Topics 4 and 6 had overlap: topic 4 seemed to be about meals and food and topic 6 about bingeing experiences. Topic 5 seemed to be about people's feelings toward their bodies. Topic 8 seemed to be about weight loss journeys, while topic 9 seemed to be about seeking help to stop binges. Finally, topic 10 seemed to focus on anorexia recovery and medicalized experiences with the disorder.

### *Top terms within each keyword group (RQ1)*

The top 30 most salient terms of each keyword group are shown in Table 9.2 (13 for keyword EDNOS due to the small number of posts related to it). Across all eating disorder keywords, posters tended to use similar terms. Common words across most eating disorder keywords included 'body', 'calorie(s)', 'pounds' / 'lbs', 'today', to name a few. Either 'help' or 'support' was a top term for each keyword. However, no singular term appeared in the top keywords across all five eating disorder keyword groups.

Certain eating disorder keyword groups had similar top words. For example, anorexia and bulimia tend to both use the word 'gain(ed)' frequently, whereas 'gain(ed)' is not in the top terms for BED, eating disorder or EDNOS. 'Friends' was common in the anorexia and eating disorder keyword groups but not others. Recovery terms were frequently used across all keyword groups except BED. 'Year(s)' was common in anorexia and bulimia keyword groups but not BED, eating disorder or EDNOS. However, other time-related words were frequently used in the BED category.

Each keyword group also had unique top terms. For instance, unique to anorexia were 'underweight', 'height', 'unhealthy', 'skinny', 'look' and 'old'. For BED, specific time-related words were common, such as 'months', 'night',

**Table 9.1** Top 20 most salient terms of 10 topics based on the 1,838 unique posts

| *Topic 1* | *Topic2* | *Topic3* | *Topic4* | *Topic5* | *Topic6* | *Topic7* | *Topic8* | *Topic9* | *Topic 10* |
|---|---|---|---|---|---|---|---|---|---|
| add | body | daughter | ate | body | binge | appreciated | body | advice | anorexia |
| anorexia | build | eat | breakfast | day | control | causes | calories | binge | anorexic |
| bulimia | cal | tknily | calorie | disorder | cravings | disorder | day | control | bones |
| disorder | class | getting | calories | eat | day | disordered | gain | day | cal |
| disorders | cutting | got | chocolate | fat | days | guys | gained | days | doctor |
| ed | day | help | day | feel | eat | heard | healthy | eat | fighting |
| friends | fat | know | days | food | food | helps | lbs | feel | hear |
| healthy | lifting | lbs | diet | good | gym | important | lose | food | kind |
| help | lower | like | dinner | know | hours | interesting | losing | hard | knowing |
| like | min | lol | eat | life | hungry | men | lost | healthy | mean |
| looking | mins | mother | exercise | like | like | new | months | help | nutritionist |
| love | muscle | old | feel | look | morning | number | past | know | people |
| new | plan | sister | food | make | night | psychological | pounds | like | person |
| people | pm | son | foods | people | pounds | reading | really | need | recovered |
| recovery | run | supposed | know | really | sugar | research | started | really | says |
| support | stone | today | like | things | time | said | time | stop | starting |
| trying | training | weight | lunch | think | tired | study | want | time | stories |
| want | week | year | meals | time | try | supplements | wei^it | want | subject |
| way | weight | years | today | want | water | topic | year | week | success |
| years | workout | yesterday | week | weight | work | use | years | weight | underweight |

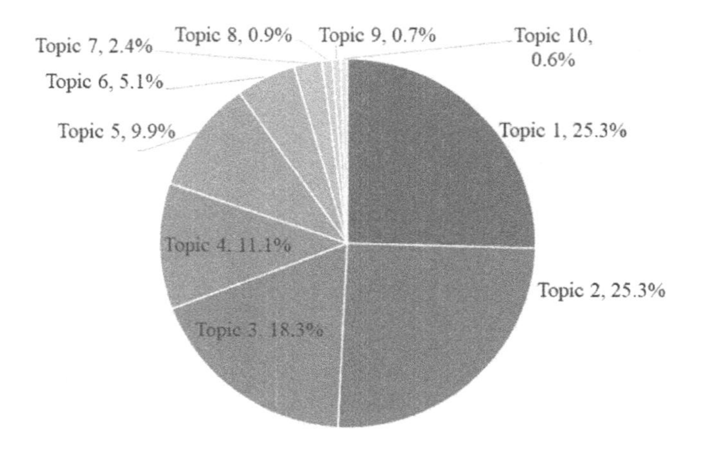


**Figure 9.2** Proportion of the dataset each topic comprises (using the 1,838 unique posts)

'daily' and 'week', as well as specific mentions around food or food content, such as 'chocolate' and 'protein'. Interestingly, 'diet' and 'exercise' were only top terms for BED. While other keyword groups contained words like 'eat' and 'eating', BED was the only one with 'ate' as a top term. Other top terms for BED included 'need', 'started', 'tell', 'tired', 'went' and 'work'. Specific to bulimia were words such as 'struggle', 'lose', 'trying', 'love', 'really', 'started', 'things', 'use' and 'way'.

## *Phase 2: Exploratory qualitative methods*

### *Types of goals across randomly sampled posts (RQ2a)*

Of the 169 posts we coded, the majority did not mention a specific health goal. Of the 62 that did mention a specific health goal, 49 posts mentioned a goal of losing weight, 9 mentioned a goal of gaining weight, 10 mentioned a goal of gaining muscle and 18 mentioned a specific health goal not covered by those categories. Specific health goals aside from weight loss or gain and muscle gain included a desire to control their eating, to regain their period, to regain their metabolism, to train for a sporting event, to improve their digestion, to maintain a specific BMI, to recover from an eating disorder, to eat more, to obtain a specific body shape, and to eat within a calorie limit (separately from a weight goal). Types of goals across the randomly sampled dataset can be seen in Figure 9.3.

**Table 9.2** Topmost salient terms of each keyword group (using all 1,941 posts)

| *Anorexia* | *BED* | *Bulimia* | *Eating Disorder* | *EDNOS* |
|---|---|---|---|---|
| anorexia | ate | ago | actually | add |
| anorexic | body | body | anorexia | disorder |
| body | **calorie** | **calories** | body | *feel* |
| **calories** | **calories** | eating | bulimia | ***food*** |
| day | chocolate | *feel* | charge | good |
| eating | daily | *gain* | disorders | *healthy* |
| *feel* | day | **going** | eat | help |
| *food* | diet | got | **friends** | *know* |
| **friends** | disorder | *healthy* | *goal* | **like** |
| *gain* | exercise | *know* | *healthy* | **recovery** |
| *gained* | *food* | **lbs** | *health* | support |
| *goal* | help | **like** | help | *want* |
| going | *know* | *lose* | little | **weight** |
| *healthy* | lbs | love | *lost* | |
| height | *meal* | *people* | *meal* | |
| help | months | really | *meals* | |
| **like** | need | **recover** | new | |
| look | night | Started | *people* | |
| low | *people* | struggle | pounds | |
| old | **pounds** | **support** | **recovery** | |
| *people* | protein | sure | relationship | |
| pounds | started | things | said | |
| question | tell | think | say | |
| recovered | tired | **today** | support | |
| **recovery** | **today** | toyme | thought | |
| skinny | *want* | *use* | thoughts | |
| sure | week | *want* | **today** | |
| *underweight* | **weight** | way | told | |
| *unhealthy* | went | **weight** | *use* | |
| year | work | years | *weigh* | |

## *Types of goals within each keyword group (RQ2a)*

Based on the 169 sample posts from users who self-disclose a mental health experience, original posters tended to share different health goals in the online community based on the eating disorder keyword groups, which can be seen in Figure 9.4.[2] It was common for posts not to include specific health goals. In fact, the highest proportion of health goals across BED, bulimia and eating

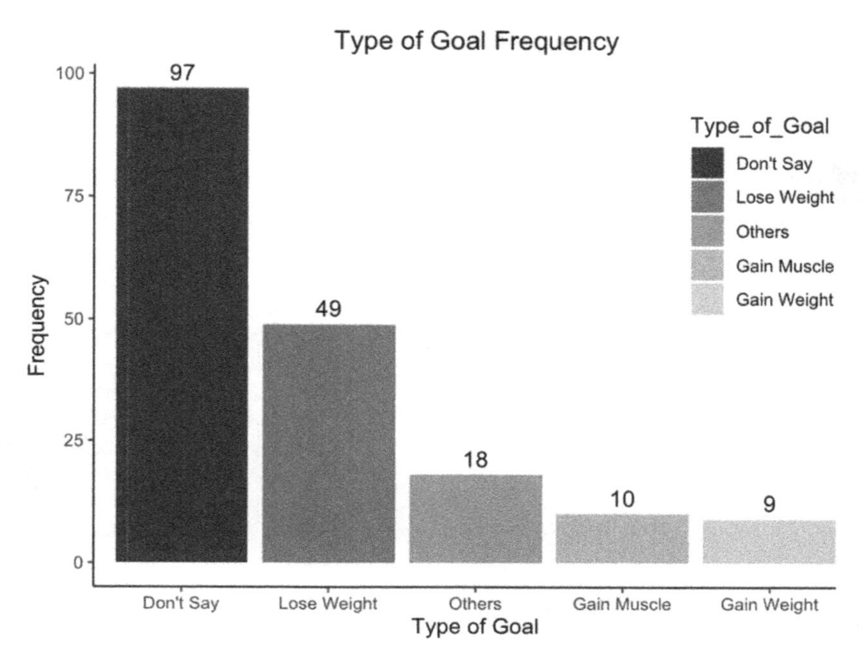


**Figure 9.3** Frequency of types of goals across 169 posts

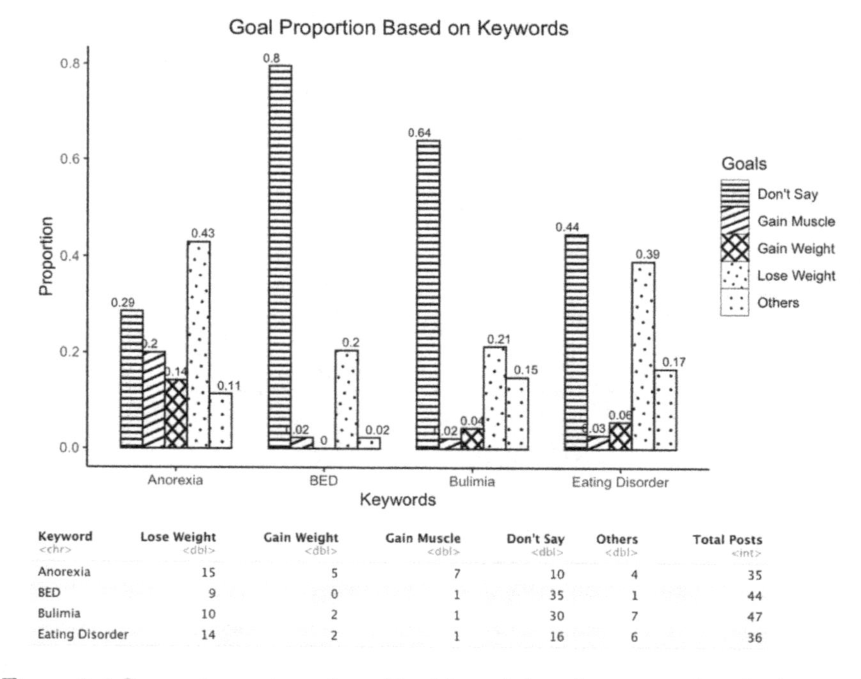


| Keyword | Lose Weight | Gain Weight | Gain Muscle | Don't Say | Others | Total Posts |
|---|---|---|---|---|---|---|
| <chr> | <dbl> | <dbl> | <dbl> | <dbl> | <dbl> | <int> |
| Anorexia | 15 | 5 | 7 | 10 | 4 | 35 |
| BED | 9 | 0 | 1 | 35 | 1 | 44 |
| Bulimia | 10 | 2 | 1 | 30 | 7 | 47 |
| Eating Disorder | 14 | 2 | 1 | 16 | 6 | 36 |

**Figure 9.4** Proportion and number of health goals based on eating disorder keyword posts

disorder keyword groups was 'don't say'. Posts within the anorexia keyword group, on the other hand, had the highest proportion of lose weight health goals. About 43% of posters using the keyword anorexia reported wanting to lose weight, 20% to gain muscle, 14% to gain weight, 11% had other goals not covered in our codebook and 29% did not state their goals.

'Lose weight' as a goal was fairly evenly distributed among all the keywords, with a slightly higher frequency in the anorexia and eating disorder keyword groups. It was a goal for 15 posters in the anorexia keyword, 10 in the bulimia keyword, 9 in the binge eating disorder keyword and 14 in the eating disorder keyword group. 'Gain weight' as a goal was also fairly evenly distributed, with 5 of the posts being from the anorexia keyword, 2 from the bulimia keyword, 0 from the binge eating disorder keyword and 2 from the eating disorder keyword. 'Gain muscle' as a goal was skewed towards posters in the anorexia keyword group. The other keywords had only one mention of gaining muscle as a goal each.

### *Needs around health goals (RQ2b)*

**Changing weight in a healthy way.** Whether users were talking about weight loss or weight gain goals, they expressed similar needs. For individuals trying to lose weight, many discussed having gained too much weight while trying to overcome extreme restriction, purging and/or low weight. Some users also mentioned concerns about their metabolism and amenorrhea from fluctuations in eating behaviours and weight. Users were interested in using the app to help them lose weight in a healthy way, but they often shared concerns about slipping back into eating disorder behaviours and extreme measures, such as restriction, purging and so on. For instance, one user with a history of anorexia nervosa mentioned wanting to lose weight in a healthy way and use the app without triggering eating disorder behaviours:

> I had eating disorders as a teen … Really I just want to lose about 20 lbs in order to reach 140–145 (at 5'9'). I find [the app] so helpful, but also it's way too easy to fall back into the controlling anorexic mindset. I'd love to hear from others who have recovered from an eating disorder and have decided to lose some weight for healthy reasons while trying to keep it healthy.

Similarly, another user mentioned needing to lose weight in healthy way but had concerns about calorie counting:

> I've been in recovery from an eating disorder for over 10 years. I was diagnosed with EDNOS because I didn't exactly fit the criteria for anorexia or bulimia … I want to lose the weight the healthy way. I don't want to go back down that road at all … I don't want to become obsessed with calories … Calorie counting works but it fuels my eating disorder.

While more users talk about weight loss, users who are trying to gain weight share similar concerns: they want to gain weight steadily but not too quickly or too slowly (as some have some immediate weight gain needs). However, they do not want to resort to extreme measures to gain weight, and some fear gaining weight, even if they recognize it as imperative for their health. Therefore, some users turn to the community for advice and support around keeping up their uptake and not slipping into restriction or purging. For instance, one user posted in the community to solicit information about how to gain weight in healthy way:

> I am a recovering anorexic, and I am hoping to get some advice on ways to gain weight in a steady and healthy way? I am starting yoga soon, and I am hoping to tone up while gaining weight. If you check out my daily intake and give me some ideas that would be awesome?

**Curbing bingeing.** Many users talked about bingeing as a key source of unwanted weight gain and/or negative feelings toward themselves and food and sought support for stopping binge eating, regardless of whether they explicitly mentioned specific health goals related to their weight or objectives with the app. For instance, one user posted to garner advice to stop binges:

> I was a bulimic for about 5 years. I decided to stop, and I started to lose weight too. I was finally happy with myself! Recently, I keep bingeing all of the time … I exercise, but I still eat more than I need … I can't stop myself from bingeing. I overeat until I want to puke. Any advice and motivation?

Similarly, another user discussed their binge eating problem and came to the community for advice:

> I have a binge eating issue, and I am seeking help and support. I think about food too much; I think being alone so I can eat whatever I choose, and I hide food I've eaten. I can binge on just about anything, but it's usually food I make at home. I eat too much or all of it. I have had this issue for as long as I

can remember. I am now at my highest weight, but I am seeking a solution. I fear admitting this, although it's to strangers. I just need some advice on how to get in control of myself again.

## Discussion

This work begins to shed light on the needs of diet and fitness app users who post about eating disorders in the app's associated online community. In general, we found that eating disorder-related posts tend to solicit social support (but for different reasons), which is unsurprising given the social nature of online communities. Regardless of type of health goal (e.g., weight loss, weight gain), users express concerns around changing their weight in a healthy way and not resorting to extreme measures or slipping back into eating disorder behaviours or unhealthy approaches. As discussed in the next chapter, diet and fitness apps can contribute to eating disorder behaviours, with users mentioning app restriction conflicting or aiding their disorder. Our research suggests that apps also have the possibility to *positively* contribute to users' recovery if greater care is taken with app design. Across eating disorder experiences, bingeing was discussed as a pain point; users felt bingeing contributed to weight gain that was either unwanted or happened too quickly, their feeling badly about themselves and/or sometimes triggering compensatory behaviours (e.g., restriction, purging and so on). Based on the consistency of users' posts within the online community, it seems the app itself may be able to better support these users' needs. Diet and fitness app designers and developers should reconsider their objectives by redefining success not as weight loss in and of itself but by supporting users in defining success for themselves and promoting healthy relationships with food and one's body, centred around users' success criteria. This also means that many diet and fitness apps must rethink what it means not to support *weight loss* but to support *healthy* eating, exercise and, if needed, weight change.

Our exploratory analyses also began to reveal differences across eating disorders, such as anorexia, BED and bulimia. Users posting about anorexia were often looking for friends and other people who share similar lived experiences as well as advice and help. Individuals with a history of anorexia may have a variety of health goals by using the app, such as gaining weight, losing weight, gaining muscle, re-establishing metabolism, regaining their period, eating enough and so on, depending on their personal circumstances. However, consistent across goals was a desire to engage in healthy practices and discussions orientated around recovery. Users also discussed these healthy practices in contrast to unhealthy ones. They talked about 'gaining' in both the sense of needing to gain weight and gaining weight—sometimes wanted, sometimes unwanted—as they work through the disorder. In general, users posting about anorexia tended to share information about their journey, as well as express hallmarks related to the disorder itself (e.g., underweight, skinny and so on). Users with BED spoke much less about their personal journey and were more centred around their binges. They tended to use time-related words and food-related words to describe their experiences with bingeing and used the online community to solicit help on ways to stop bingeing. Additionally, they discussed exercise and diet but did not focus on much recovery talk. In general, BED seemed to be more colloquial and in line with 'typical' dieting experiences rather than anorexia and bulimia that were discussed more as 'formal' eating disorders. For bulimia, users also wanted support, but they rarely mentioned looking for friends specifically. They talked about weight gain as a reason for wanting to lose weight in a healthy way. Similar to those with BED, users with bulimia also wanted to curb bingeing, but they were also concerned about the cyclical nature of binges and purges. Like anorexia, posts related to bulimia also contained personal journey details, and users tended to centre their discussions around recovery.

These findings can serve as a foundation for future research to better understand the different needs based on users who experience different types of eating disorders and eating disorder behaviours. Additionally, this work may inform not only the design of online communities to support users in finding the information they need, but it will hopefully also inform the design of diet and fitness apps themselves towards a more dynamic, personalized and holistic view of health.

## Limitations

We used keywords to find relevant data; however, it is possible that we missed eating disorder posts that used other words to describe their eating disorder experiences. Thus, while this work is a good first step, it is exploratory in nature and not exhaustive nor necessarily representative of all users with eating disorders who use diet and fitness app online communities. Further, because this study focused on exploring online community data, it may miss the needs of app users who do not utilize the online community. Lastly, interpreting the computational analysis and coding was from our own understanding of the original posters' intent. Future work should include an in-depth investigation of the needs of a broad range of users with eating disorders.

## Acknowledgements

We want to thank Yeyang Gu for the incredible work extracting and organizing data for this study.

## Notes

1 Due to the sensitivity around eating disorders, it was important to consider the ethics around conducting this research. The Institutional Review Board determined this research exempt; the name of the app and community are not disclosed and quotations are slightly edited to protect users' privacy.
2 EDNOS was removed from this part of the analysis due to the small sample size, which left us with 162 posts.

## References

Ackard, D.M., Croll, J.K., & Kearney-Cooke, A. (2002). Dieting frequency among college females: association with disordered eating, body image, and related psychological problems. *Journal of Psychosomatic Research* 52(3): 129–36. https://doi.org/10.1016/s0022-3999(01)00269-0

Bowler, L., Oh, J.S., He, D., Mattern, E., & Jeng, W. (2012). Eating disorder questions in Yahoo! Answers: information, conversation, or reflection? In ASIST 2012. Baltimore, Maryland. http://doi.org/10.1002/meet.14504901052

Eikey, E. V. (2021). Effects of diet and fitness apps on eating disorder behaviours: qualitative study. *BJPsych Open* 7(5): e176. https://doi.org/10.1192/bjo.2021.1011

Eikey, E.E.V., & Reddy, M.M.C. (2017). 'It's definitely been a journey': a qualitative study on how women with eating disorders use weight loss apps. In *ACM CHI Conference on Human Factors in Computing Systems (CHI '17)* (pp. 1–13). Denver, CO: ACM.

Eikey, E.V., Reddy, M.C., Booth, K.M., Kvasny, L., Blair, J.L., Li, V., & Poole, E.S. (2017). Desire to be underweight: exploratory study on a weight loss app community and user perceptions of the impact on disordered eating behaviours. *JMIR mHealth and uHealth* 5(10): e150. https://doi.org/10.2196/mhealth.6683

Honary, M., Bell, B.T., Clinch, S., Wild, S.E., & McNaney, R. (2019). Understanding the role of healthy eating and fitness mobile apps in the formation of maladaptive eating and exercise behaviours in young people. *JMIR mHealth and uHealth* 7(6): e14239. https://doi.org/10.2196/14239

Keski-Rahkonen, A., & Tozzi, F. (2005). The process of recovery in eating disorder sufferers' own words: an internet-based study. *International Journal of Eating Disorders* 37: 580–86. https://doi.org/10.1002/eat.20123

Krebs, P., & Duncan, D.T. (2015). Health app use among U.S. mobile phone owners: a national survey. *JMIR mHealth and uHealth* 3(4): 1–12. https://doi.org/10.2196/mhealth.4924

Levinson, C.A., Fewell, L., & Brosof, L.C. (2017). MyFitnessPal calorie tracker usage in the eating disorders. *Eating Behaviours* 27(April): 14–16. https://doi.org/10.1016/j.eatbeh.2017.08.003

Blei, D.M., Ng, A.Y., & Jordan, M.I. (2003). Latent Dirichlet allocation. *Journal of Machine Learning Research* 3(Jan): 993–1022. https://doi.org/10.1145/1015330.1015439

McCaig, D., Elliott, M.T., Prnjak, K., Walasek, L., & Meyer, C. (2020). Engagement with MyFitnessPal in eating disorders: qualitative insights from online forums. *International Journal of Eating Disorders* 53(3): 404–11. https://doi.org/10.1002/eat.23205

Neumark-Sztainer, D., Wall, M., Guo, J., Story, M., Haines, J., & Eisenberg, M. (2006). Obesity, disordered eating, and eating disorders in a longitudinal study of adolescents: how do dieters fare 5 years later? *Journal of the American Dietetic Association* 106(4): 559–68. https://doi.org/10.1016/j.jada.2006.01.003

Shisslak, C.M., Crago, M., & Estes, L.S. (1995). The spectrum of eating disturbances. *The International Journal of Eating Disorders* 18(3): 209–19. https://doi.org/10.1002/1098-108x(199511)18:3<209::aid-eat2260180303>3.0.co;2-e

Simpson, C.C., & Mazzeo, S.E. (2017). Calorie counting and fitness tracking technology: associations with eating disorder symptomatology. *Eating Behaviours* 26(2017): 89–92. https://doi.org/10.1016/j.eatbeh.2017.02.002

Stover, C.M. (2014). *Elements of a Sensibility: Fitness Blogs and Postfeminist Media Culture*. Austin: The University of Texas at Austin.

Thomas, D.R. (2003). A general inductive approach for qualitative data analysis. *American Journal of Evaluation* 27(2). https://doi.org/10.1177/1098214005283748

Tiggemann, M., & Zaccardo, M. (2015). 'Exercise to be fit, not skinny': the effect of fitspiration imagery on women's body image. *Body Image* 15: 61–67. https://doi.org/10.1016/j.bodyim.2015.06.003

Whitlock, J.L., Powers, J.L., & Eckenrode, J. (2006). The virtual cutting edge: the internet and adolescent self-injury. *Developmental Psychology* 42(3): 407–17. https://doi.org/10.1037/0012-1649.42.3.407

# 10 Using Qualitative and Mixed-Methods Approaches to Investigate Online Communication About Eating Disorders: A Reflective Account

*Dawn Branley-Bell*

## Introduction

Online communication around eating disorders (EDs) represents a common source of public concern, and the focus of many media headlines (e.g., 'TikTok: Fears videos may "trigger eating disorders"', Lantos, 2020; 'Instagram eating disorder content "out of control"', Crawford, 2019; 'Social media is fuelling eating disorders among children as young as twelve', Chalmers, 2019). There are two major concerns often expressed within the media. First is the possible reinforcement of ED behaviours through normalization of the behaviour, i.e., making the user feel that this behaviour is acceptable, justified and, in extreme cases, perhaps even desirable (Bine, 2013; Schroeder, 2010). Second is the potential for ED-related material to 'trigger' ED behaviour in vulnerable users (Branley & Covey, 2017; Eikey & Booth, 2017). These concerns have been heightened due to social media use being heaviest amongst younger users, who also represent the age group most heavily affected by EDs (Arcelus et al., 2011). However, it is crucial to recognize that online platforms can play a positive or a negative role, depending upon the context and the user(s) involved. For example,

Dawn Branley-Bell, 'Chapter 10: Using Qualitative and Mixed-Methods Approaches to Investigate Online Communication About Eating Disorders: A Reflective Account' in: *Eating Disorders in Public Discourse: Exploring Media Representations and Lived Experiences*. University of Exeter Press (2023).
 DOI: 10.47788/QSFW4482

online communication has been linked to improved mental health wellness (Asbury & Hall, 2013), increased social connectedness (Highton-Williamson et al., 2015; Naslund et al., 2016; Smith-Merry et al., 2019), increased coping (Smith-Merry et al., 2019), emotional support (Wright et al., 2003) and empowerment (Barak, 2007). Social media can also provide a platform through which users can find support and guidance on treatment and recovery (Branley & Covey, 2017; Branley-Bell & Talbot, 2020b)—this is particularly important, as individuals experiencing EDs rarely seek professional help (Ali et al., 2020; Hart et al., 2011). Further research is needed to fully understand online communication around EDs and to identify protective interventions to enable us to protect against negative impacts while avoiding disruption of positive communication networks, as the implementation of a poorly guided intervention could unintentionally disadvantage the majority of individuals.

This chapter is a reflective account of my own research experience within this field, reflecting on the use of qualitative and mixed-methods approaches. I will describe some of the techniques I have applied while striving to capture an accurate portrayal of online communication around EDs. Applied responsibly, I believe that qualitative and mixed-methods techniques can help to highlight the valuable voice of lived experience. Throughout this chapter, I reflect upon the design and ethical challenges I have encountered and aim to share some of the lessons that I have learned along the way.

## Background

Before diving into the methodological considerations, I want to first take some time to explain why research in this domain is important, and why we must strive, as researchers, to provide an accurate insight and portrayal of online communication.

Online communication about EDs is not a new phenomenon. Long before the introduction of social media, internet users have been using technology to share, discuss and access ED-related content. Although the arrival of Web 2.0 brought with it the introduction of social media platforms, prior to this, traditional websites and online forums were used for these discussions (Branley, 2015; Lipczynska, 2007). That said, as social media has become so mainstream within our society, it has helped to move online communication about EDs into the public eye. This has fuelled public concerns around negative impacts;

this section begins by discussing the driving factors behind these concerns, and how they are linked to stigmatizing public discourse. The discussion then turns to positive elements of online ED-related communication and highlights why greater awareness is needed to provide a more complete view of the 'bigger picture'.

### *Stigmatizing public discourse and fears about online communication*

The nature of EDs—particularly the behaviours associated with these disorders and the high mortality rate, alongside concerns for the wellbeing of our loved ones—can predispose us to focus on the negative aspects of online communication. The mass media helps to fuel public concerns with headlines drawing attention to the possibility of social contagion effects or extreme online content such as pro-ED websites. However, the media has been described as focusing on 'an oversimplified picture of pro-ED platforms viewed only in terms of ED maintainers' (Smahelova et al., 2020, p. 634). Just because the internet provides a communication channel for users, this does not necessarily mean that it plays a role in the development or persistence of EDs. It is for this very reason that my early ED research focused on capturing a more complete picture of online ED communication, seeking to extend beyond the narrow pro-ana focus depicted in the media.

Early research in this field tended to focus upon extreme content (e.g., Brotsky & Giles, 2007; Lipczynska, 2007; Norris et al., 2006; Tong et al., 2013; Yeshua-Katz, 2015). Before I continue, I wish to be clear that I am not disputing the existence of extreme online content; on the contrary, there are aspects of online communication that are concerning. One example is the sharing of extreme 'thinspiration' or 'bonespiration' images (Branley & Covey, 2017; Talbot et al., 2017). I completely agree that damaging or harmful content should be addressed. However, as I found in some of my earlier research, this type of communication is likely to represent the minority rather than the 'norm' (Branley & Covey, 2017). Furthermore, recent research suggests that it may not be as simple as categorizing material into either pro-ED or pro-recovery content, as user motivation may be a much bigger factor in influencing the impact that online content has upon the viewer. To quote Smahelova et al. (2020):

> Even platforms centered on nonprofessional recovery, platforms providing professional help, and platforms providing regular information about food, diet, and exercise can be used for maintaining the illness. On the other hand, in the recovery phase, nonprofessional pro-ED platforms could serve as a challenge and a 'waking up point' for some participants, and that could enhance the recovery process. As a result, the usage of each kind of online platform is intertwined with the motivation of the participants rather than the type of the platform and the purpose. (p. 634)

This suggests that to categorize online content as explicitly negative or positive may be too simplistic—the bigger picture is likely to be much more complex! I believe that research is needed to help increase our understanding and raise public awareness that society needs to move away from an oversimplified, alarmist approach. We need to understand more about users' motivations and other contributing factors related to positive or negative outcomes of online communication.

### *Raising awareness of positive aspects*

In seeking to illustrate the deeper complexity of online communication about EDs (and indeed online communication about mental health more generally), researchers need to raise awareness around positive aspects. This could feed into a more balanced societal view.

Benefits of online communication are not unique to EDs; research continues to highlight positives across many domains; for example, online communication can help to alleviate loneliness (Leavitt et al., 2019), provide a source of support for physical and mental health (Pretorius et al., 2019; Zhang et al., 2017) and help to raise awareness and address stigma (Chen & Yang, 2016). Back in 2014, as part of my doctoral research, I conducted an investigation of online communication about EDs on social media (Branley, 2015; Branley & Covey, 2017). Using ED-related search terms, I used the live firehose to capture 12,000 tweets and 73,000 Tumblr blogs over a twenty-four-hour period. I applied inductive, thematic analysis to identify indicators of user motivation(s) for sharing ED content. My results showed that pro-ana content was in the minority and that the majority of users appeared to be communicating about EDs for positive reasons, including sharing and inspiring recovery, challenging pro-ana views, raising awareness around EDs and challenging social norms. Since then, many researchers have continued to demonstrate the positive aspects of communicating about EDs online (e.g., Kendal et al., 2017; McLean et al., 2019; McNamara & Parsons, 2016).

More recently, a colleague and I researched the impact of the COVID-19 pandemic on the lives of individuals with experience of EDs (Branley-Bell & Talbot, 2020b). Our findings show how technology and online communication can play a positive role for this population, particularly during stressful and socially isolated periods such as the pandemic lockdown.

Since the start of my research career, I feel that there has been a gradual shift of opinion within the research community, with increasing awareness that online communication around EDs is not necessarily negative and that a more comprehensive view is necessary. Thankfully, professional bodies are also beginning to recognize the positives of online communication, with ED charities such as Beat (www.beateatingdisorders.org.uk) acknowledging the importance of positive online spaces and even embracing these platforms by offering their own support through Twitter and Instagram. However, there is still much work to be done in relation to addressing public opinion and that often depicted in mainstream media.

### *Implications of public and media perceptions*

I have already touched on the clear disconnect between perceptions of online communication within the research community and that within the media and society. On one side, there is negative media coverage, stigmatizing societal norms and fears about online communication, while on the other, there are researchers and individuals with lived experience who are recognizing that online communication can also be driven by positive motivations and/or lead to positive outcomes. But you may be wondering why this disconnect in opinion is so important. Well, negative public perceptions can be linked to significant negative implications. For instance, individuals experiencing EDs traditionally report experiencing feelings of being misunderstood, misrepresented and stigmatized (Ali et al., 2020), and they commonly experience loneliness and social isolation. Media and public misconceptions around online communication can worsen this, subsequently negatively impacting upon the wellbeing of this population. Furthermore, negative perceptions of online communication could lead to calls for censorship. However, research (including my own, e.g., Branley, 2015) suggests that such censorship could impact upon positive sources of support, access to recovery information and other aspects of recovery and coping facilitated by online platforms.

The internet has the potential to provide even more benefits, for instance by increasing accessibility to healthcare treatment using remote delivery (Branley-Bell & Talbot, 2020b; Talbot & Branley-Bell, 2020). Thus, broadly labelling all ED-related online communication as negative could 'create barriers in the treatment process because internet usage can also offer positives' (Smahelova et al., 2020). From my own research experiences, I strongly believe that focusing too heavily on the negative can result in us missing the 'bigger picture' and the positive opportunities that online communication affords us.

## *My experiences and perceived advantages of qualitative ED research*

Qualitative methods have a lot to offer ED research to help address the issues discussed in the previous section. Based upon my own experiences, reflections and lessons learned, I would like to discuss three key benefits of qualitative approaches: (1) staying true to the voice of lived experience, (2) understanding and adopting a shared language and (3) creating generalizable insights in a rapidly evolving online environment.

### *Staying true to the voice of lived experience*

In my opinion, one of the main benefits of qualitative research is the ability to stay true to the voice of lived experience. It is vital that we gain insight into the lived experience of individuals who communicate about EDs online. I certainly do not wish to imply that quantitative approaches do not have merit, far from it. Quantitative research can provide us with valuable insights into trends and relationships, and enable us to test the significance of predictive factors linked to recovery or relapse. Indeed, in my own research, I often apply a mixed-methods approach to allow the empirical testing of quantitative methods (including longitudinal studies which can track change over time) to be complemented by the rich insight of qualitative methods.

When wishing to capture and explore the voices of lived experience, qualitative approaches really come into their own. They provide us with the best tools to seek deeper understanding of the factors and thought processes underlying behaviours. Qualitative data can help explain how individuals make sense of their own world, their perceptions and thoughts. I have personally found qualitative approaches invaluable in allowing me to create a dialogue with the individuals taking part in my research. For instance, open-ended questions allow participants more control over the direction of the conversation and they may raise a point that I had not initially considered, but which turns out to be a valuable contribution to the research. I also find that there is immense value in being able to probe and prompt further discussion to gain clarification and/or to check my own interpretations of the individual's account. The latter can be particularly useful when paraphrasing quotes, as this provides an opportunity to check that I have interpreted the participant's words in the way that they were intended (I will return to the issue of paraphrasing later in this chapter).

### *Understanding and adopting a shared language*

I have also found qualitative approaches to be invaluable in helping me to understand and adopt a shared language with my participants and/or target audience. Qualitative methods provide insight into the language used by individuals with lived experience. I have often found it surprising just how often the terminology used in public reports or research could be perceived as shaming or inappropriate. For example, in some of my recent collaborative work, I have been investigating the 'Better Health' campaign (Talbot & Branley-Bell, 2020). Launched by the UK Government as a response to the COVID-19 pandemic, this campaign was designed to 'encourage millions to lose weight and cut COVID-19 risk' (Public Health England, 2020). The campaign was influenced by data showing that obese people are significantly more likely to become seriously ill with coronavirus compared with non-obese individuals (Docherty et al., 2020; Hussain et al., 2020). However, when it was first launched, the campaign used wording such as 'war on obesity' and 'protect the NHS, save lives' which were branded stigmatizing and shaming by ED charities and specialists (Mead, 2020). Interested in the public reaction, my colleague and I analysed tweets referencing the campaign. Our findings suggest that the use of inappropriate language may have reduced the campaign's effectiveness, and may have been harmful to vulnerable populations (Talbot & Branley-Bell, 2020). Shaming language is particularly worrying, as individuals with EDs traditionally report experiencing negative stigma and show low levels of professional help-seeking (Ali et al., 2020; Hart et al., 2011). Furthermore, during the COVID-19 pandemic (and shortly before the introduction of the Better Health campaign), individuals with EDs were already experiencing feelings of shame and perceptions that they were burdening the 'overwhelmed' NHS if they were to seek help for their ED (Branley-Bell & Talbot, 2020b). Campaigns using inappropriate and/or shaming language have the potential to decrease the likelihood of individuals seeking critical healthcare. We reflected upon the campaign placing a strong emphasis on weight loss (rather than health more generally) and its potential to trigger vulnerable populations (Talbot & Branley-Bell, 2020). This is just one example of how a disharmony in language can represent a considerable barrier between individuals experiencing EDs and those aiming to promote positive change. When conducting research, it is vital to have a shared language (Yorke et al., 2020) and qualitative approaches can help us to establish this.

### *Creating generalizable insights in a rapidly evolving online environment*

'But you need to have a backup plan, in case the internet is just a phase!' You may think this quote sounds absurd now, but back when I was proposing ideas for my doctoral research, this is exactly the type of response I received. Many academics were concerned that I was 'hedging my bets' on a technology that might simply be a passing phase. I was asked to consider what my backup plan would be if the internet fell out of favour and was no longer used by the masses. Of course, this quote is one of the extreme examples. Digging deeper, it became apparent that most of the apprehension was more accurately described as a concern over social media being just a phase. Again, this may seem unlikely now, as social media has become firmly ingrained in our everyday lives, but it was not such a stretch of the imagination back then.

Reflecting on the first two decades of the twenty-first century, it seems likely that social media will be around—in some shape or form—for a long time to come. However, there is still merit in discussing how to prolong the longevity and relevance of your research. As a cyberpsychologist, I am very aware of the rapid pace in which this research environment evolves. Platforms come and go (remember Google+ and MySpace?) and we must account for this in our research. No researcher wants to dedicate a significant chunk of their research career to a study that is resigned to the history books in a short space of time. Of course, our research is not always going to be 'cutting edge', but we can at least use the methods we have to help prolong its relevance. Qualitative insight can benefit us in this regard. For example, deeper insight into the underlying factors and user motivations behind behaviour can make it easier for us to identify if research conducted on one (perhaps since obsolete) platform may remain relevant to other platforms. Including more than one social media platform can also be beneficial; I use this approach to help me identify if there are overarching themes evident across the platforms (of course, if there are not, that also makes for interesting discussions, for instance considering what aspects of the platform environment may explain these differences).

## Methodological Considerations

Having explained why I believe qualitative approaches represent an important tool for research in this domain, I would like to use the following section to highlight my experiences and reflections in relation to some specific design challenges and considerations: (1) avoiding preconceptions and the importance of co-design, (2) ensuring confidentiality and privacy, (3) promoting openness, (4) considering language and terminology and (5) representing the bigger picture.

### *Avoiding preconceptions and the importance of co-design*

It is important for me to be critical in my research and to take the time to consider whether I am bringing any pre-existing bias or preconceptions. Although this is important for any research, I am particularly aware of this issue when working in a field that is so often sensationalized in the mass media, and one prone to societal stereotypes and stigma. Individually, both 'internet usage' and EDs can be highly emotive, controversial subjects, and this is amplified further when investigating the interaction between the two.

It is important to recognize that we are all influenced by the world around us. As responsible researchers, we need to stay alert to potential influences and choose methods which help us to capture the true lived experience of our participants. We must design our research with the aim of obtaining an accurate reflection of the target population's behaviour, motivations, experiences, attitudes and beliefs. For this reason, I generally use inductive approaches to allow themes to be generated from the data (also referred to as a bottom-up approach), rather than approaching the data with pre-determined hypotheses or themes which may lead to increased chances of misinterpretation.

In my own experience, I have found co-design to be a valuable tool to reduce potential bias or misinterpretation. Co-design (also sometimes referred to as experience-based design, participatory design or coproduction) involves end-users in the entire research process. For example, within a health context, co-design can involve patients, carers and staff (Boyd et al., 2012). I have found that this approach can really help to shape and strengthen my research designs, methods and interpretations, partly by helping to identify limitations and possible sources of bias. Using co-design to work alongside individuals with lived experience has been not only incredibly rewarding, but also essential for increasing the scientific integrity of my research.

There is another significant benefit of this approach, namely the opportunity for individuals with lived experience to be more actively involved with research (i.e., rather than limiting them to the role of 'participant'). I strongly believe that research, and interventions, should be designed alongside those with lived experience—rather than something that is imposed upon them by researchers, healthcare professionals or governmental bodies. Co-design affords those living with EDs the opportunity to help share their valuable insight to influence the body of knowledge, interventions, healthcare services and/or policy. Thankfully, the benefits of this approach are being increasingly recognized and co-design is being more widely adopted and encouraged (Talbot & Branley-Bell, 2020).

## *Ensuring confidentiality and privacy*

'But is it really public, or is it private-public?' This quote represents a dialogue I find myself revisiting when planning research which uses online data. Online platforms provide an interesting, and somewhat unique, ethical dilemma when it comes to privacy. While in offline situations it may be relatively clear cut, the distinction between what can be considered public or private often becomes blurred when talking about online environments. This becomes an issue when capturing online data that exists in the 'public' domain (e.g., social media data) where it is not always possible to obtain informed consent from the original user. Traditionally, the British Psychological Society (2014) ethical guidelines suggest that use of data in the public domain is acceptable in situations where users can reasonably be 'expected to be observed by strangers' (p. 25). However, this can be somewhat of a 'grey area' when it comes to online platforms.

Interestingly, this dilemma goes above and beyond whether the information is actually publicly accessible, as online spaces and platforms can also differ in their 'perceived public'. Privacy online has previously been described as 'less about public vs. private [i.e., privacy settings] and more about whether you are findable and identifiable by people who actually know you in real life' (Rifkin, 2013, para. 8). In my earlier research, I described a distinction between perceptions of 'private-public' and 'open-public' spaces (Branley, 2015, pp. 104–105). For example, Twitter users are generally very aware that this is an openly public domain, used by the mainstream population, and that their tweets are likely to be seen more widely. However, other platforms may be regarded as more private spaces, which it is unlikely that others besides the intended audience frequent—even though *technically* there are no privacy settings preventing public observation. There are many factors which could underpin the perception of a private-public, including platforms which are regarded as less mainstream, harder to find or those that offer more anonymity (Branley, 2015, pp. 104–105). Therefore, considering what is public from an ethical viewpoint—in the online environment—can require careful consideration. In my own experience, it can often be useful to discuss this with others who have experience in the field.

Even if data is deemed appropriate for collection and analysis, it is vital that steps are taken to ensure privacy, confidentiality and anonymity of the users. One issue I feel strongly about is ensuring anonymity when using social media data. As students, we may have been generally taught to remove names and identifiable information from data to ensure anonymity. However, this is not adequate within the online domain.

### *Removing their username ≠ anonymity!*

Due to the ability to easily and quickly search online, it is very important to avoid directly quoting online content. Even more so when the research concerns sensitive subjects. Directly quoting what someone has said online means that the user could quickly be identified by running a web search for that text. Of course, if the data was obtained with informed consent from the participant to publish their quotes, this is not an issue. However, participant consent is often not possible or feasible—and in this instance, I have relied upon two approaches in my own research. First, if it will not detract from the strength of the research, I tend to avoid the use of quotes in my papers and instead focus upon writing about the general themes and findings. However, sometimes the inclusion of quotes is particularly valuable for strengthening the research and/or improving reader comprehension. In this instance, I have used paraphrasing (e.g., Branley, 2015, p. 117; Talbot & Branley-Bell, 2020). Paraphrasing refers to rewriting the same information in a different way, by making word, sentence and/or grammar changes. The aim is to rewrite the idea(s) expressed by the original author but retain the original meaning. One lesson I have learned is that paraphrasing is not as easy as it may initially seem. Considerable care must be taken to accidentally avoid altering the meaning of the text. Paraphrasing is something I regard as a multi-person task; aim to have at least two researchers independently paraphrasing the text, and only include quotes once there is consensus between the researchers that the original meaning of the message has been retained (e.g., Branley, 2015, p. 117; Talbot & Branley-Bell, 2020).

### *Watch out for that hashtag!*

Another lesson I have learned along the way is to pay particular attention to the use of unique terms—even if using otherwise paraphrased text. One particularly unique or unusual term could result in the user being easily identifiable with a quick web search. The same applies to user-generated hashtags. Searching for a unique hashtag (e.g., #ICantBelieveIBurnedMyToast) as opposed to a mainstream, widely adopted hashtag (e.g., #Weekend) can immediately bring up the corresponding social media post—even if the rest of the quote is completely paraphrased. Once I've paraphrased a quote, I often run a quick web search to check that the original result is not easily found.

It can be tricky to know which steps to take to ensure privacy and confidentiality when conducting online data collection. For example, it is important to carefully consider the security of online platforms used to conduct interviews and/or store data. This can involve checking the platforms' terms and conditions to identify if data is accessible by any third parties and using platforms with secure data encryption wherever possible. The online environment evolves rapidly, and with it, so do the ethical considerations involved. Luckily, there are useful resources available to help inform online research, which are regularly reviewed and updated. In my own line of research, for instance, I often refer to the British Psychological Society 'Ethics Guidelines for Internet-Mediated Research', which is accessible via the guidance section of their website (www.bps.org.uk/article-types/guidelines). All researchers have a responsibility to keep up to date with recent developments and updates to ethical guidance, at least within their own field.

### *Promoting openness and selecting appropriate platforms*

Although online research methods can be tricky, they also provide many advantages and opportunities, particularly for research involving potentially sensitive subjects such as EDs. Technology provides us with many different platforms and methods for data collection, and I have found this hugely beneficial for increasing participant ease and promoting open discussion. I take time to consider the types of methods that are both suitable for my research aim(s), and also likely to be well accepted by the individuals I would like to take part. Where possible, I have found that offering a range of participation methods/platforms is beneficial, as individuals differ in their preferred type of interaction. For example, many people can feel uncomfortable taking part in telephone or face-to-face interviews—particularly if they are discussing a topic that they find difficult or uncomfortable to talk about. Of course, there are others who prefer audio and/or visual interaction, and video or audio calls can be valuable in this respect.

I have found that some participants prefer using online text-based messaging platforms. Reasons include eliminating the need for face-to-face interaction, increased anonymity and less pressure for an instantaneous response (compared, for instance, to the awkwardness of silent moments during a face-to-face interview or audio/video call). This can decrease participation anxiety and promote open and honest discussions (Branley, 2015).

From a practical perspective, with text-based platforms the data is effectively already transcribed. This can save a considerable amount of time and expense. On the other hand, there are certain language cues (such as pauses in conversation and emphasis on words) which can be lost when using a text-based platform. As with all methodologies, it is about weighing up the pros and cons and making a balanced decision which considers your specific research design, aims and participants.

### *Considering language and terminology*

I have already touched upon the importance of using appropriate language. In reality, I have found that this can be very daunting as a researcher, as you may worry about accidentally using less-than-ideal terminology. Being aware of the impact that language can have can make you acutely aware of the risk of accidentally wording something incorrectly. I find that the best way to address this is not only to understand the existing academic literature but also to speak to healthcare professionals in the field and, crucially, to the target population—i.e., individuals with lived experience. The latter are best placed to provide insight into terms that they personally find shaming, judgemental and/or inaccurate. Reassuringly, I have found that people generally appreciate that I have taken the time to ask their opinion and check their preferred terminology.

### *Representing the bigger picture (including to the media and public)*

Earlier I mentioned how I have tried to avoid focusing on extreme online communication in my research and aimed to capture the bigger picture. Within this section, I would like to share some of the methods I have used to achieve this.

When planning one of my earlier studies, I realized that existing research tended to collect data by using search terms specific to pro-ana (e.g., Brotsky & Giles, 2007; Lipczynska, 2007; Norris et al., 2006). I realized that if I was aiming to capture ED communication more generally, this had to start with my chosen search terms. I broadened the terms from pro-ana specific (e.g., #proana, #pro-ED) to include more generic eating disorder terms (e.g., #eatingdisorder, #edproblems). To help identify other appropriate terms, I used a hashtag search tool (such as hashtagify.me) to identify other words commonly associated with the term 'eating disorders'. Reflecting upon this, I am particularly grateful that I broadened my search terminology. Without doing so,

I would have only captured the extreme minority of my sample. The results would have been very negative, as the data collection would only have captured content designed/shared to *promote* disordered eating behaviours. By widening my search terms, I discovered that most users in my sample were actually using the internet for more positive reasons. In fact, most of the messages in my data set were dedicated to what I later termed pro-recovery (i.e., content designed to encourage recovery in the user and/or others) or *anti* pro-ana (i.e., content specifically challenging the pro-ana mentality). In sharing this experience, I hope that this helps to demonstrate how research findings and conclusions can be significantly impacted by the decisions we make in the early stages of our research, and how bias can be so easily, and unintentionally, introduced.

Of course, research into the negatives and/or extremes of online communication is also very important. This can lead to greater understanding, earlier intervention for vulnerable groups and improved support mechanisms. However, I feel that we should also strive to encourage balanced research designs that can help feed into a more complete societal view of online ED-related communication. Unfortunately, working within this field, I have discovered that even with the best research design, researchers may still find it difficult to ensure accurate mass media coverage of their research. All too often, I hear from fellow researchers about their research being misquoted in the media with an overly sensationalist headline (usually one that is negative and alarming). This can be particularly distressing to the researcher, who can find their valuable 'take-home message' and research implications overshadowed by the attention-seeking headline. I empathize with researchers feeling apprehensive about media coverage of their research, due to concerns of misrepresentation. Thankfully, my personal experiences of the media thus far have generally been positive. However, I have picked up a few quick tips that may be helpful for some readers.

### *Focus on the 'take-home message'*

Personally, prior to a media interview, I find it helpful to identify the key 'take-home message(s)' that I would like the media to portray, and I focus upon getting that across in a clear, concise manner. Framing my research this way also helps prevent me from attempting to cover too many aspects of my research during the interview and, in doing so, losing the emphasis on the key message.

It is important to remember that media quotes and footage will be cut down significantly during editing—and the more you talk about during the interview, the more likely it is that your take home message will be one of the bits that's cut.

### *Talk to the reporter—they're human too!*

When I receive an interview request, I find it very helpful to talk to the journalist/reporter to establish which angle they are approaching the report from. This is something I now do regularly, but prior to any interview experience, I remember being unsure whether this was an accepted thing to do. Reporters tend to be happy to discuss the best way to approach the topic, and this can really help you get a feel for the potential direction and tone of the interview. In some instances, it is also possible to request interview questions ahead of an interview, or to review the quotes or recorded footage prior to the story going live. It certainly doesn't harm to ask.

Another aspect that is easy to overlook is the imagery used by the press or other dissemination outlets when presenting your research. It can be helpful to discuss what images will be used, as an inappropriate image could portray your work in a negative or inaccurate light. For instance, it is generally advisable to avoid imagery that portrays or strengthens an ED stereotype—neutral imagery is often more suitable. Of course, imagery may not always be within the researcher's control, but it does pay to ask about these things whenever possible.

### *Don't forget to get your research 'out there'!*

I also believe that it is hugely important that researchers strive to engage with the public and other non-academic audiences to help promote increased understanding around EDs and online communication. This can help to increase awareness of positive findings, which may not always receive the media publicity of the more extreme and/or negative findings. To help achieve this, I try to disseminate my research to policy-makers and governmental bodies, for example to help improve public messages and health campaigns (e.g., Talbot & Branley-Bell, 2020). I also look for opportunities to take part in public events, to help disseminate my research findings to a non-academic audience and/or provide public reports that can be disseminated through non-academic channels such as through ED charities, public websites and blog posts (Branley-Bell & Talbot, 2020a).

## Conclusion

In this chapter, I have reflected upon some of my experiences, and personal lessons learned, during my time as a researcher investigating online communication around EDs. Online communication can play a vital role in the lives of individuals experiencing EDs, and awareness of this is growing within academic and professional contexts. Despite this, negative stigma is still common amongst the mass media and general population. Individuals with EDs still report feeling misunderstood. Qualitative and mixed-methods approaches can provide positive methods to help raise understanding and awareness. In turn, this can help to develop a shared language and identify positive approaches to treatment, more effective support mechanisms and appropriate non-shaming public health messages.

I hope the insights I have shared are helpful, or at least provide some food for thought. That said, if working in research has taught me anything, it is that every day is a lesson—and I am under no illusion that there are no more learn in the future. The online research environment is a challenging but rewarding one, with an abundance of research opportunity. As responsible researchers, we should strive to use appropriate study designs, keep up to date with ethical issues and involve those with lived experience whenever possible. Research is a continuous learning process and by sharing our experiences more openly, we can help to contribute to an ever-stronger body of knowledge.

## References

Ali, K., Fassnacht, D.B., Farrer, L., Rieger, E., Feldhege, J., Moessner, M., Griffiths, K.M., & Bauer, S. (2020). What prevents young adults from seeking help? Barriers toward help-seeking for eating disorder symptomatology. *International Journal of Eating Disorders* 53(6): 894–906. https://doi.org/10.1002/eat.23266

Arcelus, J., Mitchell, A.J., Wales, J., & Nielsen, S. (2011). Mortality rates in patients with anorexia nervosa and other eating disorders: a meta-analysis of 36 studies. *Archives of General Psychiatry*. https://doi.org/10.1001/archgenpsychiatry.2011.74

Asbury, T., & Hall, S. (2013). Facebook as a mechanism for social support and mental health wellness. *Psi Chi Journal of Psychological Research* 18(3): 124–29. https://doi.org/10.24839/2164-8204.jn18.3.124

Barak, A. (2007). Emotional support and suicide prevention through the Internet: a field project report. *Computers in Human Behaviour* 23(2): 971–84. https://doi.org/10.1016/j.chb.2005.08.001

Bine, A.-S. (28 October 2013). Social media is redefining 'fepression'. *The Atlantic*.

Boyd, H., McKernon, S., Mullin, B., & Old, A. (2012). Improving healthcare through the use of co-design. *The New Zealand Medical Journal* 125(1357): 76–87.

Branley, D.B. (2015). *Risky Behaviour: Psychological Mechanisms Underpinning Social Media Users' Engagement*. Durham: Durham University.

Branley, D.B., & Covey, J. (2017). Pro-ana versus pro-recovery: a content analytic comparison of social media users' communication about eating disorders on Twitter and Tumblr. *Frontiers in Psychology* 8: 1356. https://doi.org/10.3389/fpsyg.2017.01356

Branley-Bell, D., & Talbot, C. (24 August 2020a). People with eating disorders saw their symptoms worsen during the pandemic. *The Conversation*. http://theconversation.com/people-with-eating-disorders-saw-their-symptoms-worsen-during-the-pandemic-new-study-140487

Branley-Bell, D., & Talbot, C.V. (2020b). Exploring the impact of the COVID-19 pandemic and UK lockdown on individuals with experience of eating disorders. *Journal of Eating Disorders* 8(1): 44. https://doi.org/10.1186/s40337-020-00319-y

British Psychological Society (2014). Code of human research ethics. Leicester: BPS.

Brotsky, S.R., & Giles, D. (2007). Inside the 'pro-ana' community: a covert online participant observation. *Eating Disorders* 15(2): 93–109. https://doi.org/10.1080/10640260701190600

Chalmers, V. (December 2019). Social media is fuelling eating disorders among kids as young as 12. *Daily Mail*. https://www.dailymail.co.uk/health/article-7751201/Social-media-fuelling-eating-disorders-kids-young-12.html

Chen, X., & Yang, L. (2016). Social support within online communities: internet reach and content analysis of a cancer anti-stigma Facebook page in Mexico. *Global Media Journal* 1(1).

Crawford, A. (March 2019). Instagram eating disorder content 'out of control': BBC News. *BBC News*. https://www.bbc.co.uk/news/uk-47637377

Docherty, A.B., Harrison, E.M., Green, C.A., Hardwick, H.E., Pius, R., Norman, L., Holden, K.A., Read, J.M., Dondelinger, F., Carson, G., Merson, L., Lee, J., Plotkin, D., Sigfrid, L., Halpin, S., Jackson, C., Gamble, C., Horby, P.W., Nguyen-Van-Tam, J.S., … & Semple, M.G. (2020). Features of 20 133 UK patients in hospital with covid-19 using the ISARIC WHO Clinical Characterisation Protocol: prospective observational cohort study. *BMJ* 369. https://doi.org/10.1136/bmj.m1985

Eikey, E.V., & Booth, K.M. (2017). Recovery and maintenance: how women with eating disorders use Instagram. iConference. https://doi.org/10.9776/17024

Hart, L.M., Granillo, M.T., Jorm, A.F., & Paxton, S.J. (2011). Unmet need for treatment in the eating disorders: a systematic review of eating disorder specific treatment seeking among community cases. *Clinical Psychology Review* 31(5): 727–35. https://doi.org/10.1016/j.cpr.2011.03.004

Highton-Williamson, E., Priebe, S., & Giacco, D. (2015). Online social networking in people with psychosis: a systematic review. *The International Journal of Social Psychiatry* 61(1): 92–101. https://doi.org/10.1177/0020764014556392

Hussain, A., Mahawar, K., Xia, Z., Yang, W., & El-Hasani, S. (2020). Obesity and mortality of COVID-19: meta-analysis. *Obesity Research & Clinical Practice* 14(4): 295–300. https://doi.org/10.1016/j.orcp.2020.07.002

Kendal, S., Kirk, S., Elvey, R., Catchpole, R., & Pryjmachuk, S. (2017). How a moderated online discussion forum facilitates support for young people with eating disorders. *Health Expectations* 20(1): 98–111. https://doi.org/10.1111/hex.12439

Lantos, E. (22 June 2020). TikTok: fears videos may 'trigger eating disorders'. *BBC News*. https://www.bbc.co.uk/news/uk-wales-52919914

Leavitt, V.M., Riley, C.S., De Jager, P.L., & Bloom, S. (2019). eSupport: feasibility trial of telehealth support group participation to reduce loneliness in multiple sclerosis. *Multiple Sclerosis Journal* 26(13). https://doi.org/10.1177/1352458519884241

Lipczynska, S. (2007). Discovering the cult of ana and mia: a review of pro-anorexia websites. *Journal of Mental Health* 16(4): 545–48. https://doi.org/10.1080/09638230902946874

McLean, S.A., Caldwell, B., & Roberton, M. (2019). Reach out and recover: intentions to seek treatment in individuals using online support for eating disorders. *International Journal of Eating Disorders* 52(10): 1137–49. https://doi.org/10.1002/eat.23133

McNamara, N., & Parsons, H. (2016). 'Everyone here wants everyone else to get better': the role of social identity in eating disorder recovery. *British Journal of Social Psychology* 55(4): 662–80. https://doi.org/10.1111/bjso.12161

Mead, K. (27 July 2020). Obesity campaign branded 'stigmatising' by eating disorder specialists. *ITV News*.

Naslund, J.A., Aschbrenner, K.A., & Bartels, S.J. (2016). How people with serious mental illness use smartphones, mobile apps, and social media. *Psychiatric Rehabilitation Journal* 39(4): 364–67. https://doi.org/10.1037/prj0000207

Norris, M.L., Boydell, K.M., Pinhas, L., & Katzman, D.K. (2006). Ana and the Internet: a review of pro-anorexia websites. *The International Journal of Eating Disorders* 39(6): 443–47. https://doi.org/10.1002/eat.20305

Pretorius, C., Chambers, D., & Coyle, D. (2019). Young people's online help-seeking and mental health difficulties: systematic narrative review. *Journal of Medical Internet Research* 21(11): e13873. https://doi.org/10.2196/13873

Public Health England. (27 July 2020). Major new campaign encourages millions to lose weight and cut COVID-19 risk. GOV.UK. https://www.gov.uk/government/news/major-new-campaign-encourages-millions-to-lose-weight-and-cut-covid-19-risk

Rifkin, A. (2013). Tumblr is not what you think. http://techcrunch.com/2013/02/18/tumblr-is-not-what-you-think

Schroeder, P.A. (2010). Adolescent girls in recovery for eating disorders: exploring past pro-anorexia internet community experiences. In *Dissertation Abstracts International: Section B: The Sciences and Engineering*. Alhambra, CA: Alliant International University.

Smahelova, M., Drtilova, H., Smahel, D., & Cevelicek, M. (2020). Internet usage by women with eating disorders during illness and recovery. *Health Communication* 35(5): 628–36. https://doi.org/10.1080/10410236.2019.1582135

Smith-Merry, J., Goggin, G., Campbell, A., McKenzie, K., Ridout, B., & Baylosis, C. (2019). Social connection and online engagement: insights from interviews with users of a mental health online forum. *JMIR Mental Health* 6(3): e11084. https://doi.org/10.2196/11084

Talbot, Catherine V., & Branley-Bell, D. (2020). #BetterHealth: a qualitative analysis of reactions to the UK Government's better health campaign. *PsyArXiv Preprint*. https://doi.org/10.31234/osf.io/rmjsg

Talbot, C.V., Gavin, J., van Steen, T., & Morey, Y. (2017). A content analysis of thinspiration, fitspiration, and bonespiration imagery on social media. *Journal of Eating Disorders* 5(1): 40. https://doi.org/10.1186/s40337-017-0170-2

Tong, S.T., Heinemann-LaFave, D., Jeon, J., Kolodziej-Smith, R., & Warshay, N. (2013). The use of pro-ana blogs for online soial support. *Eating Disorders* 21(5): 408–22. https://doi.org/10.1080/10640266.2013.827538

Wright, K.B., Bell, S.B., Wright, K.B., & Bell, S.B. (2003). Health-related support groups on the internet: linking empirical findings to social support and computer-mediated communication theory. *Journal of Health Psychology* 8(1): 39–54. https://doi.org/10.1177/1359105303008001429

Yeshua-Katz, D. (2015). Online stigma resistance in the pro-ana community. *Qualitative Health Research* 25(10): 1347–58. https://doi.org/10.1177/1049732315570123

Yorke, E., Evans-Atkinson, T., & Katzman, D.K. (2020). Shared language and communicating with adolescents and young adults with eating disorders. *Paediatrics & Child Health*. https://doi.org/10.1093/pch/pxaa047

Zhang, S., Bantum, E.O.C., Owen, J., Bakken, S., & Elhadad, N. (2017). Online cancer communities as informatics intervention for social support: conceptualization, characterization, and impact. *Journal of the American Medical Informatics Association* 24(2): 451–59. https://doi.org/10.1093/jamia/ocw093

# 11 'I'll Never Be Skinny Enough': A Fantasy Theme Analysis of Pro-Anorexia Discourse

*Allyn Lueders*

## Introduction

Do you feel fat sometimes? Bloated after eating a big meal? Do you enjoy food but feel guilty for over-indulging on occasion? Are you embarrassed to eat in front of some people? A specific person? We all have different relationships to food and eating. Such feelings become a disorder when they take over your life and you simply cannot stop thinking about them. While eating disorders have ancient roots (Bemporad, 1996), they have become more prevalent in the USA and around the world in recent years (Dalkilic, 2013).

Body image and feminine or masculine identity are essential components of Western/industrialized life (Malson, 2008). Social media exacerbate both facts as technology streamlines posting pictures of yourself and looking at pictures of others in a state of constant comparison (Mabe et al., 2014; Sidani et al., 2016). Having an eating disorder is often connected with other life stressors and complications such as domestic abuse, low self-esteem, need for control and lack of interpersonal support (Le Grange et al., 2012; Martin et al., 2019; Staff, 2018).

When at a loss for a supportive relationship or mentor connection, many people look to the internet to supplement what they cannot find face-to-face. Online, they will discover many thriving eating/dieting support communities with copious offerings: nutritional suggestions, advice from top medical experts

Allyn Lueders, 'Chapter 11: 'I'll Never Be Skinny Enough': A Fantasy Theme Analysis of Pro-Anorexia Discourse' in: *Eating Disorders in Public Discourse: Exploring Media Representations and Lived Experiences*. University of Exeter Press (2023). © Allyn Lueders. DOI: 10.47788/SDQF1133 and in-home counselling to support a healthy road to recovery from the disorder. If someone would like to be on the path to recovery, there are plenty of websites to help get there. But not everyone goes to the internet with such 'healthy' intentions. Instead, a person may want 'thinspirational' workout tips, starvation dieting plans, 'hiding your weight loss' strategies and pictures of emaciated women and men to show the ultimate possibilities (Gring, 2017). If it seems offensive for someone to suggest a need to recover, or that 'lack of' eating decisions are wrong, there are plenty of websites to encourage this as well. Pro-anorexia and pro-bulimia (often termed pro-ana and pro-mia) websites are available to support these ideals. It may be difficult to find like-minded individuals who support such pursuits at school or work, but they are easily found in the online world.

Pro-ana and pro-mia sites originally gained popularity in the early 2000s (Casilli et al., 2012), but the movement was introduced to a wider audience through a *Newsweek* article of 6 December 2006 (Springen). Onlookers were immediately worried and started spreading their concerns about lasting physical, mental and societal impacts of sharing these ideas online. Many thought that webhosts should be able to shut down any site that promotes self-harm or dangerous habits, but other members of the public argued for free speech. No matter the decision, pro-eating disorder site owners continually move their content from site to site, so it is hard for authorities to monitor them and meanwhile they are ever more accessible by the public. Since these early days, search engines such as Google and Yahoo have attempted to outlaw these sites on the basis that they promote self-harm and violate search engine terms and conditions (Custers, 2015).

Not to be deterred, pro-eating disorder site owners continually re-package their sites, changing keywords and jargon so as not to be detected and censored (Casilli et al., 2012). Sites are listed under new URLs, based out of different webhosts or disguised in yet other ways. For example, pages that were originally found through a Yahoo search may have later been located through a Google search, or a site that was once a Xanga site may now be found only through WordPress (Casilli et al., 2012; Gring, 2017). Still available and growing, pro-ana/mia sites offer a community to members, a place to talk about their weight loss goals and find support to achieve those goals. These comments are often in narrative form, but participants also post pictures and videos that are referred to as 'thinspo' or 'thinspirational' to encourage members to continue pursuing their weight loss goals to an extreme level (Barnett, 2012; Tong et al., 2013).

### *Symbolic convergence theory*

Using terms like 'thinspo' or 'thinspirational' and related behaviour patterns become commonplace and well understood by a group of people through symbolic convergence. 'Individuals build a sense of community or a group consciousness' through symbolic convergence (Griffin, 2016, p. 39). It is an assumption of symbolic convergence theory (SCT) that 'meaning, emotion, and motive for action are manifest in the content of the message' (Wu, 2017, p. 24). SCT describes how groups create and share fantasies about the group and outside groups and thereby develop a shared identity (Duffy, 2003). Members know what to say and what the expected reaction is because the group shares meanings/understandings.

Indeed, symbolic convergence occurs when a group is involved in a fantasy theme or rhetorical vision (Adams, 2013). A fantasy theme is 'the content of the dramatizing message' that is repeated in various contexts and used by multiple people. Through such continuous use, a fantasy chain may be formed (Bormann, 1985, p. 5). A rhetorical vision, similarly, is a 'unified putting-together of things to give participants [in a community, like a pro-ana group] a broader view of things' (Bormann, 1985, p. 8).

Being involved in a rhetorical community where people share understanding and viewpoints (Bormann, 1985) helps members of a pro-ana community express themselves and share feelings in a group of like-minded individuals that they might not otherwise find. Put simply, they feel safe within the group. Further, the interactive nature of such social media sites and blogs solidifies visitors' influence on each other (Perloff, 2014). By reading the blog, following along with others' stories and identifying similarities between the poster and oneself, website participants adopt the rhetorical vision and fantasy therein (Duffy, 2003). They are able to develop a community to seek and exchange support that they cannot access through their offline connections (Tong et al., 2013).

Pro-ana sites are usually operated by one or more individuals who have an eating disorder themselves and seek to gain and provide emotional support (Tong et al., 2013). Results from a cross-sectional survey show that 'well over half of survey respondents' join pro-ana or pro-mia sites to give and receive emotional support (Mantella, 2007, p. 28). In fact, participants in pro-eating disorder communities have reported that they receive support from these sites that they do not receive in their offline social networks (Brotsky & Giles, 2007).

Much research has been done on pro-eating disorder sites (e.g., Casilli et al., 2012; Custers, 2015; Dias, 2003; Gring, 2017; Haas, 2010) because anorexia and bulimia are such serious disorders. Hass, Jennings and Chang (2021) point to these sites as an example of an online negative enabling support group (ONESG) because of their ability to turn a clearly negative behaviour, such as self-starvation, into a positive communal experience. In fact, anorexia is the deadliest of mental disorders (Berkman et al., 2007) so any associated behaviour is very dangerous. New research continues to be published on this phenomenon as finding the most effective solution is of paramount importance. But a panacea has yet to be found and unfortunately, exactly how the feeling of connection and safety is created within these online groups also remains unclear.

## *Fantasy theme analysis*

To examine how members of a pro-ana online community create such feelings of safety and togetherness through communication, I used fantasy theme analysis (Bormann, 1972) to analyse posts on Myproana.com (MPA).

Fantasy theme analysis (FTA) assumes that 'when individuals read or hear dramatic narratives, they participate in a social reality defined by the stories being told. That reality has characters with whom they identify and others whom they oppose; it has implied values they accept when they are moved by a character's struggle' (Kidd, 1998, para. 19). From this narration and description, FTA draws meaning and evidence of group fantasies and can 'observe, categorize, and explain group communication' (Adams, 2013, p. 72). Ultimately, FTA points to common ideas, topics or semantic clusters as evidence of fantasy themes and fantasy chains (Bauer et al., 2018; Bormann, 1972).

FTA has been used to study numerous texts including sermons of colonial Puritan ministers (Bormann, 1972), players' interactions in an online role-playing game (Hammers, 2007) and memes of the 2015 Deflategate controversy (Perreault, 2019). Each of these investigations demonstrates the explanatory power of FTA in various contexts. Bormann (1982) argues that in all contexts, group communication works through symbolic convergence, two or more symbolic worlds moving towards each other and overlapping through communication. This process is more than a rational convergence. It is an emotional understanding between people that allows and encourages group members to sympathize, empathize and connect with each other. When members find that they interpret life events in similar ways, they often also connect through shared conversational fantasies.

'Fantasy', in this theory, is not used in the same way as in normal conversation. As a colloquialism, fantasy is used to describe something imaginary or unreal. In FTA and SCT, 'the technical meaning for fantasy is the creative and imaginative interpretation of events that fulfils a psychological or rhetorical need' (Bormann, 1985, p. 5). Put simply, a person needs for something to be true to legitimize personal choices and therefore creatively interprets events to make it true.

The fantasy is taken to the next level when it becomes a fantasy theme. As Bormann explains, a fantasy theme occurs when an idea or discourse is supported within a community (Adams, 2013; Bormann, 1980). Even further, when a fantasy theme is picked up in group conversation, expanded upon and used in multiple instances, it becomes a fantasy chain (Bormann, 1985). When members gravitate towards a line of dialogue, the conversation tempo picks up, excitement grows and people start talking over each other because they just can't wait to add more, a fantasy chain is created, or the fantasy 'chains out' (Adams, 2013; Bormann, 1985).

A fantasy chain occurs most often in a rhetorical community. More than a group of people who speak the same language, a rhetorical community shares a common communication style and rhetorical vision of the future (Bormann, 1980). When a group of people get together and find common ground in their shared difficulties and disturbances with the current situation, a rhetorical community is created. Through discussion of these common hardships, individuals are likely to create meaningful social bonds. In fact, group members frequently use fantasies as a way to relieve tension within the group (Griffin, 2016) and remind group members of what they all share. Additionally, fantasies are used to describe the main tenet of a group's communication to newcomers and experienced members alike.

Bormann (1985) emphasizes that certain rhetorical visions can be quite powerful: 'Some rhetorical visions are so all-encompassing and impelling that they permeate an individual's social reality in all aspects of living. I call such all-encompassing symbolic systems life-style rhetorical visions' (p. 8). A life-style rhetorical vision is so compelling that it moves people into action:

> When a person appropriates a rhetorical vision, he [*sic*] gains the supporting dramas and constraining forces which compel the adoption of a lifestyle and to take certain action. The born-again Christian [for example] is baptized and adopts a lifestyle and behaviour modelled after the heroes of the dramas that sustain that vision. (Bormann, 1982)

It follows that a person embroiled within a pro-eating disorder community would also adopt that lifestyle, alter their eating habits and view extreme weight loss as success.

Bormann's description of how a critic can use FTA to understand a rhetorical community gives an overview of this technique:

> A critic can take the social reality contained in a rhetorical vision which he [*sic*] has constructed from the concrete dramas developed in a body of discourse and examine the social relationships, the motives, the qualitative impact of that symbolic world as though it were the substance of social reality for those people who participated in the vision. (Bormann, 1982, p. 401)

Following these investigate guidelines illuminates the driving force behind a social reality or fantasy theme in a rhetorical community.

## Method

### *Procedure*

Therefore, to uncover the rhetorical vision embedded within pro-eating disorder online communities, I conducted an FTA. Specifically, I marked repeated symbolic cues, dramatis personae (characters), plot line (action) and scene (setting) as units of analysis (Bormann, 1980; Duffy, 2003).

### *Sample*

To fuel this study, I collected data from MPA for a two-month period between 1 February 2020 and 1 April 2020. I chose his community for analysis because of the frequency and currency of posts, and the number of members. Specifically, on 1 February 2020, MPA had 416,182 members who post, reply and/or read the site daily under a screenname, which may or may not be their actual name.

During this study's time frame of analysis, five main threads stood out as hot topics because they regularly attracted attention and induced site activity. Threads included as data for this study include: 'Stupid things normies believe', 'Calories for today *High restrictors only*', 'Do you love being skinny in airports', 'Do you think you [are] skinny', and 'Have you ever ED version'. Together, these threads consisted of 1,652 posts. Each post ranged in length from 1 to 202 words, with an average length of 25 words.

Sixty-two per cent of the included posts were 'liked' on MPA, and 16% included at least one picture. I copied posts from these five main threads on the Anorexia Discussion board into a Word document and then deleted extra spaces and ads. This resulted in 845 pages of single-spaced 12 pt. text. Analysis of this text informed the current study and provided evidence of fantasy themes present.

I first began analysis by reading through all data multiple times to familiarize myself. I discerned dramatizing agents (i.e., characters, action, setting), frequently used keywords, expression of site rules and emotion description for analysis at this stage following Bormann (1982) and extant research (e.g., Simmons, 2014). To make sense of how these community members have constructed their rhetorical community, it was important to detect instances in which community members perpetuated fantasy logic.

### *Description of MPA*

As the 'About' section of MPA describes, 'MPA is a site dedicated to the support or recovery of those suffering from eating disorders or body dysmorphic disorders. Please be sensitive to this fact when creating an account and contributing to board.' There are message boards dedicated to anorexia, bulimia, four other types of eating disorders and twelve other related topics. I chose the anorexia discussion board for analysis in this study because it was the source of the most activity by far; there were 3.7 million replies on the anorexia board, and 0.9 million replies on the bulimia board as of 1 February 2020.

The site editor describes the anorexia discussion board as 'a place to discuss anything specifically related to Anorexia' (MPA). A common post that is seen on such sites includes, 'CW HW LW GW UGW' which stands for current weight, highest weight, lowest weight, goal weight and ultimate goal weight. In this format, members are able to confess their current weight, highest weight and so on, and it is expected that the listed current weight and highest weight are to be scoffed at or empathized with, lowest weight should be congratulated and goal weight encouraged.

To create an account and make contributions to the site, a person must fill out a form with a username (or screen name) and password. But as a researcher, I chose not to create an account and remain a lurker, since many others do as well. 'Lurkers' are defined as 'passive, noninteractive members' and often account for many users in any online community (Mousavi et al., 2017, p. 376). A study done by Mousavi et al. (2017) revealed that 43% of males and 57% of females were lurkers on online brand communities. Demonstrating similar percentages, on the first day of data collection for the current study, 44 members and 71 guests (lurkers) were browsing the Anorexia discussion forum at MPA. Clearly, MPA follows the lurking patterns found by other researchers.

There are many reasons people choose to remain lurkers instead of becoming members of online communities (Preece et al., 2004; Schneider et al., 2013). Preece et al. (2004) found that feeling posting was unnecessary, thinking they were being helpful by not posting and needing to learn more about the group before posting were top motivators of survey respondents. Lurking is now seen as a more legitimate research focus as the way people engage with online environments becomes clearer (Edelmann, 2013; Walker et al., 2013). Therefore, it was meaningful for the current study to analyse only posts that lurkers can read, as they likely make up more than half of site visitors per day.

Lurker or member, anyone can read posts on this site without creating an account. However, there are some forums on MPA that are members only. The ability to see a full member list is restricted to members only as well. All data I collected for this study was publicly available, so it was not necessary to submit for IRB approval for this project. Members' privacy was not threatened or imposed upon because all collected data was publicly available online.

## Findings: Results and Discussion

### *Characters*

FTA aims to demonstrate how fantasy themes come together through tracking three categories: character, action and setting (Bormann, 1982; Engstrom, 2009). The way these dramatic dynamics support overarching ideals is key for fantasy theme development. First, characters found in the MPA posts can easily be separated into two main categories. Perhaps because of the inherent conflict or defensiveness involved in pro-eating disorder websites, the Us vs. Them dichotomy is blatantly obvious in this study's data. The 'Us' category for MPA includes all references to 'I' or 'we' in the data informing this study and any descriptions of self.

### *Us*

Participants on MPA described themselves in many ways, both positive and negative.

Unsurprisingly, many commenters on this website suffer from low self-esteem and therefore often paint themselves in a negative light. For example, in answer to the 'Do you think you skinny' thread, 'Darling Nikki' responded, 'I think I look healthy or athletic, not skinny. I want to lose another 15 lbs and am hoping then I'll finally look skinny to myself. Though I know I won't ☹.' Showing that she takes things even further, 'Guest_SecretAccountImScared' asked, in the 'Have you ever ED version' thread, 'Have you ever hit your UGW [ultimate goal weight]? (If so, what was it like?)'. 'Dieanax' responded, 'yes, around bmi 11-12. but by that time i was literally at deaths door. couldn't give two shits about how i looked [*sic*].' This post received one like.

Each post at MPA was not always so dark. Participants often referred to themselves in a positive way when speaking from experience. In answer to the 'Do you think you skinny' thread, 'Hannah94' posted:

> Objectively yes. Am I satisfied? No. But I still decided to maintain because I know for sure that I will never be satisfied at any weight. So now I'm at least ok with my body andstill somewhat healthy (BMI 15.9). It still is a constant battle not lowering my goal weight any further … Food and water weight is messing with my head.

With this post, 'Hannah94' signalled to other MPA participants that she has achieved her UGW and can say from experience that it is an ugly road that others might not want to pursue.

Another post that exemplifies positive self-descriptions on MPA came from 'Grim Reaper'. While not positive from an objective standard, this post shows the poster is proud and determined: 'I figured out that I still lose [weight] on 2300k cal/day though the tdee calculator says I only need ~1700 to 1900 kcal to maintain … and my BMI is so low that I just cant function when having big kcal deficits and I kinda dont wanna die rn [right now, *sic*].'

### *Them*

The Us character, while prominent, was not alone in MPA posts. The second main character present on MPA fills out the 'Them' category. 'Them' in this data includes 'normies' and parents/family. 'Normies' is the title participants used to describe those without an eating disorder or people who do not carry out restricted eating habits. Anyone who expresses worry about a participant or tries to impede their thinness goals also fits this category.

A main thread included in this study is 'Stupid things normies believe', and it was clear that MPA members delighted in laughing about how stupid, easily tricked, and ignorant 'normies' are. For instance, 'Jinxie' wrote: 'My coworker is on the keto diet, not losing anything as shes [*sic*] eating her tdee [total daily energy expenditure] in fat. Why is CICO [calories in, calories out] so hard to understand?' Similarly, 'Daughter of the Rainbow' shared the following story about her father:

> OMG the other day my dad was saying, 'There is an eating disorder, where you hyperfocus on food and tell yourself, okay i can only eat 800 calories…'
>
> He doesn't know about my ed [eating disorder], he was talking about what kind of food should be put in the pantry for 'growing teenagers and kids.' I thought it was funny because I've just recently found that just under 700 cals a day is my sweet spot, but i used to eat like 300 or less a day for two, three, or four days and then binge enormously lol. And he has. no. ideeeaaa … mwahaha [*sic*]

With this example, 'Daughter of the Rainbow' demonstrates how she is part of the 'Us' category, and her father is in the 'Them' category. For examples, see Table 11.1A.

As an additional example of the 'Them' category, 'impmon' recalls:

> my boyfriend's mom tried to 'understand' my disorder once and made me veggies. but she cooked them in oil. so i didn't eat them. she wasnt offended but she tried to be like, 'BUT I USED (SOME HEALTHY???) OIL SO IT'S HEALTHY SO IT SHOULDNT SCARE YOU' MA'AM IT IS STILL LIKE 150 CAL PER TBSP I DON'T CARE [*sic*].

**Table 11.1** Dramatizing agents

| | *Examples* | *No. of occurrences* |
|---|---|---|
| **11.1 (A) Characters** | | |
| Us<br>Negative | • I think I look healthy or athletic, not skinny. I want to lose another 15 lbs and am hoping then I'll finally look skinny to myself. Though I know I won't 🙁<br>• I think I'm thin but I'm not happy with it because I'm still at a healthy/normal BMI and I won't be happy until I'm underweight and have a thigh gap | 1,422 |
| Positive | • So now I'm at least ok with my body and still somewhat healthy (BMI 15.9)<br>• Still losing weight so I'm over the moon! | |
| Them | • My coworker is on the keto diet, not losing anything as shes [*sic*] eating her tdee [total daily energy expenditure] in fat. Why is CICO [calories in, calories out] so hard to understand?<br>• OMG the other day my dad was saying, 'There is an eating disorder, where you hyperfocus on food and tell yourself, okay i can only eat 800 calories..behaviour He doesn't know about my ed [eating disorder], he was talking about what kind of food should be put in the pantry for 'growing teenagers and kids'. I thought it was funny because I've just recently found that just under 700 cals a day is my sweet spot, but i used to eat like 300 or less a day for two, three, or four days and then binge enormously lol. And he has. no. ideeeaaa … mwahaha [*sic*] | 82 |
| **11.1 (B) Actions** | | |
| I'm trying (to)…<br>Recovery based<br>Non-recovery based | • not to count calories, but I still estimate<br>• bump up my intake<br>• get out of severe low restriction<br>• to work my way up to high restriction (and stay there) so I'm really excited to see some examples<br>• slowly lose down to BMI 13.4<br>• eat a low tdee<br>• make up for lack of exercise with lower restriction | 11 |
| Calorie actions | • counting<br>• avoiding<br>• estimating<br>• consumed | 48 |
| Weight actions | • gaining<br>• losing<br>• maintaining<br>• being | 270 |
| **11.1 (C) Setting** | | |
| 'here' | • Only here and on my ed tumblr<br>• I'm just out here lapsing after 3 years<br>• just here to feel less crazy | 18 |
| 'place' | • A place to discuss anything specifically related to Anorexia<br>• This is a safe place for high restrictors ONLY | 13 |

Even though this woman tried to understand, she failed in the eyes of 'impmon' and thus is cast as a 'Them' character. For examples, see Table 11.1A.

### *Actions*

Besides characters, it is important to consider actions present on MPA. A commonly used semantic cluster on MPA was 'I'm trying' and this automatically calls for an action. 'I'm trying' was used most often on MPA in reference to restrictive eating habits or dysmorphic ideas. For instance, 'AyySock' mentioned on the 'Calories for today *High restrictors only*' thread, 'I'm trying to work my way up to high restriction (and stay there) so I'm really excited to see some examples (:.' This post received two likes. Similarly, 'Fatass2003' said, 'I'm trying to slowly lose (down to BMI 13,4) [*sic*].' Also, 'shrinkingviol3t' said, 'Ednos (eating disorder not otherwise specified). 27 and still trying to disappear.'

In contrast, other participants used the 'I'm trying' semantic cluster to discuss goals of recovery habits. Member 'thin&thinner' said: 'I'm at 1167 [calories] so far today and I'm very proud of myself (trying to rewire my pissant brain into eating beyond my past restriction of under 800). Hoping to get myself to eat more before bed, too!' and 'Thegymbum' mentioned, 'trying to bump up my intake for a few days'. For examples, see Table 11.1B.

### *Setting*

Characters and actions are undoubtedly large contributors to fantasy development on MPA. The setting of MPA also adds to fantasy development specifically because of the controversy and online interactions involved on the site. As mentioned above, the pro-ana movement has been in the public eye for more than ten years and, as such, MPA is just as likely to be championed as it is to be ostracized by potential onlookers (Boero & Pascoe, 2012; Hoffman, 2018; Tong et al., 2013). The influence of the feud can even be seen in comments on MPA. For example, 'idontwannabeyouanymoree' posted, 'Have you ever actually been PRO Ana?' 'BeautifullyUnreal' liked this post and then responded, 'Yes and still am. Been pro for the last 7.5yrs, but I obviously won't admit it on other sites like IG [Instagram] or FB [Facebook].' Apparently other websites are not seen to be as accepting of pro-ana ideas as MPA.

Another impactful aspect of the setting is that MPA is an online group. This inherently affords anonymity to participants, increases the opportunity for honest and frequent self-disclosure and is considered a safe place. Specifically, Tong et al. (2013, p. 408) note that blogs like MPA offer participants 'interactivity, self-disclosure, [and] masspersonal communication'. Interactivity here suggests that contributors can comment, respond and constantly make changes to the forum; it is not static. Further, self-disclosure is encouraged on forums like MPA through the anonymity they afford users. Similarly, the masspersonal level of communication online offers additional anonymity through the ability to get lost in the online crowd, but a close personal connection is still available through forums with optional one-on-one interactions.

Furthermore, participants can post pictures of themselves or share pictures that do not include the face, so as not to be identified. Being anonymous encourages increased self-disclosure, and likely more honesty, from all contributors (Ging & Garvey, 2017; Hass et al., 2010). These connections available online through MPA contribute to fantasy development amongst participants and lurkers, as can be seen through posts such as when 'Fatass2003' shared: 'My BMI is 14,2 (I know there are many people on here with lower bmis but yeah).' By referencing MPA with the word 'here', 'Fatass2003' constructs MPA as a place with a setting that influences what is shared.

The anorexia discussion board description, 'A place to discuss anything specifically related to Anorexia', also sets the reality constructed online on MPA in a location that includes certain expectations. Users are expected to say certain things at certain times and react in certain ways because of rules built in this environment. One specific instance where this became clear on the discussion board came when one user posted something that others thought was wrong, out of place, or against the rules. In the 'Calories for today *High restrictors only*' thread, a discussion broke out about the definition of high restriction. This thread was started by 'Fatass2003', who introduced the idea by stating,

> I know it can be a bit invalidating and quite frankly soul crushing to post your calories on the main thread when you are a high restrictor. But your ED is just as valid and severe as someone who low restricts or fasts. This is a safe place for high restrictors ONLY to post their calories for the day (along with what you ate, if you want). To be clear, I consider 800+ calories high restriction.

Despite these clear guidelines, 'dennniese' begged to differ:

> How is this high restriction? Or do i don't get it anymore, my highest intake is 100 kcal, today i had a hypo from to low blood sugar and i eat for the forst times in months, a slices of Bread no crost with peanut butter. But i am hoping that i am on my place here i read a lot off other people that do the same. Today 165 kcal and scared to death for the scale, workout double! Good luck tomorrow everyone. And i don't mean you guys eat healty or a lot but in my mind for me it is way to much you stil eat way to little [*sic*].

Member 'kalynn' immediately responded, 'Not sure why you felt the need to post this in a thread that's specifically meant to be a safe space for high restrictors who can get triggered by seeing low restriction posts? No one is impressed here.' This and other posts solidify the setting of MPA. For examples, see Table 11.1C.

Because of characters, actions and setting abundantly present in posts, the fact that a rhetorical community has been formed at MPA was clear upon first reading this data. Contributors do appear to have created their own reality in this community. After multiple iterations through the data, in addition to the dramatizing agents, emotions and frequently used keywords became apparent. Finally, and of utmost importance to the creation of a rhetorical community, the acceptance of a social reality of the site and of objective reality was also indisputable at MPA.

As can be imagined, a forum focused on eating disorders is an emotional place. Even so, the word 'feeling' was only present in this data eight times. However, I coded 69 posts as expressing emotion across all threads. Users expressed both positive and negative emotion on the site. Upon further analysis, I condensed the 69 posts as expressing eight main emotions. Six were negative: frustrated, disgusted, regretful, anxious, scared, guilty, and two were positive: happy, relaxed.

### *Emotion*

The emotion about which participants most frequently posted during the time of data collection was frustration. Sixteen posts were coded as expressing frustration. Posters were frustrated about their struggles with weight and food, and dealings with other people. Specifically, 'dollop' responded to another member's post about being demotivated by slow weight loss by saying, 'It's just so frustrating that it happens all the time, but also good to realise [*sic*] that I'm not the only one.' As another example, admitting that none of her clothes fit after weight loss, 'something_of_a_porkrind' said, 'It makes me both happy and incredibly frustrated.'

Another emotion frequently expressed on MPA was disgust. Specifically, I coded 14 posts as expressing disgust. Members were disgusted both with themselves and with food/eating. In the 'Have you ever ED version' thread, 'JoceyCat' admitted to suffering with a side effect of undereating. She said, 'Yes, and it's disgusting. I shed more than my cats.' In the same thread, redcola asked, 'Have you ever thrown food out to avoid eating it but then couldn't resist the temptation and ate it out of the garbage can?' Member 'anorexic.engineer' liked the question post and then responded, 'disgustingly yes lmao'.

In addition to all the negative emotions, there were two positive emotions expressed in this data: relaxation and happiness. The first was relaxation, which was mentioned twice. 'Stupid and mental' admitted that even though some foods are terrifying, the fear subsides when it is finally eaten: 'yeah, i [*sic*] can relax when i have too'. Another way participants at MPA reported achieving relaxation was through drugs. As part of the 'Have you ever ED version' thread, '9ainty' asked, 'Have you ever taken drugs to reduce appetite?' 'Bloodfloodms' responded, 'Yes, weed to relax, have a longer fast and sleep without the hunger pain. But nothing like hard drugs.'

The second positive emotion about which participants posted on MPA is happiness. Being happy was discussed on MPA as both a purely positive emotion and a retaliatory joy that something bad happened to someone else. Taken together, being happy was referenced 27 times in this study's data. For example, in the 'Have you ever ED version' thread, 'Len97' asked, 'have you ever been happy that someone close (friend or family etc) gained weight [*sic*]'. This could be a suggestion of retaliatory happiness, where you are happy because of another's 'misfortune.' 'bruhijustneedhelp' responded, 'Yes, it was a friend who also has an ed and I was happy she was recovering,' which appears to be pure positivity. For examples, see Table 11.2.

### *Frequently used keywords*

Besides emotions, there were also frequently used keywords and semantic clusters on MPA. As mentioned above, members talked about weight loss a great

**Table 11.2** Emotion

| | *Examples* | *No. of occurrences* |
|---|---|---|
| NEGATIVE | | |
| frustrated | • It's just so frustrating that it happens all the time, but also good to realise that I'm not the only one<br>• It makes me both happy and incredibly frustrated | 16 |
| disgusted | • Edit: just checked my body and Im fat and disgusting<br>• My thighs stomach and arms are disgustingly fat and jiggly<br>• Hye drunk pickles juice just to disgust yourself and not eat?<br>• Yes it was disgusting | 14 |
| scared | • I am actually scared of getting too skinny especially w all the doctors and hospitals being too busy for the next few months but for some reason I'm still continue to restrict<br>• sometimes i want to 'recover' but most of the time i like having my disorder because im scared if i dont have it i'll get even fatter than i already am | 10 |
| regretful | • sometimes I think 'well im fat anyway' then I binge and cry after in regret, lol<br>• Yep, regret it every time | 8 |
| guilty | • the gum I have is 5 calories but I do sometimes feel guilty if I chew too much of it<br>• Chew and spit or swallow completely, I feel guilty | 7 |
| anxious | • I get anxious about it sometimes but not to the point of fear, thankfully<br>• I don't like going to parties or social gatherings of any kind, they stress me out and make me anxious because of all the people I don't know | 3 |
| POSITIVE | | |
| relaxed | • yeah, i can relax when i have too<br>• Yes, weed to relax | 5 |
| happy | • And I'm relatively happy with my body. I don't know why I'm restricting<br>• have you ever been happy that someone close (friend or family etc) gained weight | 27 |

deal, and used the repeated keywords of 'CW, GW, HW, LW, UGW' or a similar combination. For instance, '-until-it-kills-' is one of many MPA members whose signature on each post included the 'cw hw lw ugw' combination with, 'cw: i'm too scared to look lw: 154 gw:110 ugw: 90'. These keywords were used 403 times during this study's data collection. While it was extremely common to discuss weight in this way on MPA, the most used phrase during data collection was 'have you ever', as part of the 'Have you ever ED version' thread. This phrase, and its abbreviated counterpart, 'hye', was used 1,157 times in this data. Participants seem to be asking if others have similar experiences to them, and if they have perhaps taken things even further. Member 'aytche' posted in the 'Have you ever ED version' thread, 'Have you ever had a panic attack that was food/calorie related?' 'Pickles the Drummer' responded, 'Yeah, more than once. Panic attacks in general are way more common when I'm restricting.' For additional examples, see Table 11.3.

### *Construction of reality*

Finally, the construction of reality was very clear on MPA, be that objective reality or the pro-anorexic reality of Myproana.com. Objective reality was most obvious when commenters would contrast what they 'should be thinking' to what they actually were. For example, 'imyourhope' said, 'technically i am healthy but i look ... heavy [*sic*]'. Reality specifically constructed on MPA was also clear on the site, and most often when one member gave suggestions to another. When one member asked about high restricting, 'Fatass2003' responded, 'you should definitely try it. It totally works, but it is slower than low restriction. But, its [*sic*] better for your metabolism, and for me it reduces urges to binge. I lose (without exercise) like 2 lbs per week, but everyone is different.' For additional examples, see Tables 11.4A and 11.4B.

**Table 11.3** Repeated keywords

| | *Examples* | *No. of occurrences* |
|---|---|---|
| Have you ever (hye) | • Have you ever ate something despite being terrified of the calorie content?<br>• HYE refused to use food-scented/flavored soap/ shampoo etc just in case there happens to be calories in it? | 1,157 |
| CW, GW, HW, LW, UGW | • cw: 158, gw: 135, hw: 165, lw: 122<br>• HW- 145 LW- 110 CW- A weight I cannot deal with Next GW- 130 UWG- 98 (For now, I am never satisfied with myself) | 403 |

**Table 11.4** Acceptance of social reality

| | *Examples* | *No. of occurrences* |
|---|---|---|
| **11.4 (A) Acceptance of social reality of MPA** | | |
| | • you should definitely try it. It totally works, but it is slower than low restriction. But, its better for your metabolism, and for me it reduces urges to binge. I lose (without exercise) like 2 lbs per week, but everyone is different<br>• I know logically 1000 is pretty low, especially with exercise on top of it, but I feel like I'm eating a 'normal' amount of food and am fighting so hard not to restrict lower because I know I might binge if I do | 4 |
| **11.4(B) Acceptance of objective social reality** | | |
| Objective | • From a dysmorphic standpoint, I think I'm super super fat, and from outside viewers/medical standpoint I'm pretty healthy, muscular, and a couple extra pounds but not fat and not even really chubby<br>• logically, i know i am. but mentally, i still believe im fat | 21 |

Using FTA (fantasy theme analysis) to analyse messages posted on MPA (Myproana.com) highlights that members have a shared rhetorical vision that points to three identifiable fantasy themes: Us vs. Them, 'I'll never be skinny enough' and 'Open to recovery'. By focusing on dramatic components of characters, actions and setting that members concentrate on in comments, the fantasy themes became clear, as did a social construction of reality. Fantasy themes are discussed below.

## *Fantasy theme 1: Us vs. Them*

As noted previously, characters on MPA are split into two main categories: Us, including other participants on the site with similar views on food/eating; and Them, including any people outside the website who express opposing viewpoints on food/eating such as family members, friends or healthcare professionals. A fantasy theme has clearly been created surrounding this point and chains out every time a member at MPA uses an insider term that people in the Them category might not understand. Also, complaints, caricatures or chastisements thrown at those in the Them category on MPA repeatedly signal that the Us vs. Them fantasy theme should be taken as fact and carried on.

### *Fantasy theme 2: 'I'll never be skinny enough'*

Another fantasy theme present on MPA was that participants will never be satisfied with their bodies and so they can always be skinnier. They must focus on food restriction, CICO, calories and so on to have a hope of achieving their unattainable goal of extreme thinness. Moreover, this fantasy theme is repeatedly seen when focusing on the actions in which members reported engaging on MPA. Specifically, when the frequently used keyword 'calorie' or its shorthand 'cal' was referenced, three main reported actions indicate this endless pursuit of weight loss: counting, avoiding and estimating.

Reported actions were not the only evidence of this theme. Another finding from the current study is that members frequently express emotions on MPA and many are emotions motivated by pro-ana goals. For instance, several members confessed that they were scared that they would never be skinny enough or that they would never be satisfied with their bodies. One participant, 'Nikki131', commented, 'Yes I am actually scared of getting too skinny especially w [*sic*] all the doctors and hospitals being too busy for the next few months but for some reason I'm still continue [*sic*] to restrict.' This comment shows that even with outside pressures and unique worries of today, 'Nikki131' and many other participants are unable to let go of their disordered thoughts.

Ultimately, it was very clear from comments posted on MPA that members engage in the rhetorical vision or socially constructed reality of this forum. Every time a member listed their 'CW HW LW GW' (or similar combination) it was as if they labelled themselves as a part of the group, a believer, a follower of this fantasy theme. It also highlights the common understanding and shared priorities members have reached in this rhetorical community.

### *Fantasy theme 3: Open to recovery*

A final fantasy theme present on MPA was their openness to recovery and encouragement of healthy eating choices. Some members reported seeking recovery or working towards recovery, thereby marking themselves as open to this idea. It can only be assumed that members simply did not comment on the dissent or disagreement between members since no such data was collected for this study. This fantasy theme can also be seen through actions in which members reported engaging. As mentioned above, use of the keyword 'calorie' and the reported actions resulted in one action that points to members' healthy eating habits and openness to recovery: consuming. Specifically, members reported trying to consume more calories, increase their caloric intake each day and so on.

Regarding the emotions that participants reported experiencing on MPA, many are recovery-motivated. For example, some members were scared but excited to enter recovery. Others were overwhelmed about increasing their intake—as 'Thegymbum' commented, 'when I try to aim for 2,000, I panic and have trouble even getting to 1,400 lol. The brain works in mysterious ways.' With this post, it is clear that 'Thegymbum' is working towards recovery, but it is still very difficult to change deeply rooted dysmorphic thought processes. Possibly, such emotions were not reported more frequently on MPA because of inner turmoil experienced by participants when they approach recovery.

## Conclusion

This study looked at members' comments posted to the anorexia discussion forum of Myproana.com. FTA has illuminated three fantasy themes present in this community: the 'Us vs. Them' theme, which perpetuates many of the comments posted on the MPA forum, the 'I'll never be skinny enough' theme, which is seen through members sharing tips and encouragement to further each other's weight loss, and the 'openness to recovery' theme, which can be seen when members congratulate each other on maintaining a higher caloric intake or other comments that support a recovery-based mindset. It is unique to discover both pro-recovery and pro-eating disorder sentiments supported on the same forum.

Looking closely at where contributors placed their energy as expressed through reported actions provided an initial indication that MPA is uncommon in its encouragement of both pro-ana and pro-recovery-focused activities. The website URL alone suggests that it would only be geared towards and encouraging of one side of this issue, yet any time a participant expressed the desire to recover, they were not ostracized and were instead encouraged to become healthy. Perhaps MPA was originally a setting to encourage a singular focus, but current participants have expanded its direction. Similarly, many user comments express both an understanding of the scientific reality of health and a counter desire to remain skinny to a dysmorphic extreme. This could be because many MPA contributors are approaching a decision to pursue recovery, or it could simply be a display of the deep-seated complications of living with an eating disorder. As Branley-Bell (2021) notes, we cannot assume individuals and the online communities they populate can be cleanly separated into either pro-recovery or pro-anorexia categories. The user's intent and motivations towards online content must also be considered for a clear understanding. In addition to these insights, there are also implications related to the healthcare field and theoretical pursuits to be drawn from this study's findings. Implications, limitations and suggestions for future research are included below.

### *Healthcare implications*

Data from the current study clearly show that some afflicted with eating disorders continue to perpetuate pro-ana sensibilities, where restricted eating is a lifestyle choice and should be congratulated. However, this study also shows that other participants on the same website proclaim the contrary sentiment and support recovery or healthy eating choices. Such a clash of ideals is rarely seen in a family, group of people or website community who remain active together without expressing any conflict.

Not only does this suggest that individuals who are extremely anti-recovery can be accepting of pro-recovery individuals, but also that they can refrain from interfering with each other's goals. Further, this data demonstrates that participants at MPA show a deep understanding of what is considered 'objectively healthy', even if they still refuse to comply. A step forward from what has appeared to be strict refusal or rejection in the past, data from the current study suggests that more individuals may be open to pursuing recovery. Perhaps more patients need to be connected with a supportive online community, like MPA, that can help push them towards recovery (despite the community's name). As mentioned above, users' motivations alone often determine the emotional valence of particular online content (Branley-Bell, 2021). Future studies should collect data to show the number of MPA members pursuing/achieving healthy habits compared to those pursuing disordered options or make a similar comparison on an additional website.

### *Theoretical implications*

In addition to encouraging healthcare implications, this study also expands the use of communication theory and offers theoretical implications for the future. First, while FTA has been used in the past to analyse pro-eating disorder websites (e.g., McCabe, 2009), posts from MPA have not been studied. Further, the combination of both pro-eating disorder and pro-recovery posts on the same site has yet to be chronicled through FTA or SCT. This study shows that a strong rhetorical community can exist on a website, and one of those strengths is its allowance for clashing fantasy themes being supported. This conclusion works to further the application of FTA and exemplifies how two groups from opposing viewpoints can successfully coexist.

### *Limitations and suggestions for future research*

As with any investigation, there were limitations to the current study. Because of inherent anonymity of MPA participants, it was impossible to discern their sexual or national identity. Therefore, the diversity of this study's sample remains unclear. Future studies could target a website with a more specific audience base or collect data on the demographics of participants to then make relevant comparisons. This would provide information to enable healthcare workers to develop more targeted programmes related to this study's findings.

Another limitation of the current study was the brief time of data collection. While only two months of collection provided copious amounts of data, there is a great chance that a limited number of participants were contributing to the data set. Future studies could collect data for one week per month for six months, for example, or one day per month for a year. Stretching out the time of data collection would likely represent contributions from a wider number of community members. If done, conclusions from the current study may be confirmed with greater strength, or disconfirmed due to additional participants. Either way, because concern over one's own weight seems to be part of the human condition, as does connecting with people online, it appears that future studies will likely be conducted concerning eating disorder websites. FTA is an illuminating method through which to do it.

## References

Adams, A.S. (2013). Needs met through role-playing games: a fantasy theme analysis of dungeons and dragons. *Kaleidoscope* 12: 69–96.

Bauer, J.C., & Murray, M.A. (2018). 'Leave your emotions at home': bereavement, organizational space, and professional identity. *Women's Studies in Communication* 41(1): 60–81. https://doi.org/10.1080/07491409.2018.1424061

Bemporad, J.S. (1996). Self-starvation through the ages: reflections on the pre-history of anorexia nervosa. *International Journal of Eating Disorders* 19(3): 217–37. https://doi.org/10.1002/(SICI)1098-108X(199604)19:3<217::AID-EAT1>3.0.CO;2-P

Berkman, N.D., Lohr, K.N., & Bulik, C.M. (2007). Outcomes of eating disorders: a systematic review of the literature. *International Journal of Eating Disorders* 40: 293–309. https://doi.org/10.1002/eat.20369

Boero, N. & Pascoe, C.J. (2012). Pro-anorexia communities and online interaction: bringing the pro-ana body online. *Body & Society* 18(2): 27–57. https://doi.org/10.1177/1357034x12440827

Bormann, E. (1980). *Communication Theory*. New York: Holt, Rinehart & Winston.

Bormann, E. (1972). Fantasy and rhetorical vision: the rhetorical criticism of social reality. *Quarterly Journal of Speech* 58(4): 396–408. https://doi.org/0.1080/00335637209383138

Bormann, E. (1985). *The Force of Fantasy: Restoring the American Dream*. Carbondale, IL: South Illinois University Press.

Bormann, E. (1965). *Theory and Research in the Communicative Arts*. New York: Holt, Rinehart & Winston.

Bormann, E. (1982). Fantasy and rhetorical vision: ten years later. *Quarterly Journal of Speech* 68: 288–305. https://doi.org/10.1080/00335638209383614

Casilli, A.A., Tubaro, P., & Araya, P. (2012). Ten years of Ana: lessons from a transdisciplinary body of literature on online pro-eating disorder websites. *Social Science Information* 12(120): 1–31. https://doi.org/10.1177/0539018411425880

Custers, K. (2015). The urgent matter of online pro-eating disorder content and children: clinical practice. *European Journal of Pediatrics* 174(4): 129–43. https://doi.org/10.1007/s00431-015-2487-7

Dalkilic, A. (2013). Psychopharmacological treatments in eating disorders and comorbid conditions. *Klinik Psikofarmakoloji Bulteni* 23: S26.

Dias, K. (2003). The ana sanctuary: women's pro-anorexia narratives in cyberspace. *Journal of International Women's Studies* 4: 31–45. https://doi.org/10.1007/s00431-015-2487-7

Duffy, M.E. (2003). Web of hate: a fantasy theme analysis of the rhetorical vision of hate groups online. *Journal of Communication Inquiry* 27(3): 291–312. https://doi.org/10.1177/0196859903252850

Edelmann, N. (2013). Reviewing the definitions of 'lurkers' and some implications for online research. *Cyberpsychology, Behavior & Social Networking* 16(9): 645–49. https://doi.org/10.1089/cyber.2012.0362

Ging, D. & Garvey, S. (2017). 'Written in these scars are the stories I can't explain': a content analysis of pro-ana and thinspiration image sharing on Instagram. *New Media & Society* Jan. 2017, 1–20. https://doi.org/10.1177/1461444816687288

Griffin, E. (2016). *A First Look at Communication*. Boston: McGraw Hill.

Hammers, M.L. (2007). Desire and fantasy in online RPGs: bridging the gap between self and other. *Texas Speech Communication Journal* 32(1): 44–52.

Haas, S.M., Irr, M.E., Jennings, N.A., & Wagner, L.M. (2010). Online negative enabling support groups. *New Media & Society* 13(1): 40–57. https://doi.org/10.1177/1461444810363910

Hoffman, B. (2018). Pro ana (1): eating disorder or a lifestyle? *Trakia Journal of Sciences* 2: 106–113. https://doi.org/10.15547/tjs.2018.02.006

Kidd, V. (3 April 1998). Fantasy theme analysis. http://www.csus.edu/indiv/k/kiddv/FTA_reading.html

Le Grange, D., Swanson, S.A., Crow, S.J., & Merikangas, K.R. (2012). Eating disorder not otherwise specified presentation in the U.S. population. *International Journal of Eating Disorders* 45(5): 711–18. https://doi.org/10.1002/eat.22006

Mabe, A.G., Forney, K.J., & Keel, P.K. (2014). Do you 'like' my photo? Facebook use maintains eating disorder risk. *International Journal of Eating Disorders* 47(5): 516–23. https://doi.org/10.1002/eat.22254

McCabe, J. (2009). Resisting alienation: the social construction of internet communities supporting eating disorders. *Communication Studies* 60(1): 1–16. https://doi.org/10.1080/10510970802623542

Malson, H. (2008). Deconstructing un/healthy body weight and weight management. In S. Riley, M. Burns, H. Frith, S. Wiggins, & P. Markula (eds.), *Critical Bodies: Representations, Identities and Practices of Weight and Body Management* (pp. 27–42). London: Palgrave Macmillan. https://doi.org/10.1057/9780230591141_2

Mantella, Dana G. (2007). 'Pro-Ana' web-log uses and gratifications towards understanding the pro-anorexia paradox. Thesis, Georgia State University.doi: https://doi.org/10.57709/1061290

Martin, J., Arostegui, I., Lorono, A., Padierna, A., Najera-Zuloaga, J., & Quintana, J.M. (2019). Anxiety and depressive symptoms are related to core symptoms, general health outcome, and medical comorbidities in eating disorders. *European Eating Disorder Review* 27(6): 603–613. https://doi.org/10.1002/erv.2677

Mousavi, S., Roper, S., & Keeling, K.A. (2017). Interpreting social identity in online brand communities: considering posters and lurkers. *Psychology & Marketing* 34(4): 376–93. https://doi.org/10.1002/mar.20995

Perreault, G., & Ferrucci, P. (2019). Punishing Brady, redeeming Brady: a fantasy theme analysis of memes from the 2015 Deflategate controversy. *Atlantic Journal of Communication* 27(3): 153–68. https://doi.org/10.1080/15456870.2019.1610761

Preece, N., Nonnecke, B., & Andrews, D. (2004). The top five reasons for lurking: improving community experiences for everyone. *Computers in Human Behavior* 20(2): 201–24. https://doi.org/10.1016/j.chb.2003.10.015

Schneider, A., Von Krogh, G., & J'aGer, P. (2013). What's coming next? Epistemic curiosity and lurking behavior in online communities. *Computers in Human Behavior* 29: 293–303. https://doi.org/10.1016/j.chb.2012.09.008

Sidani, J.E., Shensa, A., Hoffman, B., Hammer, A., & Primack, B.A. The association between social media use and eating concerns among U.S. young adults. *Journal of the Academy of Nutrition & Dietetics* 16(9): 1465–72. https://doi.org/10.1016/j.jand.2016.03.021

Simmons, B. (2014). A fantasy theme analysis of ex-Christians' online deconversion narratives. *Northwest Journal of Communication* 42(1): 117–41.

Springen, K. (6 December 2006). The dangers of pro-anorexia web sites. *Newsweek*, https://www.newsweek.com/dangers-pro-anorexia-web-sites-105601

Staff, Mayo Clinic (20 February 2018). Anorexia nervosa. Diseases and conditions. https://www.mayoclinic.org/diseases-conditions/anorexia-nervosa/symptoms-causes/syc-20353591

Tong, S.T., Heinemann-Lafave, D., Jeon, J., Kolodziej-Smith, R., & Warshay, N. (2013). The use of pro-ana blogs for online social support. *Eating Disorders* 21: 408–22. https://doi.org/10.1080/10640266.2013.827538

Walker, B., Redmond, J., & Lengyel, A. (2013). Are they all the same? Lurkers and posters on the net. *eCULTURE 3*(16): 376–93.

# 12 Lived Experiences of Parents Raising Children with Eating Disorders: A Thematic Analysis

*Emma O'Rourke and Laura A. Cariola*

## Introduction

Parents of children with an eating disorder (ED) play a central role in supporting the recovery of their children. Although there has been some attention paid to exploring the perceptions of parents caring for a child with an ED, much of this research has focused on their perceptions of family-based treatment (Halvorsen & Heyerdahl, 2007; Halvorsen & Rø, 2019; Hughes et al., 2020). As such, there is a dearth of research focusing on parents' everyday experiences of raising a child with an ED. To obtain a better understanding of the lived experiences of these parents, this study aims to focus on the language used in parents' discussions on Mumsnet, a UK online parenting community. Mumsnet is aimed at parents, but the vast majority of users are women and mothers (Pedersen, 2020). Mumsnet has a large number of users and readers, and covers a wide range of topics relevant to parenting, with more than 10 million monthly unique visitors and more than 100 million page views overall (Pedersen, 2020). It provides an anonymous space where parents can openly discuss sensitive topics, resulting in naturally occurring discourse data relating to parents' experiences, which come without the various biases of empirically generated data, such as interview schedule constraints or situational biases. An exploration of parents' voices offers an opportunity to

Emma O'Rourke and Laura A. Cariola, 'Chapter 12: Lived Experiences of Parents Raising Children with Eating Disorders: A Thematic Analysis' in: *Eating Disorders in Public Discourse: Exploring Media Representations and Lived Experiences*. University of Exeter Press (2023).  DOI: 10.47788/MMRH9260 develop new understandings of their lived experience. Rather than focusing on parents' or carers' experience of treatment, this study intends to explore parents' experiences of caring for a child with an ED, and how parents understand their child's ED and recovery.

Empirical evidence has consistently suggested that parents can both be a valuable resource and play an active role in facilitating and supporting the treatment delivered by health professionals (Honey et al., 2008). Family-based treatment for EDs, also known as the Maudsley approach, is regarded as an effective intervention for patients who are able to attend outpatient treatment (Rienecke, 2017). In the early phases of treatment, parents are empowered and temporarily given the responsibility for their child's weight restoration. In addition, parents are allowed to make the decisions about their children's food, about their eating and about the potential of interacting with their eating-disordered behaviour. Parents have an essential role in encouraging food consumption and new behaviours in their child, as well as providing reinforcements and rewards to improve and encourage progress, until a steady weight has been reached and the child is willing to eat without much resistance (Martin et al., 2011). Finally, in order for parents to aid recovery, it is fundamental that they provide a caring and compassionate environment for their child, showing empathy and an element of understanding (Treasure & Nazar, 2016).

Taking into consideration that parents are perceived as a primary resource for children's recovery, positive family functioning is a crucial factor in moderating positive treatment outcomes. Positive family functioning has been associated with the provision of supportive family interactions. This includes the provision of parental warmth, emotional attunement, problem solving skills and understanding of their child's experiences (Tan et al., 2003; Wallis et al., 2017). Negative family functioning, however, such as critical parent–child communication, entanglement resulting in blurred interpersonal boundaries, overprotectiveness and controlling behaviour, has a negative effect on outcomes (Espíndola & Blay, 2009). Negative family functioning has also been associated with intense mealtimes, characterized by arguments and 'fights for control', which impact on the strategies the parent uses to encourage food intake (Jaffa et al., 2002; White et al., 2015). Negative atmospheres at the dinner table have been associated with a reduced food intake, whereas a positive atmosphere related to an increased food intake (Koivisto, Fellenius & Sjödén, 1994; White et al., 2015). It is not unusual for parents' relationships with their child to be severely affected by an ED. Caring for a child with an ED places considerable demands on the family and is often associated with high levels of stress, worry and frustration (Svensson et al., 2013; Whitney et al., 2007). For example, a qualitative study by Perkins and colleagues (2004) identified that carers believed the ED acted as an emotional barrier between themselves and the person in their care, restricting their relationship and closeness, which made it difficult to maintain a positive relationship (Perkins et al., 2004). Similarly, a focus group and interview study by Highet and colleagues (2005) showed that EDs impacted on the family and caregiver throughout all stages of the disorder, with their child becoming increasingly detached, socially withdrawn and self-centred in an attempt to control people and exclude others, allowing them to mask their disorder. Some parents also feel that the public appear judgemental towards them, demonstrating facial expressions which suggest they believe the parents are responsible for their child's ill-health (Highet, Thompson & King, 2005). Parents often blame themselves for the illness, and perceive themselves as being helpless in promoting recovery (Whitney et al., 2005).

Other people's lack of understanding and unkind comments can be a frustrating and upsetting experience, which often results in parents socially isolating themselves, out of fear of being judged (Hillege, Beale & McMaster, 2006). A qualitative study by McCormack and McCann (2015) identified that caregivers felt the ED had 'taken over' and revealed that their lives were affected socially and financially as a direct result of the ED. Due to the stigma associated with EDs, caregivers sometimes decided not to disclose the disorder to others. This is consistent with other studies that have shown that stigmatization can lead parents to experience unwarranted shame, as well as feeling discouraged from sharing their experiences (Macdonald et al., 2011; Whitney et al., 2007).

Although some caregivers have had positive experiences with primary care services, a common experience of caregivers is that the ED has a significant impact on them, as well as on their child. Empirical research suggests that parents' self-efficacy, expressed emotions, as well as accommodation and enabling behaviour mediate improvements in distress and perceived level of functioning of the child with an ED (Goddard et al., 2011; Robinson et al., 2012). Parents' distress is not always taken seriously or validated by healthcare professionals such as general practitioners, who may respond dismissively and fail to inform them adequately about their child's care (Highet, Thompson & King, 2005;

McCormack & McCann, 2015; McMaster et al., 2004). In particular, caregivers' difficulty in coping with their child's ED can have a severe impact on their own mental health (Treasure & Nazar, 2016). The parents' symptomatology and response may then exacerbate or maintain the ED (Goddard et al., 2011). For instance, some caregivers engage in maladaptive coping behaviours, by blaming themselves for not having recognized their child's ED sooner (Cottee-Lane et al., 2004), or for underestimating the seriousness of their child's ED, resulting in feelings of helplessness and guilt (Perkins et al., 2004; Whitney et al., 2005). Some other parents avoid acknowledging that their child has an ED, as they need time to accept and process their child's ED diagnosis (Brown, 2011). In some cases, parents engage in self-distraction and portray an optimistic image in order to hide their negative emotions from their child (Honey & Halse, 2005). Parents have expressed a need for more guidance, more practical advice and the space to talk to others about their experiences (Winn et al., 2004).

## Methods

### *Data*

The data for this study were obtained from the online forum Mumsnet (https://www.mumsnet.com). A total of sixty-seven discussion threads, published between January 2010 and November 2020, were identified as pertinent to caregivers communicating and discussing their concerns about their child's ED. Using the Mumsnet advanced search function, the search used a combination of different keyword search terms and acronyms to identify discussion threads relevant to children. Keywords related to EDs (e.g., anorexia, bulimia, orthorexia) and the population (e.g., daughter, son, DD, DS). To identify relevant discussion threads, inclusion and exclusion criteria were applied. Identified discussion threads had to: (1) be published between 2010 and 2020, (2) mention the child of the user (e.g., child, daughter, son, stepson, stepdaughter) and (3) focus on an ED (e.g., anorexia nervosa or bulimia nervosa, binge eating disorder, orthorexia). Discussion threads were excluded if: (1) they were published before 2010, (2) the discussion was not relevant to a child under the care of the user, or (3) the discussion was not relevant to a diagnosed ED.

### *Ethical considerations*

Prior to the collection of the data, the administrative team of Mumsnet was contacted to seek permission to use relevant discussion threads for the purpose of this study. Permission to use any relevant post was granted, based on the premise that Mumsnet would be acknowledged as a source and the users' identities would be anonymous and confidential, including identifying details and real or usernames. Taking into consideration that it was not possible to obtain users' permission for their discussion posts to be used in this study, a post was published in the 'non-member requests' section of Mumsnet to inform readers about the study and to offer users who had contributed to a discussion relevant to the care of a child with EDs to contact us and request their post to be deleted from the data. The study was reviewed by and received ethical approval from the School of Health in Social Science's Ethics Committee at the University of Edinburgh.

### *Thematic analysis*

The organization of the coding was assisted by the qualitative software package NVivo 10. This allowed for an identification of the themes present in the transcripts, using a systematic framework to capture the complexity of meaning in the textual data (Braun & Clarke, 2006, 2014). An inductive approach was also used to identify codes and themes from the text. The thematic analysis was conducted following the guidelines as outlined by Braun and Clarke (2014). Based on their guidelines, a six-step procedure and a fifteen-point checklist of criteria were applied, which included: (1) familiarizing oneself with the data, (2) generating initial codes, (3) searching for themes, (4) reviewing themes, (5) defining and naming themes and (6) producing the report. To ensure reliability and reduce bias, the emerging codes and themes were evaluated and discussed between the researchers.

## Results

A thematic analysis of the Mumsnet discussion threads identified four themes: (1) understanding, helplessness and self-blame, (2) control of the eating disordered behaviour, (3) abusive behaviour, self-harm and communication and (4) mental health needs and lack of support.

### *Theme 1: Understanding, helplessness and self-blame*

Many parents mentioned their lack of understanding of eating-disordered behaviour. Examples related to their limited insight into thoughts and beliefs around food, reasons for food refusal and denial of being hungry. Some parents also experienced problems and uncertainty in evaluating the seriousness of early signs of an ED. One parent described her 14-year-old daughter as having developed an ED during the Covid-19 lockdown, following a restricted diet and increased exercising. The parent expressed her struggle to understand the daughter's thinking and denial of the disordered eating, leaving the mother lost and isolated with her observations:

> I'm really struggling to understand her thinking around this, to me it makes no sense. Sometimes I can see she is hungry but she constantly denies it. The eating disorder team have now requested a lot of tests including blood tests and an ECG. Dd seems oblivious to what she's doing to herself and insists she is absolutely fine.

Parents of children who were referred to a hospital indicated a lack of knowledge around inpatient hospital treatments. One parent described the emotional difficulties of coping with and handling her daughter's hospital admission. It appeared that she felt guilty and like a failure for not being able to be honest with her daughter, and she was anxious about the long-term outcomes for their child–parent relationship as a result of the hospitalization. There is a sense of the parent's concern that she might 'become a victim' for helping their daughter:

> I feel awful as she knows we are going to the hospital (inpatient ward) it's a 2 hour drive but she thinks it's a check up and a talk. I was told not to tell her as it will be far to[o] distressing. […] I doubt I'll be able to visit more than once every two weeks and I feel like a failure […] I feel like she'll hate me forever for leaving her there and DS who's 17 and very close to DD […] refuses to talk to me and called me a 'fat bitch' for leaving her in an inpatient unit. Am I an awful mother and will she hate me forever?

Some parents also described mixed experiences with healthcare professionals and inpatients, and there is a sense of desperation and helplessness around how to ensure the child receives appropriate professional help. Among some parents whose children have been diagnosed with an ED and hospitalized in an inpatient unit, there is a sense of concern and worry about the usefulness of the treatment. One parent asked for help on how to proceed after an unhelpful inpatient treatment, as it not only enforced the child's restricted eating, but had a detrimental effect on the child and the family:

> Camhs were useless, gave her more ideas about how to restrict what she eats and how to get away with it. Where can we get help. She hates her body, wants to stop having periods, scratches herself when she's frustrated. I just want her to be happy and healthy. It's destroying us all. Help, please help.

Some parents correspondingly expressed uncertainty about navigating treatment alongside school attendance:

> I suppose the experts will eventually tell me what they think she needs but usually the treatment is daily if not residential and it's about an hour from her school. There are much closer places almost next door to her school but we don't live in that county and can't access them. My plan was to do maybe weekly counselling till after the exams and then do the intense part. But would I be unreasonable to go for the daily or residential options now and forget about GCSEs?

Several parents spoke about the possible causes of their child's ED. Whereas some parents proposed a genetic link, many parents assumed that the ED was caused by environmental factors, such as stress from school and a house move, or pre-existing mental health problems. Parents also blamed themselves for their child's ED, indicating that they felt a sense of guilt due to the pain they saw their children experiencing. For example, one parent described how she felt her own dieting behaviour or eating problems might have been associated with the development of her child's ED, and that she felt she should have acted earlier to prevent her son from potentially facing the same experience as his aunt:

> I've removed the scales from the house so he can't keep weighing himself. I am pretty much constantly on some kind of diet so can't help but feel this is my fault. My older sister was anorexic as a teenager. She ended up in residential treatment. I can't believe I didn't act on my gut earlier and listened to my husband when he said I was being paranoid.

### *Theme 2: Control of the eating-disordered behaviour*

Parents emphasized the increased attention they paid to their child's food intake, weight and exercising behaviour. Some parents attempted to gain a sense of control by surveying their child's eating-disordered behaviour. Others provided elaborate lists and details about their child's daily food intake. There was a sense of parents describing behaviours and eating patterns as from an outsider's perspective, without having much insight into the child's internal experiences:

> Ds has Weetabix or porridge for breakfast Innocent smoothie with breakfast. Lunch at school—chicken sandwich no butter plain. Or pesto pasta cold. I am not sure he eats lunch as I have no way of telling if he eats lunch.

Some of the parents' concerns revolve around ensuring that their child has sufficient daily food intake to increase their bodily weight, as a means to avoid inpatient treatment and hospitalization. Both parents and children can become calorie obsessive and it can consume their everyday lives:

> Devastated..dd is 'dangerously underweight'. Despite hammering away at those damn cals, she gained 6g in a week. Hospital/camhs want progress or she is in, I think it's the best thing for her. Camhs on Thursday, dietician next Tuesday. Camhs can get her in hospital if things not going well. She should be on bed rest till Thursday but she's not having it, won't 'put her life on hold'.

There was a strong focus on controlling eating behaviours, with parents describing how restricted food intake allows the child to feel that they are gaining some control in their life. Parents are often given control over ensuring their child's weight restoration as part of treatment, but some parents struggle with this, and others reassure themselves with regards to their control of the eating schedule:

> I have probably missed loads of questions and advice but what is sticking out is the question am I in charge of her eating? The answer is yes. Team calculated that dd has been on approx 500 cals for a long time, I now have to encourage her to eat 3 calorific meals with dessert and 3 calorific snacks every day.

One parent also expressed distress about her daughter's upcoming release from an ED unit, and she described a strong sense of anxiety that she would not be able to control her daughter's food intake:

> The doctors said she will be released next week and I am worried about how to get her to continue to eat at home short of force feeding her. She has been up and down in hospital. Can anyone give me some tips?

Some parents spoke about relying on schools to support, control and enforce their child's food intake. One parent, for instance, reported how the school would let them take their daughter home for lunch, whereas another parent discussed how the school would supervise the child during lunchtime:

> PS I contact my daughter's school and they were really supportive. They offered to supervise her snacks and lunch if necessary. I think the threat of that was enough to make her eat in school! If you can work out the calorie target and organise his food to make sure he is getting that you will know if he is cheating because his weight will continue to fall.

One mother also described her observation of a shift from initially helping her daughter to control her binge eating to becoming the 'food police', who surveyed what her daughter ate. She reflected whether her 'entrenched' role of controlling her daughter's eating might have exacerbated the ED:

> I remember once she cried due to gaining weight, she felt great difficulty resisting muffins/cakes at school and I could help her to control things and buy healthy food. Gradually I've become the food police, this meaning only healthy stuff at home. The problem is that we've become entrenched in our roles. I wonder if she has always struggled to teach her own appetite and hunger and if she has always relied on me to control things.

### *Theme 3: Abusive behaviour, self-harm and communication*

Many parents described their children's challenging behaviours as being frightening and stressful. Examples of challenging behaviour included abusive language, violent outbursts, refused communication and self-harm. One parent described how her daughter's decreasing bodily weight and emotional stability were uncontrollable, and the abusive language and violent behaviour demonstrated by her daughter frightened the parent. There was a strong sense of the parent's bewilderment about the child's behaviour, and despair about the emotional impact on their family:

> She has had 6 weeks of FBT [family-based treatment] but her weight keeps dropping and her mental state is uncontrollable now and her control stronger and her aggressive and violent reaction is becoming frightening. Her foul language and abuse is now secondary to her physical behaviour. We are

> trying to find a good eating disorder counsellor or otherwise but they seem to be so busy. Anyone know anyone to recommend in surrey and or any advice? We are so worn out and feeling despair. My DD is a smart girl with so much going for her … it is so sad. Our family is under so much stress and its [*sic*] now so dysfunctional.

While most parents expressed a strong sense of despair at enduring their child's abusive behaviour, one parent described how an argument offered a cathartic opportunity to vent their frustrations at each other, allowing them to then speak openly about their true feelings and experiences:

> This past weekend was awful, we had a massive row yesterday which went on for an hour, but at the end, we were all crying and she really opened up and said how much she hated herself, her disorder and also how sorry she was for causing us pain … but she literally CANNOT eat. She is stick thin, exhausted and constantly crying or angry. She hasn't eaten since Saturday night and is currently in bed, too weak to get up.

Several parents spoke about the difficulty of engaging their child in conversation about the ED. As such, parents felt shut out and emotionally separated from their child's experiences, which affected their ability to offer appropriate support and to better understand their child's difficulties:

> Whenever I try to say anything she walks out of the room, often out of the house. It is ruining her life—she has no energy and has lost several jobs as a result of not being able to get out of bed. She will talk about the depression but flatly denies that she has an eating disorder. Any ideas for getting her to accept some support?

Similarly, some parents found it a challenge to refrain from speaking about the ED, even if the child expressed their annoyance at them speaking about food repeatedly, to the exclusion of other topics:

> Finding it hard to leave DD alone, she actually commented today that she is sick of talking about food, but it's so hard not to when you're so worried. I also feel as if I'm neglecting friends and family because this is taking up all my headspace. Actually, feel quite exhausted by it all.

Some parents surveyed their child's online use and engagement with pro-ana communities to obtain a better insight into their ED behaviour experiences:

> pro-ana chat group saying how she was skipping breakfast, hated having to eat meals in front of us, posting pictures of herself saying she wanted to see her ribs, etc.

One parent also mentioned that she felt shut out by healthcare professionals due to patient confidentiality. Parents further feel that there is a lack of communication between healthcare professionals and themselves. They found it frustrating when important appointments were missed or cancelled and, in some cases, appointments were in secret due to a lack of parent–child and parent–health professional communication; this can impact greatly on the parent–child relationship.

> We feel shut out from the professionals she talks to as they speak to her directly over the phone and appointments are sent in her name. Because of patient confidentiality we don't get to know. She's very immature, not organised and forgets to go to appointments or turns up late and she doesn't take information in easily. She never tells us about these appointments, we only find out by chance. Don't know where to turn!

Whereas some children externalized their anger by shouting abuse at their parents, some parents described how their children would deliberately hurt their own bodies through self-harming behaviour and attempted suicides, including cutting, overdoses and self-asphyxiation. Parents expressed the devastation of witnessing their child's restrictive food intake in combination with the self-harming behaviour, describing their experiences as 'unbearable' and 'heart breaking':

> Since my post, my daughter has taken an overdose of paracetamol's [*sic*] when we were 2 hours from home. A friend got into the house and stayed with her until paramedics came. The paramedics realised she had not taken enough tablets to do harm and after an hour, chatted to me and left. Half an hour later we heard a bang upstairs, and found her hanging from a cord attached to her door handle.

The above parent mentioned that her daughter was hospitalized and then sectioned under the Mental Health Act 1983, as she had intentionally injured her body. The mother described leaving her daughter in the mental health unit as 'heart breaking', as her daughter was 'begging to come home'.

Parents described their desperate efforts to maintain an open conversation with their children who were dealing with both EDs and self-harming behaviour. This posed some conflicts for parents who were deeply concerned about their child's self-destructive behaviour, but were not able to communicate their worries due to fear that it would negatively affect their child's mental health:

> She knows I know and I am trying really hard to keep ou[r] limited venue of communication open or she does have a tendency to shut everyone out, I try not to nag her about it but I really feel she needs some help, if too much pressure is applied she will just cut herself of[f] and the depression will become deeper.

### *Theme 4: Mental health needs and lack of support*

Parents described their parenting experiences as exhausting, stressful and time consuming. Several parents stated that the challenges of caring for their eating-disordered child were severally affecting their own mental health:

> My Dr diagnosed me with PTSD last Oct because of all of this. I've tried really hard to get better myself because I'm aware how much my DC need[s] me. But I'm a long way from well enough to cope with this.

Parents referred to a lack of support from their husbands, often finding themselves alone and unsupported in looking after their child. It appears that the experience of having a child with an ED differs between fathers and mothers, in the sense that mothers assume a more active supportive role and experience more overt stress, whereas fathers are described as passive, and unable to offer emotional and practical support to the mother:

> I wish DH were more emotionally supportive. I don't often turn to him for words of encouragement, I wish he could offer me a bit of kindness, I really needed that this week. I think he should get some counselling. I don't think he is just 'being a man'. I can't leave him over this but I can't manage to be the only provider of emotional support for myself and our children, I'm long since worn out with it.

In this excerpt, the mother's characterization of her husband's lack of emotional support and 'kindness' seems to represent the emotional abandonment occurring in her marriage. Her description aligns with the experiences of single parents who speak about feeling stressed and exhausted handling the emotional and practical challenges of raising a child with an ED, working without any additional support. One parent described her daughter's relapse into an ED, and her anxiety of not being able to cope with the stressors and offer the necessary support:

> She's ill again. She has dropped a ton of weight since last month, all the behaviours are back. I've just searched her room and found a massive carrier bag full of rotting food in her wardrobe. I don't want this again, I know that's unreasonable but I've tried so hard to get my life on track and have a happy family again. I'm divorced, there's only me to keep all of us okay. I just don't think I can.

For many parents, Mumsnet appears to be one of the very few places where they can ask for advice, share experiences and seek support from other parents who are directly or indirectly affected by an ED and essentially help themselves feel less isolated.

## Discussion

The current study aimed to explore the experiences parents face when caring for children with EDs. This qualitative research allowed a broad examination of differing views through a thematic analysis of Mumsnet posts, enabling in-depth consideration of the parents' experiences. The findings from this study showed that many parents go through extremely challenging experiences, supporting their child with a complex mental health condition, with minimal support and resources, while all the time being aware that the ED could be life-threatening.

The heightened emotions and distress parents encounter, while having minimal support, makes their experience of caring for their child an exhausting ordeal and responsibility. The findings of this study align to a certain extent with other qualitative research that identifies the blame and guilt that manifest themselves in parents during their struggle with their child's ED (Highet et al., 2005; Hoste, Doyle & Le Grange, 2011; Ross & Green, 2011). The results of this study also highlight the sense of uncertainty that many parents experience, which can lead to feelings of distress. Parents in this study were consistently feeling worried and frightened about their child's wellbeing, which reflected their emotional vulnerability in supporting their child with eating difficulties. Several parents described a sense of disconnection and feeling excluded from their children's ED experiences. The lack of communication impeded a supportive parent–child dialogue and any ability to develop understanding of the ED behaviour and underlying motivations. This was further exacerbated by barriers of confidentiality that prevent healthcare professionals from sharing information with the parents. Rather than speaking to their parents about their problematic eating behaviours, some children engaged with pro-ana communities, possibly as a means to share their thoughts, ask for support and seek validation within the safe space of the ED community. As discussed by Lueders (this volume), pro-ED sites create simplistic 'us' versus 'them' social categories, to the extent that 'us' includes other pro-ED site users who share similar views about food and eating, whereas 'them' includes anyone who expresses opposing views on food and eating (see also Haas, Jennings & Chang, this volume). Evidently, the Mumsnet posts indicated that some parents experienced themselves as part of the 'them' group due to their attempt to enforce their child's food intake, thus positioning them as helpless 'outsiders'. Some parents reported feeling great loneliness, and their child's ED impacted negatively on their physical and psychological health, causing self-isolation for some. This finding is supported by previous research that found parents are likely to experience a high level of burden, and tend towards developing symptoms of depression and anxiety (Zabala, Macdonald & Treasure, 2009).

The immediate impact on the families was experienced as devastating (Ross & Green, 2011). Most parents had to deal with ongoing demands made by their child and the challenging behaviours associated with the ED. Many parents felt their relationship with their child was tested on several occasions, leading to arguments, due to the parents and the child becoming hostile and angry. Some parents were also often confused when they realized that what they thought was right and what they were required to do were opposed. As such, it appeared that parents require greater support and direction from health professionals regarding their role as a parent when caring for a child with an ED. Receiving more support from health professionals would help parents to feel less distressed, helpless and exhausted (Whitney et al., 2007). Unlike in previous research by Ross and Green (2011), the parents in this study did not discuss any positives which could be drawn out from their experiences of caring for a child with an ED. This further supports the idea that it is extremely difficult for parents in such situations, and that in reality, the experience is overwhelmingly negative. Conversely, the negative perspective appeared to enable parents to cope with the unpredictability and uncertainty that came with the ED. In particular, it became clear that their understanding deepened and evolved throughout their experience; however, the remaining uncertainties were deeply unsettling for them.

Demographically, in comparison to other online parent support forums, parents on Mumsnet typically comprise mothers who are slightly older, are more likely to be employed outside the house, and have an income above the national average (Pedersen, 2020; Pedersen & Smith, 2013). In this study, the majority of threads possibly also comprised contributions from mothers rather than fathers. Future research should explore the experiences of fathers of children with EDs, to allow us to gain an understanding of their perspective. This could allow fathers to be more open about their experiences of raising a child with an ED and allow researchers to analyse the extent to which the experiences of fathers and mothers are similar or different, in order to help identify support strategies that would meet the needs of both parents. Additionally, the majority of parents on Mumsnet spoke about their daughters living with an ED, with only very few parents discussing their sons living with an ED. This could be due to EDs being more common in teenage girls, although evidence has shown that teenage boys are less likely to admit ED symptoms such as purging and weight dissatisfaction than girls (Striegel-Moore et al., 2009). This demonstrates that more teenage boys could be suffering in silence, unrecognized by the parents. In addition, the majority of threads focused on anorexia nervosa, with only a few discussions exploring bulimia nervosa, despite the fact that bulimia nervosa is more prevalent (Galmiche et al., 2019). Only one thread discussed orthorexia as part of the category of Other Specified Feeding or Eating Disorders (OSFED). This supports previous research that has shown bulimia is easier to hide compared to other EDs such as anorexia nervosa, and therefore cases are likely to remain undiagnosed (Clarke & Polimeni-Walker, 2004). Evidence has shown that bulimia and anorexia share many similarities in terms of patient experience and stigmatization (Byrne et al., 2011). There is a great need to further explore the lived experiences of parents, in order to improve both ED services and the treatment of EDs, as well as to raise public awareness of EDs in young people.

## References

Braun, V., & Clarke, V. (2006). Using thematic analysis in psychology. *Qualitative Research in Psychology* 3: 77–101. https://doi.org/10.1191/1478088706qp063oa

Braun, V., & Clarke, V. (2014). What can 'thematic analysis' offer health and wellbeing researchers? *International Journal of Qualitative Studies on Health and Well-Being* 9: Article 26152. https://doi.org/10.3402/qhw.v9.26152

Brown, H. (2011). A parent's perspective on family treatment. In D. Le Grange & J. Lock (eds), *Eating Disorders in Children and Adolescence: A Clinical Handbook* (pp. 457–60). New York: Guilford Press.

Byrne, S.M., Fursland, A., Allen, K.L., & Watson, H. (2011). The effectiveness of enhanced cognitive behavioural therapy for eating disorders: an open trial. *Behaviour Research and Therapy* 49: 219–26. https://doi.org/10.1016/j.brat.2011.01.006

Clarke, D., & Polimeni-Walker, I. (2004). Treating individuals with eating disorders in family practice: a needs assessment. *Eating Disorders* 12(4): 293–301. https://doi.org/10.1080/10640260490521343

Cottee-Lane, D., Pistrang, N., & Bryant-Waugh, R. (2004). Childhood onset anorexia nervosa: the experience of parents. *European Eating Disorders Review* 12(3): 169–77. https://doi.org/10.1002/erv.560

Espíndola, C.R., & Blay, S.L. (2009). Anorexia nervosa's meaning to patients: a qualitative synthesis. *Psychopathology* 42: 69–80. https://doi.org/10.1159/000203339

Galmiche, M., Déchelotte. P., Lambert, G., & Tavalacci, M.P. (2019). Prevalence of eating disorders over the 2000–2018 period: a systematic review. *The American Journal of Clinical Nutrition* 5: 1402–13. https://doi.org/10.1093/ajcn/nqy342

Goddard, E., McDonald, P., Sepuveda, A.R., Nauman, U., Landau, S., Schmidt, U., & Treasure, J. (2011). Cognitive interpersonal maintenance model of eating disorders: intervention for carers. *British Journal of Psychiatry* 199: 226–31. https://doi.org/10.1192/bjp.bp.110.088401

Halvorsen, I., & Heyerdahl, S. (2007). Treatment perception in adolescent onset anorexia nervosa: retrospective views of patients and parents. *International Journal of Eating Disorders* 40(7): 629–39. https://doi.org/10.1002/eat.20428

Halvorsen, I., & **R**ø, Ø. (2019). User satisfaction with family-based inpatient treatment for adolescent anorexia nervosa: retrospective views of patients and parents. *Journal of Eating Disorders* 7: 12. https://doi.org/10.1186/s40337-019-0242-6

Highet, N., Thompson, M., & King, R.M. (2005). The experience of living with a person with an eating disorder: the impact on the carers. *Eating Disorders* 13(4): 327–44. https://doi.org/10.1080/10640260591005227

Hillege, S., Beale, B., & McMaster, R. (2006). Impact of eating disorders on family life: individual parents' stories. *Journal of Clinical Nursing* 15(8): 1016–22. https://doi.org/10.1111/j.1365-2702.2006.01367.x

Honey, A., Boughtwood, D., Clarke, S., Halse, C., Kohn, M., & Madden, S. (2008). Support for parents of children with anorexia: what parents want. *Eating Disorders* 16: 40-51. https://doi.org/10.1080/10640260701773447

Honey, A., & Halse, C. (2005). Parents dealing with anorexia nervosa: actions and meanings. *Eating Disorders: The Journal of Treatment and Prevention* 13: 353–67. https://doi.org/10.1080/10640260591005245

Hoste, R.R., Doyle, A.C., & Le Grange, D. (2011). Families as an integral part of the treatment team: treatment culture and standard of care challenges. In J. Alexandra & J. Treasure (eds), *A Collaborative Approach to Eating Disorders* (pp. 136–43). London: Routledge.

Hughes, E.K., Poker, S., Bortz, A., Yeo, M., Telfer, M., & Sawyer, S.M. (2020). Adolescent and parent experience of care at a family-based treatment service for eating disorders. *Frontiers in Psychiatry* 11: 310. https://doi.org/10.3389/fpsyt.2020.00310

Jaffa, T., Honig, P., Farmer, S., & Dilley, J. (2002). Family meals in the treatment of adolescent anorexia nervosa. *European Eating Disorders Review* 10: 199–207. https://doi.org/10.1002/erv.464

Koivisto, U., Fellenius, J., & Sjödén, P.O. (1994). Relations between parental mealtime practices and children's food intake. *Appetite* 22: 245–58. https://doi.org/10.1006/appe.1994.1023

Macdonald, P., Murray, J., Goddard, E., & Treasure, J. (2011). Carer's experience and perceived effects of a skills-based training programme for families of people with eating disorders: a qualitative study. *European Eating Disorders Review* 19(6): 475–86. https://doi.org/10.1002/erv.1065

Martin, J., Padierna, A., Aguirre, U., Quintana, J., Hayas, C., & Munoz, P. (2011). Quality of life among caregivers of patients with eating disorders. *Quality of Life Research* 20(9): 1359–69. https://doi.org/10.1007/s11136-011-9873-z

McCormack, C., & McCann, E. (2015). Caring for an adolescent with anorexia nervosa: parent's views and experiences. *Archives of Psychiatric Nursing* 29(3): 143–47. https://doi.org/10.1016/j.apnu.2015.01.003

McMaster, R., Beale, B., Hillege, S., & Nagy, S. (2004). The parent experience of eating disorders: interactions with health professionals. *International Journal of Mental Health Nursing* 13(1): 67–73. https://doi.org/10.1111/j.1447-0349.2004.00310.x

Pedersen, S. (2020). Practical, everyday feminism: mothers, politicians, and Mumsnet. *Women's History Review* 30(3): 509–19. https://doi.org/10.1080/09612025.2020.1860281

Pedersen, S., & Smith, J. (2013). Mothers with attitude: how the Mumsnet parenting forum offers space for new forms of femininity to emerge online. *Women's Studies International Forum* 38: 97–106. https://doi.org/10.1016/j.wsif.2013.03.004

Perkins, S., Winn, S., Murray, J., Murphy, R., & Schmidt, U. (2004). A qualitative study of the experience of caring for a person with bulimia nervosa. Part 1: the emotional impact of caring. *International Journal of Eating Disorders* 36(3): 256–68. https://doi.org/10.1002/eat.20067

Rienecke, R.D. (2017). Family-based treatment of eating disorders in adolescents: current insights. *Adolescent Health, Medicine and Therapeutics* 8: 69–79. https://doi.org/10.2147/ahmt.s115775

Robinson, A.L, Strahan, E., Girz, L., Wilson, A., & Boachie, A. (2012). 'I know I can help you': parental self-efficacy predicts adolescent outcomes in family-based therapy for eating disorders. *European Eating Disorder Review* 21: 108–114. https://doi.org/10.1002/erv.2180

Ross, J.A., & Green, C. (2011). Inside the experience of anorexia nervosa: a narrative thematic analysis. *Counselling and Psychotherapy Research* 11: 112–19. https://doi.org/10.1080/14733145.2010.486864

Striegel-Moore, R.H., Rosselli, F., Perrin, N., DeBar, L., Wilson, T., May, A., & Kraemer, H. C. (2009). Gender difference in the prevalence of eating disorder symptoms. *International Journal of Eating Disorders* 42(5): 471–74. https://doi.org/10.1002/eat.20625

Svensson, E., Nilsson, K., Levi, R., & Carballeira Suarez, N. (2013). Parents' experiences of having and caring for a child with an eating disorder. *Eating Disorders* 21(5): 395–407. https://doi.org/10.1080/10640266.2013.827537

Tan, J., Hope, T., Stewart, A., & Fitzpatrick, R. (2003). Control and compulsory treatment in anorexia nervosa: the views of patients and parents. *International Journal of Law and Psychiatry* 26: 627–45. https://doi.org/10.1016/j.ijlp.2003.09.009

Treasure, J., & Nazar, B.P. (2016). Interventions for the carers of patients with eating disorders. *Current Psychiatry Reports* 18: 16. https://doi.org/10.1007/s11920-015-0652-3

Wallis, A., Miskovic-Wheatley, J., Madden, S., Rhodes, P., Crosby, R.D., Cao, L., & Touyz, S. (2017). How does family functioning affect the outcome of family based treatment for adolescents with severe anorexia nervosa? *Journal of Eating Disorders* 5: 55. ttps://doi.org/10.1186/s40337-017-0184-9

White, H.J., Haycraft, E., Madden, S., Rhodes, P., Mikovic-Wheatley, J., Wallis, A., Kohn, M., & Meyers, C. (2015). How do parents of adolescent patients with anorexia nervosa interact with their child at mealtimes? A study of parental strategies used in the family meal session of family-based treatment. *International Journal of Eating Disorders* 48: 72–80. https://doi.org/10.1002/eat.22328

Whitney, J., Murray, J., Gavan, K., Todd, G., Whitaker, W., & Treasure, J. (2005). Experiences of caring for someone with anorexia nervosa: qualitative study. *British Journal of Psychiatry* 187: 444–49. https://doi.org/10.1192/bjp.187.5.444

Whitney, J., Haigh, R., Weinman, J., & Treasure, J. (2007). Caring for people with eating disorders: factors associated with psychological distress and negative caregiving appraisals in carers of people with eating disorders. *British Journal of Clinical Psychology* 46: 414–28. https://doi.org/10.1348/014466507x173781

Winn, S., Perkins, S., Murray, J., Murphy, R., & Schmidt, U. (2004). A qualitative study of the experience of caring for a person with bulimia nervosa. Part 2: carers' needs and experiences of services and other support. *International Journal of Eating Disorders* 36: 269–79. https://doi.org/10.1002/eat.20068

Zabala, M.J., Macdonald, P., & Treasure, J. (2009). Appraisal of caregiving burden expressed emotion and psychological distress in families of people with eating disorders: a systematic review. *European Eating Disorder Review* 17: 338–49. https://doi.org/10.1002/erv.925

# 13 'Anorexia is Seen as a GOOD Thing When You're Fat!': Constructing 'Eating Disorders' in Fat Acceptance Blogs

*Wendy Solomons, Kate Davenport and Joanne McDowell*

## Introduction

Cultural expectations of body size and shape form a familiar topic in discussions about eating disorders (EDs). Arguments against unrealistic portrayals of bodies, whether in conventional or online social media, are extensive and well known. Yet cultural pressures to achieve the 'thin ideal'—with associated stigmatization of fatness, and social sanctions for those who fail to conform—persist and have become taken for granted within many societies, with consequences for health and wellbeing.

However, dissenting voices increasingly talk back to dominant discourses, through 'fat acceptance' (FA) positions. Within this chapter, critical discursive approaches are used to explore how marginalized speakers negotiate this contested terrain: constructing and arguing alternative positions within online FA forums, and positioning themselves as credible voices worthy of attention. More specifically, we consider how users of FA spaces construct the topic of 'eating disorders' and the identities of those involved, in ways that reflect but also perturb existing understandings.

Wendy Solomons, Kate Davenport and Joanne McDowell, 'Chapter 13: 'Anorexia is Seen as a GOOD Thing When You're Fat!': Constructing 'Eating Disorders' in Fat Acceptance Blogs' in: *Eating Disorders in Public Discourse: Exploring Media Representations and Lived Experiences*. University of Exeter Press (2023). © Wendy Solomons et al. DOI: 10.47788/UHLM5757

## *Cultural representations of fatness*[1]

In reference to bodies, 'fat' refers to adipose tissue used to store energy and insulate the body, and to the overall corpulence of the body. Precisely what constitutes a 'fat body' varies across time, place and culture, with often contradictory meanings. As an adjective, 'fat' can also imply richness and abundance; yet, for many, the word is an insult. While acknowledging that the notion of a 'thin ideal' obscures intersectional complexities, within many Western/ized societies, there is arguably a demonization of the fat body and those who fail to conform (Nash & Warin, 2017; see also López-Rodríguez, and Gulec, this volume).

These representations are woven through with powerful medical and neoliberal discourses which construct particular levels of fatness as a health concern. Public health campaigns and media coverage of an 'obesity epidemic', and a 'war on obesity', foreground not only health 'risk' to individuals, but the societal and economic burdens of failure to do so (Gard, 2011). Critics note that societal attempts to regulate fat bodies predate such medicalization, and relate more clearly to cultural preoccupations with 'civilization' and supremacy, race, class and gender prejudice (Erdman, 2011; Strings, 2019). There is growing evidence of complex relationships between adiposity and health, structurally 'obesogenic environments' and the social determinants of health, and the limitations of dieting for long-term weight management (Campos et al., 2006; Toomath, 2016). Yet current discourse continues to portray being overweight as an 'obvious' medical concern primarily caused by poor individual health behaviours—a failure to 'eat less and move more'—underpinned by laziness, ignorance or lack of willpower (Nimegeer et al., 2019; Puhl & Heuer, 2010). Popular press and weight loss reality shows perpetuate stereotypical portrayals (see also Bowen & Waller, Parrott et al., and Bates, this volume) and oversimplified notions that weight is individually controllable by anyone prepared to 'do the work', enhancing negative attitudes, societal 'fatphobia' and 'weight stigma' towards fat people (Monson et al., 2016).

## *Weight stigma and its consequences*

Graham (2005) argues that Western societies have become 'lipoliterate': 'reading' bodies for insight into their bearers' histories and supposedly inferior intellectual, psychological and moral nature. Thus fat bodies become visible markers of an assumed individual failure to uphold societal standards, and—bearing personal responsibility—are punished by stigmatization and social marginalization. Systematic literature reviews highlight persistent weight-based stigmatization and discrimination, not only in media portrayals but in interpersonal and family relationships, education, employment and healthcare across many countries and cultures—including from professionals working in ED services (Brewis et al., 2018; Pearl, 2018; Puhl et al., 2014). Those already marginalized by race, gender, class and sexuality appear especially penalized (Fikkan & Rothblum, 2012; Van Amsterdam, 2013).

This has serious consequences. Interplays of direct and indirect discrimination, shaming, bullying, marginalization and internalized weight stigma impact on socioeconomic, social, psychological and physical wellbeing (Pearl, 2018; Pearl & Puhl, 2018), including the development and maintenance of disordered eating and EDs (Puhl & Suh, 2015). Despite these devastating consequences, and an increasing empirical evidence base countering assumptions about the relationships between behaviour, weight and health (Hunger et al., 2020), many (including some health professionals) maintain that stigma and 'fat shaming' are justified to motivate fat people to alter their behaviour (Nath, 2019; Puhl & Heuer, 2010; see also López-Rodríguez, this volume).

## *Forming a resistance: fat acceptance*

However, other voices are raised in resistance. 'Fat acceptance' (FA) movements arose in the USA in the 1950s and 1960s alongside broader civil rights movements, challenging anti-fat discourse and the medicalization of obesity. There is no universal position of FA, but a gathering of people who question prevailing positions on health and obesity (including the role of the weight loss industry and other vested interests), rejecting the notion that bodies are only acceptable if they conform to societal ideals (Cooper, 2008; Dickins et al., 2016). There is overlap and divergence from related movements, including broader 'size acceptance' and 'health at every size' (HAES), which promotes focusing on health rather than on weight (Bacon & Aphramor, 2011). FA challenges current weight-centred health policy as a violation of human rights which contributes to inequality, oppression and discrimination, and perpetuates obesity and health inequalities (Tomiyama et al., 2018). However, FA faces medical, media and popular criticism from those who suggest FA activists are in denial, biased and promote obesity (Muttarak, 2018). Given that the work of FA is often taken up by fatter people, the systematic discrediting of FA arguments is facilitated by the prejudices of a 'lipoliterate' society that assumes fat people to be less intelligent or credible, particularly on matters relating to health and eating (see also Cariola & Lee, this volume).

More recently, FA has moved into digital spaces, through blogs and forums on social media platforms self-titled the 'fatosphere'. Members of the public are no longer simply the audience or object of media attention, but active in creating, curating, sharing and commenting in the co-construction of multimedia content within complex and fast-evolving platforms. While attention often focuses on potential threats to wellbeing posed by social media (see Haas et al., this volume), more nuanced approaches acknowledge ways in which the fatosphere offers possibilities for resistance and contestation of oppressive mainstream cultures (Lupton, 2017). Though critics note the predominance of white women and lack of attention to intersectionality, there remain opportunities for marginalized people across geographical boundaries to come together and reclaim some control over their identities and bodies within a relatively safe space that allows group identification (Harding & Kirby, 2009; Nash & Warin, 2017; Branley-Bell, this volume).

Striley and Hutchens (2020) report multiple motivations for engagement, encompassing intra/interpersonal (e.g., support) and systemic aspects (e.g., commitment to social justice). Users, including those who would not identify as fat activists, report a sense of social connectedness and validation within an online community of people who share lived experience: of struggling with societal body ideals; of societal and internalized fatphobia; of discrimination and degradation, and the daily challenges of living alongside 'thin privilege'. Users report improvements in mental and physical health, and a sense of empowerment as they develop alternative discourses of FA, but note the complexities of maintaining these ideals in 'real life', where societal and long-internalized pressures persist, and where expression of FA ideas can trigger relational conflict (Afful & Ricciardelli, 2015; Dickins et al., 2016; Donaghue & Clemitshaw, 2012).

Language-based research has highlighted the adoption and resistance of different discourses relating to FA, both within the fatosphere and mainstream digital spaces (see Cain et al., 2017) and, to a lesser extent, discursive strategies for achieving rhetorical impact (Davenport et al., 2018). We argue that there is further need to understand ways in which marginalized people manage the presentation of their positions in discussion with others: not only *what* they talk about, but *how*, if they are to compete with more established discourse. Relatedly, we consider speakers' construction of their *identities* in talk, to achieve the difficult task of legitimizing their positions in the face of opposition; presenting themselves as credible speakers who should be heard, while also maintaining valued relationships.

Additionally, we turn to an area that has received little scholarly attention: representations of EDs within the fatosphere. Given other research showing that a significant proportion of fat people report disordered eating, and a significant proportion of people diagnosed with EDs have histories of overweight (Puhl & Suh, 2015), there is a strong likelihood that a proportion of people using FA forums live with historical, current or future risk of EDs. Hence our research question: how are EDs, and those who live with them, constructed within the fatosphere?

## Method

### Materials

Data was drawn from group blogs identifying themselves explicitly as fat acceptance (FA) sites. These blogs provide a space where multiple authors share and comment on each other's posts, within a collaborative and specified arena. A purposive sampling approach was used to identify suitable material, originally for a wider study on use of FA sites (for details, see Davenport et al., 2018). Three blogs identifying themselves as FA were selected to represent different types of platform (Tumblr, Wordpress, Blogspot), and time-sampled to provide forty-five days of data across 2010–2015, providing a robust and varied dataset of over 90,000 words. Although blogs contained photos and images, these were not analysed. For this chapter's specific focus on EDs, the original corpus was narrowed using search terms such as 'disorder', 'ED', 'anor(exia/ic)', buli/mia/ic', 'purge', 'puke', 'restrict', 'diet', 'weigh/t' and 'cal/orie', producing a smaller dataset of approximately 20,000 words.

### *Ethical considerations*

Ethical issues arise when drawing from sensitive material online, where explicit consent cannot be obtained from historic online users and, given the nature of the internet, quotes could potentially be traced back to original sites (see Branley-Bell, this volume; Heilferty, 2011). Legal and professional guidelines permit research into online content if websites are, like the ones sampled here, in the public domain; i.e., 'open access', without membership or passwords, and where people could 'reasonably expect to be observed by strangers' (BPS, 2017). Bloggers used pseudonyms, but additional steps were taken to anonymize user-names, sites and identifying features (including removal of hashtags). Ethical approval for research was gained from the University of Hertfordshire.

### *Analytic approach: critical discursive psychology*

This work uses critical discursive psychology (CDP) to analyse discourse found in FA blogs. CDP is underpinned by a social constructionist epistemology: that is, understanding that language and talk do not simply represent events 'out there' in the world, or provide a window into people's subjective experiences, emotions or identities; rather, that language, through social exchanges, actively *constructs* social reality (Burr, 2015). Discourse is thus not treated as a route into something else, but becomes the focus of analysis, exploring how particular understandings of the world are brought to bear.

CDP (Edley, 2001; Wetherell, 1998) draws together two strands of analysis that have often been employed separately: post-structural or Foucauldian-inspired discourse analyses (FDA) (e.g., Willig, 2008) and discursive psychology (DP) (e.g., Edwards & Potter, 1992). FDA typically explores ways in which culturally available discourses construct different understandings of the world, considering the interplay of discourse, power and subjectification: how certain versions become more dominant than others, and whose interests are served by this. Though citizens can make choices about which discourses (or versions of reality) to adopt, the focus is on the availability of discourses at a 'macro' level. By contrast, DP considers 'micro' practices of interpersonal talk: how people actively construct particular versions of reality within their talk; managing interactional and identity-related concerns like being understood as a 'moral' person, and performing social actions like explaining and positioning their own versions against other possible understandings (Wiggins, 2017).

CDP synthesizes these two approaches. Drawing from FDA, it considers how socioculturally available discourses (or 'interpretative repertoires') shape possibilities for understanding the world, identities and social actions at a given time and situation; but also (drawing from DP) understands people as social agents who use discursive resources in talk to achieve different social actions, including the negotiation of identities:

> Critical discursive psychology acknowledges that people are, at the same time, both the product and the producers of discourse [...] It aims to examine not only how identities are produced on and for particular occasions, but also how history or culture both impinge upon and are transformed by those performances. (Edley, 2001, p. 190)

Analysis therefore attends to both of these processes, as they are seen in texts and talk. Integral to this is the identification of interpretative repertoires, ideological dilemmas and subject positions (Edley, 2001). Interpretative repertoires (Potter & Wetherell, 1987) are culturally familiar ways of representing and evaluating aspects of the social world (objects, events, arguments, relationships and so on). Similar to the Foucauldian concept of discourses, IRs are, however, seen as smaller and more fragmented (Edley, 2001), offering many possibilities for speakers to take up and use to different effect. Significantly, IRs can construct different and conflicting versions of the same phenomena, leading to ideological dilemmas to be negotiated (Billig et al., 1988). IRs also open up different subject positions—particular (though fluid) identities or 'ways of being'—which, given their implications for how individuals are viewed societally, must then be negotiated in talk (van Langenhove & Harré, 1999).

Thus, CDP attends to processes of construction within discursive work, and what this accomplishes, both locally and in wider sociocultural practice. It is particularly valuable in considering constructions of contested or 'difficult' topics, where marginalized voices attempt to challenge more established and powerful positions, or where the identities of speakers may be in some ways at risk (e.g., being evaluated as not credible). As such, it was deemed particularly appropriate for the topic of this chapter.

### Analytic process and quality

Following Locke and Budds (2020), texts were read repeatedly to enable familiarization with the discursive terrain, and identify different discursive constructions of topics of interest, i.e., the categories (objects, practices and people) being invoked, and when and how. Identification of ideological dilemmas and interpretative repertoires followed, locating pervasive, culturally understandable patterns and divergences across the corpus, and what these constructions accomplished in the context of interactions: what kinds of 'reality' were being constructed and resisted. Relatedly, analysis explored the subject positions made available by these different repertoires, with implications for subjectivity, experience and practice. Shifting to a more 'micro' level of analysis (and drawing on the tools of DP) then allowed more detailed consideration of discursive accomplishments: the use of linguistic tools and processes to achieve rhetorical functions, such as 'talking back' to other arguments, positionings or interpretations. Finally came a stepping back to consider the broader 'macro' implications of the constructions: what they achieve and mean for the topic ideologically, speaking to wider discourses and contemporary movements.

While this analytical approach may appear linear, the actual practice is messier, with recursive movement between steps, and revising of earlier codings. Acknowledging the complex and subjective nature of constructionist qualitative research, the quality of the work was reviewed with reference to established criteria (Tracy, 2010). This was supported by reflexive group working, drawing on different personal and professional frames of understanding to consider 'blind spots' and alternative interpretations (Willig, 2008). As part of this, reviews considered how our personal positions as white European women with different relationships to weight/loss, fat/phobia and body image influenced our engagement with the words and worlds being studied.

## Analysis and Discussion

Analysis draws out two interwoven threads running in tension through this corpus: EDs as a marginalized topic in FA spaces; but also, EDs as an important, if problematic, topic for fat people and FA.

### *Eating disorders as a marginalized topic for FA sites*

Our first observation was that EDs formed only a small proportion of the FA talk sampled. Further, two of the three platforms contained almost no talk on EDs. In order to understand the meaning of talk—or its absence—CDP stresses the importance of attending to the *contexts* of its production. This is not simply 'talk about EDs', which *happens* to be drawn from FA sites; this is talk *constructed on and for* particular FA sites, for particular audiences, within frameworks that encourage and discourage certain types of talk based on the sites' reasons for existence. So we ask first: how does this contextualize our interpretation of what is said (and how)—and what is *not* said?

### *Eating disorders as... not what we're here to talk about?*

In a world where being fat is denigrated, FA sites aim to offer alternative spaces where activism against a 'fatphobic' world, and the positive affirmation of fat people—physically, psychologically, socially—can take precedence. A relative paucity of ED talk might be understood simply as reflecting its lack of relevance to participants, or to FA's main aims. In the words of one contributor explaining a parallel lack of discussion of weight loss on the site, 'that's not what we're about'. However, further exploration suggests a more complex picture.

### *Eating disorders as... not 'our' problem?*

The following exchange is not initially 'about' EDs, but part of a wider topic questioning the need for a specific FA movement rather than the more inclusive 'size acceptance':

> **Alasia:**[2] *I'm fat and I'm all about accepting the way I am, but why fat acceptance? Why can't it just be size acceptance? I realize that fat people are absolutely persecuted, don't get me wrong, but [...] if people start insulting slimmer people, it makes it okay for them to insult us.*
>
> **Azha:** *That's a really good question. I didn't name the movement (and some people DO call it size acceptance, I'm just not one of them [...])*
>
> *We live in a society that inherently privileges the thin. Very thin people do frequently have to live with the suspicion of having an eating disorder or get told to 'eat a sandwich' but that's nothing compared to the shit that fat people get thrown at them. With the cries of OBESITY EPIDEMIC BOOGA BOOGA BOOGA and the health concern trolling and the just plain fucking rudeness that fat people face every day [...] they're faced with prejudice and difficulties. I don't mean to trivialize the way that super thin*

*people are treated, I'm sure it really sucks to have people think that you have an eating disorder, but until 'wow, you look really skinny today!' ceases to be a compliment, I really can't sympathize that much.*

In many ways, this exchange can be viewed as part of the routine co-construction of both FA and the identities of FA community members. Even before asking their question, Alasia works to establish claims to speak and be accepted as a member of the FA community, as 'fat', 'accepting' and understanding the context of fat discrimination. With a disclaimer and hedge to mitigate any implied criticism (Wiggins, 2017), Alasia is positioned as a 'learner' seeking clarification from a more experienced community member. Being part of this community appears important, and talk simultaneously questions and reinforces constructions of '*slimmer people*' as the out-group ('them') in comparison to 'us'.

Azha responds within this frame, as an 'educator' repeating an established FA repertoire: that, while SA does theoretically encompass FA, society raises specific issues for ('we') fat people, who need additional representation. In doing so, though, Azha draws on a common repertoire of EDs as associated with the world of 'very/super thin' people, dismissing this as of little concern to a fat person battling a thin-privileging society.

This construction of EDs as the preserve of thin people is clearly not the only one, but of enough concern to form the topic of blogs elsewhere in the fatosphere:

**Capella:** *What do you think of when you hear the words 'anorexic' or 'bulimic'? What mental picture do you have? This?*
[Photograph of a severely emaciated young white woman]

Here, established blogger Capella adopts the educator role speaking directly to her FA audience, challenging anticipated preconceptions that EDs—even anorexia—are relevant only to the very thin. Her extended post is complex and provokes heated debate. But in a part of the fatosphere where 'us' and 'them' is sometimes reduced to 'fat' and 'thin', or FA vs. fat-stigmatizing, the post and responses highlight that the topic of EDs can complicate these group identities.

### *Eating disorders as... dangerous even to talk about?*

*This is a fat positive space. This is not a porn or fetish blog. There will be no discussion of weight loss.*

Other aspects of FA sites also contextualize ED talk. Though sites differ, most state rules (as those above) about permissible topics and forms of discussion. Most take the position that topics like weight loss—ubiquitous in the outside world and argued to be harmful—are not allowed, to create a place of respite.

However, this creates a dilemma: if the fatosphere aims to be a place where fat people can have their experiences validated, bans on certain topics could exclude those they are intended to support. Partly to manage this, blogsites have developed systems of disclaimers and 'trigger warnings' at the start of entries, alerting users to topics that would otherwise be off-limits, and they may choose to avoid:

> *Trigger warning: Discussion of feeling the urge to diet and other disordered eating behaviours.*
> *Serious trigger warning: Frank discussion of health, weight loss, weight loss surgery and eating disorders.*

In using these, bloggers demonstrate their position as insiders to the community who know the rules and seek to protect fellow users, while also giving 'balance' and choice (Wiggins, 2017). Simultaneously, they reinforce certain topics as 'dangerous'. The concept of a 'trigger' draws on repertoires of risk, responsibility, trauma and psychological harm that might be precipitated or reactivated even by discussion (see also Branley-Bell, and Eikey et al., this volume). The collocation of weight/diet talk with 'disordered eating' and EDs in some of these alerts makes clear that EDs *are* a topic of relevance for FA sites, and a troubling one. The relative lack of ED talk on other sites (two of the three sampled here) now seems less an indication of irrelevance, more (like diet talk) a topic that is almost too risky to discuss easily—yet one that some FA users want to discuss.

## Eating disorders as relevant to fat people and FA

Headed by trigger alerts, blogs on a minority of FA sites provide detailed personal accounts of living with EDs; and, more specifically, living *as a fat person* with this experience—in ways that highlight relevance for the FA community.

### Eating disorders as... linked to thin culture and fatphobia

> **Diya:** *Trigger warning: This post is all about eating disorders*
> *Eating disorders (EDs) are something I have a hard time understanding outside of my own personal experience [...] I've said before that I'm in*

> *recovery for EDNOS (eating disorder not otherwise specified, which is the diagnosis they give when you're fat even if you meet the criteria for anorexia or bulimia).*
>
> *See, for me, fatphobia was the center of my experience. The hatred of my own fat was everything to me. I recognize that there were aspects of control involve too [...] an amazing sense of having power over my own life. But the real reason wasn't control. No, it was fat. I had to be thin! Not because thinness showed control over my body, but because thinness was what was accepted by society. Despite people saying 'it's not about being thin!' well... it was an awful lot about being thin. I know it's a mental illness, not just something 'normal' men and women get from social pressure, but I can't help but think that social pressure was a huge fucking chunk of what triggered it for me.*
>
> *And when I look into the windows of ED forums everywhere I see the same thing. I rarely see someone saying they feel out of control; I see them saying they feel fat [...] freaking out because they gained a few pounds. See, here's where I really need help understanding eating disorders, despite my own struggle with one. If it walks like fatphobia, talks like fatphobia, and acts like fatphobia, then how come it's not fatphobia?*

From the outset of the post, this regular FA blogger makes relevant her personal experience of this topic—as someone with an ED diagnosis, and (in multiple posts) as 'fat'. In a move increasingly recognized within contemporary discourse, this opens up a subject position of someone who is 'expert-by-experience', so can claim experiential authority for her argument while also fostering community with others who have similar experiences (Dawney, 2013; Lyons et al., this volume). The ability to present oneself as a credible speaker takes on particular importance for fat people, habitually discredited within 'lipoliterate' society—particularly when speaking against more powerful voices on topics relating to health or diet. Here though, within a FA site, it is the work of talking about eating disorders that requires justification.

Both the content and discursive construction of what follows attends to this. A key message here—that societal fatphobia is central to personal experience of ED—makes relevant and then extends a central repertoire of FA that will be understood by site users: that 'social pressure' to be thin underpins problematic experience, and for fat people in particular. Initially, Diya makes a purely personal ('*for me*') knowledge claim for this extension to EDs, with extreme case formulations ('*fatphobia was* ***the centre*** *of my experience*', '***everything*** *to me*') adding discursive force (Pomeranz, 1986).

But might others see things differently, and be persuaded by other repertoires of ED? While claims made from personal experience hold a particular type of authority, they remain vulnerable to assertions that they are biased, too clouded by subjectivity, not generalizable. Diya's words attend to this possibility, in ways similar to other blogs. First, experiential narrative is combined with switches to an educator voice that demonstrates her knowledge of biomedical and psychological repertoires: explaining the medical diagnostic EDNOS acronym used at the time (since revised); and acknowledging alternative repertoires of EDs as '*not about the weight*' but '*control*'. Her ability to reflexively '*recognize*' and acknowledge '*aspects*' of personal relevance acts as a form of 'stake inoculation' (Edwards & Potter, 1993), positioning her as knowledgeable, self-aware and equipped to balance possibilities.

The persuasiveness of Diya's argument is then enhanced further as personal introspection is supplemented by positioning her as an external observer, more akin to a researcher '*look[ing] into*' ED forums. From these she cites corroboration by '*them*' of her perspective: that this is not simply an idiosyncratic personal view and neither, she implies, is it just a FA view. The extract ends with rhetorical force: if '*they*' are '*complaining about being fat*', surely this is about fatphobia—an issue highly relevant to the FA community? (The question of who exactly 'they' are will be returned to shortly.) Her credibility as a source of understanding provides the backdrop to emphasize her point: '*the real reason*' ('*despite*' what others might say). And if this speaker, knowledgeable on multiple counts, has '*a hard time understanding*' EDs, an implicit rhetorical question arises: are people *without* personal experience in any position to contradict her?

The post gains many positive responses that confirm the relevance of Diya's post to the FA community. Some emphasize links to the broader FA repertoire: that dieting, underpinned by weight stigma and fatphobia, is ineffective and leads, through yo-yo dieting/weight-cycling, to progressive obesity:

> **Felis:** *I think you hone in on and clarify a very important truth [...] I have been researching the topics of nutrition and obesity for over three years [...] One of my conclusions [...] is that most obesity seems to be a reaction to previous caloric restriction. Other than children who are made to restrict*

> *calories by their parents or the insane anti childhood obesity movement, there are all of these normal weighted people going on weight loss diets due to body image problems and voila, they end up with obesity issues due to their attempts at caloric restriction [and] yo-yo dieting [...] I believe that it all comes down fat phobia, this is what motivated these people to go on weight loss diets in the first place.*

Others illustrate the 'theory' with moving personal testimony, building consensus and community in linking societal fatphobia and EDs:

> **Heze:** *I had a bit of 'puppy fat' about 10.*
>
> *My father, between 10 and 12 until nearly 17, started me on a severely restrictive diet [gives details] My mother disagreed but she 'nagged' and was happy enough to tell me that 'Fatties are a waste of time / space', 'Fatties are stupid' (much like my father) etc.*
>
> *Subsequently I had bulimic behaviour for 18 years, but instead of controlling my weight I ballooned massively and now have to contend with morbid obesity.*
>
> *Now I have to deal with the consequences of that.*

Like Heze, many contributors draw on recognizable psychosocial repertoires (e.g., of oppressive societal and parental pressure), linking these temporally to 'subsequent' behaviour associated with EDs. Amid societal injunctions for fat people to 'take responsibility', Heze's words decentre her (as a child) from culpability in weight gain or EDs, simultaneously positioning her as an unfortunate but good citizen who now must '*deal with the consequences*'.

While this repertoire of ED as underpinned by fatphobia is strongly drawn upon, it is not the only one. An alternative repertoire of ED as about *control*, referenced though contested by Diya, is returned to by one responder who maintains this is congruent with her FA position:

> **Intan:** *I will likely always be fat. And that's okay. Because my eating disorder had nothing to do with the want to be thin. It had to do with, and still does, with being in control. It's an illusion.*

Most, though, construct EDs as complex, combining psychological and biomedical repertoires of 'mental illness' while maintaining the frame of cultural fatphobia. Notably, all these contributors have begun by positioning themselves as people who have lived with EDs, so have experiential authority for their knowledge claims:

**Kaveh:** *I don't think it isn't entirely about weight. I think that life stress and being a coping mechanism for abuse is definitely a big player, though, for most with EDs.*

**Libertas:** *I do not believe I would have developed an ED if I wasn't afraid of becoming fat. Yes, I've got probably got some genetic predispositions- underlying tendencies toward anxiety and depression which made me more vulnerable- but I strongly believe my eating disorder was fueled by my family and cultural environment.*

**Maia:** *Eating disorders are mental illnesses brought on by society. They wouldn't exist without the pressure to be thin at all costs.*

### *Eating disorders as... different for fat people*

Beyond talk about *development* of weight issues and EDs, FA bloggers also stress that the experience of *living with* EDs is different for fat people compared with those of lower weight—including what is even acknowledged as an ED.

**Sika:** *Fat people torture themselves and are told 'go on keep doing it fatty' while thin people are told 'ooh poor you, you look like Barbie, but what pain you must be in'.*

**Polaris:** *This is exactly why I never sought help for my ED. Anorexia is seen as a GOOD thing when you're fat. Curing fatphobia would change so many aspects of ED's, how they're treated, and the ED community.*

Bloggers suggest that severe restriction and behaviours that would otherwise raise serious concern and diagnosis are not only ignored but societally encouraged for fat people. Further, this stigma and discrimination are depicted as present within professional systems, leaving them vulnerable to further physical and psychological harm:

**Intan:** *At 350 lbs. I was hospitalized with severe malnutrition, severe anemia (in fact, needed 6 units transfused) and my hair had fallen out. Diagnosis: Restrictive anorexia. They came into my room to look at me like a carnival*

> *exhibit. Who could imagine a fat anorexic? And better yet, one who didn't binge or purge?*

And, in a further complication of 'us' and 'them' positions, bloggers speak of their additional vulnerability within 'the ED community', and the impact of fatphobia here. Continuing her post on fatphobia (above), Diya continues:

> *Okay okay [...] Let's assume that eating disorders are all about control and not about being skinny. Isn't it still inherently fatphobic? They use fat as a stand in term for disgusting, unwanted, unlovable, ugly, or worthless. They (and understand when I say 'they' I'm not by any means referring to all people with EDs, just those I've observed) use photos of people like me as thinspiration [...] to perpetuate their disease, to validate their feelings that fat is the worst thing on the planet you can be. Being fat is so bad that death and sickness are better than being that. Than being me [...]*
>
> *These people are my comrades, yet I constantly feel outside of the community because I'm fat.*
>
> **Kaveh:** *I used to help moderate the only ED group on [platform] that supposedly accepted bigger girls with EDs. I noticed that 'big' seems to mean 160-170 lbs. And most of them were just using the forum to discuss their eating habits, etc. and not try to get better. I would make posts telling people to respect others' EDs, since I have struggled with all of them at one point or another myself [...] Nobody listened to me, of course, and they continued to disrespect the people with BED or who were fatter [...]*
>
> *I am really hoping that there can at least be an insular community formed to protect those with BED and people with EDs that are heavier. Because when I was inpatient my treatment was compromised by a lot of bullying.*

Both have made explicit their own diagnoses with EDs, yet these and other posts position other people with EDs (or at least '*those I've observed*') as the outgroup: the category of 'fat' takes precedence over that of slimmer/other ED sufferers, and the implicit 'us' here appears to be the FA community. Posts convey painful stories of stigmatization and rejection. Lists of examples, extreme case formulations and rhetorical questioning of the audience build a discursively compelling case, allowing for affective resonance to build experiential authority and community (Dawney, 2013; Wiggins, 2017). The fatphobia that is so prevalent in society, it is argued, unsurprisingly invades even the ED communities where people should be getting support. While societies arguably portray those with EDs as emaciated and fragile, Kaveh counters that '*bigger girls*' here are particularly susceptible to bullying from others with EDs, and need particular protection as an '*insular community*'. Thus, a claim is made of the need for a more specific 'us', even as others acknowledge that an appreciation of societal fatphobia should, in theory, lead to a joining of forces with others living with EDs; those who should be 'comrades' within a broader 'body acceptance' movement.

### *Eating disorders as… requiring ongoing resistance—with the support of FA*

> **Maia:** *I'm bulimic, though its currently under control. To my dismay, I know the old programming will never go away […] No matter how I try, that voice is still there.*

Within these blogs, EDs are often constructed as conditions that are being 'managed' or resisted by speakers, in an ongoing struggle. Diya (above) positions herself from the start as 'in recovery' from an ED, drawing on a repertoire often associated with addiction or psychological ill-health: no longer all-consuming, but requiring ongoing vigilance against the threat of relapse.

> **Tiaki:** *I have been practicing HAES since 2010. I'm not saying it has been easy or that I got it perfectly. I've been working on different aspects of myself ever since.*
>
> *Since I have struggled with eating disorders before, It's been a long way. So far I have manged my self-image and understood my hunger signals. Still, I struggle with diet mentality.*

Popular discourse associates dieting with struggle, to lose weight or maintain loss, within culturally valued frames of self-improvement. In contrast, FA advocates are often depicted as passively 'giving up', if not downright lazy and irresponsible; not caring about (or even promoting) poor health for fat people (Muttarak, 2018). Talk on FA sites subverts these repertoires. FA and HAES are constructed, not as passive 'acceptance', but as practices that require work to maintain in real life. Here, the struggle of FA practice is tied to the struggle to prevent relapse, not simply into '*diet mentality*', but into poor mental health and

EDs. FA and HAES are thus constructed, not as a dangerous promotion of fatness, but as the alternative to more dangerous EDs—something that health professionals need to attend to:

**Maia** [responding to Diya's post on fatphobia and EDs]: *My experience and mindset were very similar before discovering size acceptance and HAES.*

*I started bulimic behaviour when I was 12. It was in control on and off throughout my 20's and 30's, although I continued with yo-yo dieting until I was in my mid-forties and discovered HAES and Size Acceptance (thank all that's holy!)*

**Navi:** *I came to FA via an ED. I was a regular on [an ED forum]. Then [...] I left [...] I had outgrown it by working with a therapist who advocated HAES etc.*

*A lot of ED recovery is messed up and promotes thinness, vs truly being underweight, as the ideal. Even anorectics are encouraged to gain some weight but to be careful about becoming overweight.*

Discursively, talk takes the form of culturally powerful 'quest' narratives (Frank, 1995) of personal growth through struggles with adversity, and the authority to speak on the basis of this hard-won learning. In talking back to '*a lot*' of ED programmes, the corroborative power of another professional adds weight. However, while some bloggers adopt an almost evangelical tone in portraying HAES/FA as the solution, most hedge with more caution: this is a long-term struggle. FA and HAES communities, though, are constructed here as the support that members need:

**Libertas:** *FA blogs were beginning, baby steps toward my recovery. For awhile it was something I read to comfort myself for not being thin—but I still could not internalize the messages. Only after I was formally treated and stopped engaging in behaviours for extended periods of time did I start to slowly internalize the message toward myself. Now I feel much more supported in FA communities than I do eating disorder communities*

**Vega:** *I avoid ED Recovery communities that aren't FA and HAES friendly. I find it triggering and toxic [...] and I think these places are doing their members a great disservice by keeping the focus on weight rather than health and sanity.*

FA blogs are thus constructed as a legitimate site for talk about EDs, and a unique space in which to support those who are excluded by their fatter bodies from wider, fatphobic ED communities. And, in keeping with the ethos of FA, repertoires of learning through struggle reinforce subject positions of authorities and activists who not only 'talk back' to detractors, but seek to offer this understanding to those who are in need:

> **Zhang:** *I blog because if one of my posts can wheedle its way into just one person's awareness who is on the road to an eating disorder due to self-loathing and body dissatisfaction, and give them an opportunity to reconsider that there is another point of view, then it is a worthwhile use of my time.*

## Conclusions and Further Reflections

This work provides insight into under-researched intersections between EDs and FA movements, foregrounding the words of those with lived experience of both, and highlights tensions in representing EDs within this section of the fatosphere. We conclude that the relative absence of talk about EDs in some FA sites reflects personal and ideological dilemmas for site users in portraying their experiences while maintaining valued positions within FA communities, within a context where their status and credibility is already threatened by a fat-denigrating society.

Bloggers within these FA sites negotiate difficult discursive terrain, constructing EDs as relevant and dangerous to the worlds of fat people and FA; underpinned by societal fatphobia; experientially different for fat people because of this, societally and even within ED communities; and posing distressing and ongoing threats to fat people, in which the work of FA can provide valuable support towards recovery. Our analysis extends research into other digital communities, particularly mental health service user, survivor and recovery movements, in which marginalized individuals draw together in peer support, self-help and activism. As in these arenas (e.g., Näslund et al., 2020), personal narratives of experience form a foundation for activity within FA sites. Bloggers construct authority as 'experts-by-experience', able to talk back to detractors from positions of privileged insight while also demonstrating institutional knowledge. Narratives of vulnerability reinforce experiential authority and draw together communities, stimulating and drawing further rhetorical strength from corroborative accounts, allowing the personal to be made political (Noorani, 2013). However, while research into other movements has often focused on contestation between 'service users' and professionals, the current study highlights a need to bridge potential divisions *within* as well as beyond a support community.

Talk about EDs is complex in the fatosphere. The advocated use of 'trigger warnings' constructs EDs as dangerous even to talk about, risking re-traumatization and threats to personal wellbeing, while presenting FA communities as offering protection to the vulnerable. The most consistent and least contested accounts construct experience of living as a fat person with EDs in line with central FA repertoires of societal fatphobia and discrimination, in which EDs are ignored or even encouraged, and fat people suffer inadequate professional treatment, marginalization and even bullying from thinner peers within ED treatment and online forums. Speakers thus legitimate their right to post within FA (rather than ED) forums. Alternative psychological repertoires of EDs are sometimes acknowledged, but (in this space at least) more marginalized.[3]

Perhaps most importantly, in making links between EDs and FA, these blogs draw on but subvert medical and social discourses of 'danger' and risk, responsibility and recovery. In a world where fat people must contend with accusations that their fatness is a dangerous personal failure—and that FA is a dangerous movement that promotes 'giving up' on health—these blogs construct a counternarrative in which the dangers of EDs outweigh those of fatness; and FA/HAES provides active, though hard-to-achieve, strategies to resist the ongoing threat of both fatphobia and EDs. This, site users argue, is a message which the public and health professionals need to understand.

Relatedly, these blogs speak to a context where online communities, especially around EDs, are viewed with public and professional suspicion (see also Haas et al., and Branley-Bell, this volume). Over-simplistic distinctions are often made between 'pro-disorder' (e.g., pro-ana) and 'pro-recovery' sites (Firkins et al., 2019; Lupton, 2017). While FA proponents sometimes challenge ideologies of health as a personal moral obligation, here FA is drawn on as part of the toolkit in personal (though increasingly collectivized) fights against EDs, highlighting again the complex relationship between FA and neoliberalism (Guthman & Dupuis, 2006). In this, these blogs align most with 'pro-recovery' rhetoric—though redefining the 'problem', the 'recovery' here relates to mental health, not fatness.

So why is this message not voiced more widely across the fatosphere? Why, as has been alleged (Glen, 2008), might FA forums discourage talk about EDs? This warrants further research attention, with many possibilities and implications. However, talk about EDs within FA communities may be viewed as threatening not only personal wellbeing, but also the broader identity and ethos of FA movements. In a society that denigrates fat people, FA strives to challenge notions of fatness as a 'problem', and/or question whose problem this is, relocating the problem away from widely assumed moral or psychological flaws of fat people, back to the society that perpetuates harm through sociocultural and fat-related discrimination. EDs are psychiatric classifications: though acknowledging the impact of societal pressures, these primarily (and contentiously) construct individual 'psychopathology' (Gelo et al., 2015). Contrary to FA aims, a focus on EDs within its forums risks reinforcing perceived links between fatness, individual behaviour and/or 'psychopathology.' And in societies where mental health difficulties generally, and EDs in particular, are stigmatized (Puhl & Suh, 2015), talk about personal experience of EDs presents further challenges to the identities of speakers and communities. For those already discredited by their larger bodies within a lipoliterate society, the threat to credibility is arguably deepened. This may then be a topic that FA advocates, already under siege, have good reason to avoid.

However, others with lived experience of EDs *and* ongoing fat stigma make a compelling case for acknowledgement, inclusion and support from FA communities, as well as the need for ED programmes to incorporate FA/HAES principles. Questions remain about why some areas of the fatosphere appear more fertile sites than others for talk about EDs. The sampling technique of this research attempted to capture different FA philosophies and approaches (e.g., to curation), and it can be argued that this was successful in highlighting some differences. Beyond ideological differences, there are methodological implications for research within the digital world. Further work could usefully explore other aspects of digital communities that facilitate particular constructions (e.g., encouraging image-based vs. word-heavy posts; blogger-led vs. chat-based forums).

Further, there is a need to expand the cultural focus of research in the fatosphere. All the sites sampled here were culturally limited by being English-speaking, and their anonymized format can also obscure users' cultural differences. Many users appeared to be from the USA, making relevant aspects of specific food, healthcare and political systems. In other posts, some spoke directly about their ethic/cultural background (e.g., as Black, European or Hispanic) and other aspects of their identities (e.g., regarding gender, as LGBTQ+, as socioeconomically disadvantaged or as disabled), but many did not; and, intriguingly, these topics were largely absent in the posts about EDs. This raises questions about what aspects of personal identities can be brought to different digital forums, and also—as considered elsewhere in this volume—the importance of not assuming findings to be 'universal' across cultural contexts, or constructing the experience of white people as the 'norm'. While many areas of the fatosphere may be dominated by white women, other voices are increasingly heard highlighting the impact of heritage, but also racism and other forms of social injustice on constructions of body ideals, different EDs, and mental health (Johansson, 2021). Future research must now apply intersectional lenses to understand these important areas, attending to the voices of the marginalized people most affected.

## Notes

1 Many fat acceptance advocates reject terms such as 'obesity' or 'overweight' as part of the medicalization of normal variation, preferring to reclaim the term 'fat' to describe bodies. We adopt this language here, unless reporting studies that specifically use medicalized terms.

2 Pseudonyms have been given. Original names and pseudonyms on FA sites often obscure preferred gender or cultural background of participants, so these pseudonyms (names of star systems) are intended to be gender- and culture-neutral. Additionally, we use ungendered pronouns (they/their) unless participants themselves make this clear in their contributions.

3 Here it is important to repeat the boundaries and implications of the constructionist epistemology being used: it does *not* make realist claims for what is said (for example that EDs *are* caused by fatphobia, or something else); nor does it even claim unproblematic insight into what speakers *really* believe or experience. Rather, it focuses on what can be said, by particular speakers in particular contexts; how this is done; and the social actions accomplished by constructing topics and identities in particular ways.

## References

Afful, A., & Ricciardelli, R. (2015). Shaping the online fat acceptance movement: talking about body image and beauty standards. *Journal of Gender Studies* 24(4): 453–72. https://doi.org/10.1080/09589236.2015.1028523

Bacon, L., & Aphramor, L. (2011). Weight science: evaluating the evidence for a paradigm shift. *Nutrition Journal* 10(9). https://doi.org/10.1186/1475-2891-10-9

British Psychological Society (2017). *Ethics Guidelines for Internet-mediated Research.* Leicester: BPS.

Billig, M., Condor, S., Edwards, D., Gane, M., Middleton, D., & Radley, A. (1988). *Ideological Dilemmas.* London: Sage.

Brewis A, Sturtz-Sreetharan, C., & Wutich, A. (2018). Obesity stigma as a globalizing health challenge. *Global Health* 14(1): 20. https://doi.org/10.1186/s12992-018-0337-x

Burr, V. (2015). *Social Constructionism* (3rd edn). London: Routledge.

Cain, P., Donaghue, N., & Ditchburn, G. (2017). Concerns, culprits, counsel, and conflict: a thematic analysis of 'obesity' and fat discourse in digital news media. *Fat Studies 6*: 170–88. https://doi.org/10.1080/21604851.2017.1244418

Campos, P., Saguy, A., Ernsberger, P., Oliver, E. & Gaesser, G. (2006). The epidemiology of overweight and obesity: public health crisis or moral panic? *International Journal of Epidemiology* 35(1): 55–60. https://doi.org/10.1093/ije/dyi254

Cooper, C. (2008). *What's Fat Activism?* University of Limerick Department of Sociology Working Paper Series: University of Limerick.

Davenport, K., Solomons, W., Puchalska, S., & McDowell, J. (2018). Size acceptance: a discursive analysis of online blogs. *Fat Studies* 7(3): 278–93. https://doi.org/10.1080/21604851.2018.1473704

Dawney, L. (2013). The figure of authority: the affective biopolitics of the mother and the dying man. *Journal of Political Power* 6(1): 29–47. https://doi.org/10.1080/2158379x.2013.774971

Dickins, M., Browning, C., Feldman, S., & Thomas, S. (2016). Social inclusion and the Fatosphere: the role of an online weblogging community in fostering social inclusion. *Sociology Health & Illness* 38(5): 797–811. https://doi.org/10.1111/1467-9566.12397

Donaghue, N., & Clemitshaw, A. (2012). 'I'm totally smart and a feminist … and yet I want to be a waif': exploring ambivalence towards the thin ideal within the fat acceptance movement. *Women's Studies International Forum* 35(6): 415–25. https://doi.org/10.1016/j.wsif.2012.07.005

Edley, N. (2001). Analysing masculinity: interpretative repertoires, subject positions and ideological dilemmas. In M. Wetherell, S. Taylor, & S.J. Yates (eds), *Discourse as Data: A Guide to Analysis.* London: Sage and the Open University.

Edwards, D., & Potter, J. (1992). *Discursive Psychology.* London: Sage.

Edwards, D., & Potter, J. (1993). Language and causation: a discursive action model of description and attribution. *Psychological Review* 100(1): 23–41. https://doi.org/10.1037/0033-295x.100.1.23

Erdman, A. (2011). Fat shame: stigma and the fat body in American culture. New York: New York University Press.

Fikkan, J.L., & Rothblum, E.D. (2012). Is fat a feminist issue? Exploring the gendered nature of weight bias. *Sex Roles: A Journal of Research* 66(9-10): 575–92. https://doi.org/10.1007/s11199-011-0022-5

Frank, A. (1995). *The Wounded Storyteller: Body, Illness and Ethics.* Chicago: University of Chicago Press.

Gard, M. (2011). *The End of the Obesity Epidemic.* London: Routledge.

Gelo, O.C.G., Vilei, A., Maddux, J.E., & Gennaro, A. (2015). Psychopathology as social construction: the case of anorexia nervosa. *Journal of Constructivist Psychology* 28(2): 105–25. https://doi.org/10.1080/10720537.2013.858087

Glen, L. (1 January 2008). Big trouble: are eating disorders the lavender menace of the fat acceptance movement? *Bitch Media*, https://www.bitchmedia.org/article/big-trouble

Graham, M. (2005). *Fat: The Anthropology of An Obsession.* New York: The Penguin Group.

Guthman, J., & DuPuis, M. (2006). Embodying neoliberalism: economy, culture, and the politics of fat. *Environment and Planning: Society & Space* 24: 427–48. https://doi.org/10.1068/d3904

Harding, K., & Kirby, M. (2009). *Lessons from the Fat-o-Sphere: Quit Dieting and Declare a Truce with Your Body.* New York: Pedigree.

Heilferty, C.M. (2011). Ethical considerations in the study of online illness narratives: a qualitative review. *Journal of Advanced Nursing* 67(5): 945–53. https://doi.org/10.1111/j.1365-2648.2010.05563.x

Hunger, J.M., Smith, J., & Tomiyama, A.J. (2020). An evidence-based rationale for adopting weight-inclusive health policy. *Social Issues and Policy Review* 14: 73–107. https://doi.org/10.1111/sipr.12062

Johansson, A. (2021). Fat, black and unapologetic: body positive activism beyond white, neoliberal rights discourses. In E. Alm et al. (eds), *Pluralistic Struggles in Gender, Sexuality and Coloniality.* London: Palgrave Macmillan.

Locke, A., & Budds, K. (2020). Applying critical discursive psychology to health psychology research: a practical guide. *Health Psychology and Behavioural Medicine* 8(1): 234–47. https://doi.org/10.1080/21642850.2020.1792307

Lupton, D. (2017). Digital media and body weight, shape, and size: an introduction and review. *Fat Studies* 6(2): 119–34. https://doi.org/10.1080/21604851.2017.1243392

Monson, O., Donaghue, N., & Gill, R. (2016). Working hard on the outside: a critical discourse analysis of 'The Biggest Loser Australia'. *Social Semiotics* 26(5): 524–40. https://doi.org/10.1080/10350330.2015.1134821

Muttarak, R. (2018). Normalization of plus size and the danger of unseen overweight and obesity in England. *Obesity* 26(7): 1125–29. Actions

Nash, M., & Warin. M. (2017). Squeezed between identity politics and intersectionality: a critique of 'thin privilege' in fat studies. *Feminist Theory* 18(1): 69–87. https://doi.org/10.1177/1464700116666253

Näslund, H., Sjöström, S., & Markström, U. (2020). Service user entrepreneurs and claims to authority. *European Journal of Social Work* 23(4): 672–84. https://doi.org/10.1080/13691457.2019.1580249

Nath, R. (2019). The injustice of fat stigma. *Bioethics* 33(5): 577–90. https://doi.org/10.1111/bioe.12560

Nimegeer, A., Patterson, C., & Hilton, S. (2019). Media framing of childhood obesity: a content analysis of UK newspapers from 1996 to 2014. *BMJ Open* 9(4). https://doi.org/10.1136/bmjopen-2018-025646

Noorani, T. (2013). Service user involvement, authority and the 'expert-by-experience' in mental health. *Journal of Political Power* 6(1): 49–68. https://doi.org/10.1080/2158379x.2013.774979

Pearl, R. (2018). Weight bias and stigma: public health implications and structural solutions. *Social Issues and Policy Review* 12(1): 146–82. https://doi.org/10.1111/sipr.12043

Pearl, R., & Puhl, R. (2018). Weight bias internalization and health: a systematic review. *Obesity Reviews* 19: 1141–63. https://doi.org/10.1111/obr.12701

Pomerantz, A.M. (1986). Extreme case formulations: a new way of legitimating claims. *Human Studies* 9: 219–30. https://doi.org/10.1007/bf00148128

Potter, J., & Wetherell, M. (1987). *Discourse and Social Psychology: Beyond Attitudes and Behaviour*. London: Sage.

Puhl, R., & Heuer, C. (2010). Obesity stigma: important considerations for public health. *American Journal of Public Health* 100: 1019–28. https://doi.org/10.2105/ajph.2009.159491

Puhl, R.M., Latner, J.D., King, K.M., & Luedicke, J. (2014). Weight bias among professionals treating eating disorders: attitudes about treatment and perceived patient outcomes. *International Journal of Eating Disorders* 47(1): 65–75. https://doi.org/10.1002/eat.22186

Puhl, R., & Suh Y. (2015). Stigma and eating and weight disorders. *Current Psychiatry Reports* 17: 552–61. https://doi.org/10.1007/s11920-015-0552-6

Striley, K., & Hutchens, S. (2020). Liberation from thinness culture: motivations for joining fat acceptance movements. *Fat Studies* 9(3): 296–308. https://doi.org/10.1080/21604851.2020.1723280

Strings, S. (2019). *Fearing the Black Body: The Racial Origins of Fat Phobia*. New York: New York University Press.

Tracy, S.J. (2010). Qualitative quality: eight 'big-tent' criteria for excellent qualitative research. *Qualitative Inquiry* 16(10): 837–51. https://doi.org/10.1177/1077800410383121

Toomath, R. (2016). *Fat Science*. Auckland: Auckland University Press.

Tomiyama, A.J., Carr, D., Granberg, E.M., Major, B., Robinson, E., Sutin, A.R., & Brewis, A. (2018). How and why weight stigma drives the obesity 'epidemic' and harms health. *BMC Medicine* 16(1): 123. https://doi.org/10.1186/s12916-018-1116-5

Van Amsterdam, N. (2013). Big fat inequalities, thin privilege: an intersectional perspective on 'body size'. *European Journal of Women's Studies* 20(2): 155–69. https://doi.org/10.1177/1350506812456461

Van Langenhove, L., & Harré, R. (1999). Introducing positioning theory. In R. Harré and L. van Langenhove (eds), *Positioning Theory: Moral Contexts of Intentional Action* (pp. 14–31). Oxford: Blackwell.

Wetherell, M. (1998). Positioning and interpretative repertoires: conversation analysis and post-structuralism in dialogue. *Discourse and Society* 9(3): 387–412. https://doi.org/10.1177/0957926598009003005

Wiggins, S. (2017). *Discursive Psychology: Theory, Method and Application*. London: Sage.

Willig, C. (2008). Discourse analysis. In J.A. Smith (ed.), *Qualitative Psychology: A Practical Guide to Research Methods* (2nd edn) (pp. 160–85).

# Synthesis of Group Discussion

The discussion that follows places the individual chapters of this volume in the context of group discussions that took place among the contributing authors. The aim of these conversations was to facilitate critical dialogue and reflective understanding between the different disciplinary perspectives and language-based approaches, and to open a way to a more inclusive and pluralistic understanding of presentations of eating disorders (EDs). The discussions also explored strengths, limitations and future research directions to advance understanding of the experience of EDs, and their broader social and cultural dimensions, by those directly and indirectly affected. The discussions were chaired by the editor of this volume, Laura A. Cariola, and the first authors of the contributing book chapters, many of whom provided significant input to the dialogue by sharing their views and insights.

A starting point for discussion was that EDs, like many other mental health disorders, are typically conceptualized through a medical lens that outlines the classification, aetiology and specific symptoms, making it possible to think and speak of EDs as 'real' and 'true' ontological entities. As such, the clinical framework assumes that EDs and any other mental health disorder are diagnosable with the same certainty as physical health conditions. One major benefit of any classification system of psychopathology is that it provides language for the grouping together of a set of common symptoms. Conversely, although the medical lens offers concepts that provide the possibility of conceptualizing EDs, it also frames how we ought to understand EDs, and limits the availability of alternative ways of thinking of, speaking of and experiencing of problematic eating behaviours. By acknowledging that representation of EDs is strongly affected by available medical knowledge and ideas that structure our reality

'Synthesis of Group Discussion' in: *Eating Disorders in Public Discourse: Exploring Media Representations and Lived Experiences*. University of Exeter Press (2023). © Laura A. Cariola. DOI: 10.47788/QOOC5977

and influence how we think and speak, it is also possible to recognise that EDs do not exist as 'true' entities that undisputedly exist based on value-free objective scientific observation, but are socially constructed through discursive practices that are positioned as authoritative, in particular medical discourses. As such, the medical discourse offers a dominant version and interpretation of the 'reality' of EDs, but not a real and objective reflection of reality. For example, the taxonomy of the DSM is to a large extent informed by psychiatric and psychological evidence, yet essentially it is based on the subjective agreement of a medical panel rather than scientific and unmediated objectivity.

This was the consensus view among the authors who contributed to this volume, which made it possible to use language-based approaches to critically explore the elements that constitute the social and discursive constructions of EDs. In particular, we investigated those associated with the various media, including the UK and international newspapers, social media, online communities, blogs and forums, apps and in-depth interviews about lived experiences. The chapters in this volume demonstrate how the application of different language-based approaches can span the entire continuum from positivism to constructivism. It provides ground to explore the tensions between prescribed ways of thinking, speaking and experiencing that are facilitated and delimited by the medical discourse, and the possibility of alternative discourses and perspectives on EDs. The absence of these alternative discourses creates a gap between the public perception of what EDs ought to be and how they are experienced. It also means that individual experiences of ED are not acknowledged, which results in those affected by an ED feeling isolated, lonely and as if nobody understands them. The tension between these positions and discourses is evident in the chapters of this volume, which provide a compelling insight into the role of language in representing and constructing EDs, the associated sociocultural norms and values within the larger societal context and the social interactions and constructions of EDs within the boundaries of online communities among like-minded affected people. The studies in this volume highlight and raise further questions that generate new understanding of the contrast between the languages and voices of lived experiences and those of the predominant, medically informed public discourses; meanwhile, they illuminate the role of stigma and its production and reproduction through language.

The central theme of the 'scientific' medical discourse, which describes the way EDs are constructed in public discourses, is evident in the five chapters that explore ED representations in newspaper and magazines using content analysis, metaphor analysis and frame analysis. Of these, two studies identify that newspapers use a predominantly medical frame, positioning EDs as medical disorders that require medical intervention. For instance, Matt Bowen and Rhian Waller's study utilizes their novel media frame matrix to code aetiological and media-specific representations of anorexia nervosa in the UK newspapers. Their results show that the illness model was the commonly used frame, which emphasized the importance of treatment and the failings of the healthcare system. Although the illness model is the most commonly used, there is a balance between the three most commonly used, including the social, personal stressors and trivialization.

The prevalence of the illness frame was also evident in Carolina Figueras Bates' cross-cultural metaphorical analysis of Spanish and US newspapers that predominantly constructs EDs through the metaphorical schema 'AN ED IS A PROBLEM', implying the urgent need for a solution. The framing of eating disorders as in need of 'repair' alludes to the 'THE BODY IS A MACHINE' schema as a central tenant of the biomedical model. Contrary to previous research that stressed the relevance of medical conceptualizations of EDs to appropriately inform the public (e.g., O'Hara & Smith, 2007; Shepard & Seale, 2010), this fine-grained metaphor analysis provides insight into how medical frames of ED are powerful devices that reinforce existing societal structures of control, and how these produce a complex dynamic of social frames that underpin the representation of ED pathology. Within the medical frame, newspapers categorized EDs as 'abnormal' and therefore alluded to sensationalist perceptions of EDs that reinforce stigmatizing attitudes in the public. The study's analysis of metaphors also highlights the availability of extended and generalized metaphorical schemas that underpin a common conceptualization of EDs, nested within a medical perspective that privileges the 'expert' doctor's opinion and meanwhile undermines the voice of those with lived experiences and the possibility for contested discourses. As these metaphorical frames are easily understood and recognized by the public and shape the broader societal view on EDs, they are also the hardest to change.

The emphasis on a medical cause, however, was not present in all studies. For example, with a focus on the overlooked and neglected topic of representation of men with EDs, Scott Parrott, Kimberly Bissell, Nicholas Eckhart and Bumsoo Park's qualitative content analysis of English-language newspapers in Canada, the UK and the USA shows that in all three countries, eating disorder aetiology was most frequently attributed to the mass media, stress, genetic factors and pressure from family and friends. Of these articles, nearly a third featured a first-person account from a man with an ED, and they often reported men's experiences of EDs, including their social dimensions, such as prejudice and discrimination. In particular, this study demonstrates how newspapers can be powerful advocates for those with EDs by communicating stories to the public, with a focus on themes such as educational aspects and the lived experiences of those who are often overlooked (e.g., men with EDs), as a means to challenge societal assumptions and stigma around ED.

Hayriye Gulec's qualitative content analytic study of two broadsheet Turkish newspapers highlights the predominant emphasis on individual factors (e.g., perfectionism and self-discipline) and social factors (e.g., internalized thin ideal, body dissatisfaction, dieting) when presenting EDs. The Turkish press also categorized EDs as 'abnormal' and placed blame on the affected individuals as vulnerable victims who lacked agency and succumbed to societal pressures to achieve a thin body ideal. Meanwhile, references to Western celebrities also trivialized and glamourized eating disorders, while seducing and encouraging readers to aspire to the thin body ideal. Stigmatizing representations are also made visible in Irene López-Rodríguez's analysis of animal metaphors in women's magazines in Canada, the UK and the USA. Women's eating experiences were depicted through the use of stigmatizing and shaming zoomorphic metaphorical schemas to describe women's eating behaviour and overweight bodies. Such bestial iconography marginalizes and dehumanizes women's bodily experiences and further legitimizes the act of dehumanizing those with problematic eating behaviour, or those who do not comply with society's body or beauty ideal. Such an objectification of humans also encourages the notion of perfectionism as virtuous rather than self-destructive. This becomes particularly problematic in women's magazines, where women are exposed to a range of contradictory communications, ranging from messages about perfectionism and advertisements for beauty products, on the one hand, to articles on self-empowerment and self-love, on the other. In the context of mental health, this discourse positions those with EDs and non-conforming body shapes as 'other' and further ignores that EDs are not narrowly confined to a restricted anorexic type but also include binge eating disorder. In particular, binge eating disorder should not be conceptualized in simplistic terms of 'excessive eating' as a choice or indicator of lacking control over food consumption, but as an ED that should be understood within the broader and complex context of biological and psychosocial factors.

Overall, the book chapters provide a mixed picture of ED presentations, and are only partly consistent with recent longitudinal studies of mental health representations in newspapers that showed a reduction in stigmatizing newspaper content, possibly due to the intervention of anti-stigma campaigns (e.g., Time to Change) (Anderson et al., 2018; Rhydderch et al., 2016; Thornicroft et al., 2013). Although representations of individuals with EDs have tended to be significantly less stigmatizing compared to those of other diagnoses, such as schizophrenia or personality disorders (Bowen et al., 2020; O'Hara & Smith, 2007; Shepard & Seale, 2010), the studies in this volume indicate that news coverage of EDs in the global West has shifted from depicting EDs as a trivial issue to a serious societal public problem that affects both women and men. Such a shift has potentially significant implications for how readers can obtain a better understanding of EDs, which may positively affect their accessing of treatment and recovery. Conversely, there is a continuous need to ensure balanced reporting of EDs to reflect their multifaceted aetiology, and further, to regulate newspaper and magazine coverage through reporting standards (e.g., the National Union of Journalists) to protect readers from the harm associated with shaming normal bodily experiences, such as hunger and eating.

The way in which medical frames can assume an authority that silences the voices of ED experiencers is examined in two chapters that explore individuals affected by EDs and their feelings and attitudes towards media representations. The lived experiences of individuals with an ED, and how they make sense of newspaper representations of EDs, is the focus of Laura A. Cariola and Billy Lee, who use an interpretative phenomenological approach. Their study shows that individuals perceived newspaper reporting as sensationalized, and trivializing EDs by narrowly focusing on a medical lens, such as physical appearance and weight loss. These stereotyped representations affected individuals' intra- and interpersonal experiences by creating a sense of loneliness and self-stigma, and an inability to communicate their authentic experiences to others, whose perceptions of EDs are firmly anchored in stereotypical assumptions that are reinforced by the media. Similarly, Gareth Lyons, Sue McAndrew and Tony

Warne used a narrative inquiry approach that offered an insightful perspective on the lived experiences of men with EDs in relation to their encounters with the broader media. Their findings show that participants felt that there was a lack of representation of men with EDs in the media, and that the stereotype of EDs predominantly affecting young teenage girls would marginalize those who do not fit this clichéd medicalized portrayal. Participants who had worked with the print media witnessed how journalists would ignore their personal experiences in favour of writing sensationalist and stigmatizing stories with a focus on weight, catchy headlines and shocking pictures, thus actively silencing more authentic lived ED experiences.

The media, such as newspapers, appear to force the voices of those with lived experiences to fit to existing stereotypes: young, female, white. These discourses silence the presentation of individuals who are part of other, marginalized groups in society, including men with eating disorders and LGBTQI individuals, to the extent that the narrowness of reporting leads to misinformation about EDs and a stereotypical perception in the wider society that EDs mainly affect young white women. This highlights the necessity for these marginalized voices to be given a platform and to be heard in newspaper discourses, as EDs, just like any other mental health problem, can affect anyone regardless of gender, ethnicity, economic factors or any other demographic characteristic. An under-reporting in the media of men with EDs, and of other underrepresented populations, has serious and far-reaching repercussions in terms of offering appropriate access to support and resources which resonate with individuals from diverse backgrounds, and the provision of education to improve understanding of EDs within the larger society.

Simplistic representations also permeate newspaper portrayals of ED recovery through the use of a dichotomous differentiation between a healthy and an unhealthy person, without acknowledging that recovery is often a lengthy process that requires consistent vigilance and monitoring to avoid relapse. Although the medical frame tends to reduce EDs to a set of medical symptoms, recovery from EDs cannot be reduced to merely establishing healthy eating habits and bodily weight. Thus, EDs are complex, with a strong psychological basis that may include protective responses to deal with adverse environments and coping mechanisms to manage complex emotions, including anxiety, daily stressors and trauma. Such traumatic experiences are often associated with systematic societal problems, including sexual abuse, violence against girls and women, discrimination against minority populations (e.g., Black and LGBTQI populations) and expectations imposed by toxic masculinity (Mekawi et al., 2021; Parker & Harriger, 2020). As such, the development and maintenance of EDs are influenced by an individual's unique life experiences and sociocultural circumstances.

The strong tendency of the media to avoid critical examination of the political dimensions of EDs creates and reinforces stigma, misunderstanding and miscommunication. Alternative media discourses should focus on exploring the sociocultural causes of EDs and deepening empathic understanding of the relationship between EDs and the lived experiences of abuse and trauma, rather than framing and victim-blaming individuals with EDs as frivolous and over-focused on attaining beauty standards.

Several studies in this volume explore newspaper and magazine representations of EDs, and the impact of these representations on individuals with EDs, providing insight into how narrow and stereotypical discourses superimpose a narrative on individuals with EDs or problematic eating. The loss of the individual voice and the predominant authoritative tone and assumed objectivity of the medical frame create a distance between the unique experiences of individuals affected by EDs and public discourses such as newspapers, which further creates a public discrepancy between the medical expert opinion and the actual individual experience that remains silenced. As such, individuals with EDs often find themselves being spoken about like objects and exposed to the gaze of the public, whose function is to obtain satisfaction and entertainment from the exposed 'other'. It highlights the need for journalism to engage in responsible practices that value the voice of lived experiences—with the aim to empathically educate and raise public awareness about EDs and encourage conversation, rather than relying exclusively on professional opinions and insights that tend to unempathically oppress the voices of those with EDs.

Similarly, the notion of the oppressed voice of the individual with an ED calls attention to the necessity for academic research in the field of EDs to involve individuals with lived experiences as a fundamental and essential part of the research process, and not merely as a token gesture. For example, Dawn Branley-Bell's thoughtful account explores the importance of the self-reflective researcher and the use of methodological and ethical strategies relevant to qualitative and mixed-methods approaches. Based on her experiences and lessons learned using qualitative methods to analyse ED online communication, she reflects on her role as a researcher engaging in a dialogic encounter with participants in a shared space to explore how participants make sense of their world, and how to create generalizable insights into the underlying factors or motivations of their behaviours. Through this dialogical researcher–participant encounter, it is possible to adopt a shared language beyond the medicalized and often shame-based language associated with EDs. In relation to methodological considerations, she highlights the need for researchers to remain critical and self-reflective, and the value of co-designing research with individuals with lived experiences to reduce possible biases; the ethical importance of ensuring confidentiality and privacy; and the need for openness and selection of appropriate online platforms to engage with participants. Arguably, individuals with lived experiences who are contributing to the development of a research project should also receive appropriate acknowledgement as part of the process—for example, being offered co-authorship on a publication and access to conferences at accessible rates.

In contrast to the pervasiveness of the medical perspective that dominates how EDs are talked and thought about in the public domain, meanwhile silencing the experiences of those affected, online ED forums and communities provide a containing space in which individuals are able to talk about their experiences using their authentic voices and language. ED online communities provide support and a sense of social connection to individuals with EDs who otherwise may feel socially isolated. Although online communities as communicative spaces are shielded from the dysfunctional discourses of the public, these communities are dysfunctional in their own way and perhaps even dangerous—yet it remains difficult to determine whether the oppressive discourse of the mainstream public is less, equal or more dangerous to individuals' health and wellbeing than ED online communities. Stephen M. Haas, Nancy A. Jennings and Pamara F. Chang's theoretical discussion outlines six core communication characteristics that form Online Negative Enabling Support Group (ONESG) theory, to conceptualize online communicative message exchanges between members of pro-ana communities as extreme online communities that promote anorexic health behaviours. They propose that these communicative features may be present in other online community contexts and that they hold heuristic potential to promote and enable other types of negative health behaviours, including self-injury and pro-suicide behaviours. ONESG theory provides valuable insight into the communicative processes of pro-anorexia online communities as a subculture that promotes negative (health) behaviours. Subcultures may be perceived as a countermovement through rebelling against the dominance of hegemonic cultures and pushing back against ED stigma, and highlighting the tension between the languages and voices of lived experiences and those of the narrow and predominant medically informed public discourses.

Although ONESG theory demonstrates how anonymity in these communities drives self-disclosure, negative health behaviours are also reconstructed as positive behaviours. Within the boundaries of online ED community space, individuals feel that they are able to be and experience themselves, and engage in supportive and empathic communication with other community members who make them feel understood and less isolated. These communicative interactions in the online community appear far removed from the oppressive and judgemental stereotypes that individuals with EDs encounter in their offline experience. These online community spaces also draw on the notion of individuals with EDs exercising the right to have a conversation about their experiences with like-minded people, and to fulfil their need to feel accepted as human beings and for their voices to be heard and understood. Allyn Lueders's fantasy theme analysis of pro-anorexia discourses demonstrates how members of the pro-ana site Myproana.com (MPA) talk about themselves, reply and read about others' ED experiences, all while enjoying the anonymity inherent in online worlds. ED communities such as pro-ana spaces have existed on the internet since the 1990s, providing a space where participants connect with others who share their beliefs, engage in empathic encounters and find encouragement/motivation for their lifestyle, something they are almost certainly not hearing from other loved ones. Community members construct their social reality based on a set of fantasy themes through the affordance of character creation, expected actions and the pro-ana setting. For example, members have usernames and sometimes avatars, and share the ED experiences that set them apart from those who do not have an ED or engage in restricted eating habits, so-called normies (e.g., parents, family). MPA members encourage unhealthy eating behaviours, such as achieving the ultimate weight goal; however, there was also evidence of openness to recovery and encouragement of healthy eating choices.

Based on the fantasy analysis of MPA, it appears that a safe community space is guided by explicit rules that function to create and reinforce group conformity among its members. Perceived rule transgressions may be then interpreted as a threat to group cohesion, reflecting that acceptance in online pro-ED communities is not necessarily unconditional. This may represent challenges, in particular for newcomers who may be unfamiliar with pro-ED community expectations and share information that is perceived as 'forbidden' on the site, and as a result receive aggressive and unempathic responses from experienced members. Such a potential backlash reflects tensions between existing and new community members, which is a barrier to developing a feeling of community acceptance and belonging that potentially may complicate the journey to recovery. Consistent with online ED community rules and ideologies, it is not necessarily unusual for some individuals not to feel accepted, as they do not fit the expected or required body shape and size, despite having an ED. Conversely, there might also be cultural differences related to online ED communities in terms of their provision of support or competitive eating behaviours, which to some extent reflect expectations, judgements and constraints on the appearance of women's bodies by enacting a power dynamic that determines whose experiences are validated or invalidated, and who is given a voice or denied their voice, or how this voice is interpreted.

Based on a corpus of three fat acceptance (FA) blogs representing the voices of those with lived experiences, Wendy Solomons, Kate Davenport and Joanne McDowell's study using a critical discursive psychology (CDP) approach provides an insightful understanding into how FA discourses represent a powerful and marginalized voice that challenges the homogenous societal 'thinness' conversation. This study highlights the diversity of ED presentations, to the extent that individuals regarded as 'fat' may also present with anorexia nervosa. In contrast to medical discourses that present fatness as a risk to health, FA discourses provide a powerful counter-discourse, which underpins the FA community that perceives ED to be a greater risk to health than fatness. Talk in these online FA forums functions to form identities of FA community members based on 'us vs. them' constructions, with slimmer people representing the out-group. Conversations in these FA forums are guided by community rules around what topics and conversations are encouraged and discouraged. Topics related to weight loss or EDs associated with the 'outside' reality are perceived as 'dangerous', to the extent that they are carefully negotiated using trigger warnings. These reaffirm the poster's position as an in-group member who shows awareness of the community rules that aim to protect members from the re-traumatization of fat stigma, meanwhile making relevant their lived experiences with EDs by positioning themselves as an expert-by-experience.

ED discourses are also part of a discussion subforum in Elizabeth V. Eikey, Oliver Golden, Zhuoxi Chen and Qiuer Chen's mixed-methods study, which combines quantitative and qualitative analysis to explore nearly 2,000 posts within an online diet and fitness app. ED conversations in the app represented individual experiences with a focus on bodily perceptions and aspirations, and trying to gain or lose weight in a healthy way. The way forum members talked about their bodies and their needs closely reflected the companies' goals of encouraging weight loss rather than supporting users' mental health or ED recovery. Conversely to other online community discourses with a shared common ground of ED behaviour that may not necessarily challenge unhealthy eating behaviour, discourses in diet and fitness app community forums reflected tensions between the perceptions of healthy dieting and fitness on the one hand, and ED behaviours on the other, with the latter positioned as a subtopic within that community. To avoid anticipated backlash by other community members, EDs are framed through the use of qualifiers, for example, 'I am in recovery from anorexia and I want to lose weight, but I want to do it in a healthy way. Can you help me?'

Online community studies typically explore the topics of how community members talk with each other, construct their individual and group identities, offer support to each other to engage in healthy or unhealthy behaviour and discuss their thoughts and experiences of recovery. There is little research on the experiences of family members and friends positioned as online ED community antagonists and outsiders. As pointed out by Haas et al. (this volume), family members of individuals who are affected by EDs or are part of pro-ED online communities often experience anxiety and frustration in dealing with challenging health behaviours, and a range of complex emotions such as feelings of shame and guilt, and experiences of social isolation. As these difficulties reduce family ties and support, those affected by a family members with an ED may be attracted to joining online pro-ED communities to meet like-minded peers for socializing and support. With a focus on the experiences of parents positioned as outsiders, Emma O'Rourke and Laura A. Cariola's thematic analysis provides a view into the lived experiences of parents raising children with EDs. Parents reported feeling helpless and assumed an outsider perspective when describing their child's eating behaviours and an absence of insight into their child's internal experiences. This position was further reinforced by parents feeling attacked and verbally abused by their child, concurrent with a breakdown of conversation that resulted in a weakening of the parent–child bond and loss of control over the child. This diminished the parents' own sense of wellbeing and positioned them as helpless witnesses to the increasing grip of the ED on their child, meanwhile facing the uncertain future of their child's health.

## Limitations of this Book and Future Directions

This volume uncovers insights into how language is used to represent EDs in public discourses, the ways in which individuals experience EDs and how they are affected in their lived experiences through media texts and societal stigma. Any attempt to organize a topic related to mental health, language and stigma will be oversimplified and limited in its attempt to capture the underlying complexity. As such, this volume presents an insightful collection of contributions that examine ED discourses from different perspectives, but it has its limitations. One of the main limitations is the focus on more prevalent EDs, including anorexia nervosa and bulimia nervosa, rather than Other Specified Feeding and Eating Disorders (OSFEDs) or Unspecified Feeding or Eating Disorders (UFEDs), which are also common and even more misunderstood than other types of ED. This further reflects the arbitrary notion of clinically diagnosed and undiagnosed EDs, as outlined in the DSM-5. Nevertheless, it is important to note that OSFEDs and UFEDs are often the target of social stigma. For example, individuals with orthorexia who restrict their diet to clean and pure food are often targets of negative evaluation (Nevin & Vartanian, 2007). It is evident that the field of EDs is an evolving process that is closely linked to medical consensus on differentiation between medical and non-medical conditions. Considering that this volume includes studies that exclusively explore prevalent and medically recognized EDs, it is acknowledged that language-based studies should also focus on OSFEDs and UFEDs to contribute to generating new knowledge in relation to these little understood areas of EDs.

Although the book offers some perspectives on marginalized groups in the discussion of EDs, such as men, there is a lack of investigation into the role of cultures and ethnicities in relation to media and language-based approaches. For example, there is a marked under-representation of individuals of marginalized groups, including the BAME population. Another related limitation is that this book does not feature any contribution from BAME scholars, which mirrors existing racial inequalities in academia and contributes to an erroneous notion that EDs might not be relevant to scholars of colour. Although the editor of this volume cast their net wide and far to invite as many scholars with an interest in EDs and the media as possible, non-Western scholars were not found or did not respond to the invitation. This highlights the value of identifying scholars publishing through alternative outlets, including blogs, which might not be listed on journal databases.

Future research would need to explore these dimensions more closely, to take advantage of the key strengths of language-based approaches in shedding light on the representations and lived experiences of individuals from under-represented and marginalized populations, who are often not the focus of studies that assume a medical frame in the conceptualization of EDs.

Nevertheless, despite these obvious limitations, this volume may offer a cohesive insight into how ED discourses are constructed, experienced and realized in various media. By doing so, it might highlight areas that are still under-researched but appeal to academics with an interest in furthering language-based approaches in the context of EDs, in order to increase understanding of EDs in the public, and to help practitioners better understand EDs and meet the needs of those experiencing them.

One possible vision for the future is for individuals to be able to talk openly about their everyday stressors and mental health problems, and to be met with empathic understanding and validation of their experiences, rather than being judged, blamed and marginalized. The ability of the public to offer empathy and space for individuals with difficult psychological experiences would promote a safer society that makes obsolete the need for creating anonymous online ED communities. As much as individuals with EDs should not be reduced to their unhealthy eating behaviour, equally EDs should not be reduced to a set of discrete clinical symptoms, but should be understood from the viewpoint of a multiplicity of selves that live within their broader sociocultural context—with particular focus on individuals who are vulnerable to experiencing adverse and traumatic experiences, such as abuse and discrimination, as part of their daily life. EDs are also influenced by biological factors which are not often highlighted in public discourses. To create more balanced representations of EDs that create empathic public understanding, and socially and psychologically safer environments that challenge the dominant medical discourse, journalistic practices and newspaper discourses should follow recommendations for ethical journalism characterized by integrity, empathy and accountability. This includes accurate and well-researched news stories that provide balanced perspectives on EDs, reporting on real-life stories of resilience and recovery, reporting EDs within their emotional context, including a diversity of people affected, stories that encourage open communication about EDs and emphasizing an educational focus consistent with mental health research. Thus, journalists should assume a constructive stance that is aligned with the premises of positive psychology, to enhance people's lives by promoting understanding and empathy, meanwhile avoiding negativity and sensationalism (Aitamurto & Varma, 2018).

This volume highlights the usefulness of language in identifying ED stigma, and in generating knowledge outcomes that are useful for tackling stigma. Future research with a focus on ED discourses in the media could, for example, explore the use of language-based approaches in conducting chronological comparisons of content over time, investigating changes in ED representations and patterns of stigmatizing language found in newspapers, for instance. In particular, the use of standardized content analysis schemes would allow one to quantify and compare frequencies of language content over time and across cultures, and to assess the effectiveness of mental health campaigns and anti-stigma campaigns on newspaper reporting and the reduction of stigma. In particular, computational approaches provide a reliable method to explore topics across large data sets, which would not be possible with manual qualitative analysis, whereas qualitative approaches make possible in-depth exploration of an individual's lived experiences and how they talk about those experiences. As demonstrated in this volume, a variety of language-based approaches and disciplinary perspectives appear to offer a promising lens to analyse and interrogate ED discourse in the media—thus, moving away from a methodological and conceptual polarization and towards a holistic and pluralistic stance would enable us to gain a better understanding of ED representations in public discourse and the lived experiences of those affected.

## References

Aitamurto, T., & Varma, A. (2018). The constructive role of journalism. *Journalism Practice* 12: 695–713. https://doi.org/10.1080/17512786.2018.1473041

Anderson, C., Robinson, E.J., Krooupa, A.M., & Henderson, C. (2018). Changes in newspaper coverage of mental illness from 2008 to 2016 in England. *Epidemiology and Psychiatric Science* 4(29): e9. https://doi.org/10.1017/s2045796018000720

Bowen, M., Lovell, A. & Waller, R. (2020). Stigma: the representation of anorexia nervosa in UK newspaper Twitter feeds. *Journal of Mental Health* 15: 1–8. https://doi.org/10.1080/09638237.2020.1793128

Mekawi, Y., Carter, S., Brown, B., Martinez de Andino, A., Fani, N., Michopoulos, V., & Powers, A. (2021). Interpersonal trauma and posttraumatic stress disorder among black women: does racial discrimination matter? *Journal of Trauma and Dissociation* 22: 154–69. https://doi.org/10.1080/15299732.2020.1869098

Nevin, S.M., & Vartanian, L.R. (2007). The stigma of clean dieting and orthorexia nervosa. *Journal of Eating Disorders* 5: 37. https://doi.org/10.1186/s40337-017-0168-9

Parker, L.L., & Harriger, J.A. (2020). Eating disorders and disordered eating behaviors in the LGBT population: a review of the literature. *Journal of Eating Disorders* 8: 51. https://doi.org/10.1186/s40337-020-00327-y

Rhydderch, D., Krooupa, A.-M., Shefer, G., Goulden, R, Williams, P., Thornicroft, A., Rose, D., Thornicroft, G., & Henderson, C. (2016). Changes in newspaper coverage of mental illness from 2008 to 2014 in England. *Acta Psychiatrica Scandinavica* 134: 45–52. https://doi.org/10.1111/acps.12606

Shepard, E., & Seale, C. (2010). Eating disorders in the media: the changing nature of UK newspaper reports. *European Eating Disorders Review* 18(6): 486–95. https://doi.org/10.1002/erv.1006

Thornicroft, A., Goulden, R., Shefer, G., Rhydderch, D., Rose, D., Williams, P., Thornicroft, G., & Henderson, C. (2013). Newspaper coverage of mental illness in England 2008–2011. *British Journal of Psychiatry* 202: s64–s69. https://doi.org/10.1192/bjp.bp.112.112920

# Index